C000145576

GLOBAL CHALLENGES FOR INNOVATION IN MINING INDUSTRIES

People have been digging in the ground for useful minerals for thousands of years. Mineral materials are the foundation of modern industrial society. As the global population grows and standards of living in emerging and developing countries rises, the demand for mineral products is increasing. Mining ensures that we have an adequate supply of the raw materials to produce all the components of modern life, and at competitive prices. Innovation is central to meeting the diverse challenges faced by the mining industry. It is critical for developing techniques for finding new deposits of minerals, enabling us to recover increasing amounts of minerals from the ground in a cost-effective manner, and ensuring it this is done in a way that is environmentally responsible. This book provides the first in-depth global analysis of the innovation ecosystem in the mining sector. This book is Open Access.

ALICA DALY is an experienced IP professional, currently working as a Senior Policy Officer in the Division of Artificial Intelligence Policy of the World Intellectual Property Organization (WIPO). Prior to her time at WIPO, she spent ten years working at IP Australia. Her most recent position there was as its first Head of Patent Analytics. During this time, she was responsible for co-authoring a number of reports published by the Patent Analytics Hub.

DAVID HUMPHREYS is an Honorary Lecturer at the University of Dundee, Scotland, and former Chief Economist at Norilsk Nickel and Rio Tinto. David has written and lectured extensively on the economics of the mining industry, authoring over 200 articles and papers on subjects ranging from commodity markets, trends in the mining sector, resource availability, sustainable development, Russian mining and the impact of China on mining, to national minerals policy.

JULIO D. RAFFO is Head of the Innovation Economics Section at the Department for Economics and Data Analytics of the World Intellectual Property Organization (WIPO). His research interests include the economics and metrics of innovation and intellectual property, with a particular focus on their intersection with socio-economic development.

GIULIA VALACCHI is based in the Department for Economics and Data Analytics of the World Intellectual Property Organization (WIPO). Before joining WIPO, she worked for the Centre of International Environmental Studies as a Research Assistant in the Sinergia Project. Her research interests include innovation, technology diffusion, climate change and environmental economics.

INTELLECTUAL PROPERTY, INNOVATION AND ECONOMIC DEVELOPMENT

Intellectual property is at the heart of modern economic life. In many countries, investment in intangible assets is growing faster than investment in tangible assets. Policy makers – whether in rich or poor economies – seek to promote an intellectual property framework that is conducive to innovation and economic growth.

The series *Intellectual Property, Innovation, and Economic Development* intends to inform such policy initiatives through rigorous scholarship. Each book in the series examines a major aspect of the interface between IP, innovation, and economic development. Economic analysis is complemented by contributions from other academic disciplines to present the latest scholarship and consider its real-world implications. The series builds on studies by the World Intellectual Property Organization, reflecting the research interests of the international policy-making community.

Series Editor

Carsten Fink,
Chief Economist, World Intellectual Property Organization

Editorial Advisory Board

Megan Macgarvie, Associate Professor, Markets, Public Policy and Law, Questrom School of Business, Boston University, USA
Beth Webster, Director of the Centre for Transformative Innovation, Professor and Pro Vice-Chancellor for Research Impact and Policy, Swinburne University, Melbourne, Australia
Mark Wu, Henry L. Stimson Professor, Harvard Law School, Faculty Director, Berkman Klein Center for Internet and Society, USA

Books in the Series

GLOBAL CHALLENGES FOR INNOVATION IN MINING INDUSTRIES

Edited by

ALICA DALY
World Intellectual Property Organization

DAVID HUMPHREYS
University of Dundee

JULIO D. RAFFO
World Intellectual Property Organization

GIULIA VALACCHI
World Intellectual Property Organization

CAMBRIDGE
UNIVERSITY PRESS

CAMBRIDGE
UNIVERSITY PRESS

University Printing House, Cambridge CB2 8BS, United Kingdom

One Liberty Plaza, 20th Floor, New York, NY 10006, USA

477 Williamstown Road, Port Melbourne, VIC 3207, Australia

314–321, 3rd Floor, Plot 3, Splendor Forum, Jasola District Centre,
New Delhi – 110025, India

79 Anson Road, #06–04/06, Singapore 079906

Cambridge University Press is part of the University of Cambridge.

It furthers the University's mission by disseminating knowledge in the pursuit of
education, learning, and research at the highest international levels of excellence.

www.cambridge.org
Information on this title: www.cambridge.org/9781108842785
DOI: 10.1017/9781108904209

© World Intellectual Property Organisation 2022

First published 2022

A catalogue record for this publication is available from the British Library.

ISBN 978-1-108-84278-5 Hardback

CONTENTS

FIGURES

TABLES

BOXES

CONTRIBUTORS

ROHAN AMBURLE is acting Director of Data Front Door and Analytics team and a former patent analyst at IP Australia, Australia.

MAXWELL ANDERSEN is an international economics researcher at the Graduate Institute of International and Development Studies' Center for International Environmental Studies in Geneva, Switzerland.

MAZAHIR BHAGAT is a data scientist at the Canadian Intellectual Property Office (CIPO), Canada.

DOMENICA BLUNDI is the coordinator of partnerships and management of RD&I at Vale S.A., Brazil.

CATRIONA BRUCE is Head of the Patent Analytics Hub at IP Australia, Australia.

BRUNO CASELLA is Senior Economist at the Trends and Data Section in the Division for Investment and Enterprise of the United Nations Conference on Trade and Development (UNCTAD), Switzerland.

SERGIO M. PAULINO DE CARVALHO is an intellectual property senior specialist at the Brazilian National Institute of Industrial Property (INPI), Brazil.

ELIAS COLLETTE is Director of Business Improvement Services and Chief of the Economic Research and Strategic Analysis unit at the Canadian Intellectual Property Office (CIPO), Canada.

ALICA DALY is Senior Policy Officer on Artificial Intelligence and Data at the World Intellectual Property Organization (WIPO), Switzerland, and former Research Fellow in the Innovation Economics Section at the Department of Economics and Data Analytics of WIPO.

FRANCESCO DIONORI is Chief of Transport Networks and Logistics Section of the United Nations Economic Commission for Europe (UNECE), Switzerland.

BAHARAK COURTNEY DOAGOO is a fellow at the Centre for International Governance Innovation (CIGI) and a former

xv

post-doctoral fellow in the International Law Research Program CIGI, Canada, and is a CIGI Fellow.

MARINA FILGUEIRAS JORGE is Chief of the Economic Affairs Advisory at the Brazilian National Institute of Industrial Property (INPI), Brazil.

JAMES FORMAN is a data scientist at Google, Inc. and a former patent examiner detailee at the Office of the Chief Economist at the United States Patent and Trademark Office (USPTO), United States.

LORENZO FORMENTI is an associate expert at the Division of International Trade and Commodities of the United Nations Conference on Trade and Development (UNCTAD), Switzerland.

EMMA FRANCIS is an IP data expert at the World Intellectual Property Organization (WIPO), Switzerland, and former patent analyst at IP Australia, Australia.

DAVID HUMPHREYS is an honorary lecturer at the University of Dundee, Scotland, and former Chief Economist at Norilsk Nickel and Rio Tinto.

MICHIKO IIZUKA is a professor at the National Graduate Research Institute on Policy Studies (GRIPS), Japan.

AMIRA KHADR is a policy analyst at Innovation, Science and Economic Development Canada and a former research economist at the Canadian Intellectual Property Office (CIPO), Canada.

ALMA LACKEN is an Assistant Director and former patent analytics project manager at IP Australia, Australia.

GREG MALONEY is an IP searcher and analyst at the Commonwealth Scientific and Industrial Research Organisation (CSIRO), Australia, and former patent analyst at IP Australia, Australia.

SEAN MARTINEAU is interim manager of IP Analytics and Data Dissemination at the Canadian Intellectual Property Office (CIPO), Canada.

MARC NEVILLE is a senior economist at the Canadian Intellectual Property Office (CIPO), Canada.

JOËLLE NOAILLY is a lecturer in International Economics and Head of Research of the Centre for International Environmental Studies (CIES) at the Graduate Institute of International and Development Studies in Geneva, Switzerland.

ANA CLAUDIA NONATO is a researcher at the Brazilian National Institute of Industrial Property (INPI), Brazil.

VITORIA ORIND is an economic affairs advisor at the Brazilian National Institute of Industrial Property (INPI), Brazil.

CLAUDIO BRAVO ORTEGA is an associate professor, director of the Master of Innovation and head of the Innovation, Entrepreneurship and Sustainability Group, at Adolfo Ibañez University, Chile.

CARLO PIETROBELLI is a professor of economics at University Roma Tre, Italy; a professorial fellow at UNU-MERIT, The Netherlands; and an adjunct professor at Georgetown University.

JUAN JOSÉ PRICE is a researcher at the Macquarie University and the Copenhagen Business School, Denmark.

JULIO D. RAFFO is Head of the Innovation Economics Section at the Department of Economics and Data Analytics of the World Intellectual Property Organization (WIPO), Switzerland.

ASRAT TESFAYESUS is a transfer pricing senior consultant at Deloitte US and former economist at the Office of the Chief Economist at the United States Patent and Trademark Office (USPTO), United States.

ANDREW A. TOOLE is Chief Economist at the United States Patent and Trademark Office (USPTO), United States; and a research associate at the Centre for European Economic Research (ZEW), Germany.

DEANNA TRAINHAM is a spatial data analyst at the Australian Government Department of Industry, Science, Energy and Resources, and a former data analyst at IP Australia, Australia.

GIULIA VALACCHI is an external consultant and former research fellow in the Innovation Economics Section at the Department of Economics and Data Analytics of the World Intellectual Property Organization (WIPO), Switzerland.

FERNANDO VARGAS is Competitiveness, Technology, and Innovation Specialist of the Inter-American Development Bank (IADB).

FELIPE VEIGA LOPES is Head of Statistics Division at the Brazilian National Institute of Industrial Property (INPI), Brazil.

MARYAM ZEHTABCHI is an economic officer at the Innovation Economics Section at the Department of Economics and Data Analytics of the World Intellectual Property Organization (WIPO), Switzerland.

ACKNOWLEDGEMENTS

The preparation of this book benefited greatly from the support of several institutions. National intellectual property offices of Australia, Brazil, Canada, Chile and the United States provided national data, expertise and feedback. IP Australia generously allowed Alica Daly to participate as a co-editor of the book. WIPO's Committee on Development and Intellectual Property (CDIP) contributed funding for the Experts Meeting on Global Innovation Patterns in the Mining Industries (May 2017, Geneva) and the contributions of Brazil and Chile under the Project on Intellectual Property and Socio-Economic Development– Phase II (CDIP/14/7).

We are most grateful to many people who greatly contributed to this book. First, we thank all the volume's contributors for their inspiring chapters and the time, dedication and patience they all committed to this project. Second, we also thank Bassen Awad, Graham Davis, Nicolas Depetris-Chauvin, Samo Gonçalves, David Kaplan, Marcela Paiva Véliz, and Catalina Olivos-Besserer, who participated in the above-mentioned expert meeting and whose perspectives enriched the direction of the book. Third, we are grateful to Alvaro Gonzalez Lopez, Sergio Escudero, Steve Melnick, and Pilar Trivelli, who contributed valuable expertise to the project.

Finally, special thanks to Samiah Do Carmo Figueiredo, Caterina Valles Galmès and Cécile Roure, who provided valuable administrative support.

Alica Daly, David Humphreys, Julio Raffo and Giulia Valacchi

FOREWORD

CARSTEN FINK

Chief Economist
World Intellectual Property Organization

BENJAMIN MITRA-KAHN

Chief Economist & General Manager
IP Australia

Innovations in mining do not make the same headlines as innovations in, say, electronics and cars. That is partly because it does not immediately lead to fancy new consumer products but, more deeply, it reflects a lack of appreciation for the importance of mining innovation. The productivity of extracting minerals from the earth has vastly improved since steam engines were introduced to clear water out of mines more than 200 years ago. The extraction and refinement of minerals now spans many fields of research and technology, from under-sea mining robots to chemical refinement methods. Raw mineral materials are at the root of industrial supply chains and the ability to supply ever-larger quantities of such materials has been a key contributor to the growth of the world economy. What's more, mining innovations have contributed to improved public health, by enhancing the safety of mining workers and limiting their exposure to harmful substances. Mining innovations have also reduced the adverse environmental impact of extraction activities, to which societies have rightly paid increasing attention.

Looking into the future, the importance of mining innovation will be no less important. With growing populations and growing economies, the demand for mineral products is set to increase. New "upstream" technologies generate new demands for certain minerals – such as lithium for battery-powered vehicles. Yet digging minerals from the earth is getting harder. The quality of existing mineral reserves is declining, rendering their extraction more difficult and complex. At the same time, the need to protect the environment and prevent climate change has become an even greater imperative. Technological innovation holds the key to addressing these challenges. There is promising potential in a number of technology fields relevant to mining, ranging from mechanical engineering to biotechnology. New digital technologies promise to take the automation of mining tasks to a new level.

Opportunities for technological progress are hard to predict. Only time will tell how successful future mining innovations will be in raising mining productivity. There is an important role for governments in shaping the innovation ecosystem in which opportunities for technological progress are realized. Companies operating in the mining sector are at the forefront of innovation. Their incentives to innovate depend on a wide range of policies, including the tax treatment of R&D investments, the protection of intellectual property rights, environmental regulations, and safety standards. In addition, companies draw on knowledge generated by academia and specialized research institutes, many of which are publicly funded.

Charting a government strategy in support of mining innovation requires solid evidence on the effectiveness of different policy approaches as well as their wider pros and cons. Unfortunately, just as mining innovation itself is under-appreciated, there is a dearth of economic research for policymakers to use as an empirical basis for decision-making. It is with this background in mind that IP Australia and WIPO joined forces in 2017 to contribute to a better understanding of the nature and drivers of mining innovation. Patent data offered an obvious entry point to study mining-related technologies, but it soon became clear that a broader approach was needed to study this field of innovation. In addition, other countries expressed interest in pursuing this line of research, leading to a set of studies that eventually gave rise to this edited book volume. Anyone interested in the multifaceted dimensions of mining innovation will find this book worthwhile reading. We hope that policymakers in particular will draw inspiration from the evidence presented in the various chapters to promote policies that contribute to vibrant mining innovation and, ultimately, to a more productive mining sector that supports economic growth as well as broader societal objectives.

Global Challenges for Innovation in the Mining Industries

ALICA DALY, DAVID HUMPHREYS, JULIO D. RAFFO
AND GIULIA VALACCHI

Introduction

People have been digging in the ground for useful minerals for thousands of years. Stone Age people dug for flints, Bronze Age people for copper. But the manner in which they have dug for minerals has changed out of all recognition. While early miners hacked small amounts of mineral from the ground with antler horns, some of today's mines employ 300 tonne trucks driven and scheduled by computers. Innovation lies at the heart of the story of mining.

Mineral materials are the foundation of modern industrial society. They are used in vast quantities to construct the infrastructure of our lives – the roads, the power stations, the airports and our homes. They are used for the durable products that we employ within this infrastructure – the cars, the planes, the hospital equipment and the refrigerators, as well as in the machinery required to produce these things. And they are used in the sophisticated gadgets that underpin the technology economy and the security products that keep us safe. The ordinary smartphone contains no less than seventy different mineral elements.

Mining ensures that we have an adequate supply of the raw materials to produce all these things, and at competitive prices. As the global population grows and standards of living of people in emerging and developing countries rises, so is demand for these mineral products increasing. In 1990, world demand for copper stood at 10.7 million tonnes. In 2017, it was over 23 million tonnes. If this rate of growth persists, by 2030 it will be 36 million tonnes.

Adding to the challenge that miners face in meeting this growing demand are two other factors. For many mineral commodities, the quality of the resources being worked is deteriorating, resulting in increased energy use and more waste. Second, the world is increasingly, and rightly, concerned about the social and environmental impacts of mining.

Innovation is central to meeting these diverse and challenging objectives. It is critical to developing techniques for finding new deposits of minerals, to enabling us to recover increasing amounts of minerals from the ground in a cost-effective manner, and to ensuring that this is done is a way that is environmentally responsible. How the industry and governments are addressing this challenge, and what they still need to do, is the subject of this book.

In this chapter, we begin by describing the mining industry and its major economic characteristics. We then discuss the role of innovation in the industry and the environment in which it takes place, and, finally, we summarize some of the major findings to emerge from the subsequent chapters in the book.

1.1   The Mining Industry

Mining is the business of recovering minerals from the ground and converting them into useable industrial materials and consumer products. The minerals we are talking about here are generally "hard" minerals, which is to say we exclude oil and gas but include the energy minerals coal and uranium. Within the category of hard minerals, the major subcategories are metals (and, within this, ferrous [iron-related] minerals, nonferrous metals and precious metals) and nonmetallics (construction minerals, industrial minerals and precious and semiprecious stones).

Although economically smaller than the oil and gas industry, the mining industry is still a very large, and very global, industry. Relative to the oil industry, the mining industry is much more diverse in its nature and much more geographically dispersed. Moreover, minerals are used in a much wider range of products. Whereas oil and gas are predominantly used in energy applications, minerals are used in everything from construction to soap powders. They are also the key constituents of the battery systems, wind turbines and solar panels used for the production and storage of renewable energy.

Determining the exact scale of the industry economically is not straightforward and, of course, valuations inevitably fluctuate from year to year along with the prices of mineral commodities. It has been estimated that the value of global mine production, at the mine gate, was around $1.3 trillion in 2014 (Lof and Ericsson, 2016). Coal accounted for around half of this, with the next biggest contributions coming from iron ore, gold and copper. If one looks at the market capitalization of the mining industry as determined on global stock markets, this is estimated to have been around $1.2 trillion at the end of 2016 (S&P Global, 2017). This equated to around 1.8 percent of the value of the global stock market at the time. It should be noted, though, that stock markets do not cover state-owned companies or the large number of small private mining concerns.

However, such broad valuations fail to capture the full economic significance of the industry for two reasons. Mineral raw materials are the starting point of long supply chains that involve substantial value adding through processing, fabrication and marketing. While the raw materials may represent only a small fraction of the value of the final marketed product, without the mineral raw material there would be no chain and no product. The value of the mineral at the mine gate is therefore just that. It says nothing about the form in which the mineral is eventually delivered to the end user or the value that has been added along the way. Very occasionally this value adding takes place at the mine but much more usually it takes place somewhere remote from it in an urban industrial center.

The second reason that global valuations offer only a partial per-spective on the mining industry's economic importance is that esti-mates of global value fail to capture the specific importance of the mining industry to individual countries. Mining typically accounts for only a relatively small proportion of GDP (less than 10 percent) and employment (less than 5 percent) even in the world's largest mineral producing countries. However, the sector's contribution to foreign direct investment, to exports and to public finances can be very sub-stantial indeed. The International Council on Mining and Metals (ICMM) lists 41 countries where minerals account for over 25 percent of exports by value, including 10 where they account for over 50 per-cent. And it lists 14 countries where receipts from mining account for more than 10 percent of government revenues (ICMM, 2016). Many of these countries are in Africa, although countries in Asia and Latin America are also represented. Such "mineral-driven" economies often have relatively few practical alternatives to mining for the promotion of their development.

As regards the corporate structure of the mining industry, this is divided between a relatively small number of large companies and a large number of much smaller companies. An analysis conducted by the ICMM suggests that there are around 150 global and large-scale companies, often referred to as "majors"; maybe 350 intermediate companies operating in one commodity or one country, these possibly on a pathway to becoming majors; and perhaps 1,500 companies having just one mine. In addition, there are upwards of 2,500 small exploration companies, some with serious prospects and others largely speculative (ICMM, 2012a, 2012b).

The two poles of the industry have markedly different functions. The larger companies are *production focused*. They account for most of the capital of the industry, a large part of this coming in the form of debt financing, and a high proportion of its mine production. The small companies work smaller deposits or operate in niche minerals, while *exploration companies* are essentially focused on discovering and proving up mineral deposits, often with a view to selling them on to a major for development. The high risk of exploration generally means that banks will not lend to these companies, so they have to raise their finance in stock markets. The most important stock markets specializing in this kind of financing are located in Toronto, Sydney and London.

In addition to companies directly engaged in finding and developing mines, there are a large number of companies supplying the mining industry with equipment and technology, a sector commonly referred to as the mining, equipment, technology and services (METS) sector. These companies work very closely with mining companies to understand their requirements and to develop innovative solutions, be these in the design and manufacture of large earthmoving trucks or in the provision of process software. Because METS companies cover a wide range of activities and do not conveniently fit traditional industrial sector categories, the precise scale of the METS sector is hard to assess. However, for some countries it is economically significant. In Australia, which has one of the world's most developed METS sectors, it is estimated that the sector accounts for A$90 billion of sales, including A$15 billion of exports. The industry association catering for METS companies, Austmine, has over 450 members (Austmine, 2018).

Beyond the formal mining sector, there is a significant informal mining industry, populated by so-called ASMs (artisanal and small-scale miners). These are very low-tech operators, employing little capital and often unregulated. Except for a few commodities such as tin, tantalum, gold and precious and semi-precious stones, ASMs account for only a very small proportion of global mineral production. The sector does, however, employ a very large number of people and attract a lot of public attention. The low-tech nature of the activity means that it does not play too much of a part in the more sophisticated types of innovation which are the primary focus of this book, but there is a strand of innovation relating to so-called frugal technologies which is relevant to this sector.

1.1.1   Mining Activities

While mining, as noted, is normally thought of as the business of recovering minerals from the ground, the actual digging up of minerals is in fact only one step in the process in which the mining industry engages, and only one of the spheres offering scope for innovation. The full process is illustrated in Figure 1.1. All these steps are essential for the creation of a successful mine.

The first step, and in fact the step where a lot of the value of a mineral deposit is created, is discovery. Exploration is a challenging and high-risk activity and a very small proportion of deposits looked at ever make it into production. The initial process of exploration can take many forms: the painstaking study of geological maps (where these exist), the interrogation of geological models, fly-over geophysical surveys, on-the-ground geochemical analyses and, perhaps, some exploratory drilling. Exploration can be thought of as part of the industry's R&D in as far as it represents a search for new products.

It is only if these initial investigations suggest that there might be a deposit with sufficient size and grade to make for a commercial mining operation that the project will be taken to the next stage, that of trying to prove up the deposit and establish a resource. This involves some serious drilling and, since drilling is costly (upwards of $100 a meter), it is only warranted if there is a good chance of establishing a commercial deposit. Otherwise, the exploration company would do better to cut its losses and look elsewhere.

In the event that this hurdle is surmounted, then the next task is to undertake a whole lot more drilling, at greater density, to establish

Figure 1.1   Simplified view of the life of a mine
Source: Author's elaboration.

a reserve (that part of the mineral resource which might provide the basis for an operating mine). At this point, the would-be miner will also have to give consideration to all the other elements that need to go into the creation of a working mine, the type and scale of the operation, where power to the mine will come from, how the product will be transported from the mine to market, and the establishment of a constructive dialogue with communities liable to be impacted by the mine and which might provide employees to it. The culmination of this process is usually a bankable feasibility study, an extensive and detailed analysis of the project showing that every aspect of the mine project has been addressed and demonstrating how it can make money for its owners and lenders. This is an acid test and, inevitably, a number of projects fail it.

For those projects that obtain financing then comes the matter of actually developing the mine. Given that this will commonly involve building supporting infrastructure (for example, roads, ports, power lines), the purchase of large amounts of equipment, the construction of plant and waste disposal facilities, the preparation of the ore body (for example, removal of overburden) and the training up of staff, this process can easily take three to four years.

It is only at this point that mining, as the term is commonly understood, takes place, where the digging and the bringing to the surface of the mineral-containing ore can proceed. Beyond this is the stage of processing. Very few minerals can be shipped and sold in the form in which they come out of the ground. Most need to be subject to some kind of treatment – referred to in the industry as "beneficiation" – whether this is the relatively simple matter of washing and screening (as in the case of coal) or the upgrading of the ore into a mineral concentrate through a process involving crushing, grinding and froth flotation (as in the case of copper sulfides).

For reasons of transportation costs (it is uneconomic to carry large amounts of dirt long distances), this processing stage typically takes place at the mine site and is considered integral to the activity of mining, since, without it, mined products cannot be sold. Thus the product at the mine gate will typically be an upgraded product that can be transported elsewhere for further processing or that can be sold to a third party for such processing. For metals, this further processing generally means smelting into metal and then refining to increase its purity. In some instances, the availability of local infrastructure (for example, power and ports) and relevant skills favor doing smelting and refining at or near the mine but often it does not, so these activities are carried out elsewhere, remote from the mine.

The final stage in the life of a mine is its closure. Historically, many mines were simply abandoned when they ran out of ore, with environmentally disastrous consequences. Today, this is unacceptable and companies have to start preparing for the closure of their mines in a socially and environmentally responsible fashion right at the outset of mining. Indeed it may well be the case that permission to mine in the first place is contingent on the miner satisfying the licensing authorities that they have a plan and have made sufficient financial provision for the mine's closure.

Naturally, the precise path a project follows will depend on the mineral commodity being produced. Moreover, different stages in the process are more important for some commodities than for others. For copper and gold, the value of the final refined metal product is largely (90 percent plus) created through exploration and mining. For aluminium and steel, most of the value is created through processing, the ores from which they are made, bauxite and iron ore, being relatively abundant in nature.

There are also some important geographical aspects to the process described. Mining supply chains are truly global. As already noted, while the final processing of a mineral product into finished form sometimes takes place near to the mine, in many cases it does not. A substantial proportion of the world's iron ore and copper concentrates is converted into metal – steel and refined copper respectively – at a distance from the mine and very often in another country, giving rise to a large global trade in these products. A similar situation arises with the technologies and equipment employed in mining, international products commonly developed in one country and applied or sold in another. Accordingly, to understand how the industry works, and track the influences upon it, one necessarily has to adopt a global perspective.

1.1.2   Economics of the Mining Industry

The mining industry has some very specific economic characteristics which it is important to understand since they shape the way the industry works and the behavior of policy-makers toward it. They also have important implications for the targeting of innovation in the industry.

Minerals Are Non-renewable. Minerals are subject to depletion. Once mined, they cannot be mined again, although it may be possible to recycle the elements recovered by mining. Moreover, the quality of some mineral resources – which is to say their grade, the size of deposits, their depth and their ease of processing – is deteriorating as the better resources are worked out. To remain competitive, the industry has to battle continually to offset the effects of depletion through increased efficiencies and cost reductions.

Minerals Are Unevenly Distributed Geographically. Occurrences of minerals at sufficient concentrations to support viable mining operations are scarce. Their distribution follows the dictates of geology so miners do not have the luxury of choosing to go only to places with sound and stable institutions where infrastructure is readily available. They have to go to where the minerals are and they have to build the required plant and infrastructure in those locations, using the best available technologies wherever in the world these may have been developed. This can add substantially to upfront costs and to political risk. Minerals often have to be transported significant distances for processing and for fabrication, resulting in lengthy and complex value chains.

Mining Is Capital Intensive. The establishment of a mine involves large-scale expenditure, long before any revenues are generated. It is critically important to the economics of mining projects therefore that they are constructed as tightly and cost effectively as possible and that the mine and associated plant function as anticipated when the project was committed. The capital intensity of mining is also a factor encouraging the exploitation of economies of scale and in favoring projects with long lives. Given the long life of many mines, it is important to get production technologies right because, once committed, these are effectively baked into the operation for a very long time.

Miners Are Price Takers. Miners sell their products into global markets over which they have little or no control. Prices in the industry tend also to be highly volatile, reflecting both the sensitivity of mineral demand to changes in the rate of global economic growth and to the slow response times of mineral supply, which follows from the capital intensity of the industry. In the absence of any influence over prices, producers are required to focus on the matters over which they do have control to ensure their profitability, namely their capital spend and operating costs.

Mining Has Intense Local Impacts. Mining can be a powerful force for local and regional economic development, creating infrastructure, stimulating local businesses and providing jobs. However, it can also be socially and environmentally disruptive. Mining involves the removal of billions of tonnes of earth and the generation of large quantities of solid and liquid wastes. These problems are likely to get more challenging over time as mineral demand increases and public expectations of the industry rise. In addition, the generation of waste from mining is growing faster than the growth of mine production as the quality of resources being mined deteriorates. This will add to pressures on the industry to develop innovative ways to deal with the environmental consequences of mining as well as to work more closely with affected communities.

Collectively, these characteristics add up to an industry that requires a close focus on production costs and on operating in a socially and environmentally responsible manner. Moreover, the challenge of doing these things is getting greater as a result of resource depletion and growing restrictions on where and how companies in the industry can operate.

The key to unlocking cost reductions and reducing waste in a world of depleting ore resources is productivity growth – which is to say, growth in the output of mines per unit of factor inputs – driven by innovation. Historically, the industry has been remarkably successful in growing its productivity and in offsetting the effects of depletion, as evidenced by the fact that, over a very long period, the cost of producing minerals has not generally risen, and in a number cases has actually declined (Humphreys, 2013). Given the nature of mining, these advances have often come in the form of gradual and incremental improvements rather than through major breakthrough technologies. The physical laws governing mining militate against the sort of productivity improvements achievable in the technology sector as represented, for example, by Moore's law which holds that processing power for computers doubles every two years. But, over time, like compound interest, the cumulative effect of these incremental improvements has delivered dramatic increases in the mining industry's productivity.

History may or may not prove to be a reliable guide to the future. It could be that the industry will continue to deliver advances in productivity which offset the effects of depletion well into the future. But this is not something that can be taken for granted. There are strong upward pressures on capital and operating costs in the industry (Humphreys, 2015). Worryingly, it would appear from the data presented in Figure 1.2 that productivity in some major mining countries has actually declined since around 2000. There may be a cyclical element to this. Typically, industry productivity declines when commodity prices are high and producers are focused on the volume of

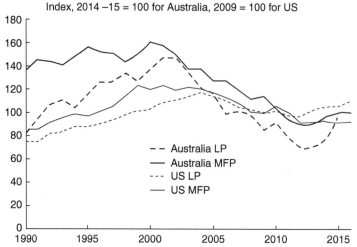

Figure 1.2 Productivity in the Australian and US mining industries
Notes: Labor productivity (LP) measures industry output per unit of labor input.
Multifactor productivity (MFP) measures output per unit of total combined inputs,
including labor, capital, energy and materials.
Sources: ABS (2018) and BLS (2018).

output rather than productivity. The last few years have seen a modest reversal of the negative trend, but it cannot yet be ruled out that there are longer-term structural forces at work here too. It should also be noted that there is mounting evidence of a decline in the productivity of exploration spending. It has been estimated that the cost of discovering an ounce of gold or a tonne of base metals has roughly doubled since the 1980s (BCG, 2015).

Miners may have to look in new places for their productivity growth in future. In the past, economies of scale have provided a major contribution to productivity growth but the industry may be reaching the limits of what these can contribute. Mines are not getting bigger and the growth in the scale of mining equipment has slowed. In future, productivity growth will have to come from other sources, particularly from innovative technologies that enable miners to work "smarter." These may include the application of high-powered computing and big data, the "Internet of things" and operating technology–information technology integration, increased automation and robotics, and the use of high-powered satellites in exploration (Mining Magazine, 2016). The challenge is a substantial one and the scope for the application of innovation considerable.

1.2 Innovation in the Mining Industry

Innovation has been an intrinsic part of the mining industry for many centuries. History offers plenty of examples of breakthrough innovations developed for, or pioneered by, the mining industry. There is evidence of use of wooden railroads in mines as far back as the sixteenth century. The first commercial use of a steam engine was for pumping flood water from mines in the early 1700s. Alfred Nobel's dynamite rapidly spread in the mining industry after its invention in the second half of the 1800s. This is also the case of energy generation technologies applied to new infrastructures – such as dams and power plants – as mining sites often require access to large amounts of energy in remote areas. Likewise, the mining sector is a key stakeholder in transport infrastructure investments (e.g. new railways and ports), where innovation can play an important part. In recent years, mining has been the focal point for the development of autonomous haulage trucks.

Innovation in other sectors also has a "pull effect" on mining activities. The growth of certain industries feeds back up the supply chain, increasing the demand for specific mining outputs. This was the case for coal and uranium for the energy sector, iron and aluminium for the transport and construction industries, and copper, lithium and the rare earth elements for the information and technology (ICT) sector. Every spike in the specific demand of a mineral generates an opportunity for new mining activities and innovation.

As discussed in Section 1.1, innovation's main goal in the mining sector was, is and will be about improving productivity. Simply put, mining firms can increase productivity in three ways: (i) by improving efficiencies at existing mining sites, (ii) by opening new sites with a higher yield or (iii) by closing those with a lower yield. Innovations can contribute to all three ways. Innovation can increase efficiencies and reduce costs in production, processing and delivery to market at a given mining yield. It can increase the accuracy of the exploration for new mine sites or reduce the costs of the mine development. And it can reduce the financial, social and environmental impact of the closure of mines.

1.2.1 Applying the Innovation Economics Framework to the Mining Sector

The following chapters in this book will address different elements of innovation economics as they apply to innovation in the mining industry. What follows is a broad depiction of the innovation economics framework that gives a conceptual base for these analyses. It focuses principally on the different types of mining innovation and the mining innovation ecosystem.

Types of Mining Innovation

As in any other sector, mining firms innovate in their products, production processes or organizational practices (OECD/Eurostat, 2019; Schumpeter, 1942).

With regards to product innovation, the mining industry is a little different to other economic sectors. Many mined products – such as copper and zinc – are simple commodities with a demand insensitive to product differentiation and branding. The discovery of entirely new products is extremely rare, suggesting that the scope for product innovation in mining is very limited. However, some industrial minerals – such as borates, fluorspar or kaolin – are sold on the basis of their chemical and physical properties rather than on their elemental content, creating opportunities for the development of product variations. Precious and semi-precious stones also offer scope for developing new product variants. Furthermore, there can be new and innovative uses found for existing products, as, for example, has occurred in the new technology field. The use of rare earth elements and lithium in green energy applications might be examples of this.

However, while the discovery and development of new mined products may be rare, the discovery of new commercial deposits of existing products through exploration is an important part of the economics of the industry. In fact, when talking about product innovation in mining, there is a case to be made that the deposit or the mine is really the "product" rather than the mineral recovered from them.

Viewed in this way, a company's expenditure on exploration becomes a part of its R&D, in the sense that it is expenditure aimed at finding new, commercially exploitable, sources of a mineral, even though such expenditure may not be recognized formally as R&D. There are interesting parallels here with other industrial sectors. Mines open up, operate and close down, very much in the way that manufactured products are invented and produced before moving through to obsolescence. Similarly, just as industries like pharmaceuticals spend large amounts of money on trying to discover new marketable drugs, despite the long odds against them, so mining has to battle equally long odds in its search for commercially viable "greenfield" (i.e. new) sources of a mineral commodity. Very broadly, it has been estimated that for every thousand mineral occurrences identified, only one will be subject to exploration and of every thousand deposits explored, only one is likely to become a mine (Kreuzer and Etheridge, 2010).

Process innovation and organizational innovation are critical to the mining industry and are generally aimed at cost reduction. In many industries, the boundaries between innovation in the production processes and the organizational ones are often blurred. This is certainly the case for the mining industry. Typically, process innovation refers to any improvement of the production process within the industrial plant. These include changes to the layout, machinery and any method employed to produce a good or service. Organizational innovation includes everything that happens outside of the production plant. These include the logistics, management, financial and similar innovations.

In the case of mining, process innovation refers to any improvement happening within the mining site, while organizational innovation is any improvement of operations outside the mine premises. However, several mining innovations will easily fit both definitions. For instance, new exploration methods (e.g. a drone sending images to a computation facility) or new transport systems (e.g. a controlling system loading deep inside the mine and offloading in a port far away) are likely to happen both at the mine site and elsewhere.

Mining Innovation Ecosystem

At the industry level, these individual innovative behaviors will combine to what can be described as a mining innovation ecosystem. The economic conditions and existing stakeholders will shape the technological development and dynamics of this ecosystem.

The constant need for cost-reducing processes and organizational innovations in the context of a scale-intensive commodity industry determines, to a large degree, how mining firms innovate (Pavitt, 1984). According to Pavitt's taxonomy, innovative mining firms are typically larger and produce a relatively high proportion of their own process technology, to which they devote a relatively high proportion of their own innovative resources. These larger companies have a relatively high level of vertical technological diversification into equipment related to their own process technology and make a relatively big contribution to all the innovations produced in their principal sectors of activity.

The mining innovation ecosystem does not only include innovative mining firms but any other stakeholder contributing to the innovation being undertaken in or for the sector. In addition to the mining companies, private companies supplying very specialized mining equipment and technology services – the METS companies referred to earlier – are active actors in this ecosystem. Mining companies are increasingly sourcing for cost-reducing innovations from such specialized suppliers (Bartos, 2007). As in many other large-scale industries, mining companies acquire new technologies embedded in the heavy machinery and equipment they require for their operation. Innovation may also arise from outsourced R&D and other technological services. METS innovations were and are a substantial part of the innovation being deployed in mining activities.

There are also public stakeholders such as universities, public research organizations (PROs) and government agencies participating in this ecosystem. Universities and PROs contribute to the generation of scientific and technical knowledge that eventually will crystallize into mining innovation. Universities and other higher education institutions also contribute to the diffusion of knowledge by training skilled labor to be employed in the mining industries.

Government agencies contribute by providing supporting innovation-related policies and institutions. Well-designed innovation and industrial policies aim at changing the economic incentives within an innovation ecosystem to attain a given policy objective. Governments in mining countries often attempt to make better use of their comparative economic advantage in mining-related commodities to generate spillovers downstream of mining or in other sectors. The industrial policies of industrialized mining economies such as Australia or Canada seem to have been more successfully implemented than have those in other mining developing and least-developed countries (Venables, 2016).

Similarly, innovation-related institutions such as finance, standards, safety and intellectual property, provide support for, and impose requirements on, the mining innovation ecosystem. In many countries, current regulatory frameworks have increasingly limited certain production practices both in terms of labor security and environmental practices. Such environmental and safety regulations are a motivation for innovation in the mining sector (Popp, 2003; Warhurst and Bridge, 1996). Innovations related to water treatment, CO_2 emissions, fracking and safety are among the typical examples. These external constraints can affect the innovation rate through the increase of cost but also through the direction of innovation projects. New environmentally friendly technologies may require a totally different approach regarding the existing technological path of given firms.

1.2.2   Ecosystem Interactions and Intellectual Property

Technology transfer and diffusion plays an important role in increasing the impact of innovation on productivity. As described above, a substantial part of the innovation occurring within the mining innovation ecosystem happens through knowledge and technology flows among and within stakeholders. Typical manufacturing and technology companies will often have large centralized R&D functions, while mining innovation often arises from the specific conditions in which individual operators work and are driven through collaborations between individual business units and METS companies.

Large mining companies can centralize innovation activities up to a certain point. There are substantial cost-saving innovations that can be achieved by internalizing and centralizing R&D activities in one place. But, eventually, at least some of these innovations are transferred and adapted to the different mining sites around the world. Local adaptation of mining technologies can shift innovation incentives of stakeholders. Mineral specificities and mining sites development are likely to be more similar around the same location. Mining companies sharing the location of the same mineral may observe economies of scale in pooling R&D and engineering resources in local hubs where the technological challenges are similar. Such scenarios may shift incentives not only of private stakeholders, as governments and universities may also see the advantage of investing in common technological solutions. These common solutions only increase technological flow within and across stakeholders.

Technological flow can be part of a codified exchange, a tacit one or simply embedded in the goods or services being exchanged. The innovation ecosystem conditions shape how knowledge and technology can be appropriated. The mining sector – as many other large-scale industries – relies on a mix of know-how lead advantage, process secrecy and patents.

Keeping know-how advantages is easier when the knowledge is not easily codifiable or embeddable in a good or service. Such tacit knowledge can be crucial to mining-related innovation. The deployment of mining sites requires technical know-how and adaptability embedded in human resources (e.g. engineers) operating on site. However, technological transfer and diffusion of tacit know-how occurs from one site to the other through the mobility of skilled labor. Mining firms often include secrecy clauses in their labor contracts to avoid undesirable leakage of tacit knowledge that may reduce their lead advantage. But the enforceability is often limited according to the jurisdiction.

The increasing need for external interaction among stakeholders pushes for a higher use of the patent system. Global mining firms needing to deploy technologies at the global scale can rely on the internationalization of their patent protection for a more standardized appropriation. Locally, joint ventures to develop technical solutions with academia and competitors for the same minerals and mine site types also foster the institution of appropriation formalities such as patents. METS companies transposing other technologies to mining sector needs will also protect their technologies of reverse engineering with patents.

1.3   Summary of Content and Findings

The subject of mining and innovation has many facets, few of which have been subject to rigorous investigation historically. The growing interest in mining innovation and the increased availably of tools for its analysis provide an opportunity to rectify this. The contributions to this book explore what has been going on in mining innovation around the world with a view to identifying patterns and trends. To do this, they use a wide variety of approaches, datasets and methodologies. Some of the contributions focus on global industry themes; others look at individual country experiences. The combined result is a rich and original perspective on a topic of critical importance to the future direction and performance of mining.

Chapter 2 provides a broad overview of recent trends in innovation in the mining sector. It finds that R&D in the mining industry is low by comparison with many other industrial sectors although the interpretation of this finding is complicated by the matter of whether mineral exploration should considered a form of R&D. It also finds that a major part of the R&D – and innovation – in the sector is carried out, not by the mining companies themselves, but by suppliers of equipment and services to the industry, the METS sector. The chapter then proceeds to a discussion of the use of patents as a proxy for innovation before employing WIPO's database on patent filings to explore recent trends in innovation. Considering both mining companies and METS companies, it finds that the rate of patenting rose sharply in the mid-2000s: this at least partly explained by China's growing interest in mineral raw materials and its increased participation in the global patenting system. The chapter also looks at patterns of innovation in different countries in light of their particular economic characteristics and competitive advantages. Thus it finds, for example, that a mining country like Canada has a strong focus on innovation in upstream activities like exploration and blasting, whilst the Republic of Korea, a major importer of mined products and a supplier of mining equipment, focuses on metallurgy and automation.

Chapter 3 takes a look at the role played by foreign direct investment in the transmission of innovation in mining. More specifically, it looks at the role of mining multinational corporations in promoting innovation in the least economically developed countries. Although, for a variety of reasons, investment in mining by multinational miners in developing countries has not always proven an unqualified blessing from a development perspective, the authors of the chapter find that there is ample evidence that developing countries have generally benefited from spillovers from technologies introduced by global miners. For the full benefit of such technology transfers to be realised in the local economy, it is appears to be important that global miners and their suppliers develop their technologies in collaboration with local partners. An incentive to do this arises from the fact that mining requirements can be very site specific, creating opportunities for local technology developments. To extract the maximum benefit from technology transfer, countries need to implement policies on foreign direct investment that not only encourage the deployment of innovation but help promote linkages between foreign investors and local companies, encourage the transfer and embedding of skills in the local economy and assist with the cultivation of a local R&D capability.

The focus of Chapter 4 is innovation in the mining value chain, a term that refers to the full range of activities that firms and workers carry out to bring a mined product from its conception to end use, recycling or reuse. The topic is addressed from the perspective of Latin America, one of the most important mineral-producing regions in the world but one that has historically been heavily reliant on technologies developed elsewhere. The growing sophistication of mining in recent years has been accompanied by growth in the importance of METS firms in the value chain. While this has complicated the dynamics of the mining industry, it has also created opportunities for mining countries like those in Latin America to play a more active part in the value chain. The authors consider how innovation can be developed through the interaction of mining companies, their suppliers and other organizations active in the innovation system, such as universities and government research centers. They provide examples of technologies that have been developed in Latin America, some of these in response to specifically Latin American challenges – an example is the development of technologies for mining at high altitudes – and conclude by looking at schemes introduced in Chile (the World Class Suppliers and Alta Ley programs) to strengthen linkages in the value chain and to promote innovation through information exchanges between innovators and those with problems to solve and through constructive interaction amongst mining industry stakeholders.

Mined products are often bulky and transport, whether by conveyor, truck, rail or ship, can account for a substantial proportion of the delivered cost of a mineral product. The continuing globalization of mineral markets, and in particular the growing impact of China as a buyer of minerals, has further increased the importance of mineral transport, both by land and sea. Innovation is important for developing new and better ways to move mineral products around and to reduce or contain costs. This is the subject of Chapter 5, in which the authors examine in detail mining-related transport patents since 1990. They find that the share of transport-related patents in total mining patents has grown in recent years and that China has accounted for a large part of the increase, having a particular impact on innovation in conveying and rail technologies. The authors provide several specific examples of recent transport innovation. They also find a rapid increase in the rate of patenting for transport automation since 2009. An examination of forward and backward citations for mining-related transport patents reveals that there are strong flows of innovation between mining and non-mining sectors.

Mining activities are often very physically disruptive and Chapter 6 shifts the focus to mining and the environment. Its particular interest is the impact of public policy and, more specifically, the stringency of public policy on innovation in "clean" technologies in mining. To test out the relationship statistically, the authors break out from the general body of mining-related patents held by WIPO those that have a specifically environmental character. They then compile data from the OECD on the stringency of environmental policy in a range of countries, further distinguishing between policies which are market based and those which are nonmarket based ("command and control"). The statistical analysis reveals a clear association between policy stringency and innovation in clean technologies, pointing up the importance of good public policy to stimulating innovation in the mining sector. Slightly less predictably, the analysis seems to suggest that nonmarket policy instruments have been more effective in stimulating innovation than have market instruments.

Chapter 7 studies mining innovation in relation with price cycles. Two hypothesis are raised: mining innovation may be pro-cyclical therefore rising in periods of high commodity prices or countercyclical therefore boosting in periods of low prices as a cost-reducing innovative effort. The pro-cyclical effect is found to be stronger than the countercyclical one, even though the two mechanisms may coexist. In addition, long price-cycle variations affect more mining innovation than short-cycle ones. This is coherent with the long decision-making timeline associated with the mining sector, where a bulk of the technological changes happen when mines are opened or closed.

The remaining chapters of the book explore the issue of innovation and mining from a country perspective, spanning both emerging economy and advanced economy experience.

The first of these, Chapter 8, focuses on Brazil, one of the world's most important mining countries. In this chapter, the authors examine mining patents filed in Brazil over the period 2000–15. The data show local mining companies filing more patents than foreign ones, but these number are dwarfed by the patenting activity in the METS sector, a sector where foreign companies, notably those from Japan, USA, Germany and Finland, totally dominate. The authors then consider what the data reveal about the mechanisms for mining innovation in Brazil. A major contribution comes from foreign companies contracted to supply equipment and technical services to domestic mining companies or the local subsidiaries of foreign ones. With respect to innovation by local miners, this field is very much dominated by Vale, Brazil's largest mining company. A case study on Vale shows the company pursing innovation through its own in-house research, through partnerships with local METS companies, through collaboration with other domestic research bodies and universities and through its import contracts with foreign technology suppliers. The authors suggest that Brazil's high dependence on imported innovation results in an undue focus on short-term cost-reducing operational technologies and insufficient attention being paid to longer-term technologies bearing on industry fundamentals like exploration, automation and the environment.

Staying in Latin America, Chapter 9 looks at Chile, the world's largest copper producer. Chile has in recent years seen several policy initiatives intended to encourage innovation in the mining sector. The authors first examine patterns of patenting activity in Chile and note the increasingly important role played in mining innovation by the METS sector. They then employ the results of a survey undertaken amongst METS companies participating in a recent government scheme for promoting innovation, the EXPANDE program, to explore these companies' innovation practices and how they protect their innovations. The survey reveals that while most companies responding to the survey consider themselves to be innovative, only a minority of them rely on IP rights to protect their innovations. This result reflects not ignorance of the IP system amongst innovators but the cost of patenting and the perceived complexity of the registration process. Other factors mentioned are the preference for other forms of protection such as trade secrets or trademarks and a lack of incentive in academic institutions to engage in technological innovations. The authors suggest that a scheme for increasing the returns on IP investment might be effective in promoting an increase in IP protection.

Chapter 10 returns to the matter of how public policy helps to shape innovation, in this instance in the USA. The particular question posed here is how the MINER Act of 2006, an act intended to raise safety standards in US mines and to incentivize the development of safety technologies, impacted innovation on health and safety in US mining. The question is of considerable importance given the high-risk nature of the mining industry. To explore the topic, the authors use advanced statistical techniques to extract from WIPO's patent database a subset of data for patents relating to mineral mining in the USA and, within that, another subset relating specifically to safety-related mining patents. Using a mixture of graphical, text-based and statistical methodologies, the authors conclude that the MINER Act did indeed have a measurable impact on innovation in the sector. They are also able to point to specific safely technologies which have emerged as a result of the implementation of the Act and to demonstrate how the increase in innovation stimulated by the Act has resulted in a numeric decline in injuries and lost workdays in the US mining industry.

In Chapter 11, the authors use patent data to explore patterns of innovation in the Canadian mining sector. The patents data show that Canada has a strong upstream (exploration, blasting, processing) focus in its patenting activity, a fact that follows logically from Canada's global leadership role in mineral exploration and its use of tax incentives to promote exploration. Some innovations in the area of exploration, the data reveal, come as spillovers from the oil and gas sector. Given that innovations tend not to be discrete events but are linked thematically, the authors develop some original 3D "landscapes" to show the relationships between different patent families and pinpoint where the emphasis on patenting activity lies. Further graphics explore where in Canada patenting activity takes place and identify areas where there is evidence of innovation clusters. A final topic analyzed is the linkages between companies and other relevant institutions engaged in the patenting process. This reveals extensive collaboration between innovators, a tendency which the authors believe is leading toward a more open environment for innovation, this despite the mining industry's traditional protectiveness of their IP rights.

The final chapter, Chapter 12, looks at innovation and IP use in Australia, arguably the most dynamic country in the field of mining innovation today, and one that benefited considerably from the mining boom triggered in the 2000s by China's rapid industrialization. Australia is further distinguished by the extent to which government has been involved in the promotion of mining innovation, through the sponsorship of research institutions such as CSIRO and the CRCs (Cooperative Research Centres) and its R&D Tax Incentive scheme. The authors of the chapter employ patent data over the period 1997–2015 to investigate who has been filing mining-related patents in Australia, for what purposes and in which parts of the country. As in Canada, the data show that the primary focus of patenting in Australia is in upstream activities like exploration, mining and processing rather than in smelting and refining. They also show evidence of high levels of patenting by foreign companies (notably from the USA, the UK and Japan) in Australia, and of extensive collaboration between these foreign companies and Australian ones. While the trend in patenting has been strongly upwards through most of the period covered by the data, since 2012 the rate of patenting has dropped sharply, more sharply than the authors would have expected.

1.4   Concluding Thoughts

The issue of innovation in mining has never been more important. Growing mineral demand coupled with the declining quality of existing reserves and demands for increased environmental performance, require a continuous effort to raise the productivity of mining and to improve the manner of its operation. Several themes emerge from the pages of this book that can help achieve a better understanding of how innovation operates in different parts of the world and where attention should be focused to meet the demands of the future.

It is evident that the technological basis of the industry is changing. The acceleration of mining-related patenting from the mid-2000s onwards may partly reflect the impact of China but probably also reflects the advent of a new technological wave, sometimes referred to as Industry 4.0. Modern (digital) technologies offer significant potential to boost the productivity of exploration and to optimize mine-operating practices, amongst other things. This requires mining companies to supplement their traditional discovery and earth-moving skills with skills drawn from other technologies and other fields. The shift in the techno-logical basis of the industry is illustrated by statistical analysis showing that the METS sector is playing a growing role in the mining industry, a role that appears destined to get still larger.

This undoubtedly complicates the supply chain of the industry but it also creates opportunities. Historically, mining companies have brought technologies they need with them and have been responsible for signifi-cant technology transfers to mineral host countries in developing coun-tries. This has not always however been a very efficient or effective process. Since much mining technology is not generic, but needs to be developed in relation to a specific problem in a specific location, there is a growing opportunity for host countries to play an active part in innov-ation and in the development of new technologies.

Another theme to emerge from the book is the important role that governments can play in the promotion of innovation. One obvious way of doing this, of course, is through the operation of effective and well-administered patents systems. However, it goes much further than this. As the examples of Australia, Canada, Brazil and Chile in the book show, government can play a positive part in the promotion of innovation through targeted tax incentives, through support for research institutions and by sponsoring schemes that bring together those with a part to play in the innovation process whether these be miners or policy-makers with problems to solve, or METS companies or research bodies (including universities) with solutions to offer.

What is clear from the analyses presented here is that, while there is much good work going on, there is much that remains to be done. Innovation holds the key to the mining industry's ability to continue to deliver a reliable supply of mineral raw materials in a cost-effective and socially acceptable manner. This book does not hold all the answers as to how this can be done but it hopefully makes a small contribution to this by shedding light on recent trends in innovation, highlighting some of the key issues to be addressed and providing some pointers on what those in industry and government should be doing to promote creative think-ing and innovative behaviours.

References

ABS (2018). Estimates of industry multifactor productivity, Australian Bureau of Statistics. www.abs.gov.au

Arundel, A., and I. Kabla (1998). What Percentage of Innovations Are Patented? Empirical estimates for European firms. *Research Policy*, 27 (2 June), 127–41.

Austmine (2018). www.austmine.com.au

Bartos, P. J. (2007). Is Mining a High-Tech Industry? Investigations into innovation and productivity advance. *Resources Policy*, 32 (4 December), 149–58.

BCG (2015). Tackling the Crisis in Mineral Exploration, Boston Consulting Group 30 June 2015. www.bcgperspectives.com

BLS (2018). Data for "Mining, except oil and gas" (NAICS 212) US Bureau of Labour Statistics. www.bls.gov

Canuto, O. (2014): The Commodity Super Cycle: Is this time different?, in World Bank Economic Premise Series 2014 (150).

Francis, E. (2015). The Australian Mining Industry: More than just shovels and being the lucky country, IP Australia.

Freeman, C. (1994). The Economics of Technical Change. *Cambridge Journal of Economics* 18 (5), 463–514.

Humphreys, D. (2013). Long Run Availability of Mineral Commodities. *Mineral Economics*, 26 (12), 1–11.

Humphreys, D. (2015). The Remaking of the Mining Industry. Basingstoke: Palgrave Macmillan.

ICMM (2012a). The Role of Mining in National Economies. London: International Council on Mining and Metals (ICMM). www.icmm.com

ICMM (2012b). Trends in the Mining and Metals Industry. www.icmm.com

ICMM (2014). The Role of Mining in National Economies (2nd ed.). London, UK: International Council on Mining and Metals (ICMM). www.icmm.com

ICMM (2016). Role of Mining in National Economies. www.icmm.com

IMF (2015). World Economic Outlook, October 2015: Adjusting to lower commodity prices, Washington, DC: International Monetary Fund.

Kreuzer, O., and M. A. Etheridge (2010). Risk and Uncertainty in Mineral Exploration: Implications for valuing mineral exploration properties. AIG News, 100, May 2010. www.aig.org.au

Lof, O., and M. Ericsson (2016). Extractives for Development, UN University/ WIDER. www.wider.unu.edu

Mining Magazine (2016). Mining Technology and the Culture of Change, September 2016.

OECD/Eurostat (2019). Oslo Manual 2018: Guidelines for Collecting, Reporting and Using Data on Innovation, 4th ed., The Measurement of Scientific,

Technological and Innovation Activities. Paris/Eurostat, Luxembourg: OECD Publishing. https://doi.org/10.1787/9789264304604-en

Pavitt, K. (1984). Sectoral Patterns of Technical Change: Towards a taxonomy and a theory. *Research Policy* 13 (6, December), 343–73.

Popp, D. (2003). Pollution Control Innovations and the Clean Air Act of 1990. *Journal of Policy Analysis and Management* 22 (4, September 1), 641–60.

Radjou, N., and J. Pradhu (2014). Frugal Innovation: How to do more with less. *The Economist.*

S&P Global (2017). State of the Market: Mining Q4-2016. https://pages .marketintelligence.spglobal.com

Scherer, F. M. (1982). Inter-Industry Technology Flows in the United States. *Research Policy*, 11 (4, August 1), 227–45.

Scherer, F. (1984). Using Linked Patent and R&D Data to Measure Interindustry Technology Flows, in Zvi Griliches (ed.), R&D, Patents, and Productivity. Chicago: University of Chicago Press, pp. 417–64.

Schumpeter, J. A. (1942) Capitalism, Socialism and Democracy. London: Routledge Classics. Reedited in 2015.

Townsend, J. (1980). Innovation in Coal-Mining Machinery: The case of the Anderton shearer loader, in Pavitt, K., (ed.), Technical Innovation and British Economic Performance. London: Palgrave Macmillan, pp. 142–58.

Venables, A. J. (2016). Using Natural Resources for Development: Why has it proven so difficult? *Journal of Economic Perspectives* 30 (1 February), 161–84.

Warhurst, A., and Bridge, G. (1996). Improving Environmental Performance through Innovation: Recent trends in the mining industry. *Minerals Engineering* 9 (9), 907–21. https://doi.org/10.1016/0892-6875(96)00083-0

Recent Trends of Innovation in the Mining Sector

ALICA DALY, GIULIA VALACCHI, AND JULIO D. RAFFO

2.1 Introduction

Products of the mining industry are an essential part of our lives. We need them to satisfy our everyday needs. The growing worldwide population, together with the rising living standards, increases the demand for minerals. The mining industry faces continuous challenges to meet such demand and to fulfill the sustainability requirements imposed by policymakers. Innovation is a key instrument to address these challenges.

Traditionally, innovation economists have not considered the mining sector to be very innovative (Bartos, 2007; Scherer, 1984). According to this view, mining firms are more likely to be large and capital intensive to benefit from economies of scale when facing a demand that relies mostly, if not entirely, on the price of mining commodities. Mining firms have few incentives to differentiate through product innovation or branding. Most innovations are related to cost-cutting processes, aiming to improve their narrow margins. As a result, mining firms source new technologies from their own production engineering departments or embedded in products and services obtained from specialized suppliers (Pavitt, 1984).

Nevertheless, there is compounding evidence to suggest not only that the mining sector is innovative but also that, recently, it is increasingly so. In most mining countries, this sector often contains a disproportionate number of innovative firms compared to other sectors (Arundel & Kabla, 1998). In addition, the sector has observed a dramatic increase in all innovation indicators since the early 2000s.

In Europe alone, around USD 657 million was spent on research and development (R&D) in mining in 2015. Although it is still much lower than so-called high-tech sectors, such as pharmaceuticals (USD 10,868 million) or chemical manufacturing (USD 7,416 million) in the same year, it is still higher than agriculture (USD 654 million) and consumer electronics manufacturing (USD 347 million) (Eurostat, 2018).[1]

We also observe that intellectual property (IP), particularly patents, is increasingly important for the mining industry. There were more mining-related inventions looking for patent protection in the last five years than all those accumulated from 1970 to 2000. Large mining enterprises and firms specialized in mining equipment, technology and services (METS) increasingly use IP to pursue their internationalization strategy. Both mining and METS companies operate in different countries and patents may help them secure their IP across jurisdictions and appropriate the knowledge embedded in new products and processes.

This chapter analyzes this recent uptake in mining innovation. We document in detail the innovation ecosystem behind this surge and discuss what it may represent for the future of the industry. We make use of a newly assembled patent database focusing on mining innovation, which enables us to study the change in mining innovation ecosystems before and after the surge.

The rest of this chapter is structured as follows. Section 2.2 defines technological innovation in the mining industry, presenting trends that show evidence of a change in innovation around the first half of the 2000s. Section 2.3 presents the results of our analysis identifying which factors are behind the mining patents boom and Section 2.4 offers concluding remarks.

2.2   Increased Global Mining Innovation

As in any other sector, mining firms innovate in their products, production processes or organizational practices. As input for these innovation outputs, mining firms perform research and development (R&D) activities, acquire off-the-shelf technologies – typically embodied in equipment and machinery – or acquire disembodied technologies such as outsourced R&D or other technological services. However, measuring these innovation traits is not always straightforward and this is particularly the case in the mining industry. We discuss the general global trends

---

[1] See Daly et al. (2019) for details on the calculation.

of mining innovation in the following, including some limits of these standard indicators.

Discerning an unequivocal global R&D expenditure trend is an almost-impossible task. The global mining-related R&D expenditure of the last decade is likely to be around USD 140 billion.[2] China (47%), the United States (22%), Australia (17%), Canada (8%) and Europe (5%) are the largest contributors to this global figure.

However, a national R&D series may be able to shed some light on how the trend might look. Figure 2.1 shows the spectacular increase of Australian mining R&D expenditure in the 2000s. In the first half of the last decade, the Australian mining sector more than doubled R&D investment. In the second half, the investment in R&D by the sector increased at a much higher rate than before. In contrast, we also observe that mining R&D expenditures have declined recently, coinciding to some extent with the recent global financial crisis and slowdown.

It is worth noting that aggregate mining R&D statistics often also include expenditure for the oil and gas industry. In the case of Australian mining R&D expenditures in 2015–16, about 33 percent relates to oil and gas R&D expenditures. Similarly, many of these aggregate R&D figures may or may not include R&D performed by firms outside typical mining industry definitions. For instance, the Australian

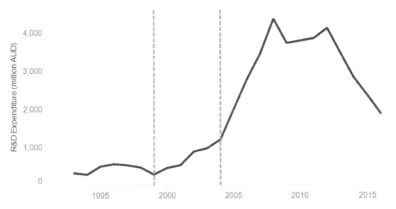

Figure 2.1   R&D expenditure in mining in Australia, 1993–2016
Note: Business expenditure on R&D for ANZSIC Division B.
Source: Australian Bureau of Statistics, Research and Experimental Development, Businesses (cat. no. 8104.0).

[2] Estimation based on OECD (2019) data in constant 2010 US dollars.

statistics include R&D expenses incurred by METS firms but do not include R&D expenses relating to mining technologies incurred by firms that are not classified as mining or METS nor public R&D related to mining.

Regarding product innovation, the mining industry is a little different from other economic sectors. The discovery of entirely new products is extremely rare, suggesting that the scope for product innovation in mining itself is very limited.[3] While the discovery and development of newly mined products may be rare, the discovery of new commercial deposits of existing products is a key element of mining activity. In fact, when talking about product innovation in mining, it could be argued that it is the deposits or the mines that are really the "product" rather than the mineral recovered from them. Viewed in this way, a company's expenditure on exploration becomes a part of its R&D expenditure, even though such expenditure may not be recognized formally as R&D (Kreuzer & Etheridge, 2010).

While typical aggregate R&D figures do not include the exploration investments, there are some estimations of the global magnitude of exploration expenditure. The rise in exploration expenditure in the first half of the 2000s is also remarkable and similar to the R&D trend in Australia. This noteworthy increase happened across all types of minerals (Figure 2.2). The early 1990s also show an increase in the level of exploration expenditure, but of a much smaller magnitude compared to what was observed in the next decade. We also observe a substantial decline after 2012.

These exploration figures have some limitations as well. First, they include all the activities related to exploration, many of which might not be innovative. Second, exploration is only one of the many mining supply chain segments where innovation can occur. Third, it is not uncommon that mining companies outsource exploration efforts to smaller companies specializing in prospecting. Mining companies take over or invest in these smaller companies only in the case of successful deposit identification, much like large pharmaceutical companies do with small biotechnology companies.

An alternative innovation indicator is patenting activity, which is an output indicator as it measures potential innovation outputs.[4] Figure 2.3 shows the number of patent families relating to mining

---

[3] Most mine products are simple commodities, but there are some exceptions, such as industrial minerals sold based on their chemical and physical properties, precious and semi-precious stones and new uses of existing mining products.

[4] A patent is an exclusive legal right granted for new, useful and fully disclosed inventions.

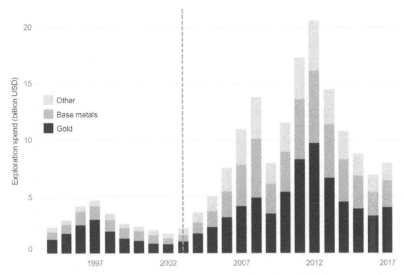

Figure 2.2   Worldwide mineral exploration expenditure (US $ bn) by commodity, 1994–2017

Source: S&P Global Market Intelligence, World Exploration Trends.

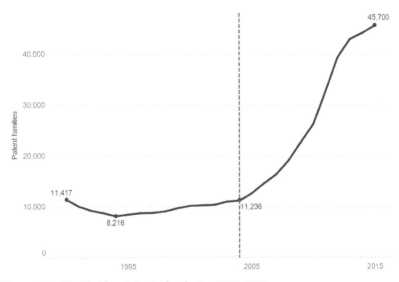

Figure 2.3   Worldwide mining technologies, 1990–2015

Source: WIPO Mining Database (technology subset).

technologies filed since 1991. It shows a relatively steady number of inventions filed between 1990 and 2003, with an exponential growth observed from the second half of the 2000s. Differently from R&D and exploration figures, we observe a slowdown but not a reverse of trend after 2012.

Patent data has many advantages when measuring mining innovation, but also limitations. First, patent publication data is rich in bibliographic information allowing for a detailed breakdown of the analysis, ranging from complete mining innovation country-year series to in-depth analysis of mining innovation stakeholders. Second, the body of patent literature reflects the entire technological developments related to the mining industry, including those produced by entities not defined as mining companies in industry classifications. This second advantage allows for a thorough examination of the mining innovation ecosystem and the different segments of its supply chain. On the other hand, not all mining innovation output necessarily ends in a patent document. Indeed, trade secrets and tacit knowledge are part of the innovation process of the mining sector. These limitations are not specific to mining innovation as the economics of innovation literature has discussed at length the use of patents as a proxy for innovation (Lerner & Seru, 2017).

One existing concern about using patent indicators relates to the overall surge in patent applications in the same period that we observe an increase in mining-specific patents (Fink et al., 2013). However, as shown in Figure 2.4, mining patents have outpaced the overall patenting activity since 2004. After more than a decade of decline in the 1990s and early 2000s, we observe the share of mining patents almost doubles from 2004 to 2013. We can also see a slight fall since 2013, when the share fell back to 2009–10 levels in 2015 compared to 2004.

All in all, the different indicators do refer to a similar global picture. Mining innovation increased in a rather spectacular fashion in the early 2000s for about a decade. We also observe at least some signs of a slowdown in the last years. But these aggregate series tell us very little about the geography of innovation or the technological changes that may be happening in the mining supply chain structure. To provide answers to these open questions, we will analyze in detail the patents associated with mining activity as follows, describing the different parts of the mining value chain and the different technological contributions to the mining industry.

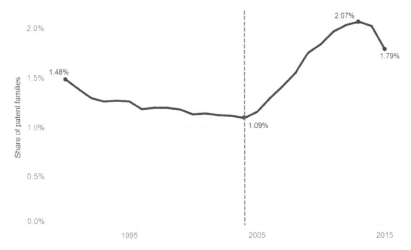

Figure 2.4   Worldwide mining technologies as share of technologies, 1991–2015
Source: WIPO Mining Database (technology subset).

2.3   What Is Behind the Mining Innovation Boom?

The understanding of mining innovation and the recent surge using patent data entails going beyond the patenting activity of mining firms, but also going beyond patents in the mining sector. There are well-known challenges in defining mining industry innovation using only a technological approach to patent data (European Commission, 2016; Francis, 2015; INAPI, 2010). These challenges include defining the non-core mining industries and deciding how much they contribute to the definition of mining. However, it is necessary to define mining technologies because mining firms also appear to innovate in industries other than mining, and therefore have patents in other technology areas. Moreover, mining innovation is also done by METS firms, making it challenging to rely on mining firms alone to define mining innovation.

Our data confirms such concerns (Figure 2.5). Between 1990 and 2015, there were 663,322 inventions filed for patent protection related to a mining technology.[5] Mining and METS companies filed for fewer than half – 239,065 patent families – of those. However, mining firms patented many of their inventions out of the mining-related patent

---

[5] These include patent and utility model applications seeking protection in one or more jurisdictions. To avoid double counting, our statistics always refer to patent families as a unit, unless otherwise stated (see Daly et al., 2019).

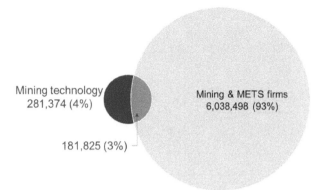

Mining technology
281,374 (4%)

Mining & METS firms
6,038,498 (93%)

181,825 (3%)

Figure 2.5   Patent families potentially related to mining by source
Source: WIPO Mining Database.

classes. These companies applied for 5,981,258 patent families not relating directly to mining technologies. From these results, we can see clearly that mining technologies can start from stakeholders other than mining-related firms, while mining firms can be very active beyond mining innovation. While neither approach can be considered fully comprehensive, we will use these depending on the type of analysis performed.

Mining Innovation Spurs on the Mining Production Life Cycle and Value Chain

We base our definition of mining technology on the different stages of the mineral extraction process – the mining life cycle – and how its supply chain is organized accordingly (Figure 2.6).

The mining life cycle consists of several distinct stages, starting with the exploration and discovery of an ore-body, moving to the extraction, refining and shipping of minerals and finalizing with the mine closure to its natural state. Each stage of the mining life cycle can include innovation inputs in multiple areas of technology. The exploration stage includes activities such as ore-body discovery, mineral determination, resource estimation and feasibility studies. The mining operation stage includes activities such as mine planning, design and development, mine construction, and mineral extraction and processing. Once the ore has been processed, then refining can occur. Services such as transport, waste treatment and energy generation support and add value to each stage of the process.

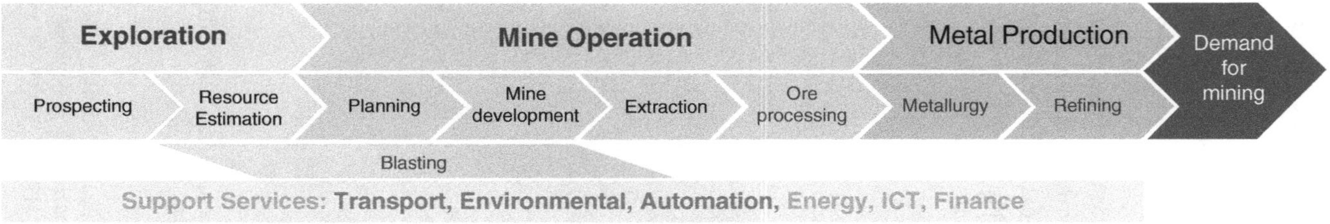

Figure 2.6 Simplified view of the lifecycle of a mine

Source: Author's elaboration.

Note: The mining sub-sectors presented in red text indicate the subsectors defined in the patent mining taxonomy.

Based on the knowledge domain required for each stage of the mining life cycle and patent classifications, we define all mining technology-related patents in nine mining subsectors: automation, blasting, environmental, exploration, metallurgy, mining/mine operation, (ore) processing, refining and transport. The overlap of our technology subsectors, as defined by patents with the mining life cycle, is indicated in red text in Figure 2.6.[6]

We observe mining innovation all across these subsectors. The mining subsectors with more innovation are exploration (24.8% of total mining innovation) and refining of extracted materials (19.1%). Other fields involve less innovation: blasting (0.6%), environmental improvements (12.6%), metallurgy (1,1%), mining (31.1%), processing (4.6%) and transport (6%) (Figure 2.7).

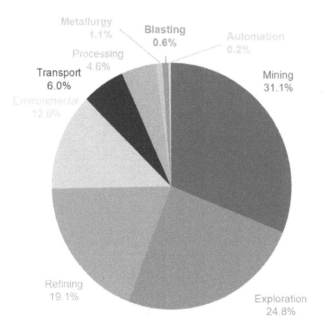

Figure 2.7   Mining technologies by subsectors, 1990–2015
Source: WIPO Mining Database (technology subset).

---

[6] Only mining for minerals and coal are included, while quarrying and oil & gas extraction are excluded. The data may still contain oil & gas–related patents if they are developing refining techniques that may also be applied for minerals (see Daly et al., 2019). Figure 2.6 is based on this definition.

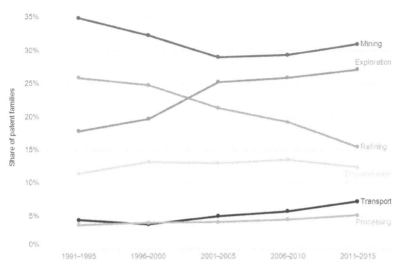

Figure 2.8   Distribution of mining technologies in subsectors by period, 1990–2015
Note: Only the six top subsectors included.
Source: WIPO Mining Database (technology subset).

Some subsectors have contributed to the recent mining innovation uptick more than others. Comparing the distribution trends, there has been a switch from refining mostly to exploration and transport (see Figure 2.8). There is also a smaller share increase from environmental innovation and processing subsectors. The industry's technological response to the extractive products demand surge seems to have put less emphasis on improving refining methods. This may be a consequence of the declining quality of mined ores, making it inefficient to invest in new refining techniques. Firms could prefer to dig new mines instead. The increase in exploration and transport probably relates to the industry's increasing need to discover new deposits in more distant locations to face rising demand (see Chapter 5). Similarly, the increase in the share of environmental technologies is probably linked with wider social and industry awareness of the environmental impact of mining activities (see Chapter 6).

In addition, the so-called fourth industrial revolution – namely advances in information technology and artificial intelligence – may offer even more potential for raising productivity in knowledge-based activities like deposit modeling (exploration), logistics (transport) or

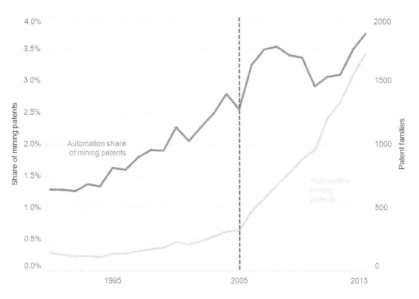

Figure 2.9   Patents families in automation class over time
Source: WIPO Mining Database (technology subset).

waste management (environmental), among many other examples. Interestingly, automation innovation in mining increased both in volume and share during the 1990s and early 2000s, when overall mining innovation activity was relatively flat (see Figure 2.9 and Figure 2.3). Automation innovation had a slow start when mining innovation started to pick up its pace in the second half of the 2000s. However, we now observe a spectacular second boom of automation in both volume and proportion of mining patents, which is likely related to the spread of digitalization.

Where Is All This Mining Innovation Originating?

The distribution of economies contributing to mining technologies does not match one-to-one with the typical mining-producing ones (Figure 2.10). Only China and the United States gather more than 10% in both mining output and innovation. The Russian Federation is the only other economy to have more than 10% of mining output, but it generated less than 1% of the mining innovation. Japan, generating more than 10% of the innovation but producing less than 0.1% of the output, is the opposite

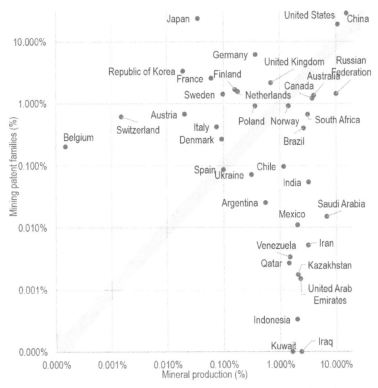

Figure 2.10 Mining production and innovation by country, selected countries
Note: Sample contains only top mineral-producing and top mining-patenting
countries. Axes are expressed in logarithmic scale.
Source: WIPO Mining Database (technology subset) and Reichl et al. (2018).

case. On a different scale, some other economies have a relatively balanced output–innovation ratios, such as China and the United States.
Australia, Canada and Norway produce more than 1% of the mining
output and generate about 1% of the innovation. Conversely, the United
Kingdom generates more than 1% of the mining innovation and produces slightly less than 1% of the output. One order of magnitude lower,
Spain having about 0.1% of both output and innovation is another
example.

Countries such as Brazil, Chile, India, Indonesia, Iran, Iraq,
Kazakhstan, Kuwait, Mexico, Qatar, Saudi Arabia, South Africa and
Venezuela – in addition to the already mentioned Australia, Canada,
Norway and the Russian Federation – produce substantially more mining

output than Japan or even the United Kingdom, but they produce much less mining innovation. On the contrary, countries such as Austria, Belgium, Denmark, Finland, France, Germany, Italy, Netherlands, Poland, Republic of Korea, Sweden and Switzerland join Japan and the United Kingdom in their disproportionate contribution to mining innovation given their production. It is also important to note that these economies – including the United States, China, Australia, Canada and Norway – not only generate most of the mining technologies but they are also where most of the patent protection is sought. Very few mining technologies seek patent protection in countries with high mining output but relatively low innovation.

What explains these different patterns between mining production and innovation? One of the most plausible explanations is that mining innovation – particularly breakthrough patentable innovation – is more likely to happen in functioning innovation systems not necessarily based on mining-operating countries. The United States, Japan, Republic of Korea, Germany, the United Kingdom and, lately, China are well-known technological hubs where innovation across sectors spurs more rapidly than the rest of the world (WIPO, 2018). These innovation systems – and those from other OECD economies – host innovative stakeholders from different industries that are likely to develop mining innovation. Many METS companies originate and conduct their R&D in countries that are not necessarily where they apply the technology, such as Japan, Switzerland or the Republic of Korea.

Undeniably, China, Japan, the United States, the Russian Federation and Germany were the largest contributors in volume to the recent mining innovation upsurge (Figure 2.11). The top ten economies account for roughly 90 percent of all mining technologies. Within these, China observes the highest increase during the last decade.

Contribution to the Mining Innovation Boom Did Not Come from the Usual Suspects

Despite China's impressive growth in volume, this is not what explains the rapid increase in the world's mining innovation relative to all innovation depicted in Figure 2.4. Indeed, China's rapid innovation increase for all technologies outpaces its mining innovation trend.

This is because the concentration of absolute mining innovation tells very little about the countries' technological specialization in mining. Many nations where mining operations are conducted may have

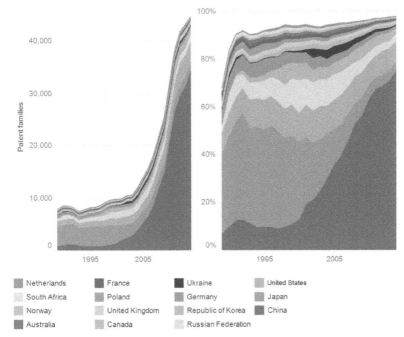

Figure 2.11   Mining innovation by top country of origin
Source: WIPO Mining Database (technology subset).

a disproportionate amount of mining innovation compared to their overall innovation. Moreover, given different country sizes and propensities to patent, comparing overall levels of patenting activity between countries can be, to some extent, misleading about where the most specialized mining innovation may reside.

Looking at each countries' mining patents as a share of the overall patents in that country, the picture begins to change (Figure 2.12). This graph shows that while China dominates mining patents in overall numbers, in terms of the share of China's patents, mining patents is between 2 and 3 percent, and is only slightly larger than the share of mining patents in the United States, Brazil and France. In contrast, countries that have economies that are heavily reliant on the mining industry, such as Chile and South Africa, and to a lesser extent, Australia, Canada and the Russian Federation, have a much higher share of mining patents.

In order to further normalize these effects, we use the relative specialization index (RSI), which indicates countries where mining innovation

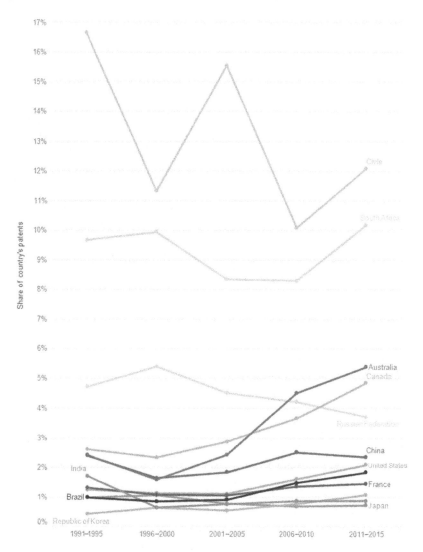

Figure 2.12   Mining patents share by country, selected countries
Source: WIPO Mining Database (technology subset).

is more important than the average (Figure 2.13).[7] A positive RSI means
that mining innovation is dominant compared to innovation in other

---

[7] The RSI measures the relative share of mining innovation of a given country with respect
to the share of mining innovation of all countries. See Daly et al. (2019).

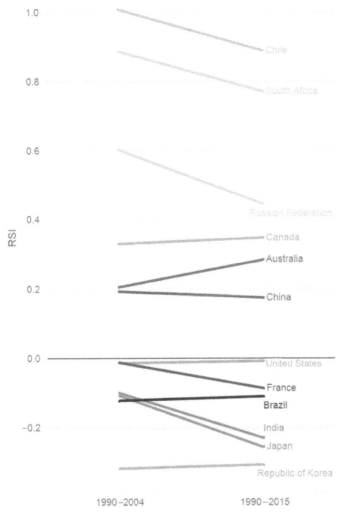

Figure 2.13   Mining relative specialization index (RSI), selected countries
Source: WIPO Mining Database (technology subset).

industries, whereas a negative RSI indicates a country is not specialized in mining innovation.

It is not surprising that countries where mining represents a significant part of the economic activity are relatively specialized in mining innovation. Chile, South Africa, Australia, Canada, the Russian Federation and China are mining-producing economies where the share of mining innovation exceeds the world's average. Brazil and India, however, are notable exceptions to this pattern. The United States, another top producing mining economy, has slightly negative specialization. While the relative ranking of countries did not change radically before and after the mining innovation surge, we do observe that the degree of specialization of many countries did change. This is also indicative of their contribution to the recent surge relative to all technologies.

In this respect, we observe that traditionally mining producing and specialized economies such as Chile, South Africa, the Russian Federation and China have diminished specialization in mining innovation; and, thus, these economies have not contributed to the recent relative upsurge. Australia and Canada, on the other hand, have increased their relative mining specialization, which implies that these contributed to the overall surge. Even if still not specialized in mining innovation, the United States and Brazil have also contributed to the recent relative boom. During the last decade, these economies decreased their negative relative specialization, becoming almost positive. Japan and India have continued to specialize outside of the mining domain, also contributing negatively to the recent relative surge.

As discussed previously, the increase of mining innovations related to exploration, transport and automation explains, in part, the recent surge (Figure 2.8). We now dig deeper to understand which countries contribute the most to these thriving subsectors (Figure 2.14). The first stylized fact is that mining subsector specialization within countries is fairly stable in rank, but the countries can vary substantially in their relative intensity.

Most of the increase in the exploration subsector is not coming from the traditionally specialized economies. Some specialized economies in exploration – namely China, the Russian Federation and the United States – diminished their relative specialization. China almost recorded a negative index after the surge. Australia and Chile increased their relative specialization in this subsector and are probably among the largest contributors to exploration booming relative to other sectors.

Among these economies, Australia was the only country that deepened its specialization in mining transport. While still not very specialized in transport, Australia was the only other selected country to improve its relative specialization in this subsector. Canada, Chile and China remain specialized in mining transport but have diminished their relative specialization. The Russian Federation, the Republic of Korea and the

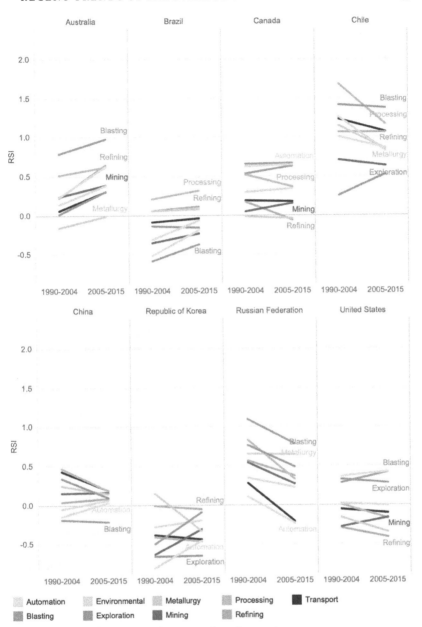

Figure 2.14   RSI by mining sub-sector, selected countries
Source: WIPO Mining Database (technology subset).

United States have been specializing even more outside of the transport domain.[8]

Australia, Canada, Chile and the United States are more specialized in automation compared to lower-middle-income and upper-middle-income nations such as China, Brazil, Mexico and India. This is also the case in countries which are not particularly mining oriented, such as France, Finland and the Netherlands. This is also because mining automation innovation is concentrated in METS firms (96.8 percent) rather than mining firms. It seems that mining firms prefer to outsource this type of innovation. METS firms innovating in automation do not need to be located in mining countries. They can conduct their R&D abroad and then sell their technologies to operating miners. High-income countries have an advantage in high-tech industries favoring the development of automated technologies. In addition, higher-income economies producing mining output have stronger economic incentives to make use of automation technologies in order to mitigate higher labor costs.

These patterns only apply partially to the dynamics of automation specialization within these economies. Australia, the Republic of Korea and Brazil increased their relative specialization in automation in a remarkable fashion during the mining innovation booming period. In contrast, the Russian Federation and Chile's specialization in automation reversed in a similar spectacular way. Canada still is fairly specialized in automation but lost some of its intensity during the last decade. The Russian Federation only deepened its lack of specialization in automation. Even if still not extremely specialized in automation, China improved its automation RSI substantially.

The selected economies are particularly weak in environment specialization. Only Chile shows a high positive RSI for environmental technologies, but declining during the last decade. However, most of these economies improved their specialization in the last decade. In particular, Australia deepened its environmental specialization. Conversely, Chile, the United States and the Russian Federation are the only ones in this sample that worsened their environmental specialization.[9]

---

[8] For more in-depth discussion on mining transport innovation, see Chapter 5.

[9] For an in-depth analysis of the impact of environmental regulation on the innovation activity in mining, see Chapter 6

A Complex Mining Innovation Ecosystem

Companies and other stakeholders are accountable for the mining innovation boom. Established companies – both mining and METS – created about two-thirds of the mining-related technologies in our data. Individuals – likely on behalf of startup and micro-companies – originated almost a quarter of these technologies. Academic institutions produced the remaining technologies, where public research organizations (PROs) and universities generated 9 and 6 percent, respectively.

Companies and individuals mostly carried out mining innovation. However, in recent years, there has been a rise in the participation of universities in the innovation ecosystem (Figure 2.15). They were almost totally absent from the scene before the twenty-first century. This may be the result of the increasing number of collaborations between universities and companies. More and more mining firms finance university programs focused on mining studies to shape high-skilled human capital, for example, the collaboration between Vale and many universities in Brazil (Chapter 8); the historical collaboration between Noranda and McGill

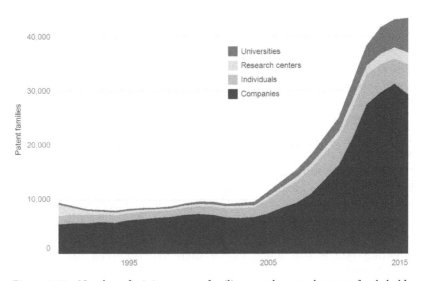

Figure 2.15   Number of mining patents families over the years by type of stakeholder
Source: WIPO Mining Database (technology subset).

University in Canada (Chapter 11); or the success of Cooperative Research Centres in Australia (Chapter 12).

In most cases, mining companies establishing collaboration with academia hired highly qualified human capital directly, creating channels for the development of innovations. This also explains why we observe very little co-patenting activity. In the period 1970–2015, only 4 percent of total mining patents had two or more applicants. This share has been constantly decreasing over time, from 9.3 percent in 1970 to almost 1 percent in 2015. Most of the collaboration activity relates to individuals (71.7 percent) and private companies (25.7 percent). PROs (1.7 percent) and universities (0.8 percent) rarely appear as co-applicants, despite the many above-mentioned collaborations with the private sector. This may be due to specific and reserved contractual agreements among the parties involved, which may assign the patent only to the private partner.

Within the academic sector, PROs have seen a comeback in the mining ecosystem in recent years. Historically, these institutions have been a large promoter of mining innovation from the mid-70s to the beginning of the 90s. They were particularly present in the Soviet Union, where 80 percent of PRO mining patents originated in the period 1970–1989. Since 1990, PRO innovation activity slowed down greatly until 2010. The fall of the Soviet Union largely explains this sudden drop of PRO patents. But many other state-funded research organizations in the West also closed or diminished their operations during the 1990s, such as the US Bureau of Mines in 1995 and the UK's Warren Spring Laboratory in 1994. Accounting for 56 percent of PRO mining patents in the period 2000–15, China-based PROs explain at large their recent trend.

Although private companies are the largest contributor to mining technologies, only a small portion of mining and METS firms file for patents and METS firms are around 10 times more likely to file for patent protection than mining companies (Table 2.1). About 3.4 percent of METS firms file patents compared to only 0.4 percent of mining firms. Mining firms patent significantly less than firms in other sectors, such as pharmaceuticals (5.8 percent), chemical manufacturing (2.5 percent) and manufacturing of consumer electronics (5.5 percent). However, their patenting rate is still much higher than that observed for firms in agriculture (0.05 percent).

The fact that mining companies get exclusive operation rights as a result of exploration may partly explain this low. Firms finding new mineral deposits can obtain exclusive and time-limited rights over those resources in a manner similar to the patent system. Investments

Table 2.1 *Mining firms with and without patents*

	Firm sector	Number of firms			
		With patents		Without patents	
METS		4,712	3.8%	125,011	96.4%
	Coal	174	0.3%	49,897	99.7%
	Metal ore	321	0.4%	77,584	99.6%
Mining	Nonmetallic mineral	53	0.9%	6,218	99.2%
Oil & Gas		838	1.5%	57,421	98.5%
Quarrying		649	0.3%	192,086	99.7%

Source: Orbis and WIPO Mining Database (firm subset).

in exploration innovation may be fully appropriated with such exclusive rights without the need to get patent protection. This parallel may help explain the low number of mining firms with patents. However, mining firms file most of their mining technologies in the exploration subsector (Figure 2.16).

Still, most of the patenting activity by mining firms is not related to mining technologies. An analysis of the WIPO technology fields shows that electrical machinery, apparatus and energy is the largest field for mining firm patents in non-mining technologies (Figure 2.17).[10]

2.4   Concluding Remarks

This chapter explored the recent boom in mining innovation. Even if an elusive target for typical innovation measurements, mining innovation has been booming for more than a decade. Australia, Canada, China, Europe and the United States concentrate the largest share of global innovation measured as mining R&D expenditures, exploration expenditures or mining technologies in patent data.

We then turned to the technological changes happening in the mining innovation supply chain structure and in the geography of innovation. For this purpose, we created a novel dataset which is employed in many chapters of this book. This data includes the patenting activity of mining

---

[10] Civil engineering contains IPC classes broadly related to mining including also oil and gas drilling (see Daly et al., 2019).

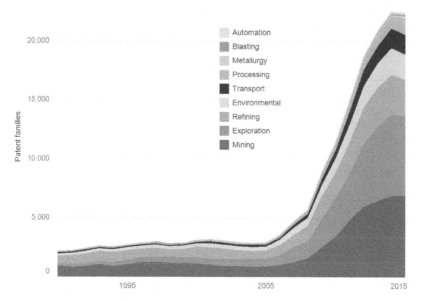

Figure 2.16   Mining Firms by technology, by earliest priority year
Source: WIPO Mining Database (firm subset).

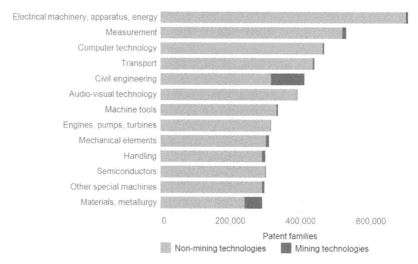

Figure 2.17   Patent families of mining firms by WIPO technology field
Source: WIPO Mining Database (firm subset).

firms and the mining-related patents not necessarily filed by these firms. We documented how mining technologies can spur on stakeholders other than mining-related firms and how mining firms can be very active beyond mining innovation.

Our analysis showed how mining innovation spurs on the mining production life cycle and value chain. In particular, recent mining innovation focused on exploration and refining technologies. However, some subsectors have contributed to the recent mining innovation uptick more than others. In particular, there has been a decrease in refining technologies shares in favor of exploration and transport technologies. We interpret these results as a direct consequence of the demand surge of mineral products in the same period. We also observe an increase in automation innovation in the mining sector. These trends are not new for the industry, which observed an increase in the 1990s and early 2000s. Nonetheless, we now observe a remarkable automation uptick.

The distribution of economies contributing to mining technologies does not correspond with the typical mining-producing ones. Only China and the United States lead both in mining output and innovation. Australia, Canada and Norway also offer a relatively balanced mining output and innovation. Other typical mining economies struggle to be present in the innovation spotlight. The Russian Federation, Brazil and Chile are probably the best among these, while other countries generate very limited innovation outcomes. Indeed, mining innovation is more likely to spur on functioning innovation systems not necessarily based on mining operation countries. Many developed economies not particularly relevant in mining production contribute greatly to global mining innovation. Japan, the Republic of Korea and many European economies are top among these.

Despite China's impressive growth in volume, it added little to the rapid increase in the world's mining innovation intensity, which has grown rapidly in all technologies. This was not only the case in China. Traditionally mining producing and specialized economies such as Chile, South Africa and the Russian Federation have all diminished their mining innovation specialization. Conversely, Australia, Canada, the United States and Brazil have increased their relative mining specialization, which also means they contributed more to the global mining innovation intensity surge.

Most of the increase in the exploration subsector is coming from the increase in specialization. Australia and Chile increased their relative specialization in this subsector and are probably among the largest contributors to the exploration boom relative to the other sectors. On mining transport, Brazil and Australia were the only countries improving their mining transport specialization. The United States, Canada and Australia are more specialized in automation compared to lower-middle-income and upper-middle-income nations. The selected economies are fairly weak in environment specialization.

Companies and other stakeholders are accountable for the mining innovation boom. Established mining and METS firms created about two-thirds of the mining-related technologies in our data. Academic institutions produced the remaining technologies, where public research organizations (PROs) and universities generated 9 and 6 percent, respectively. Although private companies beingare the largest contributor of mining technologies, only a small portion of mining and METS firms file for patents.

References

Arundel, A., & Kabla, I., 1998. What percentage of innovations are patented? Empirical estimates for European firms. *Research Policy*, 27 (2), 127–141.

Bartos, P. J., 2007. Is mining a high-tech industry? Investigations into innovation and productivity advance. *Resources Policy*, 32 (4), 149–158.

Daly, A., Valacchi, G., & Raffo, J., 2019. *Mining patent data: measuring innovation in the mining industry with patents*, s.l.: WIPO Economics Research Working Paper No. 56.

European Commission, 2016. *Raw Materials Scoreboard*, s.l.: s.n.

Eurostat, 2018. *Science and technology database, Business expenditure on R&D by NACE Rev. 2 activity*, s.l.: s.n.

Fink, C., Khan, M., & Zhou, H., 2013. *Exploring the worldwide patent surge*, s.l.: WIPO Economics Research Working Paper No. 12.

Francis, E., 2015. *The Australian Mining Industry: More than Just Shovels and Being the Lucky Country*, s.l.: IP Australia Economic Research Paper No. 4.

Griliches, Z., 1998. Patent Statistics as Economic Indicators: A Survey, in Z. Griliches (ed.). *R&D and Productivity: The Econometric Evidence*. s.l.: University of Chicago Press, pp. 287–343.

INAPI, 2010. *Patentamiento en el cluster mineria del cobre: Análisis de presentaciones realizadas en Chile*, s.l.: s.n.

Kreuzer, O., & Etheridge, M. A., 2010. Risk and Uncertainty in Mineral Exploration: Implications for Valuing Mineral Exploration Properties. *AIG News*.

Lerner, J., & Seru, A., 2017. *The Use and Misuse of Patent Data: Issues for Corporate Finance and Beyond*, s.l.: NBER Working Paper No. 24053.

OECD, 2019. *Research and Development Statistics: Business enterprise R-D expenditure by industry – ISIC Rev. 4*, OECD Science, Technology and R&D Statistics (database): https://doi.org/10.1787/data-00668-en (accessed March 23, 2019).

Pavitt, K., 1984. Sectoral patterns of technical change: Towards a taxonomy and a theory. *Research Policy*, 13(6), pp. 343–373.

Reichl, C., Schatz, M., & Zsak, G., 2018. *World Mining Data*. Vienna. ISBN 978-3-901074-44-8.

Scherer, F., 1984. Using Linked Patent and R&D Data to Measure Interindustry Technology Flows, in Z. Griliches (ed.). *R&D, Patents, and Productivity*. s.l.: University of Chicago Press, pp. 417–464.

WIPO, 2018. *World Intellectual Property Indicators 2018*. Geneva: World Intellectual Property Organization.

3

Mining Foreign Direct Investments and Local Technological Spillovers

BRUNO CASELLA AND LORENZO FORMENTI

Introduction: Motivation and Structure

The purpose of this chapter is to examine the book's main theme of innovation and intellectual property rights in the mining industry through the lens of foreign direct investment (FDI).[1] Specifically, it looks at the role of mining multinational enterprises (MNEs) as promoters of international mine production and as drivers of technological development in host countries. Indeed, the issue of FDI spillovers, both technological and of another nature, has a particularly critical development dimension in the mining industry where the bulk of investment takes place in developing countries, often LDCs (least developed countries).

The content of this chapter benefits from the expertise developed within UNCTAD Investment and Enterprise Division on the main trends and issues related to mining FDI (see e.g. *World Investment Report 2007*, chapters III to V: UNCTAD, 2007a) as well as on the link between FDI, technology and innovation (*World Investment Report 2005*, chapters III to VIII: UNCTAD, 2005c). The direct experience gained by UNCTAD through technical assistance to developing countries rich in mineral resources (see e.g. *Investment Advisory Series*: UNCTAD, 2011) also integrates the theoretical discussion with policy lessons learned 'in the field'.

Section 3.1 describes the broad context of mining FDI. Section 3.2 introduces the development dimension of mining FDI, and briefly discusses the different types of impacts that mining FDI have on host economies, with

---

[1] Foreign direct investment (FDI) is defined as an investment involving a long-term relationship, and reflecting a lasting interest and control, by a resident entity in one economy (foreign direct investor or parent enterprise) in an enterprise resident in an economy other than that of the foreign direct investor (FDI enterprise or affiliate enterprise or foreign affiliate) (UNCTAD, 2009a).

a focus on poor and vulnerable countries. Section 3.3 focuses on the innovation and technology dimension, the core theme of this chapter. It introduces a framework to analyze the role of mining MNEs as agents of innovation and triggers of technological spillovers in host countries. Section 3.4 presents an empirical assessment of how conducive the current context of mining FDI is to the transfer of technology and innovation to host countries. Finally, Section 3.5 provides policy insights and recommendations to host countries on how to leverage the technological and innovation potential of mining FDI for sustainable development.

3.1 Mining Foreign Direct Investment: An Overview

3.1.1 Multinational Enterprises (MNEs) in the Mining Industry

Investments in extractive industries have special features that make them very different from other kinds of productive investment. Long gestation periods and high capital expenditures are required to reach a minimum efficiency scale and this entails a significant degree of risk. They also have uncertain returns, due to the volatility of international commodity prices, as well as high sunk costs of project-specific assets that can hardly be transferred or sold.

Such kinds of investment, especially when taking place in developing countries, generally require the involvement of a large multinational enterprise (MNE) or a state-owned enterprise (SOE) that can rely on financial support from the government. As developing countries may lack the stock of knowledge and capital necessary to exploit their mineral endowments, a large number of investment projects is undertaken by foreign affiliates of MNEs. It follows that mining production is predominantly transnational: FDI plays a key role in enabling world mineral production, and MNEs in orchestrating it.

An analysis of the 100 largest (publicly listed) mining corporations confirms a prominent role of MNEs, at almost 70 percent of the sample, and a significant share of state-owned enterprises (17 percent) (Figure 3.1, left-hand side). In terms of geographic presence, a remarkable 60 percent of the subsidiaries of the largest 100 mining firms are located abroad (Figure 3.1, right-hand side). In other words, more than half of the operations of the largest mining MNEs are foreign owned. Also evident is that Chinese mining plays a major role in the domestic component of the statistics. Excluding Chinese firms from the sample leads to an increase in the share

The world's 100 largest mining firms

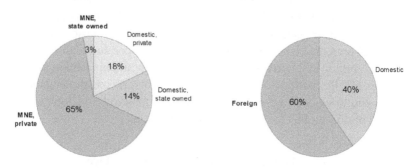

Figure 3.1   Ownership profile of (large) mining firms. Largest 100 mining companies based on operating revenues (distribution based on number of firms)
Note: Extraction from ORBIS Bureau Van Dijk, December 2018. Includes publicly listed firms operating in mining, based on US Standard Industrial Classification (SIC) (primary codes: 10 – Metal mining, 12 – Coal mining, 14 – Mining and quarrying of non-metallic minerals, except fuels). Relevance of each company for the purpose of the analysis was assessed against ORBIS trade description and, in some cases, company websites. Top 100 firms are ranked by operating revenues in the latest available year (2017 or 2018). For each company, ORBIS provides the list of *majority-owned subsidiaries* (direct or total ownership equal or above 50%). 'MNEs' are classified as companies with 10% or more of majority-owned subsidiaries located outside the home country. Companies with partial ownership information, dual-listed companies and entities part of the same corporate group were omitted.
Source: Author's calculations.

of MNEs to 76 percent and in the corresponding share of foreign subsidiaries to 64 percent.

Not only are large mining companies predominantly transnational, but mining multinationals also tend to have a more pronounced international footprint compared to other MNEs. This can be seen by comparing mining with non-mining multinationals in UNCTAD ranking of top 100 MNEs, including very large MNEs from different industries.[2] Mining MNEs (Glencore, BHP Billiton, Rio Tinto, Vale, Anglo-American) are the most internationalized in the sample according to the UNCTAD *transnationality*

2   UNCTAD ranks the largest non-financial MNEs by their foreign assets and presents data on assets, sales and employment in two top 100 lists, respectively global and from developing and transition economies. The rankings are released on an annual basis as annex tables to the flagship *World Investment Report*. For analytical insight on the role and relevance of these MNEs in the global economy, see UNCTAD (2017).

index or TNI (see the note to Table 3.1 for the TNI definition). Furthermore, they are relatively more present in developing countries. Some 35 percent of foreign affiliates of mining in UNCTAD ranking are located in developing economies, half of which are in Africa (17 percent), a share four times larger than manufacturing and services in the same group, at 5 percent and 4 percent respectively (Table 3.1).

3.1.2   Recent Trends in Mining FDI

Against the backdrop of an industry 'structurally' transnational, the level of cross-border mining investment has been dramatically falling in recent years. Since 2012, and partly due to declining commodity prices, global mining FDI has decreased by almost 90 percent, after having surged throughout the boom and hit a long-time high in 2011.[3] A pronounced downward trend has been involved in both FDI modes of entry, green-field FDI and cross-border M&As. Such a drop reflects quite closely the decline in commodity prices and its impact on investment decisions (Figure 3.2). As of 2012, MNEs found themselves bearing the costs of a decade of large-scale, growth-led investments, without the support of the high operating margins blessing the industry during the 2000s commodity super-cycle. The fall in commodity prices and consequent erosion of operating margins have forced mining MNEs to rethink their international investment model, shifting the focus from growth and investment to efficiency and productivity. Between 2012 and 2016, the operating profits of the largest five mining MNEs declined by over 60 percent, with net income falling even more (–90 percent), squeezed by weak prices and high levels of debt. For three of the top five mining MNEs (Glencore, Vale and Anglo-American), cumulative net income was even negative in the period. These very challenging operating conditions are the root causes of the abrupt retreat in mining international investment in the most recent years.

---

[3] Based on the sum of the value of FDI greenfield investment from the Financial Times Ltd, FDI markets and cross-border M&As from Thomson Reuters. Greenfield FDI relates to 'investment projects that entail the establishment of new entities and the setting up of offices, buildings, plants and factories from scratch,' while cross-border M&As involve 'the taking over or merging of capital, assets and liabilities of existing enterprises' (UNCTAD, 2009a). The use of project data on FDI greenfields and of data on cross-border M&A deals is well-established in the analysis of FDI (see UNCTAD *World Investment Report,* various editions). In particular, these two sources usefully integrate and complement Balance of Payments (BoP) FDI data in sectoral analysis as official BoP statistics are generally poor, especially for developing economies, and only available with a lag of two years.

Table 3.1 *Mining MNEs in UNCTAD Top 100 ranking of the largest global MNEs*

| | | TNI index | | | | | Ownership structure | | | | | |
| | | Domestic vs foreign affiliates | | | | | Geographic breakdown of foreign affiliates | | | | | |
Sector	# of MNEs	Avg share of foreign assets	Avg share of foreign sales	TNI index	Share domestic subsidiaries	Share foreign subsidiaries	Share developed	Share developing	Africa	Asia	LAC	Share transition
Primary, mining	5	73%	79%	0.76	14%	86%	64%	35%	17%	8%	9%	1%
Primary, oil & gas	6	82%	66%	074	13%	87%	74%	24%	5%	13%	8%	2%
Manufacturing	64	57%	72%	065	20%	80%	66%	30%	5%	18%	9%	4%
Services	25	62%	47%	0.55	29%	71%	70%	28%	4%	14%	10%	1%

Source: Author's calculations.

Note: The list of top 100 MNEs is based on UNCTAD ranking of 2016 (UNCTAD, 2017). For each MNE, the share of foreign asset and the share of foreign sales were derived from financial reports. The transnationality index (TNI) is calculated as the arithmetic mean of the share of foreign assets and the share of foreign sales. TNI is a firm-level measure of international exposure, e.g. the degree to which a MNE's interests and operations are embedded within the home country or retained abroad. It ranges from 0 (no transnationality) to 100 (full transnationality). Note that this is a simplified version of the full UNCTAD TNI that includes also the share of foreign employees in the average. The ownership structure of UNCTAD top 100 MNEs was extracted using ORBIS Bureau Van Dijk's ownership information. Subsidiaries included in the analysis are majority-owned (directly or in total) by the corporate parent.

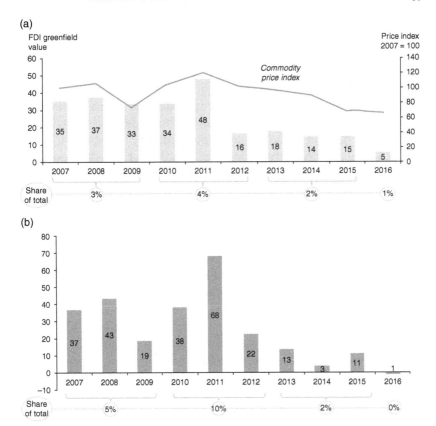

Figure 3.2   Recent trends in mining FDI
Note: Greenfield FDI and cross-border M&As are from UNCTAD FDI/MNE database, based on original data from Financial Times Ltd, fDI Markets and Thomson Reuters respectively. The same analysis based on number of projects and deals (instead of values) produces similar results.
Source: Author's calculations.

A long period of falling investment has led the global weight of mining FDI to become increasingly marginal (see shares in Figure 3.2). Yet, some developing, particularly low-income, countries still heavily rely on mining FDI. In the period 2012 – 2016, mining investment still represents 10 percent of greenfield FDI flowing to developing countries, relative to 4 percent for developed economies. This share surges to 18 percent for the groups of least developed countries (LDCs) and, in many of those economies, it exceeds 30 percent. These figures expose the development dimension of mining FDI, whereby a sizable part of fresh foreign investment flowing into some of the most vulnerable countries is tied to the exploitation of mining resources. These countries so far have been unable to diversify and attract other types of FDI.

With the bulk of economies untouched by mining FDI and few, mainly low-income countries heavily dependent on it, major developments are instead taking place on the investor side. The most visible effect is the growth of some developing country investors, such as China, India and Brazil, replacing most traditional investor countries from the developed world, particularly Canada and Australia (Figure 3.3). The most prominent case is China. Greenfield FDI investment from China between 2012 and 2016 have doubled relative to the comparable period 2002–6, positioning China as the third largest investor in cross-border greenfield projects after Canada and the United Kingdom. Chinese growth in cross-border M&As is even more impressive. In a decade, the total value of cross-border acquisitions by Chinese MNEs has increased by almost thirty times, from a cumulative 200 million US$ in the period 2002–6 to almost 6 billion US$ in 2012–16. During this period, Chinese companies have been by far the most active in acquiring foreign mining companies, with the share of China in (outward) cross-border M&As jumping from 1 percent (in 2002–6) to 25 percent. One out of four dollars spent in M&A of foreign mining companies has come from China. Around 60 percent of the value of cross-border M&As concluded by Chinese investors have targeted local companies, while 40 percent involved the acquisition of foreign affiliates of non-Chinese MNEs. The expansion of Chinese MNEs has been particularly pronounced in Africa where, between 2012 and 2016, around 20 percent of the value of FDI greenfield projects and more than 40 percent of cross-border M&As was financed by Chinese capital.

3.2   Mining FDI and Development

At the core of the critical link between mining FDI and sustainable development is the objective evidence that foreign affiliates of mining MNEs operate in some of the poorest and most depressed areas of the world. According to our preliminary analysis, more than half of the large mining exporters (with a share of mining exports in total exports above 10 percent) lie in the bottom quartile of the Human Development Index (HDI), a composite measure of achievement in key human development

Greenfield FDI project in mining, top ten investors 2012–2016

Average annual investment, billion US$, 2012–2016 and 2002–2006	Share of total

		Share of total
Canada	3,751	27%
	13,893	51%
United Kingdom	2,478	18%
	3,522	13%
China*	2,011	15%
	988	4%
Switzerland	1,062	8%
	240	1%
India	926	7%
	–	0%
United States	847	6%
	1,747	6%
Brazil	800	6%
	–	0%
Australia	540	4%
	3,526	13%
Poland	178	1%
	10	0%
Luxembourg	166	1%
	–	0%

Cross-border M&As in mining, top ten investors 2012–2016

Average annual investment, billion US$, 2012–2016 and 2002–2006	Share of total

		Share of total
China*	5,727	25%
	179	1%
United Kingdom	2,484	11%
	1,325	7%
Australia	2,118	9%
	199	1%
Canada	1,964	9%
	3,265	17%
Russian Federation	1,659	7%
	884	5%
United States	1,412	6%
	2,140	11%
Korea, Republic of	1,041	5%
	13	0%
Japan	918	4%
	281	1%
Cyprus	905	4%
	10	0%
Poland	682	3%
	–	0%

Figure 3.3 Largest investors in mining FDI
Note: Greenfield FDI and cross-border M&As are from UNCTAD FDI/MNE database, based on original data from Financial Times Ltd, fDI Markets and Thomson Reuters respectively. The same analysis based on number of projects and deals rather than values produces similar results.
Source: Author's calculations.

dimensions. Importantly, in the group of mining exporters, better HDI performance is observed in countries with lower shares of mining FDI relative to total FDI. On the other hand, countries highly dependent on mining FDI exhibit, on average, a lower level of development, substantially comparable to that of countries with negligible or no foreign investment at all.[4] In other words, while extractive FDI is crucial for mining-oriented economies, in that it represents the springboard for economic growth, countries that manage to diversify their FDI footprint across sectors tend to achieve (relatively) better development outcomes.

The impact of mining FDI on development is complex, as it spans multiple dimensions, and has historically produced controversial outcomes (UNU-WIDER, 2018). In principle, FDI can work as boosters to mineral production in countries where enabling conditions are weak. MNE entry can help overcome key constraints, such as the lack of investment financing, limited capabilities and poor access to markets. By generating tax revenues and export earnings, MNEs can also contribute to higher national income, as well as creating business and employment opportunities (UNCTAD, 2007a). However, the potential impact of mining operations, including FDI, goes well beyond the financing dimension, involving at least four different areas: i. economic impacts; ii. environmental impacts; iii. social and political impacts; and iv. technological impacts (Figure 3.4).

The rest of this section will briefly discuss the first three dimensions (economic, environmental and social and political impacts), before tackling the technological dimension, the main focus of this chapter, in Sections 3.3 and 3.4.

Economic impact. Mining FDI do not automatically generate economic gains in host countries. Research has historically pointed at an

---

[4] More specifically, the analysis of trade data for the 10 years period 2007–16 revealed 46 developing countries with an average share of exports in mining above 10% of total exports. The median HDI ranking for this group was 148 against 122 for the overall group of developing economies (based on 2015 HDI ranking). After further segmenting the group of 46 mining exporters in three sub-groups according to their FDI footprint – 22 countries with relatively low mining FDI (less than 20%), 18 countries with relatively high mining FDI (above or equal 20%) and 6 countries with negligible total FDI (at less than US$1 billion in the ten years) – the median HDI ranking for the group with relatively low mining FDI was higher than in the other two groups, at 138 against respectively 157 and 164. While merely descriptive and not implying any causal relationship, this analysis hints at a separate role of FDI in the complex and controversial link between commodity dependence and development. We believe that such dimension warrants further attention in future research work.

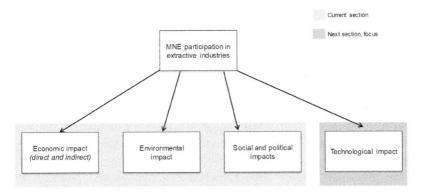

Figure 3.4   Development impact of mining FDI, multiple dimensions
Note: Based on UNCTAD (2007a).

ambiguous relationship between natural resources and economic growth. Prebisch (1950) and Singer (1950) were first to observe a long-term decline in the relative price of commodities, causing the terms of trade of commodity exporters to deteriorate. Since then, many have pointed to a negative relationship between resource abundance and economic development. Corden and Neary (1982) shed light on the recurrent link between an expanding commodity sector and de-industrialization within countries, commonly known as the 'Dutch disease'. Similarly Auty (1993) and Sachs and Warner (2001) have advanced the 'resource curse' concept, demonstrating how resource-rich countries tend to grow slower than their resource-poor peers. Others, such as Cavalcanti et al. (2011), argued that price volatility, rather than abundance per se, would be the main force behind the curse.

Most recently, the emergence of global value chains and major changes happening in the industry have led some scholars to reexamine natural-resources-based development through the lens of modern globalization. Some, including Farinelli (2012), Kaplinsky (2011), Morris et al. (2012), Ramdoo (2013), Ramdoo and Bilal (2014) and UNECA (2013), have provided new arguments for commodity-based development, emphasizing the cross-border nature of modern industrialization and the potential it entails for the extractive sector. Still, evidence at the country level is controversial, as 'blesses' and 'curses' cohabit the same regions. In sub-Saharan Africa, for instance, the breadth and depth of linkages in the extractive sector differ widely (Farooki et al., 2016; Morris et al., 2012).

Downstream activities in diamond processing have developed in Botswana, prompted by joint support of the government and foreign investor De Beers (Mbayi, 2011; UNCTAD, 2016). Spurred by FDI, a mining equipment cluster has developed in South Africa, making it a regional hub that has become, in some areas, globally competitive (Fessehaie et al., 2016). In some cases, however, potential remained untapped. In industries such as oil drilling in Angola (Teka, 2011) and gold mining in Tanzania (Mjimba, 2011), linkages of foreign affiliates with local firms are weak, limited to the sourcing of low-value services; and value addition is limited to the labor content.

Environmental impact. Environmental degradation and pollution of mine-surrounding areas are also major concerns related to mineral investment. The net environmental impact of mining FDI is the result of an interplay of factors, including project features (commodity, technology, scale and location), the quality and enforcement of regulation in the host country, and the MNE attitude towards environmental responsibility (UNCTAD, 2007a). Environmental degradation linked to mining operations is a well-documented phenomenon, particularly in countries that lack well-developed institutional ecosystems. In line with the 'race to the bottom' argument, some (e.g. Doytch and Uctum, 2016) have found mining FDI having worse environmental effects in low-income countries. Weak framework conditions, such as institutional capacity and law enforcement, but also aggressive investor lobbying, have historically been major bottlenecks to effective environmental safeguards in host countries (Appiah and Osman, 2014; Boocock, 2002; UNCTAD, 2005b). However, research also pointed at FDI as conducive to better environmental practices. In some cases, MNE entry has facilitated the inflow of environmentally sound technology (Borregaard and Dufey, 2002) and led to improved environmental standards (Mwaanga, 2017). Recently, some top MNEs have also started improving their environmental conduct as part of their commitment to advance the sustainable development agenda (UNDP/WEF/Columbia/SDSN, 2016).

Social and political impact. Finally, mining FDI have profound social and political implications in host countries, particularly for local communities residing in the vicinity of mines. Adverse social impacts affecting communities include the use and management of land in areas used for other activities, the displacement of indigenous populations, and accordingly, the loss of land and livelihoods (UNCTAD, 2012). Weak institutional capacity (ACET, 2014; Adu, 2018) and investor focus on host governments over local stakeholders (Greenovation Hub, 2014) have been major determinants behind deteriorating social conditions at mines. In addition, concerns have been raised on MNEs contributing to adverse political developments, often related to the distribution of rents. These include the perpetuation of, or the provision of incentive for, conflict (UNCTAD, 2007a) and adding to illegal practices, such as corruption (OECD, 2016a). In Africa, MNE activity in exploitative sectors has been found having a positive impact on the likelihood of conflict, particularly via large-scale land acquisitions (Sonno, 2018). In response to an increased scrutiny by the international community, however, top MNEs have been multiplying their efforts to gain a 'social licence to operate'. Global partnerships and corporate social responsibility (CSR) initiatives have been proliferating in recent years, defining new models of FDI-led community development (Gifford et al., 2010; IFC, 2014).

3.3 Mining FDI as a Vehicle of Technological Development

3.3.1 Theoretical Background

The issue of technology spillovers of FDI (i.e. the diffusion and appropriation of foreign technology, know-how or skills that may not be available locally), has been extensively studied. Literature usually links technology spillovers to productivity enhancements (or 'premia') experienced by local firms, as their most immediate and measurable effects. In general, research has found a positive relationship between inflows of FDI and the performance of domestic firms (Blomström and Kokko, 1998; Haskel et al., 2007; Keller and Yeaple, 2009). Receiving firm characteristics are important determinants of technology spillovers. Many pointed at the role of *absorptive capacity*, the stock of technology and know-how embedded in the local firm base, in ultimately determining their readiness to 'absorb' foreign assets (Fu and Gong, 2011; Kinoshita, 2000). Yet, benefits from FDI are sector-specific and increase with absorptive capacity only up to some threshold levels (Girma, 2005). The position in the supply chain and the size of receiving firms are also important factors at play. Suppliers in upstream industries enjoy productivity gains, while downstream customers tend to incur losses (Jude, 2016). Irrespective of productivity levels and technology gaps, spillovers most frequently appear in small and medium-sized firms (Damijan et al., 2013). Spillover effects also depend to some extent on foreign-investor characteristics, such as ownership and nationality. Wholly owned foreign operations are found to have more moderate (Farole and Winkler, 2014) or no productivity spillovers (Smarzynska-Javorcik, 2004) on domestic firms compared to projects involving shared domestic and foreign ownership. Industries that are more diverse in terms of FDI origin, for example, those attracting foreign investors from a larger number of nationalities, tend to have more productive domestic firms (Zhang et al., 2010). In the case of R&D investment, FDI-led productivity growth is larger when MNEs from OECD countries invest in emerging economies than in the case of R&D investments carried out by emerging country MNEs in OECD countries (Amann and Virmani, 2015).

Literature on drivers and determinants of technology spillovers is largely composed of country-level or multi-country empirical studies lacking a clear sector focus. Only some, such as Kokko et al. (1996) and Globerman (1979), have focused on the manufacturing sector of distinct countries. Spillovers in the mining sector have been only partially addressed. Discussion has been centred on the potential of MNE-SME linkages for local value addition, with the technology dimension treated as tangential to the match-making issue (OECD, 2016b; CCSI, 2016; Kaplinsky, 2011, among others). Most of these contributions take a purely qualitative approach. To our knowledge, only two studies have looked at the R&D and technology angle empirically (Farole and Winkler, 2014; Ghebrihiwet, 2019). Both of them provide statistical insight using country-level survey data, with no global assessments available to date.

In a multi-country survey, Farole and Winkler (2014) have identified two channels of technology spillovers: licensing of patented technology and R&D collaboration. On average, licensing of patented technology was listed by respondents (domestic suppliers) among the top five forms of assistance provided by foreign customers, while R&D collaboration involved up to 65 percent of respondents. In this context, joint product development has reportedly resulted in upgrading of equipment and improved quality of inputs for 'a significant number of companies'. However, there is strong variability across countries. The use of licensing and R&D collaboration is much more frequent in countries with relatively developed mining industries (and a minimum sufficient stock of absorptive know-how). Ghebrihiwet (2019) found R&D collaboration with foreign clients or suppliers having a positive and significant effect on the likelihood that firms introduce new product and process innovations. In line with the spillover literature, the likelihood and ultimate impact of collaboration on indigenous innovations differs based on the role of firms in the value chain. Suppliers are 0.5 times more likely to introduce product innovations compared to mining companies and downstream firms. In addition, continuous in-house R&D efforts (e.g. local firms' absorptive capacity), has a highly significant effect on the probability of introducing new methods of production.

3.3.2   A Framework for the Analysis of Innovation and Technological Spillovers in Mining FDI

The spectrum of mining innovations is relatively wide and varied. It not only includes frontier technology solutions developed within and for the mining industry – such as new exploration, extraction or processing techniques – but also widely applicable technologies that, despite originating in other industries, are largely used in mining supply chains (Chapter 2). These include, for instance, special transport systems connecting mines to ports, or data centres for remote operations management. Depending on intellectual property rights and contractual arrangements, technologies may, at least theoretically, transcend firms' boundaries and 'spill over' into the rest of the economy.

In the absence of a comprehensive and established approach, we introduce here a framework for the analysis of the technological impact of mining FDI (Figure 3.5). The purpose of this framework is to identify the main channels through which mining FDI can help move the technological frontier in host countries. We have identified three main channels and assessed them based on the impact on the host country's technological development (from low/indirect to high/direct).

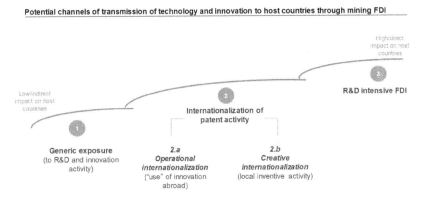

Potential channels of transmission of technology and innovation to host countries through mining FDI

Figure 3.5   An analytical framework
Source: Author's calculations.

First, and most obviously, R&D and innovation activity performed by mining MNEs, even in remote locations, and often in the home country, may generically contribute to technological development across all MNEs' international operations and therefore create spillovers in the host country. This type of channel qualifies nothing more than a 'generic exposure' of host countries to R&D and innovation activity taking place at the corporate level. The impact of this channel is unclear and indirect. In fact, on the one side, FDI do establish a preferential and stable link ('ownership-based') between the local economies and MNEs' technological and innovation capital. On the other, however, no necessary transfer mechanism ensures inclusive access to such intangible assets from the operational peripheries of the multinational group.

The second channel entails a more proactive role of MNEs in technology diffusion. This occurs when inventive activity explicitly spans beyond national borders and internationalizes as MNEs demand IP protection outside the home country. MNEs protect intellectual property abroad where they retain strategic business interests. This may be done to prevent competitors from accessing and using fundamental know-how, or to ensure protection of ground-level incremental innovations. In practical terms, internationalization happens at two levels. On the one hand, in field operations, foreign affiliates can make use of innovation generated elsewhere – most likely at headquarters (operational internationalization) – and indirectly contribute to its diffusion via licensing or other non-contractual forms of third-party relationship. More impactfully, they can trigger local inventive activity, by hiring locals in key R&D functions or via collaborative R&D with local firms (creative internationalization).

Finally, the 'frontier' of technological impact lies with R&D-intensive FDI, where the core motivation and value proposition of an FDI is to gain competitive advantage in innovation and technology development. Companies establish R&D activities in strategic locations where they have better access to knowledge-based assets that may not be easily available elsewhere. Situations of this type involve, at least theoretically, the most direct and stronger form of local impact. Indeed, not only do knowledge-intensive FDI add to the domestic stock of knowledge and call into play local economic actors, but (likely) imply frontier innovation and technology creation. If scaled, they may be at the foundation of new clusters of economic activities and ultimately shape domestic patterns of innovation.

3.4 Empirical Assessment of the Main Channels of Technological Development

The framework and channels' classification of Figure 3.5 is valid in principle and can be applied to FDI in all industries. However, when it comes to R&D and innovation, the mining industry is quite peculiar. Despite signs of change, it has historically been less oriented to transformative innovation than other industries, as largely centred on cost-cutting incremental innovations (Bryant, 2015; Deloitte, 2016 and 2017).

Compared to other industries, mining MNEs' contribution to global R&D is limited and sensitive to external shocks, such as commodity price cycles (Figure 3.6). In 2016, top mining companies invested only 0.4 percent of their sales in R&D activities, compared to 5 percent for MNEs in other, non-extractive sectors.[5] Furthermore, R&D expenditure by mining MNEs has witnessed a declining trend since 2012, as opposed to investment by other MNEs, including in oil and gas. In less than ten years, from 2008 to 2016, following a very challenging industry conjuncture since 2012, the R&D expenditure of large mining MNEs in UNCTAD ranking has decreased by 70 percent. This suggests that R&D investment in mining may not only be relatively limited compared to other sectors, but also sensitive to endogenous shocks, such as commodity price movements (see Chapter 7).

In this context, it is therefore particularly important to assess how feasible and/or realistic each channel is *in the mining context*. In the next sections, we attempt such an assessment by undertaking an empirical investigation of the current status and dynamics of R&D and innovation activity within mining MNEs. We focus on three key questions, each providing empirical background to one of the identified channels in Figure 3.5: (i) To what extent is innovation activity taking place within mining MNEs? *(channel 1)*; (ii) Does such innovation activity cross the frontier of the home country and spreads throughout the MNEs transnational borders? *(channel 2)*: (iii) Are mining MNEs directly investing in R&D projects abroad or seeking for knowledge intensive FDI? *(channel 3)*.

---

[5] It must be noted that the analysis may underestimate the overall contribution of the industry to global R&D, as figures only account for the R&D expenditure of top mining MNEs. Indeed, an important portion of mining R&D is conducted by mining equipment, technology and services (METS) companies (Daly et al., 2019; Steen et al., 2018). In addition, mine exploration can also be deemed a form of R&D. The matter is discussed in more detail in Chapter 2.

R&D expenditure as a share of sales, average in the group

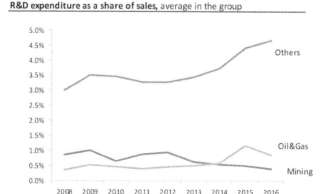

Trend in R&D expenditure, total by group, indexed 100 = 2008

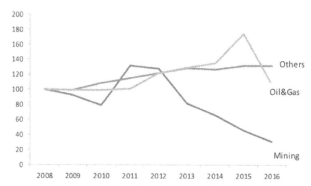

Figure 3.6   R&D expenditure of MNEs in UNCTAD top 100 ranking
Note: The sample of top 100 MNEs is based UNCTAD ranking of 2016 (UNCTAD, 2017). It includes five mining MNEs, six oil and gas MNEs, and eighty-nine other MNEs (operating in manufacturing and services, excluding financial services). Historic information on R&D expenditures and sales were extracted by ORBIS or derived from companies' financial reporting.
Source: Author's calculations.

3.4.1   R&D and Innovation Activity within Mining MNEs (channel 1)

One of the main features generally ascribed to multinational enterprises is superior technological standards. The better innovative performance of MNEs is documented by several studies. In 2002, 98 percent of the 700 largest R&D-spending firms were MNEs, accounting for more than two-thirds (69 percent) of the world's business R&D (UNCTAD, 2005c). At the country level, foreign-owned companies are found to be more innovative than domestic firms, with difference in size largely explaining the gap (Falk, 2008). Foreign affiliates also innovate more indirectly, by acquiring the most innovative domestic firms (Guadalupe et al., 2012).

In the mining industry, much innovation originates in the METS sector, with miners being largely consumers of it (Steen et al.,2018). While mining supply and service providers, particularly junior companies, tend to be more innovative than majors, frontier practices in technological, environmental, business model, and social innovation are pioneered by few top MNEs (IGF, 2018).

WIPO assembled a database containing patents for the mining sector from 1900 to 2015[6] (Daly et. al., 2019). According to the database, in the period 1990–2015, more than 600,000 patents[7] were filed in mining. Applicants were corporations in 64 percent of the patents, while in the other cases they were individuals (23 percent) or research institutions and universities (13 percent). We focus on the corporate applicants to analyze to what extent innovation is driven by MNEs. More specifically, we've compiled a global ranking of the top 100 corporate applicants of mining patents and cross-referenced it with ownership and location information to derive information on their ownership profile and locations (Figure 3.7). The analysis reveals that MNEs are the main source of innovation in the industry, with privately owned entities being the most active IP applicants. Around 60 percent of the applications in the twenty-five-year period covered by the database were filed by MNEs, mostly private owned (55 percent) (Figure 3.7, left-hand side). Interestingly, large multinational innovators (sixty MNEs), are equally split between developed economies (thirty) and developing and transition economies (thirty) (Figure 3.7, right-hand side). The latter are relatively more 'productive', as they make up 57 percent of MNE-filed applications.

3.4.2 *Internationalization of MNEs Patent Activity* (channel 2)

To what extent is the MNEs innovation activity reflected by the almost 300 thousand patent applications of Figure 3.7 (right-hand side; see note to the figure) really 'transnational'? (i.e. involving to some degree MNE host countries). Building on the classification introduced in Section 3.2 (Figure 3.5), we explore two types of internationalization of the patent

---

[6] For further details on how WIPO database has been assembled, please refer to Box 1.
[7] The numbers refer to first families' unique applications.

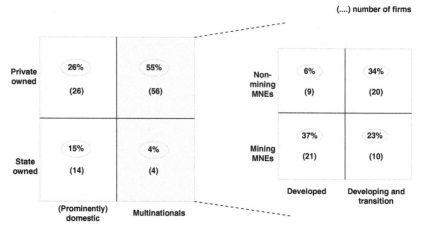

Figure 3.7   The ownership profile of the top 100 applicants of mining patents Number of applications in the period 1990–2015, share to total
Note: Patent data from EPO PatStat database. Total number of patent applications filed by top 100 corporate applicants in the period 1990–2015: 472,692 (left-hand side matrix). Total number of patent applications filed by (sixty) MNEs in the top 100 selection of corporate applicants: 277,978 (right-hand side matrix). 'MNEs' are companies with 10% or more of majority-owned subsidiaries located outside the home country. Companies with partial ownership information were omitted. The distinction between 'mining MNEs' and 'non-mining MNEs' is based on a qualitative assessment of company trade descriptions in ORBIS Bureau Van Dijk.
Source: Author's calculations.

activity: the operational internationalization and the creative internationalization.

The first and most simple channel takes place through the plain 'use' of MNE foreign-licensed technology by its foreign affiliates. We call it *operational internationalization.* Operational internationalization may occur via a number of channels, the most prominent being technology licensing within buyer–supplier relationships (UNCTAD, 2005a). Other less direct, but equally important forces, such as imitation, competition and demonstration effects, may be at play. In this context, MNEs bring the industry's more advanced technologies into developing countries and contribute to diffusion via the operations of foreign affiliates.

Recent research found that mining MNEs rely to a larger extent on local rather than central decision-making in procurement (Farole and Winkler, 2014). This attitude results both from MNEs strategic decisions and CSR mandate, where developing a local supply base has become critical to not only maximize operational efficiency, but also obtain a *social licence* to operate. In this way, local firms may end up successfully adopting superior technology when entering into contractual relationships with foreign affiliates. While operational spillovers seem to be quite indirect and uncertain, they are the most common type of technological spillovers in mining. Under the right circumstances (i.e. when a conducive policy mix is in place), they can effectively spur indigenous technological upgrades. Hence, they are a key motivation why many countries seek to attract FDI into their extractive industries (UNCTAD 2007a, 2011).

Mining FDI not only provides fertile ground for foreign-licensed technology spillovers, but also boosts local inventive activity (*creative internationalization*). Local firms may absorb foreign-licensed technology, and even develop it in-house. The increase in local inventive activity may happen at the level of foreign affiliates, when locals are hired in key R&D functions and contribute to product and process development; or when local firms end up producing new in-house innovations, as suppliers/contractors of foreign affiliates or within joint R&D ventures.

To empirically assess these two channels, we further examine the information provided by the EPO PatStat database, reporting for each patent not only the name of the applicant (i.e. the information used to perform the analysis in Figure 3.7), but also the country where the application is filed and the name and country of residence of the inventor. Such detailed information allows us to map patterns of MNE cross-border innovation, along the two main channels defined by our framework: the operational and the creative ones.

As for the operational channel, out of 277,978 mining patent applications filed by top applicant MNEs in the period 1990–2015, some 18 percent are registered in countries other than the parent's (Figure 3.8, blue shade). While MNE demand for IP protection abroad is not directly attributable to cross-border R&D (perhaps very limited in the mining industry) and may be done for purely competitive purposes, yet these data reveal the existence of some degree of internationalization in the 'use' of innovation. This is a necessary condition for the development of technological spillovers in the local economy.

It is important to notice that this type of transmission mechanism is enabled by the transnational nature of MNE activity. Not only MNEs do tend to be more proactive in developing innovations (Figure 3.7) but their transnational operating model favours innovation access and

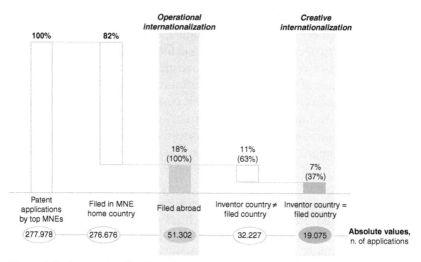

Figure 3.8   Internationalization of patent activity: evidence from WIPO patent statistics

Note: See Box 3.1.

Source: Author's calculations.

sharing across countries. Not surprisingly, the share of foreign-filed patents in the set of non-MNE top patent applicants is very limited, at 0.4 percent of the total number of patent applications.

Moving from the operational to the creative stage of patenting internationalization, one third of foreign fillings (37 percent) – corresponding to 7 percent of the total number of patent applications – reports inventor(s) whose nationality coincides with the country of filing (Figure 3.8, orange shade). While not automatic (inventor nationality may match with the country of filing for reasons other than direct involvement of local actors in the innovation process), such correspondence is interpreted as a strong hint to some kind of MNE-led local inventive activity, as implied by our definition of creative internationalization. This figure suggests that the applicant MNE may not only retain some lasting business interest in filing countries, but also conduct inventive activity involving country nationals; for example, MNE-led local innovation.

This analysis (methodological details are reported in Box 3.1) adds an important element to the discussion of technological impact of FDI in host countries. On the one hand, it confirms that innovation activity mostly takes place at the level of the parent company; however, and more

BOX 3.1 TRACKING R&D INTERNATIONALIZATION IN MINING FDI
USING PATENT STATISTICS

WIPO mining databases extract patent data from the European Patent Office's PATSTAT database. Patents belonging to the mining sector were identified through a triangulation approach which combines industry classification (two-digit ISIC Rev. 4 codes), list of mining companies provided by partner IP offices (Australia, Canada, Chile, Brazil and the US), and a combination of patent classification (IPC codes) and keywords.* The year of first filing of each patent is taken into consideration. For each patent, it identifies: the country where the patent is filed (filing country), the home country of the firm which files it (applicant country), and the residence country of the inventor/s of that patent (inventor country).**

The sample of top 100 patent applicants used in the analysis is derived from a ranking based on total mining patent applications from 2006 to 2015. The ranking only considers the last ten years of the sample because it aims at identifying top innovators based on recent performance. Additionally, singletons have not been taken into consideration for elaboration. Singletons, as highlighted in Chapter 2, are often considered innovation of lower value given that their invention is protected in a unique jurisdiction and not in multiple ones. Only entities that could be matched with Bureau Van Dijk's ORBIS were selected. The selection includes private and state-owned enterprises according to the type of global ultimate owner (GUO). For the purpose of this work, companies were classified in two homogeneous groups – multinational enterprises (MNEs) and (prominently) domestic – based on insight into their international activity. If at least one of the following criteria is satisfied, the company is labelled as MNE:

  I. *Country of incorporation of entity and GUO:* entity home country ≠ GUO home country
 II. *Ownership structure of entity:* entity home country ≠ home country of at least 10 percent of affiliates
III. *Ownership structure of GUO:* GUO home country ≠ home country of at least 10 percent of affiliates
 IV. *Desk research:* In cases where ownership analysis produced ambiguous results, information published on company reports, websites and the press was used to validate selection.

Information attached to patent applications of top applicant MNEs has been used to build proxy measures of two types of technology spillovers that may originate from MNE activity. The interpretation of each involves specific assumptions:

• Foreign filing (filing country ≠ applicant country) as a proxy of *operational internationalization*. Typically, the main reason for a firm to file for a patent in a country different from the home one is strategic. The company may or may not sell its product there but, in any case, it wants to exclude its competitors from the appropriation of the knowledge embedded in the patented

BOX 3.1 (Continued)

innovation. After the innovation is patented, this knowledge, which cannot be appropriated from entities other than the applicant, is disclosed.

• Coincidence between filing country and inventor country as a proxy of *creative internationalization*. This is a subset of the operational spillovers. In this case not only is the invention protected in a country different from the home country of the firm, but also at least one of its inventors resides in that country.*** This is a stronger form of spillover as not only the knowledge is disclosed through the patents but there is also at least one physical person residing in that country with the know-how necessary to develop such technology.

* For a detailed description of the methods used to assemble the database, please see Daly et al. (2019).
** Home country is defined as the country where the filing entity is incorporated.
*** While inventors are usually employees of the filing company, they could also be contractors temporarily working for the firm with the only purpose of developing the innovation.

notably, it also reveals a non-negligible flow of innovation from the centre to the periphery, not only at the operational level but also at the creative level. Albeit limited, such diffusion of innovation and technology is highly critical in developing countries, where economic resources other than mineral endowments are few.

3.4.3   R&D-Intensive FDI (channel 3)

FDI in mining are traditionally natural-resource seeking, driven by the availability, price and quality of natural resources, infrastructure-enabling resources to be exploited and investment incentives. In this context, there is little scope for technology or innovation-driven FDI ('strategic asset-seeking' FDI). As confirmed by the analysis of FDI greenfield projects from 2007 to 2016, mining FDI are mostly concentrated in the activity of material extraction (68 percent), while a residual portion (32 percent) involves other types of activity such as sales (14 percent) and manufacturing (12 percent). R&D-oriented FDI are very limited, at 1.5 percent of the total number of projects (Figure 3.9, left-hand side). Noticeably, low development of R&D-intensive FDI is not an issue of mining FDI strictly speaking, but also for oil and gas and manufacturing industries close to mining, such as mineral and metal

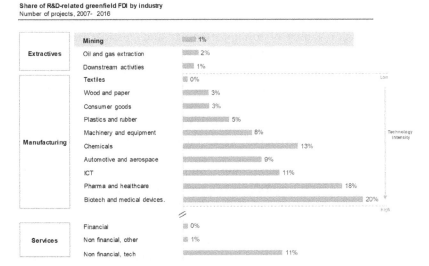

Figure 3.9 Greenfield FDI by type of activity

Note: Greenfield project data from Financial Times fDi Markets Project Database (Jan 2007–Dec 2016), December 2018. 'R&D-oriented' greenfield is any greenfield investment project conducted in 'Research and development', 'Design, development and testing' and 'Education and training' as defined by the publisher. Product groups are aggregates of fDi Markets sectors or subsectors. Ranking of technology intensity for manufacturing industries is adapted from the OECD ISIC Rev. 3 Technology Intensity Definition. *Downstream activities* include petroleum refining, iron and steel mills, ferroalloy and steel production. *Mining* includes coal mining; gold ore and silver mining; copper, nickel, lead and zinc mining: iron ore mining: non-metallic mineral mining; other metal ore mining; and support activities for mining.

Source: Author's calculations.

processing (Figure 3.9, right-hand side). More generally R&D intensive FDI are concentrated in selected industries characterized by high technological intensity, such as ICT, automotive and pharma, or high-tech services.

3.5 Concluding Remarks and Policy Implications

Despite the recent fall in mining FDI (Figure 3.2), the role of MNEs and cross-border investment in mining remains crucial. On the one side, a significant portion of global mining production is performed by MNEs through their foreign operations (Figure 3.1). On the other side, a number of countries, especially low income, heavily rely on mining FDI as a major source of foreign earnings and possible pathways to economic diversification. In a moment when the geography of investment in mining FDI is rapidly changing, particularly with the rise of Chinese MNEs (Figure 3.3), the discussion of the development implications of mining FDI becomes crucial. The impact of mining FDI on host countries is multiple, involving primarily the economic dimension, the social dimension, the environmental dimension and the technological dimension (Figure 3.4).

Focusing on the last mentioned, compared to other industries, the technological or innovation dimension of mining FDI is less visible and recognized. This is due to the fact that the mining industry is perceived as having rather poor technological content and carrying out limited innovation (Figure 3.6). In addition, a major driver for undertaking cross-border investment in mining is the access to mineral endowments, with no immediate connection to local technological development. However, insights from our analysis of the different channels of transmission of innovation and technology though FDI (Figure 3.5) suggest the existence of a link between mining FDI and technological development in host countries, which holds true across three different dimensions: (a) Given MNEs are the major source of innovation in the mining industry, FDI creates a preferential channel to their technological assets (Figure 3.7); (b) As MNE-owned patents are used and enforced by foreign affiliates in host countries, conditions are created for operational spillovers (Figure 3.8); (c) Under certain conditions, the availability, use or development of MNE technology can stimulate local inventive activity (Figure 3.8). Yet, a realistic assessment of the current FDI landscape in mining and other low-tech industries suggests that R&D-oriented FDI are still very limited and that traditional motivations (natural resource-seeking, efficiency seeking and market seeking) remain the dominant drivers of MNE foreign investment decisions (Figure 3.9).

Thus, policymakers in mining-rich countries, particularly those poor countries that heavily rely on mining, should not overlook the technology and innovation dimension when designing investment policy frameworks. At the same time, they should be aware of some intrinsic limitations of mining FDI in driving technological development and thus they should also pursue investment strategy oriented to the diversification of industries characterized by higher R&D and technological content.

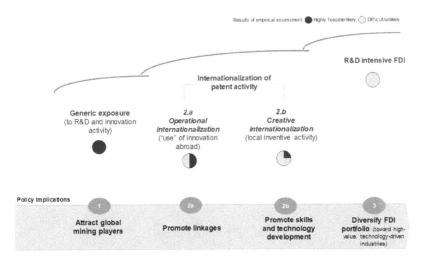

Figure 3.10   Policy recommendations: linking analysis and practice for impact
Source: Author's calculations.

Figure 3.10 relies on our framework (Figure 3.5) and the empirical assessment conducted in Section 4 to derive high-level policy options and recommendations for each channel. Policy options are briefly discussed in the following.

3.5.1   Attract Global Mining Players

Global mineral production and, ultimately, innovation, is largely undertaken by a number of global players. Not only do MNEs orchestrate most large-scale mining projects, they also lead global inventive activity (Figure 3.7). Possessing frontier technology, skills and know-how give MNEs a comparative advantage in mine construction, production and processing, which makes them desirable, if not essential partners for developing-country governments. In many cases, attracting foreign investment has not only helped host governments to secure investment financing, but has also enabled domestic exploration and extraction activities otherwise technologically unfeasible. Absent a strong comparative advantage, government efforts in this realm may be prohibitively costly and end up hindering investment, resulting in reduced production and tax revenues (UNCTAD, 2011). Following a wave of nationalizations in the 60s and 70s, attracting FDI has been instrumental in rehabilitating the declining copper industry of Zambia, initially through MNE take-overs of State-owned mines, and later through new greenfield investments (UNCTAD, 2007b).

Yet, the extra costs that governments bear in terms of resource rent sharing may be important (UNCTAD 2007a). In addition, as investment may be motivated by the need to supply foreign refineries and smelters, the flipside of relying on MNEs for mineral extraction is that refining and processing activities will often take place abroad. For these reasons, investment policy shall not work in isolation, but rather be coupled with policy instruments that seek to maximize local content and encourage the development of downstream activities.

3.5.2a   Promote Linkages

Local procurement opportunities vary widely along the life cycle of a mining project. It is estimated that procurement opportunities range between 0 and 3 percent of total spend at exploration, and up to 75 to 90 percent at production (OECD, 2016b). In order to maximize *upstream linkages*, a number of governments have imposed import restrictions or other purchase requirements on MNE affiliates. In some cases, minimum levels of local purchase are specified in contracts; in other cases, affiliates are required to state how they plan to increase local content, or submit local procurement plans (UNCTAD 2007a).

Policies to promote upstream linkages increasingly go beyond local content requirements and involve nurturing the local firm base through supplier development programs implemented jointly with foreign affiliates. Support usually includes matchmaking, as well as technology and capacity development services (UNCTAD 2005a). Analysis in Figure 3.8 points to a substantive degree of internationalization in the 'use' of mining innovation. Some 18 percent of MNE patent applications are filed in countries other than the parent, roughly a quarter of them in developing economies. Through foreign affiliate operations, MNEs bring the industry's most advanced technologies to host countries. Thus, entering into contracts or other forms of partnership with foreign affiliates can be conducive to 'operational' spillovers.

As MNEs increasingly source 'local' and corporate responsibility levels – the playing field of global business – host country governments shall look beyond pure local content requirements and set up partnership-driven platforms that enable local firms to grasp the technology benefits of buyer–supplier relationships. Success stories in this realm have been multiplying in recent years. While most remain business cases, some have spread across firm boundaries. Working closely with MNEs as contractors of exploration services, for instance, some junior domestic firms in Canada have upgraded and become world leaders in mine exploration (UNCTAD, 2011).

3.5.2b *Promote Skills and Technology Development*

Our findings (Figure 3.8) suggest that interfirm relationships not only provide a preferential channel for technology transfer and appropriation, but may also spur local inventive activity (e.g. 'creative' spillovers). As literature shows, addressing weak absorptive capacity (i.e. the lack of a sufficient stock of skills, productive and technological capabilities of receiving firms), is crucial for enabling technology spillovers. While holding true for operational spillovers, this assumption is fundamental in the case of creative spillovers that involve indigenous R&D and technology development.

When designing mineral investment policies, governments should not only attract the right foreign partners, but also invest in upgrading local productive capabilities that are necessary for matchmaking. While sound innovation policies, coupled with the availability of well-developed business ecosystems play an important role, learning may also result from locally rooted MNE activity. In Chile, foreign investors have traditionally employed Chilean workers in their mine operations, including senior managers and engineers. Over time, this helped develop a local knowledge and skills base that would become important to the broader industry. At the same time, not only did government support focus on providing skills development, innovation and R&D support services, but a part of mineral revenues were earmarked to finance indigenous innovation and R&D activities. This, coupled with the availability of an extensive network of universities specialized in mining-related education and research, have contributed to the upgrading of domestic firms to global standards (UNCTAD, 2011).

UNCTAD field practice shows that a mix of policy tools is possible. These include, for instance, matchmaking services for MNEs and suppliers, or public funds for skill development and R&D. Yet, the industry's success stories remain limited to a small number of countries, such as Canada and Chile. Specific examples of policy tools employed in these countries, with varying degrees of success, include:

- Creating public–private networks for knowledge sharing and policy formulation;
- Setting up specialized training and research institutions (joint actions by the government and industry);
- Public financing of mining R&D, including investment funds financed with mineral tax revenues.

3.5.3   Diversify FDI Portfolio (towards High-Value, Technology-Driven Industries)

While research shows potential for and, to some extent, evidence of technology spillovers in some host countries, policymakers should maintain realistic expectations in mining FDI-led technological growth. This is due to some intrinsic characteristics of mining investment. Indeed, the industry has historically been resistant to groundbreaking innovation. Cross-border investment in the sector has traditionally been 'resource-seeking', with few technology-driven investments and those only rarely transnational (Figure 3.9).

For mineral-rich countries, diversification towards non-extractive value-added activities remains crucial. While resource extraction should be at the core of their industrial development strategies, it should be intended as a pathway to economic prosperity rather than a primary source of comparative advantage. Depending on context, local content policies should aim at nurturing infant downstream activities, beyond purely encouraging local firms and individuals to link up to upstream extractives. In the long term, mineral rents shall be reinvested in the development of economic and social infrastructure, rather than be channelled into more productive activities.

Attracting (the right!) global players and establishing sound public-private partnerships may well serve to this purpose. The diamond sector of Botswana is an exceptional case in point. Against the fashion at the time of discovery (1970s), the government did not nationalize the mines, but entered into a joint venture agreement with foreign investor De Beers. The government managed to negotiate favourable rent-sharing agreements and appropriate some 80 percent of the industry profits in the form of royalties, taxes and dividends. Much of these served to finance spending in infrastructure projects, education and health (Jefferis, 2014). As a result, 'policy-driven' linkages with downstream activities, such as diamond processing and polishing, have developed over time (Mbayi, 2011). As of 2016, cutting and polishing activities count twenty active firms generating some 2,270 local jobs (UNCTAD, 2016). DeBeers has lately moved its stone-sorting operations and international sales department from London to Gaborone.

Mineral wealth can also be used to boost domestic R&D and upgrade the local skills base. While success requires some minimum absorptive capacity, the experience of Chile shows that this is actually doable. Foreign companies have traditionally employed Chilean managers and engineers in their operations, developing a local knowledge base that has become important to the broader industry. Starting from the 1980s, government support has been centred on providing services related to skills development, innovation and R&D, with revenues of the 'mining tax' being specifically earmarked to these purposes. These initiatives, coupled with the availability of an extensive network of universities specialized in mining-related education, have encouraged inter-firm collaboration and contributed to the upgrading of domestic firms to global standards (UNCTAD, 2011).

***

References

Acharyya, J. (2009). FDI, Growth and the Environment: Evidence from India on CO_2 emission during the last two decades. *Journal of Economic Development*, 34 (1 June), 43–58.

Adu, G. (2018). Impacts of Foreign Direct Investment (FDI) on Rural Poverty in Developing Countries: The case of mining FDI in Ghana, Major Papers. 19. https://scholar.uwindsor.ca/major-papers/19

African Centre for Economic Transformation (2014). Mining and the Social Environment in West Africa. ACET Policy Brief – Sustainable Resources Series.

Amann, E., and S. Virmani (2015). Foreign Direct Investment and Reverse Technology Spillovers: The effect on total factor productivity. *OECD Journal: Economic Studies*, 2104 (1), 129–153.

Appiah, D .O., and B. Osman (2014). Environmental Impact Assessment: Insights from mining communities in Ghana. *Journal of Environmental Assessment Policy and Management*. 16 (04 December). https://doi.org/10.1142/S1464333214500318

Auty, R. M. (1993), *Sustaining Development in Mineral Economies: The resource curse thesis*, London: Routledge.

Blomström, M., and A. Kokko (1998). Multinational Corporations and Spillovers. *Journal of Economic Surveys*, 12 (3), 247–277. doi:10.1111/1467-6419.00056

Boocock, C. N. (2002). Environmental Impacts of Foreign Direct Investment in the Mining Sector in Sub-Saharan Africa, in OECD (2002), *Foreign Direct Investment and the Environment: Lessons from the mining sector,* *OECD Global Forum on International Investment,* Paris: OECD Publishing. https://doi.org/10.1787/9789264199026-en

Borregaard, N., and A. Dufey (2002). Environmental Effects of Foreign versus Domestic Investment in the Mining Sector in Latin America, in OECD (2002), *Foreign Direct Investment and the Environment: Lessons from the mining fector, OECD Global Forum on International Investment,* Paris: OECD Publishing. https://doi.org/10.1787/9789264199026-en

Bryant, P. (2015). The Case for Innovation in the Mining Industry. Research report. Chicago, IL: Clareo.

Brynildsen, Ø. S., and D. Nombora (2013). *Mining without Development: The case of Kenmare Moma mine in Mozambique.* Maputo and Brussels: Centro de Integritade Publica/the European Network on Debt and Development.

Cavalcanti, T. V. de V., K. Mohaddes and M. Raissi (2011). Commodity Price Volatility and the Sources of Growth, Cambridge Working Papers in Economics no. 1112, Faculty of Economics, University of Cambridge.

Columbia Center on Sustainable Investment (2016). *Linkages to the Resource Sector: The role of companies, government and international development cooperation.* Bonn and Eschborn, Germany: Deutsche Gesellschaft für Internationale Zusammenarbeit (GIZ) GmbH.

Corden, W. M., and J. P. Neary (1982). Booming Sector and De-Industrialization in a Small Open Economy. *The Economic Journal,* 92, 825–848.

Daly, A., Valacchi, G., & Raffo, J., 2019. Mining patent data: measuring innovation in the mining industry with patents. WIPO Economics Research Working Paper No. 56. Geneva, WIPO

Damijan, J. P., M. Rojec, B. Majcen and M. Knell (2013). Impact of Firm Heterogeneity on Direct and Spillover Effects of FDI: Micro-evidence from ten transition countries. *Journal of Comparative Economics,* 41 (3). https://doi.org/10.1016/j.jce.2012.12.001

Deloitte (2016). Innovation in Mining: Africa 2016. Deloitte Touche Tohmatsu Limited. www2.deloitte.com/content/dam/Deloitte/global/Documents/Energy-and-Resources/gx-za-en-innovation-in-mining.pdf

Deloitte (2017). Innovation in Mining: Latin America 2017. Deloitte Touche Tohmatsu Limited. https://www2.deloitte.com/content/dam/Deloitte/global/Documents/Energy-and-Resources/latin-america-innovation-in-mining.pdf

Doytch, N., and M. Uctum (2016). Globalization and the Environmental Impact of FDI. Economics Working Paper 12: The Graduate Centre, City University of New York. https://academicworks.cuny.edu/gc_econ_wp/12/

Falk, M. (2008). Effects of Foreign Ownership on Innovation Activities: Empirical evidence for twelve European countries. *National Institute Economic Review*, 204 (1), 85–97. https://doi.org/10.1177/00279501082040011001

Farinelli F. (2012). Natural Resources, Innovation and Export Growth: The wine industry in Chile and Argentina, UNU-MERIT Ph.D. Dissertation – December 2012, Maastricht University: The Netherlands.

Farole, T., and D. Winkler (2014). *Making Foreign Direct Investment Work for Sub-Saharan Africa: Local spillovers and competitiveness in global value chains. directions in development–trade.* Washington, DC: World Bank. https://openknowledge.worldbank.org/handle/10986/16390

Farooki, M., D. Perkins, J. Fessahie and A. Malden (2016). Linkages in the Southern African Mining Sector: Domestic procurement challenges and context. Working Paper, Enterprise around Mining project. Hannover, Germany: Federal Institute for Geosciences and Natural Resources.

Fessehaie, J., Z. Rustomjee and L. Kaziboni (2016). *Mining-Related National Systems of Innovation in Southern Africa: National trajectories and regional integration. 2016/84.* Helsinki: UNU-WIDER.

Fu, X., and Y. Gong (2011). Absorptive Capacity and the Benefits from Global Reservoirs of Knowledge: Evidence from a linked China-OECD dataset. University of Oxford, SLPTMD Working Paper Series No. 031.

Ghebrihiwet N. (2019). FDI Technology Spillovers in the Mining Industry: Lessons from practice. Resources Policy, 62, 463–471. https://doi.org/10.1016/j.resourpol.2018.04.005

Gifford, B., A. Kestler and S. Anand (2010). Building Local Legitimacy into Corporate Social Responsibility: Gold mining firms in developing nations. *Journal of World Business*, 45 (3 July), 304–311. https://doi.org/10.1016/j.jwb.2009.09.007

Girma, S. (2005), Absorptive Capacity and Productivity Spillovers from FDI: A threshold regression analysis. *Oxford Bulletin of Economics and Statistics*, 67: 281–306. doi:10.1111/j.1468-0084.2005.00120.x

Globerman, S. (1979). Foreign Direct Investment and 'Spillover' Efficiency Benefits in Canadian Manufacturing Industries. *Canadian Journal of Economics, Canadian Economics Association*, 12 (1), 42–56, February.

Greenovation Hub (2014). China's Mining Industry at Home and Overseas: Development, impacts and regulation. The Climate and Finance Policy Centre of GHub. www.ghub.org/cfc_en/wp-content/uploads/sites/2/2014/11/China-Mining-at-Home-and-Overseas_Main-report2_EN.pdf

Guadalupe, M., O. Kuzmina and C. Thomas. 2012. Innovation and Foreign Ownership. *American Economic Review*, 102 (7), 3594–3627.

Haskel J. E., S. C. Pereira and J. Matthew (2007). Does Inward Foreign Direct Investment Boost the Productivity of Domestic Firms? *The Review of Economics and Statistics*, 89 (3), 482–496.

Intergovernmental Forum on Mining, Minerals, Metals and Sustainable Development (IGF). (2018). *Innovation in Mining: Report to the 2018 International Mines Ministers Summit.* Winnipeg: IISD.

IMF (2012). Fiscal Regimes for Extractive Industries: Design and implementation. IMF Policy Papers. Washington, DC: International Monetary Fund

International Finance Corporation (2014). Sustainable and Responsible Mining in Africa: A getting started guide. IFC – World Bank Group, Nairobi. https://www.ifc.org/wps/wcm/connect/14d1fb8c-8d63-47c9-acb7-35b20a488ff2/Sustainable+Mining+in+Africa.pdf?MOD=AJPERES&CVID=knWL6Rr

Jefferis, K. (2014). Macroeconomic Management in a Mineral-Rich Economy. Policy Note 14/0105, March 2014. London: The International Growth Centre (IGC)

Jude, C. (2016). Technology Spillovers from FDI: Evidence on the intensity of different spillover channels. *The World Economy*, 39 (12 Special Issue: Global Trade Policy 2016, edited by David Greenaway), 1947–1973. doi:10.1111/twec.12335

Kaplinsky, R. (2011). Commodities for Industrial Development: Making linkages work. Working paper 01/2011, United Nations Industrial Development Organization (UNIDO). Vienna: UNIDO.

Keller, W., and S. R. Yeaple (2009). Multinational Enterprises, International Trade, and Productivity Growth: Firm-level evidence from the United States. *The Review of Economics and Statistics 2009*, 91 (4), 821–831.

Kinoshita, Y. (2000). R&D and Technology Spillovers Via FDI: Innovation and absorptive capacity (November 2000). William Davidson Institute Working Paper No. 349.

Kokko, A. R. Tansini and M. C. Zejan (1996). Local Technological Capability and Productivity Spillovers from FDI in the Uruguayan Manufacturing Sector. *The Journal of Development Studies*, 32 (4), 602–611. doi:10.1080/00220389608422430

Liu, Z. (2008), Foreign Direct Investment and Technology Spillovers: Theory and evidence. *Journal of Development Economics*, 85 (1–2), 176–193, ISSN 0304–3878. https://doi.org/10.1016/j.jdeveco.2006.07.001

Matysek, A. L., and B. S., Fisher (2016). Productivity and Innovation in the Mining Industry. BAE Research report 2016 n.1. BA Economics: Canberra, Australia.

Mbayi, L. (2011), Linkages in Botswana's Diamond Cutting and Polishing Industry, Discussion Paper n°6, Making the Most of Commodities Programme, The Open University and The University of Cape Town.

McKinsey and Company (2015). *Productivity in Mining Operations: Reversing the downward trend.* New York: McKinsey and Company.

Mjimba, V. (2011), The Nature and Determinants of Linkages in Emerging Minerals Commodity Sectors: A case study of gold mining in Tanzania,

Discussion Paper n°7, Making the Most of Commodities Programme, The Open University and The University of Cape Town.

Morris, M., R. Kaplinsky and D. Kaplan (2012). *One Thing Leads To Another: Promoting industrialisation by making the most of the commodity boom in sub-Saharan Africa.* Milton Keynes: The Open University.

Mwaanga, C. (2017). A Study of the Economic and Environmental Impacts of Foreign Direct Investment in the Mining Sector in Zambia. *Journal of Business Administration and Education,* 9 (2), 23–47.

OECD (2016a). *Corruption in the Extractive Value Chain: Typology of risks, mitigation measures and incentives.* Paris: OECD Publishing. http://dx .doi.org/10.1787/9789264256569-en

OECD (2016b). *Collaborative Strategies for In-Country Shared Value Creation: Framework for extractive projects.* Paris: OECD Publishing. http://dx .doi.org/10.1787/9789264257702-en

Peterson, D. J., T. LaTourrette and J. T. Bartis. *New Forces at Work in Mining: Industry views of critical technologies.* Santa Monica, CA: RAND Corporation.

Prebisch, R. (1950). The Economic Development of Latin America and its Principal Problems. *Economic Bulletin for Latin America,* 7 (1 1962). United Nations Economic Commission for Latin America, Santiago de Chile.

Ramdoo, I. (2013). Fixing Broken Links: Linking extractive sectors to productive value chains, Discussion Paper n°143, March 2013, European Center for Development Policy Management, Brussels.

Ramdoo, I., and S. Bilal (2014). Extractive Resources for Development: Trade, Fiscal and Industrial Considerations, Discussion Paper n°156, January 2014, European Center for Development Policy Management, Brussels.

Sachs, J. D., and A. M. Warner (2001). Natural Resources and Economic Development: The curse of natural resources. *European Economic Review,* Elsevier, 45 (4–6), 827–838.

Singer, H. (1950). The Distribution of Gains between Investing and Borrowing Countries. *American Economic Review,* 15, 473–485.

Smarzynska Javorcik, B. (2004). Does Foreign Direct Investment Increase the Productivity of Domestic Firms? In search of spillovers through backward linkages. *American Economic Review,* 94 (3), 605–627. doi:10.1257/ 0002828041464605

Sonno, T. (2018). Globalisation and Conflicts: The good, the bad, and the ugly of corporations in Africa. Job Market Paper, February 2018. www .tommasosonno.com

Steen, J., S. Macaulay, N. Kunz and J. Jackson (2018). Understanding the innovation ecosystem in mining and what the digital revolution means for it, in *Extracting Innovations: Mining, energy, and technological change in the digital age*. Clifford, M., Perrons, R., Ali, S., and Grice, T. (eds). New York: CRC Press, pp. 3–25.

Teka, Z. (2011). Backward Linkages in the Manufacturing Sector in the Oil and Gas Value Chain in Angola. Discussion Paper n°11, Making the Most of Commodities Programme, The Open University and The University of Cape Town.

UNCTAD (2001). *World Investment Report 2001: Promoting linkages*. New York and Geneva: United Nations.

UNCTAD (2005a). *Improving the Competitiveness of SMEs through Enhancing Productive Capacity – Proceedings of four experts meetings*. New York and Geneva: United Nations.

UNCTAD (2005b). *Economic Development in Africa: Rethinking the role of foreign direct investment*. New York and Geneva: United Nation.

UNCTAD (2005c). *World Investment Report 2005: Transnational corporations and the internationalization of R&D*. New York and Geneva: United Nations.

UNCTAD (2007a). *World Investment Report 2007: Transnational corporations, extractive industries and development*. New York and Geneva: United Nations.

UNCTAD (2007b). 'Transnational corporations in the extractive industries in Zambia'. Country case study prepared for the World Investment Report 2007. Geneva: UNCTAD, mimeo.

UNCTAD (2007c). 'Transnational corporations in the extractive industries in Chile'. Country case study prepared for the World Investment Report 2007. Geneva: UNCTAD, mimeo.

UNCTAD (2009a). *UNCTAD Training Manual on Statistics for FDI and the Operations of TNCs*. New York and Geneva: United Nations.

UNCTAD (2009b). *Best Practices in Investment for Development: How to utilize FDI to improve infrastructure – electricity; Lessons from Chile and New Zealand*. Investment Advisory Series; Series B, n.1. New York and Geneva: United Nations

UNCTAD (2011). *Best Practices in Investment for Development: How to attract and benefit from FDI in Mining – Lessons from Canada and Chile*. Investment Advisory Series; Serie B, n.7. New York and Geneva: United Nations.

UNCTAD (2012). *Extractive Industries: Optimizing value retention in host countries*. Discussion paper prepared for UNCTAD XIII Conference, April 2012, Qatar. New York and Geneva: United Nations.

UNCTAD (2013). *World Investment Report 2013: Global Value Chains: Investment and trade for development*. New York and Geneva: United Nations.

UNCTAD (2015). *World Investment Report 2015: Reforming international investment governance*. New York and Geneva: United Nations.

UNCTAD (2016). *Report on the Implementation of the Investment Policy Review: Botswana*. New York and Geneva: United Nations.

UNCTAD (2017). *World Investment Report 2017: Investment and the digital economy*. New York and Geneva: United Nations.

UNDP/WEF/Columbia/SDSN (2016). Mapping Mining to the Sustainable Development Goals: An Atlas.

UNECA (2013). Economic Report on Africa 2013: Making the Most of Africa's Commodities: Industrializing for growth, jobs and economic transformation. United Nations Economic Commission for Africa. Addis Abeba. www.uneca.org/publications/economic-report-africa-2013

UNU-WIDER (2018). Extractive Industries: The Management of Resources as a Driver of Sustainable Development, edited by Tony Addison and Alan Roe. United Nations University World Institute for Development Economics Research and Oxford University Press. Helsinky and UK.

Zhang, Y., H. Li, Y. Li and L.-A. Zhou (2010). FDI Spillovers in an Emerging Market: The role of foreign firms' country origin diversity and domestic firms' absorptive capacity. *Strategic Management Journal*, 31, 969–989. doi:10.1002/smj.856

4

Innovation in Mining Global Value Chains: Implications for Emerging Economies

MICHIKO IIZUKA, CARLO PIETROBELLI
AND FERNANDO VARGAS

Emerging countries are among the largest mineral producers in the world and, in many cases, the mining sector represents a notable share of their economies. Considering their large mineral reserves and the increasing number of explorations underway, emerging countries' role in the mining sector is expected to rise.[1] In the past, the mining sector has not always been seen as an "engine of growth" despite its economic significance in emerging countries. Early analysts of economic development expected manufacturing to play a much larger role in promoting fast development (Prebisch, 1950). However, today there are signs that this may be changing. The mining sector is increasingly organized along "value chains" with a global span. Mining companies tend to outsource their intermediate inputs and services to a larger extent than in the past, and scientific and technological developments are pervasive in the industry. Importantly, the increasing sophistication of mining technologies is placing more emphasis on the technological contribution of companies, which are not themselves miners but which are nonetheless important links in the supply chain for mining. This potentially opens a window of opportunity for the structural transformation of emerging economies endowed with natural resources, and the scope for entering more

---

The authors wish to thank Beatriz Calzada and Caio Torres for their research assistance, and participants at the WIPO Conference on Innovation in the mining sector in Geneva (2017). We also appreciate the extensive comments given by David Humphreys, Julio Raffo and Giulia Valacchi.
[1] In this chapter, we use the term "emerging countries" in a broad form, to include also developing countries.

knowledge-intensive and promising activities (Anderson, 2012; Marin et al, 2015; Katz and Pietrobelli 2018; Pietrobelli et al., 2018).

This chapter discusses the innovation processes that are developing in the mining sector of emerging countries, and uses the global value chains (GVC) approach to analyze the potential available to local firms. The focus is clearly on all forms of innovation, not only those eventually subject to patenting. These include innovations in products and processes, but also in business, marketing and organizational models and practices. Moreover, the remarkable innovation that may powerfully develop through the interaction and linkages between mining companies, their suppliers and other organizations active in the innovation ecosystem, cannot be underplayed.

After briefly reviewing the relative importance of the mining sector in emerging countries – and in particular Latin America – we discuss the potential of innovation to contribute to economic development in this sector. To illustrate the types of innovation implemented, we refer to specific examples of Latin American suppliers in mining value chains. However, in developing this argument, we cannot forget that in most of Latin American mining there is insufficient supply of local knowledge. For instance, indicators of R&D expenditures and researchers involved in the Chilean mining industry show a significant lag with respect to countries like Australia (Meller and Parodi, 2017). Multinational mining companies have not traditionally conducted intensive R&D activities near their operations (Pietrobelli et al., 2018), local universities tend to specialize in scientific topics that are not directly linked to the mining industry (Confraria and Vargas, 2019), while the majority of local METS firms lack the capabilities to actively participate in innovative projects. There are still several good examples of very innovative suppliers, but their success is limited in scale and is not shared by all suppliers. In Section 4.1 we stress the importance of mining activities in emerging countries; Section 4.2 discusses mining innovation focusing on its role in emerging countries; Section 4.3 suggests how global mining value chains could affect emerging countries, looking at some specific examples from the Latin American region; Section 4.4 discusses some policy experiences related to mining innovation in Latin America; Section 4.5 concludes.

4.1   Importance of Mining Activities in Emerging Countries

The mining sector greatly contributes to the economies of emerging countries, in particular in Latin America and sub-Saharan Africa. Table 1 (upper part) shows the proportion of ores and metals in merchandise exports along with rents from natural resources by income level and by geographical regions. This confirms that natural resources are more important among lower-income countries from Middle East and North Africa (MENA), sub-Saharan Africa and Latin America and Caribbean (LAC) regions. LAC and sub-Saharan Africa are most dependent on ores and minerals, whilst the MENA region's main natural resources are oil and natural gas. In Latin America, despite a decline over the last decade, natural resources still represent a large share of GDP and exports (Table 4.1).

This general trend of the continued importance of mining resources is likely to persist, as reserves for key minerals are mainly present in emerging countries, and notably in Latin America (Figure 4.1 and US Geological Survey, 2015). Indeed, the share of production from developing countries has been increasing in the last decade (Figure 4.2).

The reserves of minerals and the proportion of mineral production do not correlate with the innovation patterns than can be observed in patent data (see Figure 4.3). This is particularly true for Latin American countries that only represent a minor fraction of the mining patents, while developed economies are very active in this domain. Emerging countries as whole have seen a remarkable increase in the number of mining patents over the last decade, but most of this increase is due to China's spectacular surge in this period.

Companies from developed countries are also disproportionally represented in the sample of larger and more international firms in the mining GVC (Figure 4.4).[2] However, companies from emerging countries have seen their participation increase in the past decade. LAC firms have grown in share in the mining segment, while other emerging economies – particularly China – have grown outstandingly in proportion of the mining equipment, technology and services (METS) segment. The increase of the Chinese METS companies correlates with a similarly impressive growth in patents. LAC companies' patenting remains very modest in both GVC segments. In 2004, LAC mining companies accounted for almost 3 percent of patenting activity, which is related to the patenting activities of large mining companies like Codelco and Vale.

4.2 Innovation in the Mining Sector

We adopt here a broad definition of innovation that includes technological and non-technological innovation to understand the mining

---

[2] The data source, BVD Orbis, is biased toward large and international companies.

Table 4.1 Natural resources matter for GDP and trade for emerging and Latin American countries

Indicators	Year	Level of income				Regions*				
		Low	L-Mid	Upper	High	EAsia&P	E&CAsia	LAC	MENA	SubAfrica
Ores & metals exports (% of merchandise exports)	2006	–	6.36	4.87	4.05	3.60	3.80	11.55	1.35	14.60
	2016	–	4.09	4.23	3.98	4.23	3.16	11.31	2.27	–
Total natural resources rents (% of GDP)	2006	15.72	8.5	9.64	1.98	2.57	1.98	7.35	31.91	16.21
	2016	12.14	3.05	3.24	1.14	1.15	1.25	3.26	16.80	8.31

Indicators	Year	Latin American countries					
		Argentina	Bolivia	Brazil	Chile	Colombia	Peru
Ores & metals exports (% of merchandise exports)	2006	4.28	22.73	10.81	63.12	2.47	57.07
	2016	3.34	36.55	10.47	51.32	1.22	52.34
Total natural resources rents (% of GDP)	2006	5.92	16.33	4.89	21.42	7.02	13.04
	2016	1.3	6.01	3.09	10.50	3.54	7.65

Source: World Bank Development Indicators. Total natural resource rents are the sum of oil, natural gas, coal (hard and soft), mineral and forest rents.

Note: L-Mid: lower middle income, EAsia&P: East Asia and Pacific, E&C Asia: Europe and Central Asia, LAC: Latin America and Caribbean, MENA: Middle East and North Africa, SubAfrica: sub-Saharan Africa

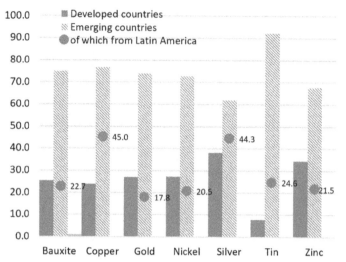

Figure 4.1   Reserves of key minerals by countries' income level (2015, %)
Note: The rest follows the IMF definitions.
Source: US Geological Survey, 2018.

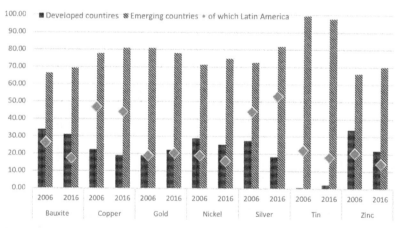

Figure 4.2   Proportion of mineral production (%)
Note: The rest follows the IMF definitions.
Source: British Geological Survey, 2018.

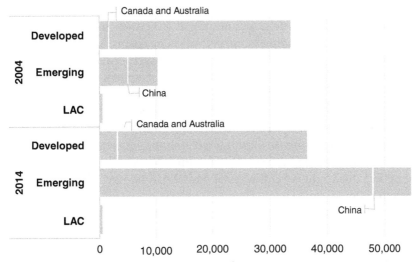

Figure 4.3 Number of mining patent families[3], by country of origin (2004, 2014)
Note: The rest follows the IMF definitions.
Source: WIPO mining database.

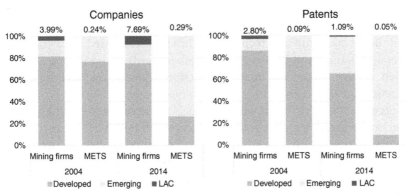

Figure 4.4 Mining GVC firms and patents by type of firm and region (2004, 2014)
Note: % at the top of the bars represent the proportion of patents by LAC. Region
determined by country of origin. Emerging countries exclude LAC. Detailed figures
refer to LAC share
Source: WIPO mining database & BVD ORBIS.

---

[3] A patent family is "a set of patents taken in various countries to protect a single invention
(when a first application in a country – the priority – is then extended to other offices)"
(OECD, 2001: 60).

sector. This includes a wide range of new products, processes, marketing methods, business models, organizational structures and new sourcing methods. Today, extending mining global value chains involves high tech equipment and service activities that require local specific knowledge and knowhow, opening up opportunities for local suppliers to upgrade their capabilities.

It is generally acknowledged that the mining sector has the following characteristics: (1) it is capital intensive, (2) miners are price takers, and (3) mining creates intense local interactions and impacts. These features greatly influence the patterns of innovation for mining companies and suppliers due to the several reasons underlined in other chapters of this volume.

First, in most cases, the capital-intensive feature of mining implies large investments upfront.[4] This self-selects those who can invest in starting a mine, limiting them to large private or public corporations. The large-scale investment is usually followed by large-scale operations whose profits tend to rely on economies of scale. These conditions limit the type of suppliers to those who can respond to large-scale demand. The large scale and long time span of operation also contribute to risk averse and conservative technology choices. The life cycle of mines – typically 20 to 30 years – further slows technological change as the change must coincide with the mine's investment cycle. The mining companies' time lag in taking up new technologies has been estimated as 13 years on average (Barnett and Lopez, 2012). In other words, technological innovation in this sector has many restrictions due to the way business functions.

Second, the price of mineral products is determined by the global market as these are undifferentiated commodities. The mining companies, therefore, are price takers. This condition makes research and development (R&D) for adding value to product highly irrelevant because the price does not reflect the efforts exerted. On the other hand, innovation could be important for cost reductions of the production process, the only factor under firms' control, especially in times of decline in global prices. Some initial evidence appears to suggest that innovation occurs in such circumstances, often in the form of better organization of works, production processes and expanding domestic backward linkages to compensate for loss of profit (Calzada and Iizuka, 2019).

---

[4] This of course does not fully apply to the small-scale, artisanal mining industry.

Improvement in production processes is mainly achieved through collaboration with external actors, often including different types of METS firms. This appears to occur in areas such as the following: (1) acquisition of technology embodied in machinery from large multinational firms (Lee and Prowse, 2014; Kaplan, 2012); (2) outsourcing (i.e. R&D spin-off) in finding fully disclosed problems with high-tech suppliers and start-ups; (3) open source collaboration, involving tech start-ups, research centers, universities and industrial organizations for finding short-term specific solutions; and (4) collaborative ventures for R&D long-term solutions, involving suppliers, universities, research centers and other mining firms (e.g. Komatsu and five research centers in Australia with Rio Tinto).

Moreover, innovation in the mining sector often faces some restrictions due to the physical infrastructure of the mine (e.g. scale of architecture, width of corridors, layout and technological level of equipment installed etc.) designed at the start of the mine's life cycle, that can set certain limits to how many changes can be introduced at a later stage (Calzada, 2018).

Third, mining activities have intense socio-economic and environmental impacts on local and regional communities. As the mines are usually located in sparsely populated regions, the large-scale operation of mining activities can create both positive and negative disruptions (Katz and Pietrobelli, 2018). The absence of appropriate regulatory measures, policies and especially institutional capabilities may cause negative impacts for the local society. This may subsequently hamper the sustainable operation of the mine. On the other hand, mining activities can generate positive outcomes insofar as they are coordinated and well integrated into the local and regional economies. Collaborative relations between miners, suppliers and other knowledge-related organizations can be achieved more easily where there is a clear and coherent regional development plan. One of the important contributions of mining activities is the generation of employment and the creation of entrepreneurial activities. As mining industries have the tendency to use the METS sector for various purposes, linking mining operations to local suppliers can encourage industrial activities and upgrade their capacities. In this context, interactions with other local actors such as R&D centers, universities, financial institutions and firms become critical. In countries like Australia and Canada, industrial associations provide various forms of support in building innovation ecosystems and promoting linkages and technological and managerial capabilities (see Chapters 11 and 12).

Innovation in the Mining Sector in Emerging Countries

The mining sector can offer new opportunities for the development of resource-rich countries via generating employment and economic activities, as well as foreign direct investment, as can be seen from the successful examples of Australia and Canada. However, it is still an open question whether it is possible to develop mining engineering, technology and services domestically in emerging countries, in light of the special characteristics of innovation.

Earlier examination of the characteristics of innovation in the mining sector revealed that this sector has both favorable and unfavorable characteristics for emerging countries. The favorable characteristics include the requirement of close collaboration between mining companies and their local suppliers in solving location-specific productive issues. Moreover, the speed of technological adoption is slow, with a focus on incremental improvements of the processes and organization of production. Local specific knowledge (i.e. geological conditions, access to public utilities, presence of indigenous population) has a special value to solve location-specific problems that may directly or indirectly affect the productive process. These characteristics could, in principle, favor firms in emerging countries because they allow learning through interaction, catching up and substantial non-technological innovation.

On the other hand, there are some features of the mining sector that could hinder firms from taking full advantage of innovation in emerging countries. The main factors include the following: (i) the large size/scale required for supplies and services, with this size asymmetry affecting the negotiation process between mining and METS companies; (ii) the large financial requirements to finance large-scale exploration and exploitation investments upfront; and (iii) the complexity of some technical problems which may require highly technical knowledge and expertise with sophisticated capital equipment and machinery. The poor access to financial resources, know-how, technical expertise and negotiation power that characterizes many firms in emerging countries, together with the difficulty of coordinating efforts and setting up collective actions, make it hard to generate innovation and benefit from it in the mining sector.

4.3   Lessons from Latin American Case Studies of Innovations in Mining Value Chains

Traditional development and innovation literature has often given a pessimistic picture of the development impact of natural resources and mining (Hirschman, 1958; Prebisch, 1950). Such an opinion has been based on various explanations, arguing that mining is often an "enclave", that large mining operations tend to be controlled by multinational corporations which perform little local innovation and govern their value chains hierarchically to the disadvantage of local suppliers, or that natural resources would induce "Dutch disease" imbalances and rent seeking (Corden and Neary, 1982; Venables, 2016). However, in recent years, mining companies have increasingly organized their activities along global value chains and this may offer the advantage of strengthening linkages among firms and other actors, and avoid the "enclave" pattern that used to prevail in the past.

Global Value Chains

The term "global value chain" refers to the full range of activities that firms and workers carry out to bring a product or service from its conception to its end use, recycling or re-use. These activities include design, production, processing, assembly, distribution, maintenance, disposal/recycling, marketing, finance and consumer services. In a global value-chain setting, these functions are distributed among many firms in different countries. In this context, "lead firms" are groups of firms that operate at particular functional positions along the chain and that are able to shape who does what along the chain, at what price, using what standards, to which specifications, and delivering at what point in time (Gereffi et al., 2005; Ponte and Sturgeon 2014).

Understanding the opportunities and drawbacks that suppliers may suffer from integration into a GVC requires knowledge of how GVCs are governed through a specific division of labor between lead firms and other actors, and how governance arises and is managed (Gibbon et al., 2008). For example, it has been noted that a more hierarchical governance of GVCs in Latin America has hindered innovation and upgrading processes in suppliers (Giuliani et al., 2005; Pietrobelli and Rabellotti, 2007). The concept of GVC governance is based on the observation that value chains are rarely coordinated spontaneously through market exchanges (Gereffi et al., 2005; Gibbon et al., 2008). Instead, they are governed as a result of strategies and decision-making by specific actors, the lead firms that manage access to final markets globally, but also at regional and national/local levels. Examining GVC governance then means studying the content and the management of these decisions across all suppliers and sub-suppliers, the strategies behind the decisions taken, the management methods chosen to implement them, and the systems through which their outcomes are monitored and implemented (Ponte and Sturgeon, 2014).

Furthermore, from a broader perspective, mining GVC governance is also shaped by actors that do not directly produce, transform, handle or trade products and services – such as civil society organizations, social movements, consumer groups, networks of experts and policymakers (Katz and Pietrobelli, 2018).

Involvement in GVCs can offer opportunities for the suppliers to innovate. In the mining sector, a new context is emerging, which is opening new opportunities for innovation and fruitful linkages between lead firms and METS firms which did not exist before (Perez, 2010; Andersen, 2012; Marin et al., 2015). These new opportunities are associated with a larger and more diversified demand for natural resources, new knowledge and technology advances applicable to these sectors and outsourcing along GVCs, together with the search for local technological solutions and an increasing pressure to innovate to reduce environmental impact (Dantas, 2011; Iizuka and Katz, 2015; Morris et al., 2012).

The results from a variety of new studies in the emerging countries of Latin America (Pietrobelli et al., 2018) indeed confirm these ideas and suggest that some local METS firms carry out important innovative activities. They have developed advanced levels of innovation capabilities, reflected in patents, new product developments, international awards, exports of goods, services and technology, and technologies in use. However, this same evidence reveals that local suppliers' innovative activity has not emerged out of rich linkages between the suppliers and the mining companies, as sometimes happens in GVCs (Pietrobelli and Rabellotti, 2011). Large mining companies have rarely built formal long-term linkages and commit themselves to joint innovation with local suppliers (Molina, 2018; Stubrin, 2018). Instead, they tended to rely on established suppliers, and when new technological challenges emerged, they relied either on solutions coming from headquarters based abroad, or on their first-tier suppliers. In other words, value chains with the typical characteristics of mining GVCs, may have governance structures that could to some degree generate a market failure for innovation. This is particularly true in emerging countries where the local and national innovation system may not provide the underlying knowledge base for the suppliers to "upgrade" into the possible technological opportunities.

In spite of these difficulties, a new potential for innovation in mining providers is apparent, and derives from demand for innovation coming from large mining companies and often related to local specific contexts. Moreover, such potential also derives from the supply side, in terms of technological opportunities related to the use and the recombination of technologies from different domains, and from the active attitude of local innovative suppliers investing in capabilities (Morrison et al., 2008).

The key for emerging countries with an active mining sector lies in successfully upgrading and diversifying economic activities. The upgrading in GVC entails three possible avenues (Gereffi et al., 2005): (1) product and process upgrading at the same stage of the chain; (2) functional upgrading, moving to higher value-added position in the chain; and (3) moving to different chains using the knowledge and capabilities acquired in a GVC. This means that overcoming obstacles and making full use of favorable characteristics of innovation in the mining sector can be a springboard for development. Collaborative innovation systems are essential to strengthen knowledge flows, fix information asymmetries and encourage interactive and continuous learning (Lundvall, 2010; Lema et al., 2018). The selected examples analyzed in the following section reveal that some opportunities are indeed emerging, and this is relevant for many other countries in Africa and Latin America with abundant mineral resources.

Incentives to Innovation Coming from Demand

Upgrading GVCs requires active investments in innovation by firms, which are usually driven by adequate incentives. Chapter 1 explained how some of the incentives for innovation in mining and METS companies come from specific demands, such as, for example, the decreasing productivity of existing mines. In Peru, for instance, due to the depletion of clean deposits (deposits with low levels of impurities), mining companies are dealing with deposits of copper, silver and gold which need to be increasingly cleaned. Moreover, mining activity in both Peru and Chile is performed at high altitudes. The La Rinconada mine, in Puno, at 5,100 meters above sea level, is the highest in the world (Molina et al., 2016) and similar conditions prevail in Chile. Existing equipment and solutions underperform, and there is a need to adapt them or develop new ones tailored to local conditions. Similarly, in Brazil, most of the activity has been moved to deeper mines, where the treatment of the mineral is more complex (Figuereido and Piana, 2016). These conditions pose pressing demands for innovation.

Additional demands for innovation come from the social and environmental challenges faced by mining companies. Local communities are concerned with livelihood security, environmental degradation and the perception that the wealth created is not fairly shared. Governments react by introducing more stringent environmental regulations and requiring some local involvement in decision-making (Katz and Pietrobelli, 2018). Again, the demand for innovative solutions and sustainable methods of production is rising fast (see Chapter 6).

The very hierarchical structure of the mining GVCs analyzed, being characterized by important power and resources asymmetry (Arias et al., 2014; Pietrobelli et al., 2018), is posing substantial problems for the upgrading of local suppliers.[5] We identified linkages with extremely poor potential to encourage innovation in mining GVCs: large mining companies are in general quite resistant to trying new solutions that have not been tested worldwide. They demand successful pre-testing conducted in several mines before even trying it, particularly when the solution comes from domestic suppliers (Pietrobelli et al., 2018). In Peru, it has been detected that the communication channels with the lead mining firm are only available for METS firms that are already working with the mining company (Molina, 2018). It is the suppliers themselves that incur the transaction costs needed to approach the mining companies and offer their services, and often lack these capabilities, even though this is intrinsically different from lacking purely technological capabilities.

In sum, at least for Chile and Peru, our results from case studies (Pietrobelli et al., 2018) confirm that exchanges of information within the mining GVCs happen, but they are mainly informal and mostly focused on the identification of the problem, rather than on finding a solution. Indeed, few exchanges were reported during the R&D stage. The experience of Brazil seems to suggest partly different conclusions. Figueiredo and Piana (2016 and 2018) found evidence of rich "learning linkages" between Vale and its suppliers, as well as between Vale, some

---

[5] On "upgrading" in value chains, see the previous discussion, and Gereffi et al., 2005 and Pietrobelli and Rabellotti, 2011. Here we rely on the standard categorization of product, process, functional and inter-chain upgrading.

Brazilian universities, and sometimes firms from different industries (e.g. Petrobras). They report that from 2009 to 2012 Vale developed 161 R&D projects with universities (151 of them from Brazil) with an estimated value of about USD 88.8 million. In some instances, it appears that Vale encouraged the development of learning linkages between other MNC subsidiaries and local mining suppliers, for example, with regard to the development of belts to transport iron ore (Figueiredo and Piana, 2016: 140). Important learning linkages also occurred with public R&D centres and sectorial institutions, for instance, with the Mineral Resources Research Company (CPRM), a government organization that seeks to generate and disseminate geological and hydrogeological knowledge in Brazil (Figuereido and Piana, 2018). Chapter 8 deepens the analysis of innovation practices in Brazil with a focus on the role of Vale.

Incentives to Innovation Coming from the Supply Side

Incentives to innovation may also come from the supply side (i.e. the new availability of scientific discoveries, new technologies and equipment, new forms of organization). Existing studies have documented how recent advances in knowledge have opened new technological opportunities also for the mining industry (Pietrobelli et al., 2018, and the studies contained in the same special issue). These are related to the massive advances in information and communication technologies (ICT), computer vision systems, satellite and other remote sensing applications, and advances in molecular and synthetic biology for bioleaching and bioremediation for copper and gold. Such supply-side incentives seem to be more effective in mining GVCs. In what follows, we will see some examples of this emerging tendency.

In Chile, the company Micomo developed highly innovative monitoring technologies through optical fiber that help extraction processes, and obtained two patents and one international award (Stubrin, 2018). Power Train technologies entered the market with new remote-control systems for trucks that operate at very high temperatures, required for performing mining at high altitudes. High Service from Chile obtained three patents related to remote monitoring and wireless communication which allows predicting wear points for key equipment and in this way anticipate replacements and avoid having to stop operations, which can cost the company around USD 150 thousand per hour. Geoambiente, from Brazil, entered the mining GVC developing sophisticated geological maps, sensors and radar images that help in the exploration phases, predicting contents of minerals and areas of erosion and are useful to monitor environmental impact (Figueiredo and Piana, 2018). The innovativeness of the company made it the largest Google partner in Brazil and helped it diversify into markets and countries beyond mining.

Another important area of new knowledge opportunity that companies are exploiting is new materials. Neptuno from Chile, for instance, developed pumps for one of the biggest open-pit mines in the world and adapted them to operate at 4,500 metres above sea level by improving materials, incorporating superior alloys and advanced engineering thermoplastic and extending the life of pumps. This gained Neptuno ten national and three international awards. One company from Brazil became a supplier of Vale developing new metal alloys, with longer durability at high temperatures (Figueiredo and Piana, 2018). Using the same kind of opportunities, Verti from Brazil developed dust suppressants that use glycerine left over from biodiesel plants, and new technological routes to recycle materials and to treat wastewater. Aplik from Chile has entered the mining GVC exploiting the technological opportunity offered by robotics. One of the main innovations of the company is a new tool for controlling irrigation at key parts of the exploitation process, helping to detect failures through irrigation maps and an alarm system. This new system is in the process of being patented and has received several national and one international awards (Stubrin, 2018).

The application of biotechnology is making the mining process more efficient and cleaner. Aguamarina is a pioneering Chilean company that managed to enter the value chain by developing first bioleaching (i.e. the extraction of metals from their ores through the use of living organisms), and then expanded into new product lines, all biotechnology-based solutions for mining companies. The main areas of activity of Aguamarina are biolixiviation, biocorrosion, bioremediation, bioreactors, water treatment and dust control (Benavente and Goya, 2011). For example, Aguamarina created unique solutions for dust control based on bacteria and microalgae. This was a new solution for a long-standing and crucial problem as mining operations create enormous amounts of dust that affect the environment, the maintenance of the machinery and even the health of mine workers and inhabitants of nearby communities. The company obtained three patents in the United States, and won five national awards.

The integration of different areas of knowledge also creates opportunities for the development of completely new or adapted products. Neptuno develops novel, innovative pumps combining knowledge about new materials, chemistry, engineering and 3D printing; Innovaxxion developed the new technology known as Earless – which reduces scrap waste in the copper mining process from 20 percent to 10 percent – by integrating knowledge about mechanical engineering, robotics and electrical engineering; Aplik integrates knowledge about electronics, informatics, mechanics and metallurgy; Geoambiente's unique results derive from combining traditional knowledge about geology with new knowledge related to communication.

Sometimes the integration of different areas of knowledge is useful to improve and upgrade existing tools and machinery. For example, Exsa in Peru, combining knowledge about engineering, explosives, new materials and chemistry developed a new method of rock fragmentation (Quantex) that generates savings of up to 20 percent of total costs and has positive environmental impact. The technology has been patented in Peru and the United States (Molina et al., 2016). Resemin developed special jumbos for narrow veins, and for coping with the extreme environmental conditions of underground mining in Peru by combining different elements of knowledge about metalworking, geology, engineering and IT (Molina, 2018). Some of the jumbos developed by the company, like the Muki, are now patented in the United States.[6] Although the largest mining suppliers have developed drilling jumbos to operate in these veins, they have faced limitations to run in sections of 1.8 m width or less; this has never been the top priority for these suppliers. Narrow veins is an important niche market that Resemin took advantage of when they introduced the Muki. This also meant increased mining productivity, drilling a 2.4 m. hole in 40 seconds, unlike traditional methods which take 7 minutes, and mechanization in tunnels, which improves safety of the operators (Molina, 2018).

One important result that emerges from studies such as those reported here is that technological opportunities appear to have been exploited mainly in areas where more experienced multinational suppliers did not have the incentive or could not meet the challenge.

Local Suppliers Strategies and Capabilities

Although new demands for innovative solutions as well as technological opportunities are emerging in mining value chains, this potential appears to have been exploited only by a handful of local firms that developed strong scientific and technological capabilities and opened specific

---

[6] Muki is a micro-jumbo of 1.05 m width created to face narrow veins and to withstand the high temperatures, lack of water, excessive corrosion, humidity and high altitude of underground mining.

channels of communication with lead firms and large first-tier providers. In other words, firm-level strategies to develop capabilities also play a central role.

In Pietrobelli and Olivari (2018), all the firms interviewed share a characteristic of substantial levels of investment in advanced levels of scientific and technological capabilities. They all perform R&D and carry out other high-level search and innovation efforts. Many suppliers from Chile invest on average almost one quarter of their sales on innovative activities and employ good shares of their total employees in R&D (Stubrin, 2018). In Peru, the interviewed firms – in different mining suppliers' sectors – declared that they employ between 3 and 4 percent of their total labor force in R&D (Molina et al., 2016).

Neptuno Pumps invested heavily in the capabilities to adapt pumps to specific geographical conditions, and thereby allowed energy savings of up to US$ 650,000 a year. A similar case is that of Power Train Technologies, which develops and sells diesel engines and other engines adapted for trucks that operate at high altitudes and in extreme weather conditions. As pointed out by the company managers, engines developed by large MNCs do not work in these conditions, and the MNC would not find it profitable to invest and adapt its engines. The engines adapted by the local Chilean supplier managed to deliver a product that saves up to 10 percent in fuel consumption, improves performance and reduces carbon prints.

One of the most successful upgrading firms is Resemin, a leading global supplier of drilling equipment in the underground mining equipment sector in Peru (Bamber et al., 2016, box 4). The company's upgrading trajectory began as parts supplier, shifting to parts manufacturer, followed by final equipment production, using reverse engineering and finally own engineering for new equipment design. The specific conditions of mining in certain areas of Peru, where veins are very narrow and the climatic conditions extreme, favored Resemin upgrading processes.

Drillco Tools develops percussion hammers and drills specially adapted to the type of rock where they are used. In the early 1990s, the company developed customized products required to enter the GVC. Interestingly, the company started adapting products to the specific conditions of Chile, but currently, and with the same approach, it sells hammers and drills through its subsidiaries in Brazil, the United States, Peru, Italy and South Africa (Stubrin, 2018). The firm exports 77 percent of its production, and offers an interesting case of upgrading into different GVCs in different countries. Linkages with clients to understand the specific requirements prevailing in each location were crucial.

In sum, there are many examples of mining suppliers in emerging economies that reached remarkable levels of innovative technological capabilities. However, many of them had to overcome the difficult challenge of managing their integration into the GVC and of creating their own markets to take full advantage of the innovations developed. This includes not only the creation of new technology but also the establishment of the conditions for the transaction (the contracts and agreement on the value of the innovation, on the rules of the game, on the distribution of benefits). This is specific to mining as well as other sectors where the availability of new knowledge and technologies from other sectors, and new forms of organization in value chains, are transforming the nature of business. This is true, for example, for precision farming and for seed production in several middle-income countries (Lachmann and Lopez, 2018). However, this process appears to be still emergent in many instances, and often hindered by the hierarchical and conservative governance of the GVCs discussed.

In conclusion, new opportunities for innovation are emerging in the mining sector. Some may be patentable, but many others are not, and they are more related to the organization of the business and of the network of transactions with different actors along the value chain. Technology opportunities coming from both demand and supply, and especially the latter, are very strong and related to basic science. Such opportunities call for advanced firm-level capabilities that are not only technological but also related to value chain integration and to the creation of a new market (Marin et al., 2016). Groups of innovative suppliers are emerging in Latin America. However, hierarchical value chains dominated by few large firms and the resulting poor linkages often block the diffusion of innovations and hinder suppliers' development. This often prevents innovation and success from spreading to a larger number of local companies.

Many research challenges remain open and deserve attention in the future. Thus, the capabilities complementary to production and necessary for market access and GVC integration need to be better understood. Similarly, the role of the various tiers of suppliers and their relationships with other local providers deserves future research. The role of public policies also needs to be explored in much greater details in a context characterized by remarkable uncertainties and by the coexistence of many actors with different and sometimes potentially clashing interests.

These include civil society and the long-term interests of sustainability and environmentally sound management of the resource, lead-firms and their tiers of suppliers, and the inter-generational distribution of costs and opportunities deriving from the mining industry.

4.4   Implications and Selected Policy Experiences in Latin America's Mining Sector

The innovation cases developed by suppliers presented in Section 4.3 have been an exception rather than the rule in the mining industry in LAC. Since these examples showcase the potential benefits for domestic suppliers of more innovation in the industry, some mining countries have made attempts to accelerate innovation by establishing programs to support innovation in mining suppliers. In this section, we focus on the lessons learned from one of the most famous examples of this type of initiative: The World Class Suppliers (WCS) program in Chile.

The WCS program was designed to try to alleviate the transaction costs and market failures that hinder the development of the innovation market. On the one hand, large mining companies know their operational problems but codifying them into terms that can be understood by external parties is a costly endeavor, which may not necessarily be always profitable. On the other hand, even when some of the operational problems are codified, potential suppliers who may have the capacity to solve them may not know of these opportunities or efforts to find these new opportunities may be too costly. Furthermore, the tacit knowledge component of each operational problem gives rise to asymmetries of information between the mining companies and suppliers. The latter is exacerbated when suppliers are providing a service (Rubalcaba, 2015). The program is built around the effort made by mining companies to codify part of their operational problems and make them accessible to potential suppliers. On top of that, the platform through which the program is organized also allows suppliers to reduce their transaction costs, since they do not need to rely only on their resources to approach mining companies and establish a new commercial relationship.

The World Class Suppliers (WCS) Program in Chile

The WCS program is a public–private initiative, launched in the late 2000s, whose primary objective is to promote the technological development of knowledge-intensive mining suppliers (KIMS) through

increasing the demand for innovations and promoting internationalization. This initiative was developed entirely by the private sector. Indeed,
the multinational company BHP Billiton created this program in 2008
and two years later Codelco, the state-owned and largest copper mining
company in Chile, joined the program.

The program works as follows (Navarro, 2018). The mining companies participating in the program identify a list of operational problems
suitable to be solved by a subcontractor. The list of problems is filtered by
considering criteria relevant to the performance of mining companies,
such as the potential economic gains, expected timeframe, and perceived
risks of new solutions, but also potential benefits to suppliers, such as
scalability of the potential solution and suitability of that solution to be
cocreated with the mining company. The final projects portfolio is
uploaded to a website, managed by the local think-tank *Fundación
Chile*, including a detailed description of the magnitude and characteristics of each of the operational challenges. Select companies are invited to
apply, but the list of challenges remains open to all potentially interested
suppliers.

Proposal submissions are collected and prescreened by the mining
company and by *Fundación Chile*, which plays the role of an honest
broker of the scheme. The preselection process is mostly based on the
estimated capabilities of applicant firms, and the mining company man-
ages the final list of proposals. When minimum criteria are met, the
mining company selects a "winner" and the process of negotiation of
a contract begins. Although the detail of the contracts of the selected
projects are kept private, because they are co-innovation projects, mining
companies are expected to provide access to facilities and non-pecuniary
resources during project development. Besides bringing its resources to
the project, the selected supplier may also apply to public financial
support. Specifically, the Chilean Development Agency, CORFO, favors
mining suppliers participating in the program when these companies
apply to innovation support schemes. A critical characteristic of the
program is that it is expected that the selected supplier retains ownership
of any intellectual property created during the project, thereby, facilitating the supplier's development through commercializing and exploiting
the new (protected) knowledge.

The implementation of the projects typically lasts between 15 and 27
months (Fundación Chile, 2012). Completed projects lead suppliers to
receive technical assistance on commercialization of the recently developed innovation. The mining company provides the financing for this

consultancy, while domestic accelerators and business consultants offer their services.

Although the program lacks a proper impact evaluation, some detailed results have been examined by Navarro (2018). Between 2009 and 2016, 92 projects were assigned to 75 suppliers.[7] The estimated pool of mining suppliers in the country ranges between 4,500 and 6,000 (Comisión Nacional de Productividad, 2017). Thirty-one of the 75 suppliers participating in the program had applied for patents before participating in the program (Navarro 2018). This high rate of patent-active firms contrasts with the 10 percent of the product innovative companies that file for patents in the rest of the Chilean economy.[8] Even within the subsample of experienced patenting companies, merely one of every five companies filed for new patents after the completion of the projects. Although only indicative, the latter reflects the non-patentable nature of a not-trivial share of the operational challenges of large mining companies.[9]

Analysis and Performance

The results of the program suggest that addressing these market failures has had some impact on a select group of suppliers. Nevertheless, the complex interaction between buyers and suppliers in the mining GVC is the subject of other market mechanisms that can be more of a deterrent to the development of domestic knowledge-intensive mining suppliers (Urzúa et al., 2017). One of the main issues however, remains the insufficient supply of local knowledge. R&D expenditures and researchers involved in the Chilean mining industry show a significant lag with respect to countries like Australia (Meller and Parodi, 2017), there appears to be low involvement of multinational mining companies in R&D activities near their operations (Pietrobelli et al., 2018), and local universities do not contribute to a large extent to the industry (Confraria and Vargas, 2019). These "symptoms" may be linked to business environment conditions that require interventions that go beyond a single

---

[7] Of all suppliers, 62 developed only one project.

[8] Own calculations using Chilean National Innovation Survey of 2017.

[9] If we assume that all suppliers that applied for patents before participating in the WCS program had used that knowledge as the main input of the solution they developed (40% of participants), and that all new patent applications are made by suppliers which did not have patents before the program (20% of participants), the results of the program imply that at least 40% of the companies participating in the WCS did not file for new patents after the completion of the project.

program to be adequately addressed. For instance, the bias of mining multinationals toward conducting R&D in home countries is a response to efficiency in knowledge management and returns on investments. This type of company conducts R&D in host countries only when there are opportunities to increase their corporate knowledge from these external sources (Belderbos, Leten and Suzuki, 2013; Belderbos, Lykogianni and Veugelers, 2008). The lack of incentives in academia to engage in industry research may also be linked to the rewards scheme of the academic system for researchers in local universities. Finally, capabilities failure in domestic suppliers limits the number of companies that would be able to engage in innovative projects that could eventually lead to knowledge-driven growth.

Although the WCS program has allowed, to a certain extent, the demand for innovations to increase, the relatively small number and size of the projects contracted under the program suggest the existence of other restrictions to innovation on the demand side. We speculate that this may be explained by the existence of principal-agent problems inside the large mining companies. While the WCS program responds mainly to a need for corporate social responsibility, and is managed by the corresponding departments, procurement decision-making is driven by operational optimization, considering risk management and efficiency. Therefore, the procurement incentives of large mining companies are not necessarily aligned with the program (Meller and Parodi, 2017).

In brief, the WCS program was an innovative initiative to lessen the asymmetries of information between mining suppliers and large mining companies, driven by the operational problems of the latter. Some results show that indeed certain companies benefited from the interaction, but generally the scheme has done little to accelerate the growth of domestic METS firms or the industry. Some other constraints in the market hinder the intensity of the collaborations between mining companies and suppliers, and the number and capacities of the latter. As Meller and Parodi (2017) remark, regardless of the design and effectiveness of the WCS program, the size of the interventions is not commensurate with the magnitude of the challenge it is seeking to address.

New Policies

Since implementing WCS-type programs is not a sufficient condition to make an impact at a more aggregate level, the Chilean government developed a new initiative to leverage the mining industry to develop knowledge-intensive companies. Backed by the learning process on WCS programs and previous national- and regional-scale policies like the Cluster Development Program and the Regional Development Agencies in the 2000s (Bravo-Ortega and Muñoz, 2018), the Chilean government launched the *Alta Ley*[10] program in 2015.

Alta Ley is a *smart specialization strategy* program (Foray, 2017), led by the public sector through CORFO, the Ministry of Economy and the Ministry of Mining. Besides focusing on promoting the development of the METS sector, this program also targets productivity increase in the industry. The board of the program is made up of members of the public sector, NGOs and universities, and more importantly, the private sector. The latter is represented by the major mining companies of the country and representatives of the mining suppliers' industry associations.

The primary function of the program is to coordinate efforts to match the supply of knowledge with the specific knowledge solutions demanded in the industry. Mining firms demand knowledge and technological solutions that are not always necessarily provided by other firms in the industry. The expansion of the WCS program aims at better matchmaking between demand and supply of mining-related knowledge. Alta Ley impacts the supply of knowledge by facilitating coordination between different industry stakeholders to increase the size and efficiency of public and club goods in the industry (Castillo et al., 2018).[11] On the demand side, the Alta Ley program identified the five main *drivers* of innovation for the industry.[12] The strategy is reflected in roadmaps that would guide the decision-making of stakeholders participating in the initiative. The implementation is made through programs designed by the Alta Ley program team. The financing comes from competitive applications to public sources.[13] One of the six programs currently implemented is the *Expande* program, which is the continuation of the WCS program (Meller and Parodi, 2017).

The *Expande* program is based on the WCS program and inspired by the open innovation strategy concept (Chesbrough, 2003) (see Chapter 9). Therefore, its operational mechanism goes beyond producing a bilateral transaction between a single innovation provider and the

---

[10] It translates literally as "high grade."
[11] Skill-based technical education, public infrastructure, institutions and regulations, and suppliers' development.
[12] Mining operations, concentration of minerals, tailings, hydrometallurgy, and smelting and refining.
[13] For example, the Strategic Investment Fund.

mining industry. Indeed, the main difference with the WCS program is that METS firms are also allowed to provide solutions to operational problems that have not been previously codified by any large mining company. On top of that, the main players of the industry are participating in the initiative and signaling the main productive challenges of the mining sector for the coming decades, and it also opens the supply side of innovation to new actors like universities, research centers and companies not previously working with the mining industry. *Fundación Chile* maintains the role of a broker but its performance becomes more critical, participating more actively in the production of information and matchmaking between mining and METS companies. *Fundación Chile* measures and surveys the local technical capacities that may be useful for the industry, while also translating the operational challenges of the industry to project-type potential suppliers. Since the *Expande* program has only been implemented for a short period of time, is it not possible to assess its outcome. However, at least in principle, by acting on both the supply and demand sides of innovation we should expect more projects than in the WCS program. However, there is no signal so far that the size of the program has been increased in a significant way, nor that the procurement policies of the large mining companies have been affected in any way.

Although Alta Ley has existed for a short time, from its design we may consider it a step forward toward solving the shortage of knowledge supply to the industry. Allowing coordination between large mining companies and signaling the main challenges of the industry to other actors of the system is expected to lower barriers to collaborative R&D and decrease the uncertainty of innovation investment decisions for the rest of the actors of the system. At the same time, better coordination between private companies and the government may increase the efficiency of the provision of knowledge and other public goods to the industry. The technological roadmaps are expected to align private and public research and innovation investments toward the leading technologies and operational challenges of the industry as a whole. Their scope and magnitude is expected to be large enough to increase knowledge investments and eventually, promote innovation to a significant extent.

In sum, as we notice the positive and original policy developments, it remains to be seen if the new public–private collaborative approach through smart specialization strategies succeeds in easing the primary constraints to get more intense and stronger interactions between domestic METS and large mining companies. Efforts like the WCS program, although valuable on its own as an innovative approach to connect mining companies with new suppliers, are not enough to lead the way toward a larger METS sector. We argue that the size of the industry and the potential gains require investments of a higher order of magnitude.

4.5   Conclusion

This chapter tries to broaden the scope and understanding of innovation in the mining sector, with a focus on emerging countries based on the experience of Latin America. The central underlying idea is that today innovation can foster growth of many countries endowed with natural resource in new ways that were not considered or not available in the past. New opportunities for innovation are emerging in the mining sector. Some may be patentable, but many others are not, and they are more related to the organization of the business and of the network of transactions with different actors along the value chain. Innovation may powerfully develop through the interaction and linkages between mining companies, their suppliers and other organizations active in the innovation system. Moreover, the new features of scientific knowledge applied to the mining sector (e.g. ICT, new materials, biotechnology) open new opportunities for new suppliers from emerging countries to enter and add value in mining GVCs.

In this chapter, we analyzed how some successful examples prove that these developments are real and offer new opportunities that were hard to visualize before. However, this does not reduce the role of public policies; indeed it promotes the need to rethink and innovate policy approaches, as the brief policy review revealed. Mining cannot become a true engine of growth for emerging economies unless linkages within mining value chains and beyond are enhanced and the system that produces the required advanced knowledge and capabilities is strengthened.

References

Andersen, A. D. 2012. Towards a new approach to natural resources and development: The role of learning, innovation and linkage dynamics. *Int. J. Technological Learning, Innovation and Development*, 5 (3), 291–324.

Arias M., M. Atienza and J. Cadenmatori (2014) Large mining enterprises and regional development in Chile. *Journal of Economic Geography*, 14, 73–95.

Bamber, P., K. Fernandez-Stark and G. Gereffi (2016). Peru in the Mining Equipment Global Value Chain. Opportunities for Upgrading, January. https://gvcc.duke.edu, accessed April 26, 2018.

Barnett, R., and L. Lopez (2012). *The Rise of the Machines*. Perth, https://www.ventureconsultants.com.au/FINAL_REPORT-Rise_of_the_Machines.pdf, accessed August 7, 2018.

Belderbos, R., B. Leten and S. Suzuki (2013). How global is R&D? Firm-level determinants of home country bias in R&D. *Journal of International Business Studies* 44 (8), 765–86. doi:10.1057/jibs.2013.33

Belderbos, R., E. Lykogianni and R. Veugelers (2008). Strategic R&D location by multinational firms: Spillovers, technology sourcing, and competition. *Journal of Economics & Management Strategy* 17 (3): 759–79. doi:10.1111/j.1530-9134.2008.00194.x

Benavente J. M., and D. Goya (2011). Copper mining in Chile, Sectorial Report, Project Opening up Natural Resource-Based Industries for Innovation: Exploring New Pathways for Development in Latin America, IDRC.

Bravo-Ortega, C., and L. Muñoz (2018). Mining Services Suppliers in Chile: A Regional Approach (or Lack of It) for Their Development. *Resources Policy*, no. May. Elsevier Ltd: 1–19. doi:10.1016/j.resourpol.2018.06.001

British Geological Survey (2018). World Mineral Production 2012–2016. British Geological Survey.

Calzada, B. (2018). Innovation in Mining, UNU-MERIT mimeo, May for Innovation in mining GVCs project.

Calzada Olvera, B., and M. Iizuka (2020). How does innovation take place in the mining industry?: Understanding the logic behind innovation in a changing context," MERIT Working Papers 2020-019, United Nations University - Maastricht Economic and Social Research Institute on Innovation and Technology (MERIT).

Castillo, J., F. Correa, M. Dini and J. Katz (2018). Políticas de Fomento Productivo Para El Desarrollo de Sectores Intensivos En Recursos Naturales: La Experiencia Del Programa Nacional de Minería Alta Ley. 218. Serie Desarrollo Productivo. Santiago.

Chesbrough, H. W. (2003). *Open Innovation: The New Imperative for Creating and Profiting from Technology*. Cambridge, MA: Harvard Business School Publishing.

Comisión Nacional de Productividad (2017). Productividad En La Gran Minería Del Cobre En Chile, no. 1: 1–445.

Confraria, H., and F. Vargas (2019). Scientific systems in Latin America: performance, networks, and collaborations with industry. *The Journal of Technology Transfer*, 44 (3), 874–915.

Corden, M., and P. Neary (1982). Booming sector and de-industrialisation in a small open economy. *The Economic Journal*, 92 (368), 825–848.

Dantas, E. (2011). The evolution of the knowledge accumulation function in the formation of the Brazilian biofuels innovation system. *International Journal of Technology and Globalisation*, 5 (3–4), 327–340.

Figueiredo, P. N., and J., Piana (2016). When 'one thing (almost) leads to another': A micro-level exploration of learning linkages in Brazil's mining industry. *Resources Policy*, 49, September, 405–414, http://dx.doi.org/10.1016/j.resourpol.2016.07.008

Figueiredo, P., and J. Piana (2018). Innovative capability building and learning linkages in new entrant knowledge-intensive service SMEs in the mining industry: Evidence from Brazil, *Resources Policy*, 58, October, 21–33, http://dx.doi.org/10.1016/j.resourpol.2017.10.012

Foray, D. (2017). The Economic Fundamentals of Smart Specialization Strategies. Advances in the Theory and Practice of Smart Specialization, January. Academic Press, 37–50. doi:10.1016/B978-0-12-804137-6.00002-4

Fundación Chile (2012). Manual de Proveedores de clase mundial. Santiago, Chile. http://desarrolloproveedores.cl/dp/wp-content/uploads/2012/10/FCh-Manual-PPCMVersion-2.0.pdf

Gereffi, G., J. Humphrey and T. Sturgeon (2005). The governance of global value chains. *Review of International Political Economy*, 12 (1), 78–104.

Gibbon, P., J. Bair and S. Ponte (2008). Governing global value chains: An introduction. *Economy and Society*, 37 (3), 315–338.

Giuliani E., C. Pietrobelli and R. Rabellotti (2005) Upgrading in global value chains: Lessons from Latin American clusters. *World Development*, 33 (4), 549–573.

Hirschman, A. O. (1958). *The Strategy of Economic Development*. New Haven, CN: Yale University Press.

Iizuka, M., and J. Katz (2015). Globalization, sustainability and the role of institutions: The case of the Chilean salmon industry. *Tijdschrift voor Economische en Sociale Geografie*, 106 (2), 140–153. doi:10.1111/tesg.12132

Kaplan, D. (2012). South African mining equipment and specialist services: Technological capacity, export performance and policy, *Resources Policy*, 37 425–433. http://dx.doi.org/10.1016/j.resourpol.2012.06.001

Katz, J., and C. Pietrobelli (2018). Natural resource-based growth, global value chains and domestic capabilities in the mining industry, *Resources Policy*, 58, October, 11–20. https://doi.org/10.1016/j.resourpol.2018.02.001

Lachman, J., and A. López (2018). Nuevas oportunidades y desafíos productivos en la Argentina: Resultados de la Primera Encuesta Nacional a Empresas de Agricultura y Ganadería de Precisión. IIEP-BAIRES, Serie Documentos de Trabajo 38, Buenos Aires, diciembre.

Lee, J., & K. Prowse (2014). Mining & Metals + Internet of Things: Industry opportunities and innovation. *MaRS*. www.marsdd.com/news-and-insights/mining-industry-iot-technology/

Lema R., C. Pietrobelli and R., Rabellotti (2018). Innovation in Global Value Chains, UNU-MERIT WP, 2018–038, UNU-MERIT, Maastricht. www.merit.unu.edu/publications/wppdf/2018/wp2018-038.pdf

Lundvall, B.-A. (1992, reprinted in 2010). User-producer relationships: National systems of innovation and Internationalization, in Lundvall, B.-A. (ed.). *National Systems of Innovation: Towards a theory of innovation and interactive learning.* London and New York: The Anthem Press, pp. 47–70.

Marin, A., E. Dantas and M. Obaya (2016). Alternative technological paths in new NR-related industries: The case of seeds in Argentina and Brazil, CENIT Working Paper. www.fund-cenit.org.ar/alternative-technological-paths-in-new-nr-related-industries-the-case-of-seeds-in-argentina-and-brazil/publicacion/392/es

Marin, A., L. Navas-Aleman and C. Perez (2015). Natural resource industries as a platform for the development of knowledge intensive industries. *Tijdschrift Voor Economische en Sociale Geografie*, 106 (2).

Meller, P., and P. Parodi (2017). Del Programa de Proveedores a La Innovación Abierta En Minería. Mimeo CIEPLAN.

Molina O. (2018). Innovation in an unfavorable context: Local mining suppliers in Peru, *Resources Policy*, 58, October, 34–48. https://doi.org/10.1016/j.resourpol.2017.10.011

Molina O., J. Olivari and C. Pietrobelli (2016). Global Value Chains in the Peruvian Mining Sector, Inter-American Development Bank IDB-TN-1114. http://dx.doi.org/10.18235/0000468

Morris, M., R. Kaplinsky and D. Kaplan (2012). One thing leads to another: Commodities, linkages and industrial development. *Resources Policy*, 37, 408–416

Morrison, A., C. Pietrobelli and R. Rabellotti (2008). Global value chains and technological capabilities: A framework to study learning and innovation in developing countries. *Oxford Development Studies*, 36 (1), 39–58. https://doi.org/10.1080/13600810701848144

Navarro, L. (2018). The world class supplier program for mining in Chile: Assessment and perspectives. *Resources Policy*, 58, October, 49–61. http://dx.doi.org/10.1016/j.resourpol.2017.10.008

Organisation for Economic Co-operation and Development (2001). Economic Analysis and Statistics Division, OECD science, technology and industry scoreboard: Towards a knowledge-based economy, OECD Publishing. ISBN 92-64-18648-4

Pérez, C. (2010). Technological dynamism and social inclusion in Latin America: A resource- based development strategy. *CEPAL Review*, N 100, pp 121–141.

Pietrobelli, C., A. Marin and J. Olivari (2018). Innovation in mining value chains: New evidence from Latin America, *Resources Policy*, 58, October, 1–10, https://doi.org/10.1016/j.resourpol.2018.05.010

Pietrobelli, C., and J. Olivari (eds.). (2018) Special Issue on Mining Value Chains, Innovation and Learning. *Resources Policy*, 58, October, 1–314.

Pietrobelli, C., and R. Rabellotti (2007). *Upgrading to Compete: Global Value Chains, SMEs and Clusters in Latin America*, Cambridge MA: Harvard University Press. www.hup.harvard.edu/catalog.php?isbn=9781597820325

Pietrobelli, C., and R. Rabellotti (2011). Global value chains meet innovation systems: Are there learning opportunities for developing countries? *World Development*, 39 (7), 1261–1269.

Ponte, S., and T. Sturgeon (2014). Explaining governance in global value chains: A modular theory-building effort. *Review of International Political Economy*, 21 (1), 195–223. http://dx.doi.org/10.1080/09692290.2013.809596

Prebisch, R. (1950). The economic development of Latin America and its principal problems. *Economic Bulletin for Latin America*, 7, 1–12.

Rubalcaba, L. (2015). Service Innovation in Developing Economies: Policy Rationale and Framework. *Emerging Markets Finance and Trade, Taylor & Francis Journals*, 51(3), 540–557.

Stubrin L. (2018). Innovation, learning and competence building in the mining industry. The case of knowledge intensive mining suppliers (KIMS) in Chile. *Resources Policy*, 58, October, 62–70. https://doi.org/10.1016/j.resourpol.2017.10.009

Urzúa, O., A. Wood, M. Iizuka, F. Vargas and J. Baumann (2017). Discovering New Public-Private Partnerships for Productive and Technological Development in Emerging Mining Countries. 5. Working Document.

US Geological Survey (2018). Mineral Commodity Summaries 2018, USGS Mineral Resources.

Venables, A. J. (2016). Using natural resources for development: Why has it proven so difficult? *Journal of Economic Perspectives*, 30 (1), 161–84. https://doi.org/10.1257/jep.30.1.161

The Role of Transport-Related Innovation in the Mining Sector

FRANCESCO DIONORI AND MARYAM ZEHTABCHI

5.1 Introduction

Mining and transport are inextricably linked. Raw materials need to get to the destination market, which could be very far away from the mine. As such, different transport modes are necessary to carry these minerals to their destinations. Shipping the mining output is expensive and, in most cases, an unavoidable component of the mining process.

The majority of raw materials that industries use today come from some form of mining, whether it be extracting from far beneath the earth's surface or from open-cut mines on the surface. Early industrializing economies drew on raw materials sourced locally. In some cases, when the location of these commodities was first identified, the most economical solution was often to build downstream factories or processing plants close to the mines and then ship the finished (or semi-finished) product to the final consumer. For example, in the beginning, it was easy and cheap to build power stations near coal mines and build an electricity distribution network than fanned out from the power station. Alternatively, industries sourced their inputs from among raw materials closest to their existing production facilities, which were not always of the highest quality but provided a ready solution.

As industrialization spread geographically and higher-quality resources were discovered remote from the main markets, the importance of transport in the logistics chain of getting raw materials to downstream users increased. This also triggered the need to innovate in the transport sector that led to making mining locations that were more remote and not moveable, more accessible. It can be said, therefore that transport became the enabler for a number of mining products to be used on a much wider scale. The development of the iron ore deposits of Western Australia and of the Amazon region were largely a result of improvements in land-based and shipping transportation. The exploitation of these high-quality resources transformed the world market for iron ore. The same applies to other minerals such as bauxite, copper and manganese.

This chapter discusses the historical importance of innovation in the transport sphere of mining and empirically assesses the recent trends. We show how technological development in the general transport sector has significantly impacted the mining sector from early on to the current days. We focus on the outstanding recent evolution of mining-specific transport innovation to shed light on what is behind this surge. We explore the differences arising both from technological changes (i.e. differences across transport modes) and from globalization (i.e. changes in the geography of stakeholders).

The chapter also looks at the recent evolution of mining-related transport innovation compared to the current trends in total transport innovation. The data shows that mining-related transport innovation (MTI) is not correlated to the overall transport trends (Figure 5.4). There is evidence of mining-specific technologies being follow-on innovations of existing transport ones (Figure 5.9), while the reverse knowledge flow is less pronounced.

Before delving deeper into these areas, the boundaries of the analysis should be clarified. When discussing mining-related transport, the discussion concerns some mining products more than others. The chapter refers mostly to those commodities that require extensive transport resources to be moved, as these are the only ones for which transport will play a key role and therefore MTI can be identified. They are usually moved in bulk and have low unit value. These include coal, iron ore, copper ore and zinc ore. Other materials with high unit value – such as gold, diamonds, rare earth, etc. – are often shipped in small quantities and their transport component will be less important and therefore not captured by our analysis. Oil and gas extraction has also been excluded from the analysis as it is not part of the core analysis in this book and it is often subject to different transport requirements.

Similarly, transport operations can be defined very widely when considering the mining environment. The discussions in this chapter will focus on transport both within the mining area and transport outside, in the form of haulage to destination. While the analysis will look at conveying as a transport means as well as innovations in logistics and above-ground transport innovations at mines, it will exclude hoisting (e.g. lifts) and other aspects that can be primarily considered as being below the ground. Once the raw materials have left the mine, the chapter will review innovations of all transport modes (land, sea and air) that are of direct relevance to the mining industry. It will also look briefly at some of the transport challenges that remain and point to some innovations that may develop in the short and medium term.

A substantial part of the analysis relies on patent data as a proxy for the MTI, which were sourced from the WIPO mining database (Daly et al., 2019) and therefore do not provide results that are disaggregated according to commodity types.

The remainder of the chapter is structured as follows: Section 5.2 describes qualitatively the importance of transport for the mining industry. Section 5.3 focuses on transport innovation in the mining sector. Section 5.4 analyses the recent trends of transport innovation using patent data and explores the direction of knowledge flows between the mining and transport sectors. Finally, future developments and challenges for MTI are discussed in Section 5.5.

5.2   The Importance of Transport for the Mining Industries

5.2.1   *Mining Output Is Always on the Move*

All mine operations are different. These differences arise from the product that is being extracted, the location of the mine, the destination of the raw material and the time within which it needs to be delivered. As a result, different mining operations require different transport solutions. For example, a coal mine situated close to a coal-fired power station (or rather, a coal-fired power station built near a mine) would need minimal transport and most of the extracted coal could be transported via a conveyor belt directly to the power station.

However, the transport of mining products is usually more complex and requires the use of multiple forms of transport. For example, the overall transport of a mined raw material will involve a conveyor belt or road transport from the mine surface to a storage or processing area within the mining premises, a road leg or, more commonly, a rail leg to a port, and then a sea leg to the destination country and finally a road or rail leg in the destination country to deliver the raw materials to the processing facility. Figure 5.1 stylizes the role of transport in the typical mining supply chain.

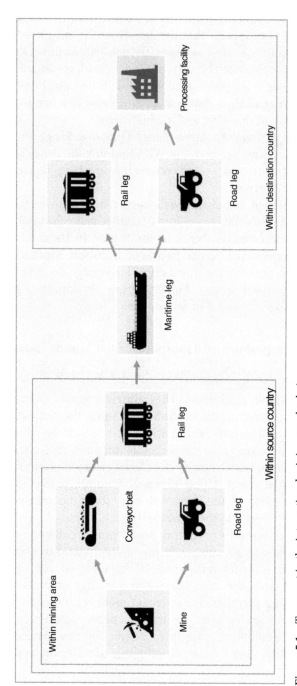

Figure 5.1 Transport in the international mining supply chain
Source: Authors' elaboration, iStock.

This movement of raw materials has a time as well as monetary cost with a typical journey from an Australian mine to China needing more than two weeks just for the sea leg,[1] while the monetary cost can be a significant share of the final delivered cost as discussed later in the chapter.

Given these multiple legs, there are opportunities to increase efficiency all along this transport chain and this is where innovation plays a key role. It could either reduce the amount of time it takes to deliver the raw materials to the customer, or the cost of doing so, or affect both of those by delivering more raw materials in a single shipment. These actions contribute to making existing sites more efficient but also make sites that were previously not economically viable, worth considering for mining operations.

5.2.2   Mining Products Are Traveling Increasingly Longer Distances

More countries are involved in the exchange of mining products today than ever. Many of these have explored their whole geography to find the most profitable mining sites. As a result, mining output is transported increasingly long distances, both within and across countries. For instance, the global production of coal – the most produced and traded mineral in volume – now has increased its geography both in its domestic and export-oriented component (The Carbon Brief, 2016).

In addition to this growing trend in production, the average distance traveled by the raw material from mine to processing facility has also increased. The global production of coal, once limited to a handful of industrialized regions producing and using it, is now produced and used by countries all around the world with different levels of industrialization (see Figure 5.2). In 2014, the largest exporter in volume was Indonesia and in value was Australia, while the largest importer was China (The Carbon Brief, 2016). This is not only the case of coal. In 2015, the largest exporter of iron ore, with over 50 percent of international exports, was Australia and the largest importer was China, absorbing 66 percent of worldwide exports.[2]

5.2.3   The Cost of Transport Operations Remain a Key Driver for Decision-Making

Given the highly competitive nature of mining operations across the world and the different modes that are used, it is difficult to pinpoint

---

[1] www.ports.com
[2] www.worldstopexports.com, data extracted on April 10, 2019.

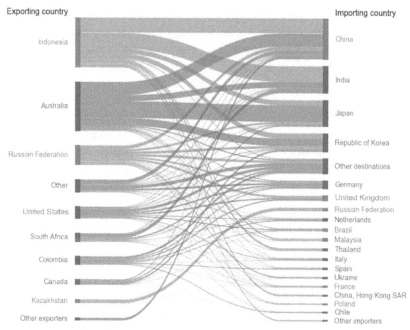

Figure 5.2 Coal and lignite imports and exports 2014
Source: UN Comtrade data, based on The Carbon Brief (2016) methodology.

the contribution that transport makes to the overall final price of the delivered raw material. Setting up infrastructure – be it rail, road or port – and buying rolling stock, vehicles and vessels impose enormous sunk-costs on firms and governments that are only worth making with a continuous and long-term revenue stream.

The cost of transporting mineral output from mine to plant is a significant component of the overall final cost. Data shows that the share of transport costs has fluctuated significantly over time. Morrow (1922) documented that the transport share in the cost of coal in the USA increased from about 22 percent in 1914 to over 50 percent in 1922. More recently, the US Energy Information Administration (EIA, 2016) estimated it to be around 36 percent and 39 percent in 2008 and 2014, respectively (see Figure 5.3). These averages hide the fact that transport cost differ substantially depending on the main transport mode utilized. The EIA (2017) estimates that the transport cost of moving coal can be 9 to 13 percent on inland waterways, about 15 percent on road, and between 41 and

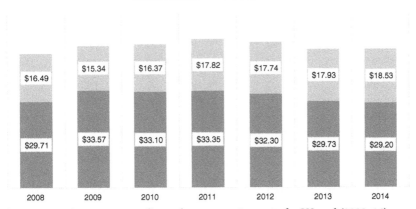

Figure 5.3 Average commodity and transportation costs for US coal (2008–14)
Source: EIA (2016).

47 percent on rail.[3] In addition to the mode of transport, the distance that the shipment of coal travels is also a significant driver of the transport cost – and hence the final price – as well the grade of the coal. A higher-grade coal (e.g. anthracite or bituminous) will bear higher transport costs but permit longer journeys than will a lower grade coal (e.g. subbituminous or lignite).

As the averages in Figure 5.3 are for relatively short distances within the USA, it is important to note that this is not necessarily representative of mining transportation – including coal – around the world. This is particularly true as they exclude a sea leg (e.g. from Australia or Brazil to China) which is a significant cost segment and proportionate to the distance traveled. Sea legs can increase the cost of transportation to over 50 percent (UB POST, 2011). For instance, transportation to Port Hedland accounts for around 20 percent of total operating costs of Western Australian producers of iron ore, and 12.7 percent of the total transport costs are incurred in the maritime leg to reach the Port of Qingdao.[4]

There is a surge in the transport cost component even in the presence of MTI activity aimed at making the transport of mining products more efficient. This is probably due to the increasing distance traveled by mining products. Indeed, the price-over-distance ratio shows that there is still room for efficiency gains through MTI. For example, the shipping

---

[3] EIA statistical data from "Form EIA-923, "Power Plant Operations Report."
[4] Assuming iron ore (62 percent Fe), delivered cost of $55/wmt and freight costs of $7/wmt.

Table 5.1 *Average distance and Capesize vessel shipping price to Port of Qingdao, China*

Selected ports	Distance (1000 nm)	Price ($/wmt)	Price–distance ratio
Port Tubarão	13.53	17.25	1.27
Port Saldanha	9.74	13.00	1.33
Port Hedland	4.06	7.50	1.84

Source: S&P Global Platts (2017) and www.ports.com.

costs from Port Saldanha (South Africa) or Port Tubarão (Brazil) are significantly higher, reflecting their longer distances (see Table 5.1). However, they are not linearly proportional to distance, indicating that there are efficiency gains in place as a result of the sunk costs being distributed over a longer distance. This is quite important because innovation developments in seaborne transport – such as the recent Valemax vessels – have been a huge factor shaping the global trade in minerals, significantly reducing the cost per nautical mile. This innovation is also essential to absorb the very volatile nature of maritime freight rates (S&P Global Platts, 2017).

To sum up, based on anecdotal evidence there is an increasing trend in the distance traveled by mining products. As a consequence, transport costs have become an increasing component of overall costs. These give mining companies strong incentives to reduce these costs and transport innovation is one important instrument to serve this purpose. The majority of the innovation in mining transport is aimed at reducing transport costs by optimizing various aspects of the transport segment within the mining value chain, namely infrastructure, rail, vehicles, containers, conveying, hauling, shipping, control and automation.

5.3   Transport Innovation in the Mining Sector

5.3.1   *What Motivates Transport Innovation in Mining?*

The main reasons for transport innovation in the mining sector are efficiency (through cost reduction, increased operation or distance reduction) and safety (through risk reduction and improved work conditions).

Efficiency (through cost reduction) remains the main driver of innovation in transport. It involves any action, investment or new process that can reduce production costs and increase the competitiveness of mines. The drive to increase efficiency targets direct costs such as cheaper inputs into the transportation process (e.g. lower fuel costs) as well as indirect costs (e.g. reducing energy consumption of vehicles or optimizing routing). The latter is the field where innovation can have the largest impact. Other examples of this type of innovation relate to the use of longer and heavier trains with which larger quantities can be moved around from the mines to the clients reducing the marginal cost of transporting the raw materials. Smart maintenance regimes (e.g. predictive instead of preventive maintenance[5]) have led to a reduction in the downtime of the network and lower maintenance costs.

Closely related to efficiency is the ability to increase output through increasing **operational times**. Any innovation that allows for 24/7 operation, in all seasons and weather, increases the effectiveness of a mine. The introduction of partial or full automation (e.g. through the use of radars) has ensured that road vehicles can work in all seasons and all weather with no need to stop for operator rest breaks.

Innovation has a direct impact on reducing **distance** (actual or perceived) to the customer. For example, new building techniques for viaducts allow them to withstand higher loads and thus reduce the direct distance between two locations; alternatively, the introduction of improved signaling intended to increase the speed of transport, or a protective coating applied to the top of loads prior to departure to reduce loss during transit.

Safety and **working conditions** are fundamental considerations in the operations of a mine to make the mining process more socially and environmentally sustainable. As such, those actions that reduce the risk of accidents and remove factors such as driver fatigue within the mining area – including through the introduction of automation and sensors/radars – are highly valued by mining companies. Innovation aims at removing staff 'from the coal face' and out of danger, as well as removing them from direct contact with extracted material. Improving the working conditions of miners could increase the attractiveness of jobs in the sector by reducing the high-risk level of these positions.

---

[5] Preventive maintenance is when maintenance is carried out according to a specific schedule identified at the time of installation. Predictive maintenance is when maintenance is carried out based on the actual condition of the infrastructure and, therefore, the actual wear and tear of the infrastructure.

Safety and working conditions go beyond the mining site as civil
society is increasingly demanding sustainability standards of mining
companies operating in their area. The key requirement is to reduce
the **environmental impact** of mining operations. Innovation has therefore focused on reducing the carbon footprint of transport operations for
mining, for example, through reducing fuel consumption. It can also help
to ensure that mining operations reduce the impact that they have on
surrounding communities.[6]

All these drivers of innovation are closely linked and a number of
synergies and positive externalities may arise from certain actions. For
example, innovation in one area aimed at reducing costs, say through
more fuel-efficient vehicles, has spill-over effects into other areas such as
environmental impact and working conditions. Furthermore, many
mines are closed systems, meaning that they have minimal or no interaction with public traffic (road or rail). This means that innovation is less
likely to be impacted by restrictive certification requirements or public
requirements set out in the national highway code.

5.3.2   How Relevant Has Transport Innovation Been for Mining?

Historically, the importance and impact of transport-related innovations
on the mining industry has fluctuated significantly. Figure 5.4 sets out the
historical evolution of mining-related transport patents as a share of all
mining patents. It shows that the share has ranged from as low as
2 percent to as high as 7 percent. Three periods emerge from this
historical analysis.

The first 15 years of the twentieth century show a period of boom. This is
likely a delayed result of the *Industrial Revolution*, when steam engines were
introduced to the transport industries to improve navigation and develop
the railways.[7] It was not until the beginning of the twentieth century and the
technological revolution, that widespread adoption of these pre-existing
technological systems – like railways, but also road-going vehicles – started.
As a benchmark, the overall share of transport innovation also experienced
a boom in the first two decades of the twentieth century. However, until

---

[6] For a discussion on mining environmental innovation, see Chapter 6.

[7] For example, steam engine technology was first introduced as pumps to remove water
from flooded mines. Jerónimo de Ayanz obtained an invention privilege from the Spanish
Crown in 1606 and Thomas Savery obtained a patent (No 356) in London in 1698. This is,
therefore, an example of a technology first developed in the mining sector and then applied
in other sectors as well.

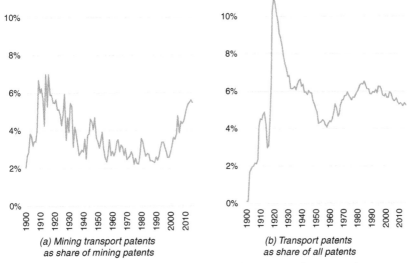

Figure 5.4   Historical change in transport-related innovation (1900–2015)
Source: WIPO mining database.

1918, it seems that MTI was proportionally more important for mining than transport innovation was for all innovations.

Despite this very innovative initial period, the share of transport-related patents compared to the rest of mining-related innovation shrunk in the following decades. This downward trend continued until the mid 1970s. As shown in Chapter 1, this trend looks to be the inverse of other mining categories such as blasting, exploration or environmental technologies whose share in the overall mining innovation pool grew steadily over this period. Related to this, metallurgy innovation using mining products did not change significantly during this period, while the processing category saw a decline similar to the transport category. Refining innovation reached a peak of almost 80 percent of total mining innovation at the beginning of the 1970s, after which it started declining steadily until the lowest point at around 10 percent in 2015.[8]

This decline of transport-related innovation in mining seems to follow the pattern of all transport innovations, which also observed a major plunge from 1920 to the late 1950s. This decline is particularly true for railways-related innovation, which has a similar trend to MTI. Part of

[8] For an in-depth analysis of the evolution of all mining categories over time, see Chapter 1.

this decline can be attributed to World War II reconstructions, which aimed at infrastructure expansion and not necessarily innovation. Indeed, MTI did not see the slight recovery that transport innovation saw from 1960 to 1985. Moreover, transport innovation has constantly been a smaller share of all mining technologies than transport innovation is for all technologies together. It seems that the mining sector has underutilized transport innovations compared to other sectors in the economy during this period. This is probably related to the small contribution of railways and shipping-related innovation observed in that period as opposed to the share of automobile-related innovation that had a relatively higher impact outside the mining sector.

Nevertheless, MTI follows a completely different trend compared to overall transport innovation and railway innovation starting from the beginning of the 1990s. While the latter two remained pretty stable as a share of all innovations in the period 1990–2015, mining transport-related innovation increased sharply as a share of all mining innovation. Almost all other mining categories lost importance in the last two decades. Their shares were absorbed by both the transport and the automation categories. Moreover, by 2014, almost a century after 1918, transport-related innovation was again proportionally higher in mining than for the average industry.

There are two potential and complementary explanations to such resurgence in mining transport patents. First, transport technologies might be benefiting from a technological push in line with the new wave of information and communication technologies (ICTs) observed in this period. Indeed, as the steam engine did in the past, ICTs are considered general-purpose technologies (GPTs) with the potential to open several avenues for further transport innovation among other industries. GPTs have had difficulties developing fully in decentralized economies (Bresnahan and Trajtenberg, 1995). However, because of the close-system characteristics of transport in the mining sector, it is possible that transport innovations related to ICTs are explored there first.

The second explanation is related to the extraordinary demand conditions in this period, which arguably led to a technological pull for transport innovation. As discussed in Section 5.2, in this period, not only was there increased globalization (e.g. increase of internationally traded goods) but also a major geographical shift of production, most notably to Asia and particularly to China. Both had a direct impact on the need for increased transport innovation. In the mining sector, this has been translated into extraordinary high price cycles and into an increase in demand for bulk minerals to feed the industrialization of Asian economies (see Chapters 1 and 7). As a result, higher prices made more remote mining sites profitable; and since China became the main destination for the output of numerous mining sites, it made the average distance to market higher in a very short period of time. Transport innovation related to mining was suddenly crucial.

5.4   What Explains the MTI Surge?

5.4.1   How Has Globalization Changed the Geography of Transport Innovation?

The geographical shift of supply and demand for certain minerals has arguably affected the technological landscape in the sector. The United Kingdom and Germany have historically been among the top innovation stakeholders of this sector, while other economies have overtaken them in more recent years. Particularly, since 1990s, the United States, the Russian Federation, Japan, China and the Republic of Korea have been the most active countries in transport innovation (Figure 5.5).

Among these new stakeholders, China is the most significant. There has been an exponential growth of Chinese mining-transport-related patents over the last 10 years, both in absolute and relative terms. This has coincided with the shift of demand for many raw materials to China. A similar trend has been documented for all Chinese mining patents (see Chapter 2). It is worth noting that China has been increasing consistently in all technological domains during the past decades (Hu and Jefferson., 2009). However, the Chinese performance in mining transport technologies is particularly astonishing. In 1990, China was responsible for less than 1 percent of all patents whilst accounting for almost 40 percent of transport-related mining patents. By 2015, China represented 53 percent of all mining patents and more than 80 percent of the MTI ones (WIPO, 2018).

5.4.2   What Are the Technological Changes across Modes of Transport?

Transport innovations related to mining cover all transport modes and all aspects of the transport chain mentioned previously. This section explores the surge of transport-related innovation according to the contribution of the main transport chain segments. These include the traditional transport modes – such as road, rail, maritime, and conveyors – and innovations applied horizontally across all these modes. Among the latter, the review focuses on containers, which could travel

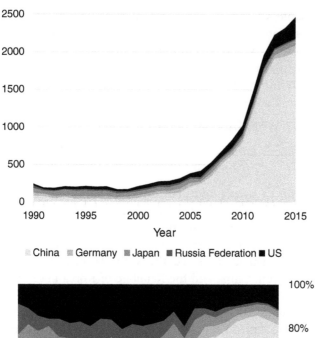

Figure 5.5   Country of origin of mining transport patents (1990–2015)
Source: WIPO mining database.

either by road, rail or sea, and control, which includes logistics and automation technologies.[9] Figure 5.6 summarizes the evolution of MTI showing the number of patent families applied in each mode of the defined categories.

[9] See annex for more details on the mining transport categories and subcategories.

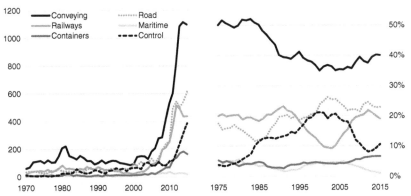

Figure 5.6   Mining transport patents by mode of transport (1970–2015)
Notes: Shares on the right are smoothed using a 5-year moving average.
Source: WIPO mining database.

A significant amount of transport innovation within the mining sector involves fixed equipment – such as conveyor belts – moving mining output within the mine site. New developments in the ***conveying technologies*** field have led to longer conveyors being installed, with lower energy consumption, higher capacity and lower running costs thanks to more durable components.

Technologies related to transporting mining output through ***conveying*** represent the largest volume of patents in the data. These have also seen the highest increase in volume during the last four decades. A cursory look at the patent pool shows that many of these patents are for detailed components of conveying systems rather than systems as a whole. This partially explains the large number of patents, but also indicates that there is considerable incremental innovation happening within this technological field.

In relative terms, innovation in this mode of transport has lost ground with respect to other categories over the period analysed, potentially pointing to an approaching technology frontier. However, the share of conveying technologies has been growing again since the 2000s as part of the mining transport surge. China's technological focus on improving this transportation tool largely explains this reverse of trend.

Recent years have seen substantial innovations in ***road transport*** within and outside the mining sector. Currently, road technologies are the second transport mode in patent volume, overtaking railways technologies. Road technologies relating to vehicles and hauling (i.e. the

trucks) explained most of this growth, while road infrastructure technologies has still grown but not as fast. Two thirds of recent road
technology advancements relate to vehicles and hauling. For example,
in the 1960s, the largest trucks in operation carried around 30 tonnes;
today there are trucks carrying 450 tonnes.

Quite a lot of transportation by trucks takes place within the mining
area, whether to crushers or to processing plants (e.g. concentrators)
before products are moved away from the mine. Part of the exponential
growth relates to the fact that transportation by truck within mining sites
is a closed system, as mentioned previously. However, some of this
growth may now have reached the limits imposed by the "real world"
outside of closed systems. For instance, truck size may have reached
a technical barrier linked to the maximum size of their tires. Tires cannot
be transported to a mine as spares if they cannot fit on or under existing
public road structures (e.g. tunnels or bridges) outside the mines. Where
these technological developments are not limited by the requirements of
public infrastructure they have also been applied outside the mining area.
For example, real-time information on the status of truck tires can be
provided to operators to allow them to change tire pressures according to
their load, reducing wear and increasing durability. Furthermore, there
are trials underway in relation to platooning technologies, where a semi-
autonomous road convoy has a lead truck driving (for the moment with
a driver, but potentially in future also autonomously) and several vehicles
following it autonomously through the use of radars.

Among the top patent-filing economies, China and Japan are more
specialized in vehicle technologies, China is also more specialized in
hauling technologies and the Republic of Korea, Japan and the Russian
Federation are more specialized in road infrastructure.

Outside the mine area though, it is not economical to transport raw
materials by road, unless the distance to destination is small (less than
80–100 km) because of capacity restrictions but also due to fuel and
maintenance costs related to the vehicles. Therefore, the transport of
mined raw materials often involves at least one rail leg to deliver the
extracted material to the customer. While railways have a significant
element of sunk costs in the building of the infrastructure and the buying
of rolling stock, the subsequent maintenance costs are manageable and as
such make the use of railways more economically viable.

The evolution of *railway technologies* resembles, in volume and trend,
that of road developments. The 1980s and 1990s saw railway technologies
decline in share, but they made a sizeable contribution to the recent MTI

boom in the early 2000s although this has dropped off more recently. China has been the largest contributor to these technologies in the recent boom, while Japan has focused on rail infrastructure in relative terms.

The railways have also seen their fair share of innovations that have benefited the mining sector. On the infrastructure side, new asset-management techniques have been introduced seeking to optimize the maintenance schedule to limit the amount of time that the line needs to remain closed for maintenance. This has been accompanied by extensive data gathering that has allowed infrastructure managers to move from preventative maintenance regimes to predictive regimes based on the actual condition of the tracks. Modular systems have also been developed to allow railways to be built and dismantled more easily if a mine needs to be operated for a shorter period of time than is usually expected for a full mining operation.

Similar to road vehicles, rail locomotives and wagons have improved their efficiency to increase the throughput for the sector. Many mining railways essentially exist in a closed system where mining traffic is the only traffic that runs on the network, which allows for more efficient techniques to be introduced. For example, a freight train traveling on the European rail network often cannot be longer than 750 m because of the requirements in relation to signaling and power, while some of the mining trains in Africa, South America and Australia are over 3 km long with the longest on record being over 7 km long.[10] To be able to haul this weight, locomotives have needed to become more powerful as well as more reliable and over the years innovation has focused on these areas. On the infrastructure side, an important factor for the railways is also the speed at which the trains are loaded and unloaded. Over the years, significant improvements have been made in this area to increase the efficiency of this process exemplified by the move from volumetric train loading systems, through gravimetric and continuous loading systems to the more modern fully automated train loading systems. These newer systems have led to improvements in loading speed, but have, more importantly, made loading more reliable and consistent in terms of train load.

Maritime technologies in the mining sector exhibit a similar trend to other transport modes, but they represent a volume at least 10 times smaller than for rail or road technologies. Among the top mining-

---

[10] See *Railway Gazette*, August 1, 2001, and Laing O'Rourke Website (retrieved 2011), Wikipedia.

transport patent-filing economies, the United States is the more special-ized in maritime technologies.

The limited number of patents is likely related to automation and innovation within ports being the more significant innovation in the maritime sector when it comes to mining industries. Vessels have seen fewer innovations as, in terms of size, they are often constrained by key shipping lanes and canals such as the Panama Canal.

Nonetheless, capacity has increased significantly over time primarily with the introduction of Capesize vessels aimed specifically at carrying bulk cargo. These vessels average around 175,000 deadweight tonnage (DWT), with the largest in operation being about 400,000 DWT.[11] This increase in size has been accompanied by an increase in the number of ports that can accept these vessels, although, given their size, the number of ports where these vessels can call is still small. In addition, vessels have become more fuel efficient and have been able to haul raw materials using better practices through improved sealing of load-carrying compartments.

In terms of horizontal technologies applied across all these transport modes, *container technologies* is the largest in patent terms. Historically, the number of patents related to containers has been very low, but more recently it grew much faster reaching more than 180 patent families in a single year. Today these technologies outrank the maritime ones. Across the years, improvements to containers have allowed the transport of mining products over longer distances and in all weather conditions. Modern containers isolate the mining load, reducing loss during transfer. Among the top filing economies, the United States, the Russian Federation and China are specialized in container technologies.

Over the past four decades, modern *control technologies* – including logistics and automation – have been deployed in the MTI sector. In recent years, new logistics practices have optimized the movement of raw materials building on common, general innovations such as just-in-time deliveries. In addition, significant innovations in the command and control sphere have occurred, with new techniques, such as the possibil-ity of predictive maintenance and better asset management for transport infrastructure, as well as more efficient management of the movement of vehicles, also through the introduction of automation.

It is clear that automation is a significant focus of innovation in more recent years and will be going forward (see Figure 5.7). Patent data shows

[11] http://maritime-connector.com/wiki/capesize/

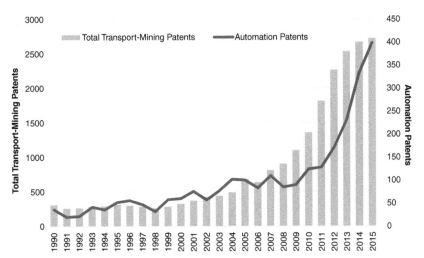

Figure 5.7   Transport patents in automation
Source: WIPO mining database.

that since the early 1990s, automation follows more or less the same increasing patterns of other transport-related patents. When focusing on more recent years, this pace has an even sharper increase. In 2015, up to 15 percent of transport patents filed globally had an element of automation. The breakdown of automation data by country indicates that the USA and Japan are the leading countries in this area. Germany and the Republic of Korea follow them by a significant margin (Figure 5.8).

Automation finds multiple applications across the different modes of transport in mining. On roads, trucks are also becoming more automated with numerous sensors and radars to optimize their movement and speed within the mining area, thus reducing congestion, diesel use and tire wear, while at the same time increasing the safety of those working on and around these vehicles. Finally, more recently, partially and fully autonomous vehicles within the mining area have been introduced. Railway transport could also benefit from automation. For example, technology can remotely operate locomotives spread along an entire train within a train consist or ensure that weight and power are distributed equally and effectively. One mining company in Australia is currently trialing an autonomous train to bring iron ore from the mine to the port for export. The trials have taken a long time mainly to ensure the service was safe as well as efficient and the service is now operational.

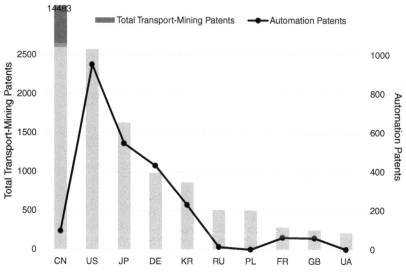

Figure 5.8   Transport automation innovation per country
Source: WIPO mining database.

5.4.3   Does Knowledge Flow In and Out of the Mining Transport Sector?

Diffusion of knowledge across industries varies and depends on its intrinsic characteristics in terms of breadth of applicability in other technological fields (Appleyard, 1996). In order to understand the role of innovation in transport and its contribution to mining innovation as a whole, it is also important to look at where MTI has come from. In the pool of 21,155 mining transport patents, more than one third have cited another patent of any technological field. For each cited patent, an analysis has been carried out on whether they are part of mining technologies or not[12] and looking also at what technology field they belong to.[13]

The aim of this analysis is to identify whether the mining transport subsector is a recipient of knowledge spillovers from other sectors – such as transport in general – or whether it produces knowledge that is then used in sectors outside mining. The pool of citations is divided into those referring to either the mining or non-mining technological fields. Figure 5.9 shows that 84 percent of the citations refer to non-mining sources, whereas only 16 percent of these refer to a mining technology.

[12] See Chapter 2 for more details on measuring mining technologies using patent data.
[13] For a discussion on measuring spillovers using patent citations and their limitations, see Trajtenberg (1990), Jaffe et al. (1993) and Michel and Bettels (2001).

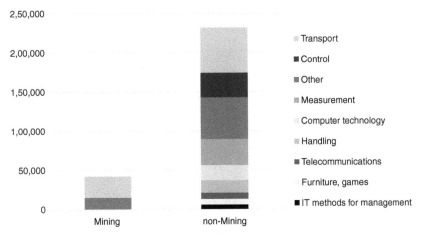

Figure 5.9   Where does MTI source technology?
Note: Patent citations from mining transport technologies by mining/non-mining and technological fields of cited patents. Fractional counting used when multiples technological fields.
Source: WIPO mining database.

Interestingly, transport is the top technological field among the patent citations from both mining and non-mining technologies. Indeed, citations to transport technologies not related to mining are an evenlarger group than those related to mining transport. Within non-mining technologies, ICTs citations as a whole – including control, computer technology, telecommunications and IT methods – are comparable in size to the transport citations. This suggests a strong knowledge flow from pure transport technology and ICTs to mining transport applications. Of those citations to other MTI (Figure 5.9, left column in grey), 74 percent refer to control technologies. This is interesting because it contrasts with the share of control in all mining transport patents, which was around 20 percent at its peak. Moreover, this reinforces the importance of ICTs as a source for mining transport technologies.

As well as understanding where MTI might come from, it is also important to highlight which other sectors use mining transport technologies as prior knowledge. The analysis therefore looked at which sectors are likely to make use of the technologies created in the mining transport subsector through the use of the citations received by mining transport patents.

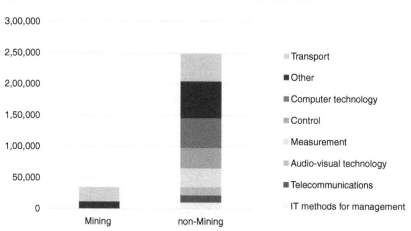

Figure 5.10   Which sectors make use of mining transport technologies?
Notes: Patent citations to mining transport technologies by mining/non-mining and technological fields of citing patents. Fractional counting used when multiples technological fields.
Source: WIPO mining database.

In the pool of 21,155 mining transport patents, almost half have received a citation from another patent. The majority of citations to mining transport technologies are from non-mining patents (88 percent). From the 12 percent that remain within the scope of mining technologies, the greater part is mining transport technologies citing mining transport patents (Figure 5.10, left column). This suggests that very little follow-on innovation spills over from mining transport to other mining technologies.

Within the non-mining citations (Figure 5.10, right column), ICTs as a whole are the bulk of citations toward mining transport technologies. In particular, citations from patents related to computer technology alone are larger than those from transport patents. Still, transport patents – not related to mining – remain one of the main categories citing mining transport patents. Both ICTs and non-mining transport gather a much larger volume of citations than mining transport ones.

These findings support the idea that transport within the mining sector might be a testbed for transport and other technologies from outside to be deployed and concept-proofed. How much this exercise benefits societies at large and mining economies in particular is a question that escapes the scope of the current research.

5.5   Future Developments and Challenges in Transport Innovation in Mining

Current technological developments both inside and, as discussed in the previous section, outside the sector can have a significant impact on MTIs and the operation of the entire mining supply chain. Patents can give us a hint on where future innovation lies and where there are still problems that need to be solved, such as empty running, that is, when a truck, train or vessel delivers the mined materials to its destination and returns empty, which essentially means that the variable cost of transport is twice as high as it could or should be. This is an issue that has affected, especially, freight transport, from early on and an innovation that minimizes this would make a significant change in relation to transport costs. The same also applies to continual improvements aimed at reducing heavy energy use.

Innovation in transport within the mining sphere has been fundamental to the growth of the sector and to increasing efficiency and safety and is also now starting to assist in reducing the environmental footprint of mining. MTI affected all possible modes of transport of mined materials within and outside the mine, namely road, rail, ships and conveyors.

The analysis has documented how important transport technologies were for mining innovation at the beginning of last century, how it declined for more than 70 years, and how it became remarkably relevant again in the last two decades. The chapter has explored the reasons behind this surge in several dimensions. For example, China has become a major player in this field, even beyond the outstanding performance that Chinese overall patenting has had. This is partially explained by the role China has played as both producer and user of mining output and the transport needs its geography and size demands. It is clear that conveying technologies made a strong contribution in the recent surge, especially given their volume. Railways and road technologies also contributed in different moments to this surge. A special mention is due to control technologies – particularly automation-related ones – which seem to be not only part of the surge but also the engine of the most recent and future developments in this sector. Interestingly, this is a domain where the impressive Chinese innovation trend has not yet had an impact.

Transport innovation – in principle more general purpose technology – seems to find an easy application in the mining sector, probably following some customization to serve mining-specific needs. On the other hand, it seems that knowledge created inside the mining transport sector then spurs ICT technologies. This result is probably driven by the recent increase in automation and digitalization, which are becoming important components of all sectors including the mining-transport one.

This could give us a hint on where future innovations are likely to go. Except for the early and more general innovations, most MTIs have been small and incremental on previous initiatives. These incremental innovations contributed extensively to increasing efficiency in transport, moving more commodities and by making the movement of bulk commodities faster, safer and more reliable.

However, there are still significant transport problems to be solved. The largest of these remains the problem of empty running mentioned previously. The continual progress of battery and alternative propulsion technology is also likely to have a positive effect on the transport of mining products, in particular in seeking to address the problem of high energy use of the mining sector, both inside the mine and outside as a partial substitute for diesel on road and rail and potentially on seagoing vessels. The growth in drone transport may also have an impact with larger, more powerful drones being used in exploring potential mining sites as well as moving equipment to those sites. Drones can also be used to inspect road and rail infrastructure from a distance, cutting down maintenance needs and reducing infrastructure unavailability.

What is clear is that innovation is often unpredictable. What has previously been considered an impenetrable frontier for technological development (e.g. automation) can be overcome from one day to the next with a milestone invention that then snowballs into further innovations that increase operational efficiency, bring down costs and increase safety.

References

Appleyard, M. M. (1996). How does knowledge flow? Interfirm patterns in the semiconductor industry. *Strategic Management Journal*, *17* (S2), 137–154.

Bresnahan, T. F., and Trajtenberg, M. (1995). General purpose technologies 'engines of growth'? *Journal of Econometrics*, 65 (1), 83–108. https://doi.org/10.1016/0304-4076(94)01598-T

Daly A., Valacchi G., and Raffo J. (2019). Mining patent data: Measuring innovation in the mining industry with patents, World Intellectual Property Organization (WIPO) Working Paper Series n. 56 (2019).

Hu, A. G., and Jefferson, G. H. (2009). A great wall of patents: What is behind China's recent patent explosion? *Journal of Development Economics*, *90* (1), 57–68.

Jaffe, A. B., Trajtenberg, M., and Henderson, R. (1993). Geographic localization of knowledge spillovers as evidenced by patent citations. *The Quarterly Journal of Economics, 108* (3), 577–598.

Michel, J., and Bettels, B. (2001). Patent citation analysis; A closer look at the basic input data from patent search reports. *Scientometrics, 51* (1), 185–201.

Morrow, J. D. A. (1922). The transportation factor in the price of coal. Proceedings of the Academy of Political Science in the City of New York, vol. 10, no. 1, Railroads and Business Prosperity, pp. 116–127.

S&P Global Platts. (2017). Capesize iron ore freight rates hit 2017 high on robust vessel demand. Singapore, August 17, 2017.

Trajtenberg, M. (1990). A penny for your quotes: Patent citations and the value of innovations. *The Rand Journal of Economics, 21* (1, Spring), 172–187.

The Carbon Brief (2016). Mapped: The global coal trade. *Carbon Brief.* May 3, 2016. www.carbonbrief.org/mapped-the-global-coal-trade.

US Energy Information Administration (2016). Rail continues to dominate coal shipments to the power sector, February 24, 2016, www.eia.gov/todayi nenergy/detail.php?id=25092

US Energy Information Administration (2017). Form EIA-923, Power Plant Operations Report

UB Post (2011). Mongolian concentrate coal exported to European market.

WIPO. (2018). World Intellectual Property Indicators, 2018. World Intellectual Property Organization.

Annex

For the purpose of the analysis, the chapter distinguished MTIs in the following categories and subcategories:

- Road
- Railways
- Containers
- Conveying
- Maritime
- Control

These were applied to the WIPO Mining Database based on the International Patent Classification (IPC) or Cooperative Patent Classification (CPC) in the patent documents. For a detailed description of the subcategories, please refer to Daly et al. 2019.

6

Environmental Regulations in the Mining Sector and Their Effect on Technological Innovation

MAXWELL ANDERSEN AND JOËLLE NOAILLY

6.1 Introduction

This chapter examines the impact of environmental policy on innovation in clean technologies for the mining sector. Mining activities pose several challenges to the environment. The extraction and processing of metals (e.g. copper, gold, aluminum, iron, nickel), solid fuel minerals (coal, uranium),[1] industrial minerals (phosphate, gypsum) and construction materials (stone, sand and gravel) is associated with air pollution, water contamination by toxic chemicals, landscape disruption and waste generation. Energy-intensive activities such as excavation, grinding of ore and the transport of material by large diesel trucks, generate substantial greenhouse gas emissions: in 2016, the mining sector accounted, for instance, for 16 percent of Australia's greenhouse gas emissions (Australian National Greenhouse Accounts, 2018), behind the energy sector (38 percent) but above manufacturing (11 percent) and agriculture (12 percent).[2] The environmental impact of mining explains why the sector is the focus of increasingly stringent environmental policies. On top of permit requirements for new mines, which typically impose an assessment of environmental impact, mining companies have to meet

---

[1] By convention, our definition of mining activities excludes fuel minerals (oil, gas, etc.).

[2] Total emissions from the mining sector can be decomposed between emissions from coal mining (42 percent of mining emissions), oil and gas extraction (40 percent) and metal ore and nonmetallic mineral mining and quarrying (18 percent). Emissions from the manufacturing of metal and other mineral products are accounted for in the manufacturing sector. Emissions from metal ore and nonmetallic mineral mining and quarrying have increased three times over the 1990–2016 period (Australian National Greenhouse Accounts, 2018).

142

stringent regulations on greenhouse gases, waste management or water pollution.

Innovation in clean technologies (i.e. technologies aiming to reduce the environmental impact of mining operations), can provide an effective solution to address these environmental challenges. Innovative technologies can help reduce water and energy consumption, limit waste production and prevent soil, water and air pollution at mine sites. Examples of such technologies are water-saving devices, electric haul trucks, desulphurization techniques to limit SO_2 emissions and underground mining technologies to minimize land disruption (Hilson, 2002).

The objective of this chapter is to estimate the impact of environmental regulations on innovation in clean technologies for the mining sector. Do more stringent environmental regulations lead to higher patenting activities in clean mining technologies? As most existing literature on this topic remains largely anecdotal and based on case studies, our analysis is the first quantitative study looking at the impact of environmental policy on clean innovation in the mining industry across a large range of countries. We rely on a novel dataset of clean patents for the mining industry provided by WIPO for 32 countries over the 1990–2015 period and investigate the impact of environmental policy stringency, as measured by the EPS index developed by the OECD on clean patenting activities. The EPS is a country-level composite index which presents the advantage of aggregating environmental policy stringency in a single indicator across a multitude of existing regulations for a large set of countries. Our analysis finds evidence that stringent environmental policies are associated with higher levels of clean patenting activities in the mining sector: a 1 percent increase in the growth rate of the EPS index is associated with a 0.3–0.45 percent increase in clean patents. These results imply that policies aiming to protect the environment are effective in encouraging mining companies to develop more environmentally friendly technologies. We do not, however, find evidence for a sizeable impact of market-based policy instruments, as often hypothesized in the literature.

The chapter is organized as follows. Section 6.2 provides some background literature and presents the conceptual framework of the analysis. Section 6.3 describes our main measures of clean technological innovation and environmental policy stringency. Sections 6.4 and 6.5 present the empirical analysis and results, respectively. Section 6.6 concludes.

6.2 Literature Review

This study relates to several strands of literature. First, it connects to the literature on the impact of environmental regulations on the development and diffusion of clean technologies (i.e. technologies that aim to reduce the environmental impact of production processes, such as energy-efficient, water-saving or renewable energy technologies). Clean technologies are characterized by a "double externality" (Jaffe, Newell and Stavins, 2005): first, just like all technologies, clean technologies generate knowledge spillovers (the knowledge externality) and second, they contribute to reducing the negative externality of pollution (the environmental externality). Due to this dual market failure, firms have few incentives to invest in clean technologies in the absence of government intervention and public policies are always justified to encourage the development of these technologies.[3]

Environmental regulations affect firms' incentives to innovate in the sense that they impact the price of production factors. According to the induced innovation hypothesis, when a factor price increases firms will develop new technologies aiming to reduce this factor (Hicks, 1932). Hence, as fuel prices increase, firms will develop fuel-efficient technologies. This hypothesis is widely supported by empirical evidence (Aghion et al., 2016; Dechezleprêtre and Glachant, 2014; Johnstone, Haščič and Popp, 2009; Noailly and Smeets, 2015; Popp, 2002) and the literature generally concludes that firms' innovation response to environmental regulation will be quick (typically within five years) and of a large magnitude. Empirical work has found that environmental policies tend to have a positive impact on clean innovation in the automobile sector (Aghion et al., 2016), electricity generation (Johnstone et al., 2009; Noailly and Smeets, 2015), the building sector (Noailly, 2012) and several manufacturing industries (Popp, 2002, 2006). So far, however, no study has more specifically looked at the mining industry.[4]

---

[3] An exception can be made for cost-saving clean technologies, such as energy-saving technologies. Profit-maximizing firms may, in this case, have incentives to innovate, even without policy intervention.

[4] Statistics and analyses on clean patents, generated for a large part by the OECD, provides some descriptive analysis of the evolution of various clean technologies over time. While some technologies have risen drastically over the last decades, such as wind energy, others which may be more relevant in the mining context such as water pollution abatement; waste management and soil remediation have instead grown much more slowly (Haščič and Migotto, 2015).

Another insight of the aforementioned literature is that the impact of environmental regulations on clean innovation depends on which specific policy instrument is used (Popp, Newell and Jaffe, 2010). Theoretical work generally concludes that market-based instruments – which set a price on the externality, such as emission taxes, emission trading or subsidies – provide higher incentives to innovate than nonmarket command-and-control regulations, such as technology and performance standards. The intuition is that market-based instruments provide more flexibility to firms on how to comply with the regulations and provide continuous incentives for technological improvements. Instead, nonmarket instruments are believed to be less effective as firms have no incentives to go beyond the standard once enacted. In addition, technological standards, in particular, may tend to lock in technological development. Nonetheless, there are also some arguments in favor of nonmarket-based regulations, in particular as command-and-control instruments may be more credibly enforced than market-based instruments. A few theoretical models also raise the possibility that command-and-control policy instruments may lead to more innovation in process innovation, rather than end-of-pipe technologies, such as waste-water treatment or flue gas scrubbers (Amir, Germain and Van Steenberghe, 2008; Bauman, Lee and Seeley, 2008). Finally, most countries have traditionally relied on command-and-control regulations and experiences with market-based instruments are still relatively recent, limiting empirical analysis. As a result, the various impacts of market versus nonmarket environmental policy instruments on innovation still need to be worked out empirically.

By its focus on mining, this study also relates to the small literature on innovation in the mining sector. Insights are quite scarce, as the sector remains largely understudied. Overall, the mining sector has the reputation of being a rather traditional and conservative sector in terms of innovation, without many examples of radical innovation over the last decades. The OECD classifies the mining and quarrying sector as a "medium-low" R&D intensity industry, together with the textile, paper and food industry and far from other high-tech (pharmaceuticals, computers), medium high-tech (machinery, electrical equipment) and medium-tech (basic metals, plastic) industries (Galindo-Rueda and Verger, 2016). Bartos (2007) similarly concludes that the mining industry is not a high-tech industry but is rather comparable to general manufacturing.

As noted in Chapter 1, the main characteristics of innovation in the mining sector are as follows: (1) most mining technologies are not developed in-house by mining companies but rather are provided by METS; (2) since mineral commodities provide little scope for product differentiation, innovation in mining is mainly aimed at cost-reduction of mining operations; and (3) profits and thus innovation in the mining industry are largely affected by booms and busts in the mineral-commodity price index (itself affected by shifts in aggregate demand[5]). The empirical evidence has mostly pointed towards a procyclical relationship between industry-specific fluctuations and innovation (Barlevy, 2007; Geroski and Walters, 1995).[6]

The specificity of competition in the mining industry has some implications for the impact of environmental regulation on clean technologies. First, as commodities are homogenous, the scope for creating a market for "green" mining products remains limited, although there are many initiatives in this direction in recent years (Laurence, 2011; Mudd, 2007; Whitmore, 2006). In the absence of a demand push for sustainably mined products, most clean innovation will have to be fostered by government regulation. A wide array of environmental regulations affects mining (Bridge, 2004): greenhouse gas regulations (fuel taxes, emission trading, etc.), water pollution legislation, regulation of land use, policies on waste management and toxic chemicals, etc. Such environmental policies may represent costly investments for mining companies as firms will need to allocate resources to pollution abatement rather than other productive investment. On the other hand, environmental policy may bring benefits if it leads to the implementation of cost-saving technologies or new profitable production processes. Although adopting environmental technologies may lead to productivity gains, the literature is inconclusive on whether these will be sufficient to offset compliance costs.[7] For now, the literature on the impact of environmental regulation on clean innovation in the mining industry is mainly qualitative and limited to a few case studies. Hilson (2002) looks at the example of the Kennecott copper

---

[5] The higher commodity-mineral prices around 2003–8 were, for instance, the result of increased demand from emerging economies and in particular China. While in theory, prices could also be affected by large supply shocks, there is no evidence that this problem has been relevant over the last decade (Kilian and Zhou, 2018). Kilian and Zhou (2018) argue therefore that indices of real commodity prices can serve as proper indicators of changes in global real economic activity.

[6] See again, Chapter 7 for a full discussion of the impact of commodity prices on innovation in mining.

[7] See the debate surrounding the "strong Porter hypothesis" (Ambec et al., 2013).

smelter in Garfield, Utah. Increasing SO_2 regulatory stringency led to collaborative innovation by Outokumpu and Kennecott into sulfur-capture technologies. Those innovations led the sulfur-capture rate at the smelter to increase from 93 percent to 99.9 percent. Crucially, that improvement led to a greater than 50 percent reduction in operating costs at the smelter. Warhurst and Bridge (1997) look at the case of the INCO Sudbury nickel smelter. Increasing stringency governing SO_2 emissions, as well as the smelter's outdated design, meant that it was no longer viable. This led INCO to invest in new smelting technologies that immensely reduced SO_2 emissions, which in turn led the smelter to become one of the world's most productive and efficient nickel smelters. As these studies are mainly anecdotal, the results cannot be generalized to other mining sites or countries.

To conclude, the literature brings important insights for our analysis. First, a large set of environmental regulations are likely to affect the development of clean technologies in mining. Second, since the scope for product differentiation is limited, there is no specific market demand for clean mining products, and we can expect environmental regulations to be particularly important.

6.3   Measuring Clean Innovation and Environmental Policy Stringency

6.3.1   Clean Patents in the Mining Sector

We measure technological innovation by patent counts, as established in the literature on clean technologies (Dechezlepretre et al., 2011). Mining patent data were extracted from the WIPO Statistics Database and the 2017 autumn edition of the European Patent Office's Worldwide Patent Statistical Database (PATSTAT) using a search strategy outlined in Daly et al. (2019) to build a comprehensive database of mining patenting.

For this analysis, the total number of clean mining patents invented in a given country-year was extracted from the database. Patents were counted by inventor.[8] The main unit of analysis is the first filing of a given invention, using the earliest filing date.

Clean mining patents were defined as mining patents having a primary focus on the environment. Table 6.1 gives the relevant International Patent Classification (IPC) and Cooperative Patent Classification (CPC) codes, some alone, some in combination and some in

---

[8] I.e., if a patent was invented by two Australians and one German, two patents in Australia and one patent in Germany were counted.

Table 6.1 *Patent classification of clean mining patents*

Sub-category	IPC, IPC combinations and IPC/keyword combinations	CPC (if different from IPC)
Reclamation of mining areas	E21C 41/32	
Treatment of waste water from quarries or mining activities	C02F 103/10	C02F2103/10
Treatment of waste water	C02F AND E21 C02F AND (mining OR mine OR mineral OR ore OR coal)	
Biological treatment of soil	B09C 1/10 AND E21 B09C 1/10 AND (mining OR mine OR mineral OR ore)	
Soil treatment	B09C AND E21 B09C AND (mining OR mine OR mineral OR ore OR coal)	
Waste Disposal	B09B AND E21 B09B AND (mining OR mine OR mineral OR ore)	
Protection against radiation	G21F AND E21 G21F AND (mining OR mine)	
Environmental		Y02 AND E21 Y02 AND (mining OR mine OR mineral OR ore)
Technologies related to mineral processing		Y02P 40/
Technologies related to metal processing		Y02P 10/

See Daly et al. (2019) for further details on the methodology. Note that while Y02P 40/ and YO2P 10/ are subclasses of YO2 (similarly COF 103/10 is a subclass of CO2F), we use an assignment system that takes only one category per patent, so patents are only counted once.

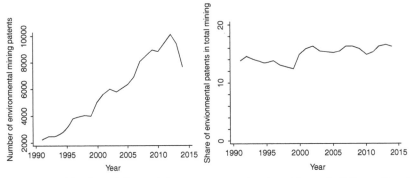

Figure 6.1   Number of clean mining patents over time in total sample (left panel) and share of clean patents among all mining patents (right panel)
Source: Author's calculations.

combination with keywords in the title or abstract. Specifically, only patents with IPC or CPC codes E21C 41/32 (reclamation of mining areas), C02F (treatment of wastewater), B09C (treatment of soil), B09B (waste disposal), Y02P (technologies related to mineral and metal processing), G21F (protection against radiation), and Y02 (general environmental) were counted as "mining clean patents". Clean patenting is dominated by four categories: metal processing, mineral processing, metallurgical wastewater treatment, and general clean patents.

As seen on Figure 6.1, on average, 15 percent of mining patents were classified as environmental mining patents over the entire data set. While the share decreased slightly over the 1990–2000 period, it increased at the end the 1990s to stabilize around 16 percent of mining patents.

Table 6.2 gives the top countries ranked by shares of clean patents in mining over the 1990–2015 period. Japanese inventors filed the highest share of clean patents, followed by Austria and Korea. While these countries do not concentrate much on mining activities, they are major providers of clean patents in general and have developed industries specialized in clean technologies – many METS companies are actually located in these countries. Major mining countries such as Australia, Brazil and Canada also appear in the top-10 of innovative countries.

Table 6.2 *Top countries as ranked according to their share of clean patents in total mining patents, 1990–2015*

Country	Percentage	Number of clean mining patents	Total mining patents
Japan	27%	30,027	113,141
Austria	26%	2,710	10,236
Korea, Rep of	22%	4,770	21,641
Italy	22%	2,030	9,407
Brazil	21%	1,140	5,327
Germany	18%	15,111	83,552
Belgium	18%	1,054	5,918
Australia	17%	2,446	14,668
India	16%	1,012	6,143
Canada	16%	6,090	38,221

Source: Author's calculations.
Note: Only countries with more than 1,000 clean patents are displayed.

6.3.2 Measuring Environmental Policy Stringency

We measure environmental policy stringency by the Environmental Policy Stringency (EPS) index developed by the OECD for 32 countries from 1990 to 2015.[9] The EPS is a composite index which summarizes the stringency of environmental policy in a given country by aggregating several sub-indicators measured on a scale from 0 to 6, with higher numbers being associated with more stringent environmental regulation. At the lower end, 0 means a policy instrument is not present in a given country-year, while 6 means the given policy instrument is the most stringent version of that policy instrument across both years and countries.

The methodology to construct the EPS is set out in detail in Botta and Koźluk, (2014) and Figure 6.2 provides a description of its main structure. The EPS index can be sub-divided into two separate indicators: (1) a component on market-based policies, which groups together

[9] Australia, Austria, Belgium, Canada, Czechia, Denmark, Finland, France, Germany, Greece, Hungary, Ireland, Italy, Japan, Korea, the Netherlands, Norway, Poland, Portugal, Slovakia, Slovenia, Spain, Sweden, Switzerland, Turkey, the UK, the USA, Brazil, China, India, Indonesia, Russia, South Africa.

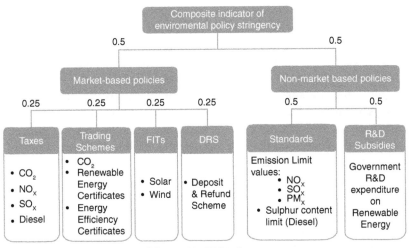

Figure 6.2   Decomposition of the OECD EPS index
Source: Botta and Koźluck (2014).

instruments assigning an explicit price to externalities such as taxes, trading schemes, feed-in tariffs and deposit-refund systems and (2) a nonmarket-based policies component, which categorizes command-and-control regulations such as environmental standards and governmental R&D subsidies (specific to renewable energy).[10] We will use both indicators at a later stage in our empirical analysis. Given our focus on the mining sector, we modify the standard index by excluding feed-in tariffs and deposit-refund systems, as these are not likely to be relevant for regulating mining activities.

The EPS index presents several advantages compared to other measures of environmental policies existing in the literature – namely: single policy changes, pollution abatement and control expenditures (PACE), surveys of executive and/or industry perceptions of stringency, or measures of environmental performance (Botta and Koźluk, 2014; Brunel and Levinson, 2013; Sauter, 2014). First, the EPS addresses the challenge of the multidimensionality of environmental policy, which targets various pollution sources and types of pollutants via a multitude of policy

---

[10]   To compute the aggregate EPS, each of these subindicators receives a weight of 0.5 as illustrated in Fig. 6.1. The nonmarket-based policies index aggregates the two subindicators on standards and R&D subsidies, each with a weight of 0.5. In our case, we abstract from feed-in tariffs (FITs) and deposit-refund systems (DRS), so our market-based indicator only aggregates over taxes and trading schemes with a weight of 0.5 each.

instruments. Such multidimensionality cannot, for instance, be captured by counts of single policy changes. Second, the EPS presents the advantage of being comparable across time and space. The aggregation strategy is admittedly a bit simplistic, particularly in its weighting of different policy measures. However, that issue can be resolved by looking at disaggregated measures of EPS, as is done in this study. By contrast, surveys based on subjective judgements cannot easily be compared across time and countries, as the perceived burden of environmental policies will differ depending on the macroeconomic and business environment of the executives being surveyed.

A main challenge when using the EPS index is that it is not specific to mining. Instead, it covers all environmental policies in an economy with a specific focus on policies addressing greenhouse gases and air pollutants. Mining pollutes through several main channels: land degradation, ecosystem disruption, acid mine drainage, chemical leakages, slope failures, toxic dusts and compounds of carbon/sulfur/nitrogen with toxic metal particulates, none of which are covered by the EPS index. Nonetheless, the EPS presents the advantage of summarizing environmental regulations in upstream activities, such as energy and transport, which are polluting inputs highly used in many sectors including the mining and extraction industry. Indeed, mining is highly energy intensive and requires the use of heavy, carbon-emitting machinery. Hence, regulations captured by the EPS are likely to be relevant for mining operations. Also, the exclusion of water or soil pollution legislation may not be as important an issue as it might appear. The OECD, in defending the validity of its index for the analysis of general environmental policy, found that other measures of environmental stringency, including measures related to water and other non-covered sectors, were highly correlated with the EPS (Botta and Koźluk, 2014).[11]

Finally, in identification issues, the non-specificity of EPS is an advantage in that it helps to address endogeneity concerns. It greatly reduces the potential for reverse causality between individual sectors and overall national EPS (Albrizio, Kozluk and Zipperer, 2017). Other measures of environmental policies, such as pollution abatement expenditures or measures of environmental performance are more likely affected by omitted variable bias, as they tend to be correlated with how efficient countries are in reducing pollution in a given year – for reasons other than environmental policies.

---

[11] These include, for example, the World Economic Forum's Executive Opinion Survey responses or the EBRD's CLIM index.

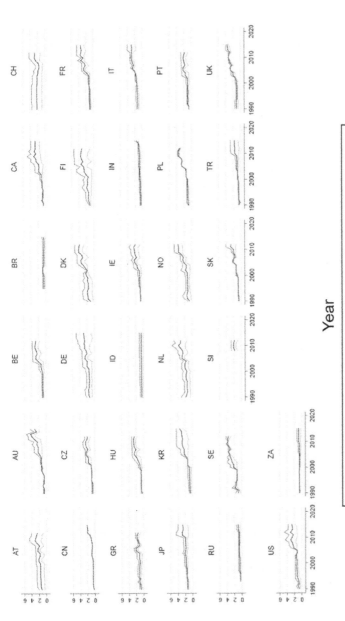

Figure 6.3 Market and nonmarket EPS
Source: Author's calculations.

Figure 6.3 plots the evolution of market (red, bottom line), nonmarket (green, top line) and overall EPS over time for the countries in our sample. We observe that the nonmarket EPS is consistently higher than market EPS across the entire dataset. Moreover, there is more and steadier growth in nonmarket EPS. Indeed, nonmarket EPS growth is considerably less volatile than market EPS (std. dev. of 0.08 vs. 0.21, respectively).

6.4   Empirical Strategy and Descriptive Statistics

6.4.1   Empirical Strategy

We estimate the impact of the stringency of environmental regulations on the number of patent applications related to clean technologies in the mining sector by estimating the following model:

$$\log\left(\frac{1}{3}\sum_{k=0}^{2}PAT_{it-k}|X\right) = \left(\frac{1}{3}\sum_{k=2}^{4}\Delta\%EPS_{it-k}\right)\beta_1$$
$$+\left(\frac{1}{3}\sum_{k=2}^{4}EPS_{it-k}\right)\beta_2 + \left(\frac{1}{3}\sum_{k=0}^{2}X\gamma_{it-k}\right)$$
$$+ c_i + p_t + u_{it} \tag{1}$$

Where PAT_i are patent counts in country i, $\Delta\%$ EPS[12] and EPS are, respectively, the growth rate and level of the EPS index and X is a vector of covariates. The remaining terms are country fixed effects c_i, year fixed effects p_t, (or a time trend depending on the specification) and the idiosyncratic error term u_{it}. All variables are expressed as three-year moving averages. The lag structure was chosen due to the nature of patenting. Since it takes time to develop a new technology once a new regulation is implemented, we consider that regulations passed in the period t-2 to t-4 will have an impact on patenting activities in the period t-2 to t, so we assume that the effect of environmental policy will occur within two years. This structure is in line with the literature, although there is some debate as to the exact lag length (Lanoie et al, 2011; Noailly, 2012; Noailly and Smeets, 2015).

We chose to include both the (logged) levels of EPS and the growth rate of EPS (in percent) in the absence of conclusive evidence from the literature. Indeed two recent studies cited in this chapter, Albrizio, Kozluk and Zipperer (2017) and Fabrizi, Guarini and Meliciani (2018) use growth and levels of EPS, respectively. Given that yearly patenting

[12] The growth rate in percentage terms was calculated according to: $\%\ \Delta EPS_t = \frac{EPS_t - EPS_{t-1}}{EPS_{t-t}}$.

data measure the flow of environmental innovative output, it seems more likely that the marginal change in EPS (i.e. its growth rate), will be more determinative of marginal output than the level of EPS.

In the second part of our analysis, we aim to compare the effect of market-based versus nonmarket-based policy instruments on patenting activities. To do so, we disaggregate the EPS index into nonmarket and market instruments (and then into their subcomponents, namely R&D support and standards, and taxes and trading schemes, respectively) and estimate equation (2) as follows[13]:

$$
\log\left(\frac{1}{3}\sum_{k=0}^{2} PAT_{it-k}|X\right) = \left(\frac{1}{3}\sum_{k=2}^{4} \Delta\%MKTEPS_{it-k}\right)\beta_1
$$

$$
+\left(\frac{1}{3}\sum_{k=2}^{4} ln\left((MKTEPS_{it-k})\right)\beta_2 + \left(\frac{1}{3}\sum_{k=2}^{4} \Delta\%NMKTEPS_{it-k}\right)\beta_3
$$

$$
+\left(\frac{1}{3}\sum_{k=2}^{4} ln(NMKTEPS_{it-k})\right)\beta_4 + \left(\frac{1}{3}\sum_{k=0}^{2} X\gamma_{it-k}\right) + c_i + p_t + u_{it}
$$

$$
(2)
$$

We use the Poisson fixed effects (FE) regression model to estimate both equations (1) and (2). The Poisson FE estimator was chosen following Allison and Waterman (2002), which identified fundamental flaws in the panel fixed effects negative binomial estimator constructed by Hausman, Hall and Griliches (1984). In the presence of overdispersion, Allison and Waterman propose using either a Poisson FE model or an unconditional negative binomial dummy variable estimator (NBDV). Poisson FE were chosen over NBDV following Wooldridge (1999), who demonstrated that a Poisson FE model remains consistent as long as the specification of the conditional mean and strict exogeneity are respected. Issues stemming from overdispersion can moreover be dealt with using robust standard errors.

The identification strategy is based on the main assumption that patenting activities in a given country are affected by domestic environ-mental policy stringency. In reality, there may be a disconnect between the geographic location of inventors and where extraction and mining operations take place. This may weaken the identification strategy, as mining firms subject to a given country's regulation can simply import

---

[13]   The major difference between this analysis and the baseline sample is that China is absent from this set of regressions because the EPS is not disaggregated into market and nonmarket-based policy for China.

patents for useful technologies from other countries. Empirically, the result of that would be a zero, or insignificant, coefficient estimate. As a result, the coefficient we find may be a lower bound estimate.

We may be worried about endogeneity concerns if, for instance, high levels of clean patenting activities facilitate the adoption of more stringent environmental policies or if countries with low levels of clean patents may successfully lobby against environmental regulation. In the estimation, this would lead to a potential reverse causality between clean mining innovation and the EPS index. Nonetheless, as discussed earlier, these concerns are likely minimized when using the EPS index: the EPS captures regulation in upstream sectors (energy, electricity and transport) and it is less likely that mining firms are active into these sectors. In addition, in the estimation the EPS variable is lagged by two years to avoid reverse causality and simultaneity issues. Finally, the estimation includes fixed effects to control for additional time-invariant confounding factors that may be omitted and affect both innovation and the level of environmental stringency (such as, for instance, the level of development of a country).

We chose a set of covariates that accounts for several factors likely to affect clean innovation in the mining industry and that relate to (1) demand-side factors not captured by policy (greenhouse gas emissions, GDP per capita, global mineral prices), (2) characteristics of a country's mining sector (net mining imports, mineral rents) and (3) technological capacity in the mining sector.

Table 6.3 gives the list of covariates used in the analysis.

Regarding demand-side factors, we include the level of greenhouse gas (GHG) emissions per capita in each country to reflect increasing concerns about pollution and the need for technological solutions to address it. We expect, therefore, GHG per capita to have a positive impact on clean mining patents. The level of GHG is also likely correlated with GDP[14] and captures the level of development of a country, so higher output and income per capita is generally associated with higher levels of innovation.

To capture the global demand for mining products, as well as the profitability of the mining sector, we include fluctuations in the global mineral price index. We use the IMF's mineral price index, which captures changes in the price of copper, aluminum, iron ore, tin, nickel, zinc, lead and uranium and which is set on the global

---

[14] Their correlation in the estimation sample is 0.46. Despite its obvious relevance to both stringency and patenting, GDP per capita was excluded from this regression, although we will include it in some specifications.

Table 6.3 *Control variables*

Variable	Description / unit	Source
Greenhouse gas emissions per capita	1,000 per unit of GDP	World Resources Institute's CAIT
Growth of GDP per capita	percent	World Bank's World Development Indicators (WDI)
Mining imports, exports	percent of all export	World Bank's World Development Indicators (WDI)
Mineral rents	percent of GDP	World Bank's World Development Indicators (WDI)
Mining net exports	1,000 USD	UN COMTRADE database
Growth of global mineral price index	percent	IMF
Total mining patents	Excluding clean patents	WIPO

Source: Author's calculations.

market.[15] This will capture business cycles effects specific to the mining sector. In line with the empirical literature and with the findings of Chapter 7, we expect innovation to be procyclical, so that higher prices and profitability will be associated to higher levels of patenting.[16]

We include covariates to control for the characteristics of the mining sector in each country. We add mining imports and exports computed as percentage of total imports, mineral rents as a percentage of GDP, and the value of net exports of minerals. These covariates aim to capture the concentration of mining activities in a given country. In general, we expect a higher concentration of mining activities (lower imports, higher

---

[15] MPI growth, as it is country-invariant, is collinear with the year fixed effects included in some specifications. They are thus principally relevant in specifications lacking year fixed effects.

[16] Note that innovation may affect the supply of minerals (through exploration activities for instance) and thereby the mineral price index, leading to endogeneity issues when estimating the impact of mineral prices on innovation. In our case, however, it is unlikely that clean patenting will affect the supply of minerals and thereby the global price index.

exports, higher share of mineral rents into GDP) to be associated with higher levels of clean innovation. Nonetheless, the results may be sensitive to multicollinearity issues if, for instance, exports are highly correlated with imports, and if mineral rents and the volume of net mining exports are correlated with the level of development of the country (GDP per capita, GHG emissions), such that a higher dependence on mineral rents would translate into lower levels of innovation.

Finally, we also include the total number of (non-clean) mining patents to control for the baseline innovativeness of a country's mining sector over time. A positive sign is expected, given that a country that is more innovative in the mining sector should also be more innovative in the specific subfield of mining clean innovation.[17]

6.4.2   Summary and Descriptive Statistics

The data set is a panel of principally developed countries, as well as the major developing country miners of Brazil, China, Indonesia, India, Turkey and South Africa. Because it does not include other developing countries with important, dominant, mining sectors (e.g. Botswana, Papua New Guinea, Zambia), results are not necessarily externally valid to all countries. Indeed, all the countries in the data set are at least middle income and all have been politically stable for as long as they have been present in the data set. The years covered are from 1990 to 2015. Table 6A in the Appendix provides summary statistics of the sample.

Figure 6.4 plots the evolution of clean mining patents and EPS growth over time for a subset of countries.[18] There is considerable commonality between these trends, particularly in the cases of the United States, France and Australia, suggesting the existence of a positive effect of tightening EPS on patenting. Figure 6.5 plots the level and growth of the IMF's index mineral prices. As can be seen from Figure 6.5, mineral prices have been quite volatile over the years covered in the data, more than doubling between 1990 and 2008, only to drop during the financial crisis, rebound and then fall rapidly again starting in 2011. There is no clear link between the evolution of the mineral commodity price index and the share of clean mining patents.

---

[17] Total mining patents were structured as a moving average with the same lag structure as clean mining patents.

[18] Specifically, a three-year, country-demeaned, moving average of logged clean mining patents is plotted against a (two-year) lagged three-year moving average of EPS index growth.

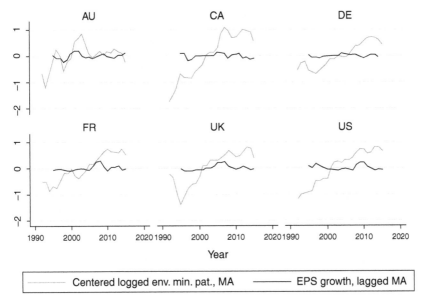

Figure 6.4   Mining patenting and lagged EPS
Source: Author's calculations.

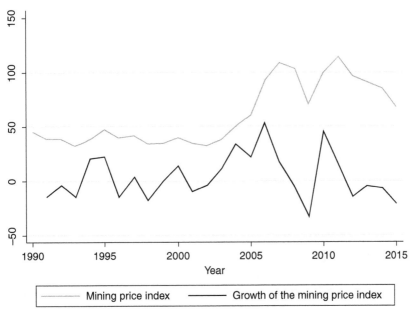

Figure 6.5   Mineral price index (MPI)
Source: Author's calculations.

6.5   Results

6.5.1   Baseline Results

Table 6.4 sets out the results of estimating equation (1). Columns (1) and (2) include only GHG emissions per capita and total mining sector

Table 6.4 *Baseline results*

VARIABLES	(1)	(2)	(3)	(4)
Level of EPS,	−0.0510	0.0480	−0.00592	0.106
(logged MA)	(0.219)	(0.209)	(0.169)	(0.188)
Percentage change in	0.434***	0.359***	0.332***	0.343***
EPS (MA)	(0.100)	(0.134)	(0.118)	(0.126)
Level of GHG per	−0.419	−0.447	−0.724	−1.061
capita (logged MA)	(0.527)	(0.596)	(0.673)	(0.710)
Total number of	0.616***	0.574***	0.585***	0.552***
mining patents	(0.141)	(0.158)	(0.137)	(0.162)
(logged MA)				
Growth of the MPI			0.263	8.535***
(logged MA)			(0.189)	(2.669)
Mining exports			−7.930**	−5.985
(percent of			(3.473)	(3.829)
GDP, MA)				
Mining imports			2.181	7.131
(percent of			(4.366)	(5.572)
GDP, MA)				
Mineral rents (percent			6.498	4.070
of GDP, MA)			(10.85)	(12.81)
Net exports of minerals			−1.33e-09	−1.59e-09
(1,000s USD, MA)			(3.01e-09)	(3.55e-09)
Time trend	Yes	No	Yes	No
Year fixed effects	No	Yes	No	Yes
Observations	553	553	503	503
Number of countries	31	31	30	30

Source: Author's calculations. The dependent variable is a moving-average of the number of clean mining patents per country from t-2 to t. All moving average independent variables are from t-2 to t-4, with the exception of total non-clean mining patents. Robust standard errors in parentheses,
*** $p < 0.01$, ** $p < 0.05$, * $p < 0.1$.

patents as covariates, whereas columns (3) and (4) add trade exposure covariates. Odd-numbered columns include year trends, while even-numbered columns include year fixed effects. As these are Poisson regressions, and the independent variables are either percentages or natural logarithms, coefficients are easily interpretable as elasticities.[19]

Across specifications, and regardless of the presence or absence of year fixed effects, there is evidence of a strongly significant, positive effect of the growth rate of policy stringency on clean mining patenting. Specifically, a 1 percent increase in the growth rate of environmental policy stringency is associated with anywhere from a 0.3 percent to 0.45 percent increase in clean patenting. Those results are significant at 1 percent level across all specifications. By contrast, we find no significant effect of the level of EPS on patenting.

As expected, there is evidence of a positive relationship between total mining patents (excluding clean) and clean mining patents, which is strongly significant in all specifications. Specifically, a 1 percent increase in overall total mining patents is associated with a 0.5 to 0.6 percent increase in clean mining patents. The magnitude of this coefficient is notably only somewhat larger than the coefficient on EPS growth, indicating EPS's important role in inducing mining innovation. The impact of fluctuations in the global mineral price index is positive and significant in column (2), although we may be concerned about issues of multicollinearity with the year fixed effects terms. Other covariates do not appear to have a statistically significant impact on clean mining patents.[20]

Several robustness checks were performed. We first considered different estimation models.[21] Poisson FE results are robust to the use of cluster-bootstrapped standard errors. Results are somewhat robust to NBDV and negative binomial "fixed effects" estimators, for which we found positive coefficient estimates with statistical significance in some specifications, but none in others.

Next, we considered different lag structures as shown in Table 6B in the Appendix. The results are robust to specifications using individual lags, as opposed to moving averages, as covariates. Interestingly, those

---

[19] With the exception of mining net exports, which could not be transformed into a logged variable due its negative elements. Its coefficient is consequently interpretable as a semi-elasticity.

[20] Although we find a negative sign of mining exports in column (3), this is not robust to including fixed effects in column (4).

[21] Results on the various estimation models are available upon request.

results find a negative impact of the level of EPS in t-2, which is offset by a similarly sized positive impact of the level of EPS in t-3. In other words, two years after legislation is passed, EPS had a negative impact on patenting, but that negative impact is counterbalanced by a positive effect as of the third year. This could indicate that in the relatively short term, environmental policy may crowd out innovation, but a positive impact occurs in the longer term. Finally, results are robust to defining variables in terms of two-year moving averages.

6.5.2   Market vs. Nonmarket Instruments

We now turn to estimating the impact of different environmental policy instruments, comparing market with nonmarket-based policy instruments. Table 6.5 reports the results of estimating equation (2), where we include both market and nonmarket sub-indicators of the EPS.[22] Column (1) includes a time trend, while column (2) includes year fixed effects. As in the preceding section, the level of the EPS variables has no statistically significant effect on patenting, while only the growth rate of EPS appears relevant. Specifically, a 1 percent increase in the growth rate of *nonmarket* EPS is associated with between a 0.25 percent and 0.5 percent increase in clean patenting. The magnitude of that effect is roughly comparable to the estimate from overall EPS, suggesting that the estimated impact on clean patenting from overall EPS is driven by nonmarket instruments. By contrast, we find no statistically significant impact of market-based instruments contrary to the theoretical insights.

To investigate this striking result further, we further disaggregate the analysis by type of policy instrument. In Table 6.6, we estimate the separate impact of the various policy instruments: namely environmental standards and government renewable R&D for nonmarket instruments and environmental taxes and trading schemes for market-based instruments – see Figure 6.2 for the construction of the EPS index across the various types of instruments. The results find evidence for a positive and statistically significant effect of the growth rate of environmental standards. Specifically, a 1 percent increase in the growth rate of the stringency of environmental standards is associated with a 0.5 percent to 0.8 percent

---

[22] A further complication is due to the fact that market and nonmarket EPS are highly correlated (0.65), as are the more disaggregated measures of EPS. That correlation does not appear to induce multicollinearity, as the inclusion of all EPS measures in the same equation caused no issues with the variance inflation factor of any of them.

Table 6.5 *Results – Impact of market vs. nonmarket EPS*

VARIABLES	(1)	(2)
Level of market EPS (logged MA)	0.0659	0.0437
	(0.151)	(0.142)
Percentage change of market EPS (MA)	−0.166	−0.162
	(0.140)	(0.130)
Level of nonmarket EPS (logged MA)	−0.0466	0.0604
	(0.191)	(0.221)
Percentage change of nonmarket EPS (MA)	0.478***	0.277**
	(0.150)	(0.137)
Level of GHG per capita (logged MA)	−1.326***	−1.875***
	(0.476)	(0.513)
Total number of mining patents (logged MA)	0.566***	0.588***
	(0.133)	(0.164)
Growth of the MPI (logged MA)	0.321	6.234**
	(0.199)	(2.869)
Mining exports (percent of exports, MA)	−3.219	−1.057
	(3.651)	(3.317)
Mining imports (percent of imports, MA)	−5.672	−3.048
	(3.848)	(4.704)
Mineral rents (percent of GDP, MA)	−2.278	−4.142
	(12.53)	(12.00)
Net exports of minerals (1000s USD, MA)	−4.38e-09**	−6.32e-09**
	(2.09e-09)	(2.75e-09)
Year trend	Yes	No
Year fixed effects	No	Yes
Observations	465	465
Number of countries	28	28

Source: Author's calculations. The dependent variable is a moving average of the number of clean mining patents per country from t-2 to t. All moving-average independent variables are from t-2 to t-4, with the exception of total non-clean mining patents. Cluster-robust standard errors in parentheses, *** $p < 0.01$, ** $p < 0.05$, * $p < 0.1$.

increase in clean patenting. This is a larger impact than the aggregate EPS index growth found in Table 6.4. Government R&D expenditures in renewable energy is found to have a negative impact on clean mining

Table 6.6 *Results – Impact of individual policy instruments*

VARIABLES	(1)	(2)
Nonmarket-based instruments:		
Percentage change in env. standards EPS (MA)	0.572**	0.811***
	(0.235)	(0.240)
Percentage change in R&D EPS (MA)	−0.192***	−0.227***
	(0.0712)	(0.0871)
Level of standards EPS (logged MA)	0.0691	0.0492
	(0.0687)	(0.0618)
Level of R&D EPS (logged MA)	−0.00322	0.0743
	(0.0573)	(0.114)
Market-based instruments:		
Pct. change in tax EPS (MA)	−0.207	−0.135
	(0.144)	(0.178)
Pct. change in trading schemes EPS (MA)	−0.0853***	−0.0485
	(0.0296)	(0.0388)
Level of tax EPS (logged MA)	−0.0156	0.00863
	(0.0179)	(0.0253)
Level of trading schemes EPS (logged MA)	0.132	0.0194
	(0.121)	(0.133)
Other covariates:		
Level of GHG emissions per capita (logged MA)	−1.801***	−1.836***
	(0.443)	(0.520)
Total non-clean mining patents (logged MA)	0.548***	0.508***
	(0.121)	(0.134)
MPI growth (MA)	0.190	5.891***
	(0.168)	(2.171)
Mining exports (percent of exports, MA)	−0.710	−1.938
	(3.429)	(3.743)
Mining imports (percent of imports, MA)	−6.208*	−3.380
	(3.707)	(4.837)
Mineral rents (percent of GDP, MA)	−8.295	−4.951
	(13.05)	(13.87)
Net exports of minerals (1000s USD, MA)	−7.38e-09**	−8.37e-09**
	(3.69e-09)	(3.93e-09)
Year trend	Yes	No
Year fixed effects	No	Yes
Observations	462	462

Source: Author's calculations. The dependent variable is a moving average of the number of clean mining patents per country from t-2 to t. All moving-average independent variables are from t-2 to t-4, with the exception of total non-clean mining patents. Cluster-robust standard errors in parentheses,
*** $p < 0.01$, ** $p < 0.05$, * $p < 0.1$.

patenting activities: a 1 percent increase in R&D EPS is associated with a roughly 0.2 percent decrease in mining clean patenting. Given that renewable energy technologies are not highly relevant for mining activities, we can expect that more spending on renewable energy will lead to some crowding out of clean innovation related to mining.

Further, we find no evidence that environmental taxes have an impact on clean patenting, while the growth in the stringency of tradable permits is associated with a very small statistically significant decline in clean patenting activities in mining in column (1), but this result is not robust to adding year fixed effects in column (2). Overall, these results confirm the ones found in Table 6.5, namely that market-based policy instruments do not appear to have a significant impact on clean innovation in the mining industry.

Just as before, we perform a set of robustness tests and find that results are robust to various estimation models and to alternative lagged structure and moving averages.[23] Using disaggregated measures of EPS, the coefficient on the growth rate of environmental standards remains significant across various moving-average specifications.

The large significant impact of environmental standards, compared to market-based instruments, may seem puzzling in light of the theoretical results. Nonetheless, as discussed in Section 6.2, a main challenge in testing the theory arises from the lack of sufficient experience with stringent market-based instruments. Environmental standards (related to air pollution in the EPS index) remain traditionally the most popular form of environmental policy and have been used extensively in many countries. In our dataset, it appears that the stringency of environmental standards has increased consistently and remained higher than other instruments over the years.[24] As seen in Figure 6.3, nonmarket EPS is consistently higher than market EPS across the entire dataset. Moreover, there is more and steadier growth in nonmarket EPS. Indeed, nonmarket EPS growth is considerably less volatile than market EPS (std. dev. of 0.08

---

[23] Results are robust to cluster-bootstrapped standard errors, to the use of a conditional random effects Poisson model using both clustered and cluster-bootstrapped standard errors. They are robust to a NBDV model as well as a conditional "fixed effects" negative binomial model in some specifications. Results are robust to alternative moving averages, specifically two- and four-year moving averages of all covariates. Those regressions find the same, positive and significant relationship between nonmarket changes in stringency and clean patent filing using two- and four-year MAs. Detailed results are available upon request.

[24] Standards have a maximum EPS value of 6/6 as compared with 4/6 and 5.2/6 for taxes and trading schemes, respectively.

vs. 0.21, respectively). In addition, the particularly positive impact of standards may also be ascribable to their high level of stability: their growth is uniformly positive, indicating that, once implemented, standards are not repealed. By contrast, environmental taxes and tradable schemes are still relatively new, have not been set at high stringency levels yet and may tend to be more geographically concentrated in Europe, rather than in regions where mining activities are prevalent.[25]

6.6   Conclusions

This chapter provides a first exploratory investigation of the impact of environmental policy stringency on clean innovation in the mining sector. Using a novel dataset of patenting activities in the mining industry developed by WIPO, we are able to identify mining patents specific to clean technologies. We combine patents data with the EPS index of environmental policy stringency developed by the OECD and conduct the analysis for a set of 32 countries over 1990–2015. Our findings show that environmental regulations do trigger mining firms to develop new clean technologies: a 1 percent increase in the EPS index is associated with an increase of 0.3 to 0.45 percent of clean patenting activities in mining. Given that the policy indicator is quite broad and abstract from water or soil regulation, our estimates are likely to be a lower bound of the impact. In further analysis, we investigate which types of policy instruments between market- and non-market-based policies, are the most effective in encouraging clean patenting. We find that nonmarket policy instruments, in particular environmental standards (mainly related to air pollution as defined in the EPS index) explain most of the effect. This may be due to the prevalence of traditional command-and-control types of regulations in countries most active in mining, with, so far, few implementations of stringent market-based policies – but a detailed investigation of this question is left for future analysis.

As our study is mainly exploratory, there are still many questions worth investigating in future work. First, the novel dataset on clean mining patents used in this study calls for a more in-depth understanding and mapping of the various types of technologies that aim to reduce the environmental impact of mining. As an illustration, the CPC Y02 classification that flags "environmental patents" is very broadly defined and could be further disaggregated. Second, an important assumption in our analysis is that domestic environmental

---

[25] Australia started with emission trading in 2016, after abolishing carbon pricing in 2014.

regulations spur innovation at home. This assumption may not hold, however, if foreign METS firms are instead important technology providers to domestic mining corporations. Third, our analysis could be extended to test the robustness of our results to other specific policy instruments for the mining sector, rather than the aggregate EPS index. Finally, it would be worthwhile to investigate whether innovation in clean technologies triggered by regulation leads to productivity gains – as a contribution to the debate on whether environmental policy may foster competitiveness of the mining industry.

References

Aghion, P., Dechezleprêtre, A., Hémous, D., Martin, R., and Van Reenen, J. (2016). Carbon Taxes, Path Dependency, and Directed Technical Change: Evidence from the Auto Industry. *Journal of Political Economy, 124*(1), 1–51. https://doi.org/10.1086/684581

Albrizio, S., Kozluk, T., and Zipperer, V. (2017). Environmental Policies and Productivity Growth: Evidence across industries and firms. *Journal of Environmental Economics and Management, 81*, 209–226.

Allison, P. D., and Waterman, R. P. (2002). Fixed-Effects Negative Binomial Regression Models. *Sociological Methodology, 32*(1), 247–265. https://doi .org/10.1111/1467-9531.00117

Ambec, S., Cohen, M. A., Elgie, S., and Lanoie, P. (2013). The Porter Hypothesis at 20: Can environmental regulation enhance innovation and competitiveness? *Review of Environmental Economics and Policy, 7*(1), 2–22. https://doi.org/10.1093/reep/res016

Amir, R., Germain, M., and Van Steenberghe, V. (2008). On the Impact of Innovation on the Marginal Abatement Cost Curve. *Journal of Public Economic Theory, 10*(6), 985–1010. https://doi.org/10.1111/j.1467-9779.2008.00393.x

Australian National Greenhouse Accounts. (2018). *National Inventory by Economic Sector 2016.* Department of the Environment and Energy, Australian Government.

Barlevy, G. (2007). On the Cyclicality of Research and Development. *American Economic Review, 97*(4), 1131–1164. https://doi.org/10.1257/aer.97.4.1131

Bartos, P. J. (2007). Is Mining a High-Tech Industry?: Investigations into Innovation and Productivity Advance. *Resources Policy, 32*(4), 149–158.

Bauman, Y., Lee, M., and Seeley, K. (2008). Does Technological Innovation Really Reduce Marginal Abatement Costs? Some theory, algebraic evidence, and policy implications. *Environmental and Resource Economics, 40*(4), 507–527. https://doi.org/10.1007/s10640-007-9167-7

Botta, E., and Koźluk, T. (2014). Measuring Environmental Policy Stringency in OECD Countries: A Composite Index Approach. *OECD Economic Department Working Papers*, 1177.

Bridge, G. (2004). Contested Terrain: Mining and the environment. *Annual Review of Environment and Resources, 29*(1), 205–259. https://doi.org/10.1146/annurev.energy.28.011503.163434

Brunel, C., and Levinson, A. (2016). Measuring the Stringency of Environmental Regulations. *Review of Environmental Economics and Policy*, 10(1), 47–67.

Daly, A., Valacchi, G., and Raffo, J. (2019). Mining patent data: Measuring innovation in the mining industry with patents. *World Intellectual Property Organization (WIPO) Economic Research Working Paper*, 56.

Dechezleprêtre, A., and Glachant, M. (2014). Does Foreign Environmental Policy Influence Domestic Innovation? Evidence from the wind industry. *Environmental and Resource Economics, 58*(3), 391–413. https://doi.org/10.1007/s10640-013-9705-4

Fabrizi, A., Guarini, G., and Meliciani, V. (2018). Green Patents, Regulatory Policies and Research Network Policies. *Research Policy, 47*(6), 1018–1031. https://doi.org/10.1016/j.respol.2018.03.005

Galindo-Rueda, F., and Verger, F. (2016). OECD Taxonomy of Economic Activities Based on R&D Intensity. *OECD Science, Technology and Industry Working Papers* 2016.4.

Geroski, P. A., and Walters, C. F. (1995). Innovative Activity over the Business Cycle. *The Economic Journal, 105*(431), 916. https://doi.org/10.2307/2235158

Haščič, I., and Migotto, M. (2015) Measuring environmental innovation using patent data. *OECD Environment Working Papers*, 89.

Hausman, J., Hall, B., and Griliches, Z. (1984). *Econometric Models for Count Data with an Application to the Patents-R&D Relationship* (No. t0017). Cambridge, MA: National Bureau of Economic Research. https://doi.org/10.3386/t0017

Hicks, J. (1932). *The Theory of Wages*. Macmillan.

Hilson, G. (2002). Eco-efficiency: Improving environmental management strategy in the primary extraction industry. *Journal of Environmental Systems, 29*(1), 1–14. https://doi.org/10.2190/KW9 M-0ER4-9W3P-96P3

Jaffe, A. B., Newell, R. G., and Stavins, R. N. (2005). A Tale of Two Market Failures: Technology and environmental policy. *Ecological Economics, 54*(2), 164–174.

Johnstone, N., Haščič, I., and Popp, D. (2009). Renewable Energy Policies and Technological Innovation: Evidence based on patent counts. *Environmental and Resource Economics, 45*(1), 133–155. https://doi.org/10.1007/s10640-009-9309-1

Kilian, L., and Zhou, X. (2018). Modeling Fluctuations in the Global Demand for Commodities. *Journal of International Money and Finance*, *88*, 54–78. https://doi.org/10.1016/j.jimonfin.2018.07.001

Lanoie, P., Laurent-Lucchetti, J., Johnstone, N., and Ambec, S. (2011). Environmental Policy, Innovation and Performance: New Insights on the Porter Hypothesis. *Journal of Economics and Management Strategy*, *20*(3), 803–842. https://doi.org/10.1111/j.1530-9134.2011.00301.x

Laurence, D. (2011). Establishing a Sustainable Mining Operation: An overview. *Journal of Cleaner Production*, *19*(2–3), 278–284. https://doi.org/10.1016/j.jclepro.2010.08.019

Mudd, G. M. (2007). Global Trends in Gold Mining: Towards quantifying environmental and resource sustainability. *Resources Policy*, *32*(1–2), 42–56. https://doi.org/10.1016/j.resourpol.2007.05.002

Noailly, J. (2012). Improving the Energy Efficiency of Buildings: The impact of environmental policy on technological innovation. *Energy Economics*, *34*(3), 795–806. https://doi.org/10.1016/j.eneco.2011.07.015

Noailly, J., and Smeets, R. (2015). Directing Technical Change from Fossil-Fuel to Renewable Energy Innovation: An application using firm-level patent data. *Journal of Environmental Economics and Management*, *72*, 15–37. https://doi.org/10.1016/j.jeem.2015.03.004

Popp, D. (2002). Induced Innovation and Energy Prices. *The American Economic Review*, *92*(1), 160–180.

Popp, D. (2006). International Innovation and Diffusion of Air Pollution Control Technologies: The effects of NOX and SO2 regulation in the US, Japan, and Germany. *Journal of Environmental Economics and Management*, *51*(1), 46–71. https://doi.org/10.1016/j.jeem.2005.04.006

Popp, D., Newell, R. G., and Jaffe, A. B. (2010). Energy, the Environment, and Technological Change, in *Handbook of the Economics of Innovation* (Vol. 2, pp. 873–937), Bronwyn H. Hall and Nathan Rosenberg, eds. Elsevier. https://doi.org/10.1016/S0169-7218(10)02005-8

Sauter, C. (2014). How Should We Measure Environmental Policy Stringency? A new approach. *IRENE, Working Paper*, *14*(1), 21.

Warhurst, A., and Bridge, G. (1997). Economic Liberalisation, Innovation, and Technology Transfer: Opportunities for cleaner production in the minerals industry. *Natural Resources Forum*, *21*(1), 1–12. https://doi.org/10.1111/j.1477-8947.1997.tb00668.x

Whitmore, A. (2006). The Emperor's New Clothes: Sustainable mining? *Journal of Cleaner Production*, *14*(3–4), 309–314. https://doi.org/10.1016/j.jclepro.2004.10.005

Wooldridge, J. M. (1999). Distribution-free estimation of Some Nonlinear Panel Data Models. *Journal of Econometrics*, *90*(1), 77–97. https://doi.org/10.1016/S0304-4076(98)00033-5

APPENDIX

Table 6A *Summary statistics of key variables*
1) All sample, MA transformed variables

Variable	Obs	Mean	Std. Dev.	Min	Max
Clean mining patents	694	173	418	0	3099
EPS level	630	1.42	0.79	0.37	3.89
EPS growth	598	0.06	0.08	−0.14	0.43
GHG emissions per capita	630	2.23	0.60	0.33	3.41
Total mining patents	694	3472	9527	0	80633
Mining exports (percent of exports)	616	0.04	0.05	0.01	0.36
Mining imports (percent of imports)	618	0.03	0.01	0.01	0.14
Mineral price index	630	55	25	34	103
Growth of GDP per capita	564	0.02	0.02	−0.04	0.08
Market EPS level	608	0.91	0.60	0	3.54
Market EPS growth	554	0.10	0.21	−0.33	1.16
Nonmarket EPS level	608	1.97	1.13	0.33	5.33
Nonmarket EPS growth	630	0.03	0.07	−0.33	0.33

Source: Author's calculations.

2) Baseline estimation sample, logged MA transformed variables

Variable	Obs	Mean	Std. Dev.	Min	Max
Clean mining patents	503	267	628.1753	0	5414
Logged EPS	503	0.27	0.583448	−0.9808292	1.35342
EPS growth	503	0.06	0.088846	−0.1489899	0.436715
GHG emissions per capita	503	2.24	0.621479	0.3430755	3.418411
Non-environmental patents	503	5.68	1.928179	0.9985774	10.14555
MPI growth	503	0.07	0.131274	−0.1067837	0.362375
Mineral exports	503	0.04	0.0568	0.0031	0.364131
Mineral imports	503	0.046	0.020141	0.0117066	0.141764
Mineral rents	503	0.00	0.009332	0	0.065297

Source: Author's calculations.

Table 6B *Robustness best of baseline estimation, using further lags and moving-average definition*

VARIABLES	(1)	(2)	(3)
Level of EPS, logged t-2	−3.895***		
	(0.719)		
Level of EPS, logged t-3	2.232***		
	(0.758)		
Level of EPS, logged t-4	1.751		
	(1.074)		
Percentage change in EPS, t-2	3.553***		
	(0.655)		
Percentage change in EPS, t-3	1.537		
	(0.970)		
Percentage change in EPS, t-4	−0.0536		
	(0.131)		
Percentage change in EPS (MA-2)		0.348***	
		(0.124)	
Level of EPS, logged (MA-2)		0.0898	
		(0.187)	
Percentage change in EPS (MA-4)			0.142
			(0.112)
Level of EPS, logged (MA-4)			0.0898
			(0.228)
Other controls	Yes	Yes	Yes
Year fixed effects	Yes	Yes	Yes
Observations	518	535	435
Number of countries	29	30	28

Source: Author's calculations.

Global Trends of Innovation in the Mining Sector: the Role of Commodity Prices

GIULIA VALACCHI, ALICA DALY, DAVID HUMPHREYS
AND JULIO D. RAFFO

7.1 Introduction

Given the boom in demand, the decreasing returns of existing mining sites and the sustainability requirements, it is not surprising that mining-related commodities have seen a remarkable increase in price over the past two decades. Equally predictable was the well-documented boom in mining production and exports that followed. What has happened to the rate of mining-related innovation during this period remains an under-studied topic.

In this chapter, we study the effect of variation in commodity prices on the innovation carried out within the mining industry. In particular, we look at whether the existence of cycles in commodity prices, distinguishing between short- and long-term cycles – the so-called super-cycles – affects innovation levels.

Given that mining companies are increasingly sourcing innovation from specialized suppliers, as noted in Chapter 1, we consider the mining industry in a broader technological sense. In addition to companies directly engaged in finding and developing mines, we include service providers that support the everyday activities of mining firms by providing specialized equipment and technology, a sector commonly referred to as the mining, equipment, technology and services (METS) sector. Innovation is proxied by patent filing. Mining-related patents filed by both mining firms and METS firms are part of the analysis.

This chapter relies on mining patent data consolidated by WIPO for the period 1970–2015. We merge the patent data with a series of indicators related to the mining sector based on data from the World Bank, namely a mineral commodity price index, an estimation of effective demand for mining production and the country's exposure to mining. We identify price cycles of different lengths using the Christian and Fitzgerald band-pass filter (Cuddington and Jerret, 2008). We conduct the analysis first using time series and then using panel data.

We find empirical evidence of pro-cyclicality between innovation and prices in the mining sector. We model innovation as a response to changes in commodity prices and test for the effects of different cycle lengths. Our results suggest that innovation reacts more to long cycle changes rather than shorter ones. We also analyze the effect on mining innovation, distinguishing between innovation generated by mining companies and by METS firms. METS companies appear as the driving force of mining innovation response to price changes. When we move to the panel analysis, we find that mining specialized countries – as opposed to countries having little mineral production – only react to changes in the long cycle components of commodity price.

The rest of the chapter is structured as follows. Section 7.2 reviews the literature and provides motivation for the chapter's main research questions. Section 7.3 presents the data while providing a descriptive overview of the mining industry innovation; it also discusses our estimation method. Section 7.4 comments on the results and the main robustness checks performed and Section 7.5 concludes.

7.2   Literature Review and Hypotheses

External macroeconomic and financial shocks certainly affect mining production, but little is known on how they translate to the sector's technological change. Mining is considered a very cyclical sector. When prices are high, new mines are opened and existing mines are exploited more intensively. While when prices are low, production slows and mines are closed (Batterham, 2004). The way innovation and technology development react to these price cycles remains, to the best of our knowledge, an unexplored topic.

As part of the commodity super-cycle, mining-related commodities have seen an outstanding increase in price over the past 15 years, accompanied by a well-documented boom in mining production and exports. This period has not only been characterized by a high increase in prices but also higher volatility (IMF, 2015). Recent work has shown that mining innovation – proxied by patent applications –has followed this boom in general, but it has also trended down after the global financial crisis (Daly et al., 2019b).

There have been many studies about trends and cycles in commodity prices (Radetzki, 2006; Tilton, 2006). A few of these, such as Labys, Achouch and Terraza (1999), have focused on mining commodities by analyzing the relationship between metal prices and business cycles. But in general, there has been less attention on the economic effects of the longer cycles of these prices. Traditionally, economic scholars have been very skeptical about the presence of these commodities "super-cycles" (Cogley and Nason, 1995; Howrey, 1968). However, a number of relatively recent studies have begun to shed some light on the topic (Comin and Gertler, 2006; Cuddington and Jerret, 2008; Solow, 2000). They find empirical evidence of substantially more volatile and persistent fluctuations in the medium- and long-term of business cycles and commodity prices, respectively.

What happened to the innovation rate of mining-related technologies during the recent period? Given the rigidity that characterizes mining sector investment, it seems plausible that R&D decisions will be based more on expectations about long-term variation of price rather than short-term ones. The existing literature has focused on how R&D expenditures vary over business cycles, although never focusing on mining or other commodity sectors. The traditional view is that recessions should promote various activities that contribute to long-run productivity and thus to growth, such as technical change (Canton and Uhlig, 1999), job turnover (Gomes et al. 2001) and human capital accumulation (Barlevy and Tsiddon, 2006). Many studies have found innovation to be pro-cyclical, measured by R&D activities (Barlevy, 2007; Fatas, 2000; Rafferty and Funk, 2004) or patents (Geroski and Walters, 1995). According to Geroski and Walters (1995), the direction of the causality seems statistically stronger for business cycles causing innovation than the opposite, although factors other than demand largely explain innovation. In what concerns the length of cycles, Barlevy (2007) argues that macroeconomic shocks are likely to have overly persistent effects due to such pro-cyclicality of R&D activities.

As highlighted in Chapter 2, the mining industry is typically considered a slow innovator (Scherer, 1984). Nevertheless, Bartos (2007) shows that its rate of innovation is comparable with general manufacturing, even if it is still lower than so-called high-tech manufacturing (Dunbara et al., 2016). The total amount of money spent on R&D by

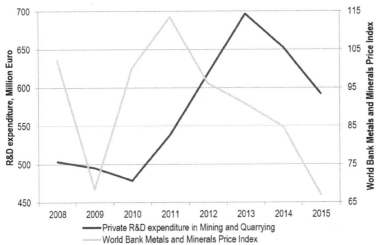

Figure 7.1   Private R&D expenditure in mining and quarrying in EU countries and World Bank Metals and Minerals Price Index
Note: EU includes Austria, Belgium, Bulgaria, Croatia, Czech Republic, Denmark, Finland, France, Germany, Greece, Hungary, Iceland, Ireland, Italy, Lithuania, Netherlands, Norway, Portugal, Romania, Slovakia, Spain, and the UK.
Source: Eurostat (2018), *BERD by NACE Rev. 25 activity.*

the sector is significant, particularly in mining-specialized countries such as Australia (Balaguer et al., 2018).

Figure 7.1 shows the private R&D expenditure in EU countries together with the Metals and Minerals Price Index from the World Bank. We can see a positive correlation between the two indicators with some delay of the R&D expenditure in reacting to price changes.

In addition to R&D expenditure, the discovery of new commercially viable mining deposits through exploration is an important part of the economics of the industry, as highlighted in Chapters 1 and 2. The existing series of worldwide exploration expenditures show a high degree of correlation with the evolution of the price index for nonferrous metals (see Figure 7.2).

METS companies contribute a substantial share of the innovation in the mining sector. These companies work very closely with mining companies to understand their requirements and to develop innovative solutions. METS firms invest, on average, more in R&D compared to mining firms (see Chapter 2). They also have lower capital expenditures than mining companies, which are required to have big initial

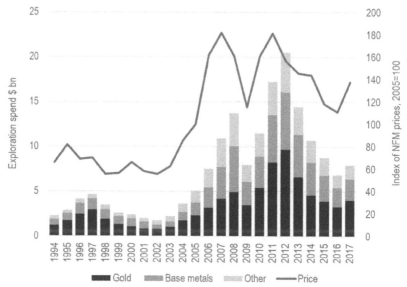

Figure 7.2   Mineral exploration expenditure by commodity and nonferrous metals price index
Source: S&P Global Market Intelligence, World Exploration Trends; The Economist.

investments both for the exploration phase and mining operations establishment. Mining firms often prefer to outsource services to specialized METS firms rather than taking it on themselves in a less efficient way. For instance, transport innovation in the mining sector is often produced by METS companies (see Chapter 5). Therefore, METS firms are an essential part of the mining innovation ecosystem.

Table 7.1 summarizes the differences between mining and METS firms along crucial dimensions of their activity. In general, mining firms are large and they operate at different stages of the mining value chain. METS firms range from big multinationals (e.g. Caterpillar or Siemens), which not only provide specialized services for the mining sector, but also serve other industries; to SMEs, which are typically specialized in the production of one product or service specially developed for the mining activity.

On average, mining firms have higher sunk costs compared to METS firms. When opening a mine, the initial investment is very big and it can only be recovered after many years of operation. Therefore, their activity is not very flexible. METS firms are more flexible. They could also have high fixed costs but this applies more to large multinationals, which

Table 7.1 *Characteristics of mining and METS firms*

Characteristic	Mining firm	METS firms (Large)	METS firms (SMEs)
Size	Large	Large (horizontally diversified)	Micro, small & medium
Diversification	Vertical (within the mining supply chain)	Horizontal (across several industries)	Horizontal (if any)
Sunk costs	Large (within the supply chain)	Large (across different industries)	Low
Innovation type	Process	Product & process	Product & process

Source: Authors' elaboration.

spread them across the different industries they serve, reducing the risk associated with their activity. Finally, mining firms produce mostly process innovation, while METS firms produce both new processes and new products that are then sold to the mining companies that use them to improve their performance.

Existing studies have shown several channels through which a price change could affect the decision to invest in innovation for other industries. Barlevy and Tsiddon (2006), Canton and Uhlig (1999) and Gomes et al. (2001) find evidence of pro-cyclicality channels between prices and innovation in other industries. These studies suggest that the pro-cyclicality can be direct or indirect, where the latter is typically through the access to finance for the firm. Conversely, Barlevy (2007), Fatas (2000), Rafferty and Funk (2004) and Geroski and Walters (1995) suggest that a countercyclical effect can arise from the cost-reducing innovative effort.

How would the pro-cyclical effect apply to the mining sector? An increase in mineral prices could directly stimulate innovation for the mining firms, which have more disposable income to invest in innovation. A price increase also indirectly affects METS firms, as they experience a higher demand for their products/services from mining firms.

Moreover, diversified METS firms may have stronger incentives to adapt technologies developed for other business.

At the same time, an increase in price also increases access to external finance of both types of firms; since financial markets' assessment of discounted future income will also be related to the new price. Similarly, increased access to finance could boost investment in innovation. Therefore, both direct and indirect effects point toward the pro-cyclicality of innovation with respect to price.

How would the countercyclical effect apply to the mining sector? A price decrease imposes cost-reduction pressure on mining firms, which already operate with tight operating margins in many mining sites. Cost-reducing technologies could be an effective way to avoid the closure of mines. Similarly, mining companies may invest in exploration, aiming to discover new deposits with higher grades, hence more cost-effective. Either the cost-reducing or exploration-related technologies can be produced in-house or sourced from METS firms. This implies a countercyclical effect, where innovation is boosted, for both mining and METS firms, in periods of low prices.

The effect of a price decrease on the access to finance for firms is instead ambiguous. On the one hand, it definitely implies reduced access to external private finance as the risk profile of these firms is now higher. On the other hand, the bigger and more diversified firms could still rely on internal resources (for the case of big vertically integrated mining firms) or on revenues from other industries that they supply (for the case of big horizontally integrated METS). Moreover, in mining-specialized countries (e.g., Chile, Australia or South Africa), the large mining companies and the sector as a whole might be, arguably, too big to fail. Policy-makers may have strong incentives to aid the sector troubled by decreasing prices and innovation financing is one valid option.

We do not know which of these effects will prevail. Still, we can argue that the countercyclical effect is more likely to occur for shorter-term price variations. Typically, a mining company can cross-subsidize activities in the short term to iron out a price fluctuation expected to be temporary. If the price variation is expected to be structural (i.e. of a longer term), companies may be limited to the countercyclical innovative actions they can undertake. A similar logic applies to public financial support, although likely with a longer horizon. In any case, we can expect the ambiguous effect is less likely in the longer cycles.

Table 7.2 *Effect on innovation and access to finance of price change*

	Mining firms	METS firms
Price increase	**+ Innovation** (+) more disposable income to invest in innovation (+) more access to external finance	**+ Innovation** (+) more demand from mining industry (+) more incentives to adapt other technologies to mining (+) more access to external finance
Price decrease	**? Innovation** (−) less disposable income to invest in innovation (−) less access to external private finance (+) cost reduction and exploration pressure (+) more access to external public finance	**? Innovation** (?) depends on mining industry demand (−) less incentives to adapt existing technologies

Source: Authors' elaboration.

Table 7.2 summarizes the channels through which a commodity price change could affect the decision of both types of mining sector stakeholders to invest in innovation.

We can formulate the main conclusions from the existing literature as four distinct hypotheses, which we are going to test in this chapter:

H1a: Higher prices generate higher disposable income (direct or indirect) that is invested to generate more (pro-cyclical) innovation;
H1b: Lower prices generate higher cost reduction and exploration pressure generating (countercyclical) innovation;
H2: Price shocks do not affect innovation unless they are perceived as structural (i.e. long lasting);

H3: As METS firms can adapt other sectors' technologies to mining, they are more likely to innovate more and faster due to price variation than mining firms; and,

H4: Mining specialized countries have stronger incentives to have counter-cyclical innovation policies.

7.3   Data and Methodology

In this section, we present and discuss the data used in our analysis. We then give an overview of the estimation methods used to study the relationship between commodity prices and innovation in the mining sector.

We use the World Bank Metals and Minerals Price Index as a proxy for an average global commodity price. This index weights the price of six commodities traded in the London Metals Exchange – aluminum, copper, lead, nickel, tin and zinc – plus iron ore, based on their world production shares. All the prices are reported in 2010 USD. The index is available from 1960 to 2017.

One limitation of such an index is that countries differ in their mining activities. Countries producing other mineral commodities than the seven minerals covered by the index or having a different weight of them, may react to other price variations than those captured by the index. In order to partially address this issue, we rely on an alternative measure of metal commodities price as a robustness check. In particular, we build a country-specific index using disaggregated commodity prices from the World Bank database,[1] weighting them based on export shares for each country. We extract data on commodity trade by country of origin from Feenstra et al. (2005). These data are classified by SITC codes. We were able to match SITC codes of export flows with products' prices from the World Bank.[2]

Following Cuddington and Jerret (2008), we decompose the natural logarithm of the de-trended commodity price in cycles of different lengths: long cycle[3] (from 20 to 70 years), medium cycle (from 10 to 20 years), short cycle (from 5 to 10 years) and a residual component (less than 5 years). Figure 7.3 plots the de-trended price index across and the

---

[1] We use prices of aluminum, copper, lead, nickel, tin, zinc, coal, iron ore and precious metals.

[2] To see, in detail, how we built the country-specific prices, read Daly et al. (2019a).

[3] Often referred to in the literature as super-cycles.

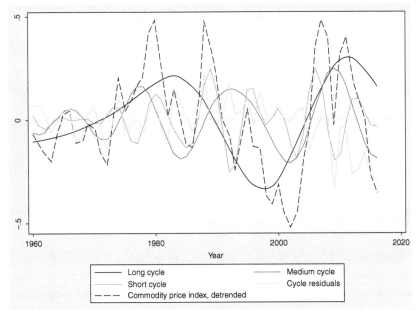

Figure 7.3   De-trended Metals and Minerals Price Index and different cycles
components
Source: World Bank Metals and Minerals Price Index.

different component cycles of the price index. The long and medium
cycles show a relatively smooth variation over time. The short cycles
exhibit more sharp fluctuation around the mean value. The residual
component exhibits the sharpest fluctuations and captures the short-
term variation of the price. All these components sum to the value of
the de-trended price index (the dashed line).

Being mineral commodities, we can expect an excess of demand to be
transferred to prices only if there is no idle supply capacity. In the short
run, mineral supply will follow those demand fluctuations with the
installed capacity limiting the effect on prices. In the long run, mining
companies can also vary capacity by opening and closing mining sites
without necessarily changing technology. So, it is important to understand how the volume of supply behaves to fully capture how prices may
affect the innovation decision. For this purpose, we also collect information on mineral rents for each country from the World Bank
Development Indicators. Given that we want to include a general measure of mineral products volume in each specification, we deflate the

mineral rents with the metals and mineral price index and create a mining quantity index based on the 2010's artificial volume.

In this chapter, we use patents as a proxy for innovation. A patent is a legal right granted for any device, substance, method or process that is new, inventive, and useful. Patents give the owner exclusive rights to commercially exploit the invention for a limited period. In return for exclusive rights, patent applications must be published and must fully disclose the claimed invention. As a result of this requirement, the body of patent literature reflects developments in science and technology. Furthermore, patent data is rich in information adjacent to technology information, such as temporal, geographic and bibliographic data. Through the extraction and analysis of data associated with patent applications, it is possible to measure aspects of invention and economic researchers have long used patent applications as a measure of inventive activity.

Chapters 2, 8 and 9 highlight the rising importance for mining enterprises to use IP instruments – particularly patents – when they pursue an internationalization strategy (see also Francis, 2015). They are often multinational companies operating in different countries and patents may help them secure their intellectual property across states and appropriate the knowledge embedded in new discoveries. Outside the mining sector, using patents as a proxy for innovation is an established practice in the literature (Acs et al., 2002; Griliches, 1998; Jaffe and Trajtenberg, 1999). In doing so, we need to acknowledge all the limitations of this approach that several studies in the existing literature have extensively raised and addressed (Lerner and Seru, 2017). In particular, we acknowledge that the innovation captured through patents is a fraction of the wider range of innovative activity in the field.

Even if not all inventions are patented, it is largely agreed that a patent embodies an original result of an R&D activity undertaken by an entity. As a result, patent data are highly correlated with R&D expenditures in the mining sector (Figure 7.4). In addition, patents offer full coverage of both application countries and years. Therefore, they are more suitable for a global study of mining innovation as this is intended to be. The rest of the chapter uses patent data as a direct measure of innovation activity in the mining sector.

Another challenge when using patent data is the lag between this variable and R&D activities. The real lag between R&D expenditures and patents has been the subject of multiple studies (Gurmu and Pérez-Sebastián, 2008; Hall et al., 1984). These studies find

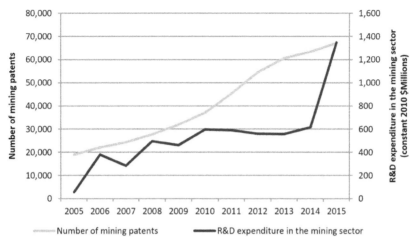

Figure 7.4   Number of patent families and R&D expenditure in the mining sector
Source: WIPO Mining Database (2018) and OECD Business enterprise R&D expenditure by industry Database.

relatively contemporaneous effects between the two variables, which justifies the use of patents as a proxy for the R&D expenditures at the firm level. We follow this approach by using a minimum lag between these two.

In the rest of the chapter, the basic unit of analysis will be the patent family, the year will refer to the first filing year of the patent family and we will use the country of origin for the country. A patent family refers to all those patents applied in different jurisdictions for the same invention.[4]

We use mineral rents as a percentage of GDP as a measure of the mining specialization in a given economy. Figure 7.5 shows the mining specialization of selected countries displaying their percentage of mining rents over GDP. Countries like Chile, Australia and South Africa have mining rents representing a large share of the GDP, which is more than nine percent for the case of Chile. These countries are considered to be more specialized in the mining sector as their income relies considerably on mining activity. On the other hand, countries like France, Japan or the Republic of Korea derive only a very minimal portion, close to zero, of their GDP from pure mining activities. By definition, countries more specialized in the mining sector have a large portion of their economy

---

[4] For all details about how we built the patent data, including patent family unique identifier and origin, refer to Daly (2019b).

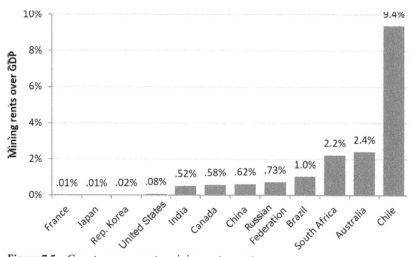

Figure 7.5   Country exposure to mining sector rents
Note: This graph has been constructed using the average mining rents over GDP for each country in the period 1970–2015.
Source: World Bank Development Indicators.

relying on these mining rents, making them more exposed to the price fluctuations of minerals and metals. Therefore, we interpret this indicator as a proxy of the country exposure to the mining industry.

This does not mean that those countries do not play any role for the mining sector. As Figure 7.6 shows, the countries with less exposure to the mining industry are oriented more towards METS firms' activities than mining firms' activities.[5] On the other hand, countries that are more exposed to mining are also more specialized in mining firms' innovation. From the same figure we can discern that innovation in the "traditional" mining fields such as exploration and blasting is more concentrated in mining firms, while METS firms develop most of the services for the sector (environment, transport and to some extent also metallurgy).

Figure 7.7 shows the evolution over time of the de-trended mining commodity price, quantity index and patents. Overall, there seems to be

---

[5] To build Figure 7.6, we calculated the relative specialization index (RSI), by country and technology for METS and mining firms' innovation. A positive RSI means that the country, within the pool of mining innovation, has relatively more innovation carried out by mining firms rather than METS, compared to the world average. For the technology, the interpretation is similar: it means that innovation in that technological field is, on average, carried out more by mining firms rather than METS.

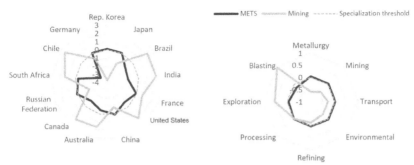

Figure 7.6   Mining and METS firms innovation relative specialization, by country and mining technology

Note: Indicator reflects the relative specialization index (RSI) based patent portfolios of METS and mining firms broken down by country and technological field.
Source: WIPO Mining Database.

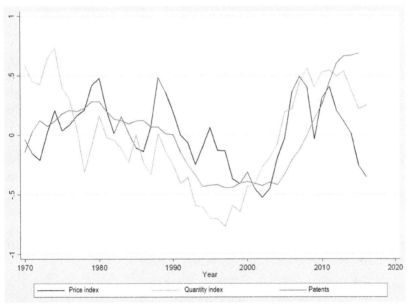

Figure 7.7   Mining price, quantity and innovation co-evolution (1960–2015)

Notes: All indicators are in logs and de-trended.
Source: World Bank Development Indicators and WIPO Mining Database.

a strong positive correlation among these three indices. To better under-stand how expectations might be formed in the short and long run and

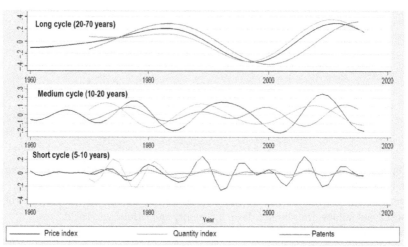

Figure 7.8   Mining price, quantity and innovation cycle decomposition (1960–2015)
Notes: All indicators are in logs and de-trended.
Source: World Bank Development Indicators and WIPO Mining Database.

what drives the observed correlation, we decompose each of these variables in the three cycles mentioned (Figure 7.8). A strong positive correlation is present for the long cycle for all three variables, although innovation seems to lag slightly. In the medium cycle, innovation seems to be correlated with price but much less than before. For the short cycle components, changes in prices seem to affect innovation in the early years of our panel but not so much in more recent ones where innovation remains relatively flat. Moreover, both innovation and quantity short cycles are in sync.

   We test the hypotheses discussed in the previous section in two main frameworks. First, we use a time-series estimation for the global mining activity and then move to a panel estimation. To see the exact model specifications, please refer to Daly et al. (2019a)

7.4   Results

Table 7.3 reports the test for H1 (first column) and H2 and H3 (second column). It finds a positive and significant effect of both commodity prices and quantity on mining innovation, validating H1a. This implies that high commodity prices, as well as high demand for mining products, boost innovation in the sector.

Table 7.3 *Time series estimation*

Dependent Variable: Log. of mining patents applications worldwide		
	(1)	(2)
Log. of Price Index	0.357***	–
(1st Lag)	(0.109)	
Long cycle component of	–	1.107***
Log. of Price Index (1st Lag)		(0.105)
Medium cycle component of	–	0.557
Log. of Price Index (1st Lag)		(0.150)
Short cycle component of	–	0.167
Log. of Price Index (1st Lag)		(0.188)
Residual cycle component of	–	−0.218
Log. of Price Index (1st Lag)		(0.237)
Log. of mining quantity	0.523***	0.202***
(2nd Lag)	(0.073)	(0.053)
Observations	44	44
Years	1970–2016	1970–2016
R-squared	0.72	0.85

Notes: The model is estimated with the OLS estimator. The dependent variable is included in logarithmic terms. All variables included in the model are de-trended. A constant is included in each specification. Robust standard errors in parentheses. *, ** and *** respectively denote significance at 10%, 5% and 1% levels.
Source: Authors' calculations.

If we look more specifically at different price cycles (second column), we realize that the price effect is mainly driven by variations in the long cycle components, which confirms H2. Shorter-term components are found not to have any effect on mining innovation.[6]

---

[6] For further details and robustness checks see Daly et al. (2019a).

Tables 7.4 and 7.5 replicate the analysis in Table 7.3, using a mining subcategory as a dependent variable instead of the full sample of mining patents. We still find an overall pro-cyclical effect of price changes on mining innovation (see Table 7.4) as predicted by H1a. H2 is also confirmed in this subcategory scenario in Table 7.5. The effect of long cycle price shocks on mining innovation is positive and significant for almost all subcategories. Only environmental mining patents seem less responsive, suggesting that other factors may play a bigger role in explaining them, for example, environmental regulation, as is discussed in Chapter 6. We find mixed evidence for H3 as the core mining technologies, namely blasting and exploration (see Table 7.4), are among the slower and faster subcategories to react to price shocks, respectively.

We also explore how mining and METS firms react to commodity price changes. In this exercise, our sample shrinks because we are only able to categorize firms appearing in Bureau Van Dijk's Orbis database under specific NACE Rev.2 codes.[7] We consider their mining patents as dependent variables and we run a similar analysis to the one carried out before. In Table 7.6, we report the same set of estimations run on two different samples: only mining firms' innovation (first and third columns) and only METS firms' innovation (second and fourth columns). Only the innovations from METS firms seem to react to price changes, while we do not find any significant effect of prices on innovation from mining firms. This points toward the validation of H3.

Nevertheless, this could also be explained by the high rate of technology outsourcing we observe in the mining industry. Given that most of the time mining firms prefer to acquire technology from specialized suppliers rather than producing it in-house, METS firms will be the ones absorbing the price variations and adapting their innovation accordingly. This may also explain why we do not observe any effect of price on patents in the shorter periods. Mining firms are the ones directly exposed to price variations. Therefore, it will take some time for this effect to be transferred to METS firms, which will then adapt their innovation decisions accordingly.

Tables 7.7 and 7.8 show the results for the panel specifications reported in the third (columns 1a and 1b) and fourth (columns 2a and 2b) equations, respectively, with the aggregate price index and with country-specific prices. The two specifications evolve quite similarly, showing that

---

[7] We classify mining firms as those companies operating in NACE sectors 0500, 0510, 0520, 0700, 0710, 0720, 0729, 0721, 0811, 0812, 0891, 0892 and 0899; and we categorize METS firms as those companies operating in sectors 2892, 2822, 0990 and 0910.

Table 7.4 *Time series estimation, different mining categories*

	Blasting	Environment	Exploration	Metallurgy	Mining	Processing	Refining	Transport
	(1)	(2)	(3)	(4)	(5)	(6)	(7)	(8)
Log. of Price Index (1st Lag)	0.095 (0.100)	0.149* (0.079)	0.345*** (0.127)	0.053 (0.120)	0.508** (0.137)	0.448*** (0.143)	0.219** (0.086)	0.491*** (0.139)
Log. of mining quantity (2nd Lag)	0.139** (0.062)	0.490*** (0.049)	0.582*** (0.079)	0.358*** (0.075)	0.439*** (0.085)	0.472*** (0.089)	0.485*** (0.054)	0.757*** (0.087)
Observations	44	44	44	44	44	44	44	44
Years	1970–2016	1970–2016	1970–2016	1970–2016	1970–2016	1970–2016	1970–2016	1970–2016
R-squared	0.18	0.77	0.69	0.41	0.62	0.60	0.76	0.77

Notes: The model is estimated with the seemingly unrelated estimator (SUR). The dependent variable is included in logarithmic terms. All variables included in the model are de-trended. A constant is included in each specification. Robust standard errors in parentheses. *, **, and *** respectively denote significance at 10%, 5% and 1% levels.
Source: Authors' calculations.

Table 7.5 *Time series estimation, different mining categories, decomposed price cycles*

	Blasting (1)	Environment (2)	Exploration (3)	Metallurgy (4)	Mining (5)	Processing (6)	Refining (7)	Transport (8)
Long cycle of Log. of Price Index (1st Lag)	0.397* (0.170)	0.232* (0.141)	1.320*** (0.143)	0.591*** (0.187)	1.513*** (0.176)	1.302*** (0.211)	0.591*** (0.140)	1.421*** (0.191)
Medium cycle of Log. of Price Index (1st Lag)	0.059 (0.173)	0.174 (0.143)	−0.224 (0.146)	−0.363* (0.190)	0.127 (0.179)	0.256 (0.215)	0.178 (0.143)	0.147 (0.195)
Short cycle of Log. of Price Index (1st Lag)	0.086 (0.182)	0.215 (0.151)	0.248 (0.154)	0.202 (0.200)	0.146 (0.188)	0.094 (0.226)	0.079 (0.150)	0.236 (0.205)
Residual cycle of Log. of Price Index (1st Lag)	−0.406* (0.237)	−0.171 (0.196)	−0.321 (0.200)	−0.463* (0.260)	−0.124 (0.244)	−0.259 (0.293)	−0.196 (0.195)	−0.246 (0.266)
Log. of mining quantity (2nd Lag)	−0.035 (0.087)	0.414*** (0.072)	0.188*** (0.073)	0.127 (0.095)	0.026 (0.090)	0.087 (0.108)	0.299*** (0.071)	0.352*** (0.078)
Observations	44	44	44	44	44	44	44	44
Years	1970–2016	1970–2016	1970–2016	1970–2016	1970–2016	1970–2016	1970–2016	1970–2016
R-squared	0.30	0.79	0.89	0.58	0.82	0.74	0.81	0.87

Notes: The model is estimated with the seemingly unrelated estimator (SUR). The dependent variable is included in logarithmic terms. All variables included in the model are de-trended. A constant is included in each specification. Robust standard errors in parentheses. *, ** and *** denote significance at 10%, 5% and 1% levels.
Source: Authors' calculations.

Table 7.6 *Time series estimation, mining vs METS firms*

	Mining firms (1)	METS (2)	Mining firms (3)	METS (4)
Dependent Variable: Log. of mining patents applications worldwide				
Log. of Price Index	−0.032	0.708***	–	–
(1st Lag)	(0.143)	(0.229)		
Long cycle component of	–	–	−0.139	1.260***
Log. of Price Index (1st Lag)			(0.259)	(0.391)
Medium cycle component of	–	–	0.124	1.047***
Log. of Price Index (1st Lag)			(0.263)	(0.398)
Short cycle component of	–	–	0.120	−0.199
Log. of Price Index (1st Lag)			(0.277)	(0.419)
Residual cycle component of	–	–	−0.368	0.518
Log. of Price Index (1st Lag)			(0.360)	(0.544)
Log. of mining quantity	0.766***	0.290**	0.744***	0.046
(2nd Lag)	(0.089)	(0.143)	(0.132)	(0.200)
Observations	44	44	44	44
Years	1970–2016	1970–2016	1970–2016	1970–2016
R-squared	0.67	0.36	0.69	0.45

Notes: The model is estimated with the seemingly unrelated estimator (SUR). The dependent variable is included in logarithmic terms. All variables included in the model are de-trended. A constant is included in each specification. Robust standard errors in parentheses. *, ** and *** respectively denote significance at 10%, 5% and 1% levels.
Source: Authors' calculations.

Table 7.7 *Panel estimation*

Dependent Variable: Log. of mining patents by applicant country				
	(1a)	(1b)	(2a)	(2b)
Log. of Price Index (1st Lag)	0.177*** (0.064)	0.191** (0.076)	–	–
Mining rent as % of GDP	–	0.045* (0.024)	–	0.014 (0.026)
Price Index x Mining rent as % of GDP	–	−0.065*** (0.017)	–	–
Long cycle of log. of Price Index (1st Lag)	–	–	0.396*** (0.126)	0.278** (0.139)
LC # Mining rent As % of GDP	–	–	–	0.196*** (0.065)
Medium cycle of log. of Price Index (1st Lag)	–	–	0.069 (0.139)	0.247* (0.126)
MC # Mining rent As % of GDP	–	–	–	−0.313*** (0.061)
Short cycle of log. of Price Index (1st Lag)	–	–	0.006 (0.096)	0.029 (0.108)
SC # Mining rent as % of GDP	–	–	–	−0.069*** (0.020)
Residual cycle of log. of Price Index (1st Lag)	–	–	−0.157 (0.143)	−0.141 (0.149)
RC # Mining rent As % of GDP	–	–	–	0.022 (0.028)
Log. of mining quantity (2nd Lag)	0.026 (0.018)	0.020 (0.017)	−0.002 (0.017)	0.001 (0.017)
Observations	1505	1505	1505	1505
No. Countries	54	54	54	54
Years	1970–2016	1970–2016	1970–2016	1970–2016

Notes: The model is estimated with the Fixed-effects estimator. The dependent variable is included in logarithmic terms. All variables included in the model are de-trended. Country fixed-effects and a constant are included in each specification. Robust standard errors in parentheses. *, ** and *** respectively denote significance at 10%, 5% and 1% levels.
Source: Authors' calculations.

Table 7.8 *Panel estimation, using country-specific price index*

Dependent Variable: Log. of mining patents by applicant country				
	(1a)	(1b)	(2a)	(2b)
Log. of Price Index	0.083**	0.086**	–	–
(1st Lag)	(0.034)	(0.034)		
Mining rent as % of GDP	–	0.044	–	0.049
		(0.039)		(0.047)
Price Index # Mining rent as % of GDP	–	−0.025	–	–
		(0.022)		
Long cycle component of log. of Price Index (1st Lag)	–	–	0.318***	0.302**
			(0.113)	(0.121)
LC # Mining rent As % of GDP	–	–	–	0.013
				(0.033)
Medium cycle component of log. of Price Index (1st Lag)	–	–	0.016	0.102
			(0.055)	(0.063)
MC # Mining rent As % of GDP	–	–	–	−0.142**
				(0.068)
Short cycle component of log. of Price Index (1st Lag)	–	–	0.018	0.038
			(0.040)	(0.043)
SC # Mining rent As % of GDP	–	–	–	−0.041
				(0.029)
Residual cycle component of log. of Price Index (1st Lag)	–	–	0.022	−0.016
			(0.080)	(0.085)

Table 7.8 (*cont.*)

	Dependent Variable: Log. of mining patents by applicant country			
	(1a)	(1b)	(2a)	(2b)
RC # Mining rent	–	–	–	0.045
As % of GDP				(0.041)
Log. of mining	0.020	0.012	0.009	−0.001
quantity (2nd Lag)	(0.019)	(0.019)	(0.020)	(0.020)
Observations	1063	1063	1063	1063
No. Countries	39	39	39	39
Years	1970–2016	1970–2016	1970–2016	1970–2016

Notes: The model is estimated with the fixed-effects estimator. The dependent variable is included in logarithmic terms. All variables included in the model are de-trended. Country fixed-effects and a constant are included in each specification. Robust standard errors in parentheses. *, ** and *** respectively denote significance at 10%, 5% and 1% levels.
Source: Authors' calculations.

the use of a World Price Index does not distort findings compared to a country-specific one. We tried the simple regression (columns a) and we then added the country exposure to the mining sector and the interaction term between the price and the country exposure (columns 1b and 2b).

Mining prices maintain a positive effect on mining innovation (as predicted by H1a), mostly capturing the long cycle component. The only main difference with the time-series specification is that the mining demand loses its significance, which is probably due to the country-fixed effects. The country exposure to the mining sector (measured by mining rents as a percentage of GDP) is found to have a positive effect on innovation only for the case of the country-invariant price index (Table 7.7), although only statistically significant at 10 percent. It is found nonsignificant for the country-specific price index (Table 7.8). Therefore, more exposed countries will, on average, innovate more in mining technologies than non-mining ones. The interaction between the price effect and exposure to the mining sector is found to be negative and significant in Table 7.7, while it loses its significance in Table 7.8. This means that less-exposed countries will be the ones that react more to price changes. An explanation for this could be found in the fact that METS companies, which are among the top innovators, are not necessarily located in mining countries. They can develop their technology in their home country and then sell it to mining firms operating in other countries.

If we have a closer look at this phenomenon introducing the distinction across price cycles (second columns), we confirm what has been found before: the long cycle component of the price is found to positively influence the innovation rate, again confirming H2. In addition, through the introduction of the interaction term, we find that mining countries react more to price changes in the long cycles (see Figure 7.9: the higher the exposure of a country to the mining sector, the bigger will be the reaction of innovation to price changes), while non-mining ones react more in the medium and short term (see Figures 7.10 and 7.11: the lower the exposure of a country to the mining sector the bigger will be the reaction of its innovation to price changes; for countries which are very exposed to the mining activity, an increase in commodity price in the

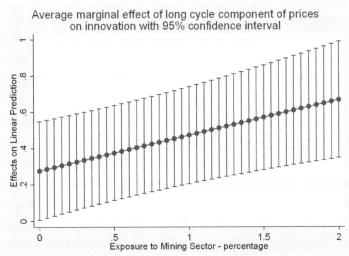

Figure 7.9   Average marginal effect of long cycle component of price index on innovation with 95% confidence intervals
Source: Authors' calculations.

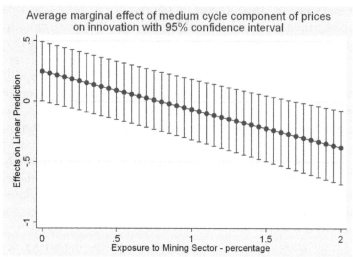

Figure 7.10   Average marginal effect of medium cycle component of price index on innovation with 95% confidence intervals
Source: Authors' calculations.

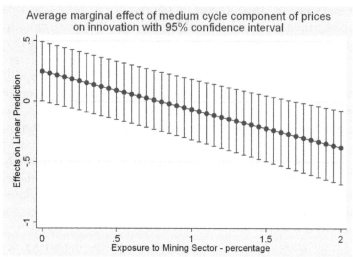

Figure 7.11   Average marginal effect of short cycle component of price index on innovation with 95% confidence intervals
Source: Authors' calculations.

medium and short term will have countercyclical effects on innovation). Mining countries are slower to absorb the price effect, compared to METS countries, which mostly affects them in the long run. This confirms our idea that mining firms are, on average, less flexible than METS firms in adapting to price changes. Therefore, there is a need for highly dependent mining countries to implement countercyclical policies able to defeat the negative effects of commodities down cycles, as anticipated in hypothesis H4. The fact that these countries rely extensively on mining rents makes them particularly vulnerable to commodity price depression, jeopardizing their ability to remain competitive in the market. This condition affects METS countries that rely only marginally on mining activity less. Their diversification becomes a strong attribute in periods of low prices.

7.5   Concluding remarks

In this chapter, we studied the relationship between economic cycles and innovation in the mining sector. In particular, we explored how the business cycle of this sector is tied in with mining commodity price fluctuation. In doing so, we focused on the impact of mineral and metal price changes on the sector's innovation.

We discussed the transmission mechanisms based on the adaptation of the existing literature on the cyclicality of innovation to the singularities of the mining sector. We hypothesized a pro-cyclical impact if the transmission is based on higher prices generating higher direct or indirect disposable income that is, in turn, invested in innovation; and, a countercyclical impact if lower prices increase the pressure to reduce cost and increase efficiency through new technologies. We also conjectured that price variation is more likely to affect innovation if perceived as long-lasting shocks, if innovators are more technologically diversified and if countries are more specialized in mining.

To test these hypotheses, we relied on novel mining innovation data for the period 1970–2015, based on patent information and a series of economic indicators related to the mining sector based on data from the World Bank. We conducted the econometric analyses using both time series and panel data. Our main contribution was to disentangle the effects of price cycles of different lengths, namely long-term, medium-term, short-term and residual. To identify them, we used the Christian and Fitzgerald's band-pass filter and isolated four components of the price.

Our setting attempted to circumvent several identification issues. We accounted for the time lag between changes in demand, commodity prices and innovation. To establish the optimal lag between these variables, we ran a series of correlation tests. We identified the price cycles using the Christian and Fitzgerald band-pass filter, as in Cuddington and Jerret (2008).

Overall, we found that mining innovation is pro-cyclical, increasing in periods of commodity price boom and slowing down during recessions. We found little evidence of countercyclical innovation. It is worth noting that these two mechanisms may coexist. Hence, a stronger pro-cyclical effect may be hiding a weaker countercyclical one. Our model cannot resolve this question, but it does indicate that if a countercyclical effect exists, it is weaker than the pro-cyclical one in most of our estimations.

We found consistent empirical evidence on long price cycles affecting mining innovation more than shorter ones. Indeed, most of the pro-cyclical effect is related to the long cycle component of the price variation. This is coherent with the long decision-making timeline associated with the mining sector, where the bulk of the technological changes happen when mines are opened or closed.

We also found evidence that the transmission of the pro-cyclical effect happens indirectly through METS firms. When comparing mining and METS firms, we found that only METS firms were responsive to adapting their innovation to price changes. Moreover, the estimations indicate that METS are more responsive and faster to adapt their innovation to price changes than the industry average.

According to our estimations, economies specializing in mining produce more mining innovation, but they are also less reactive to price changes. Nevertheless, this behavior varies substantially across the length of price cycles. More specialized economies react even more pro-cyclically to changes of the long cycle component of price than more diversified ones. Conversely, highly specialized economies may observe countercyclical responses to medium and short cycle components, while diversified economies may observe pro-cyclical responses also for the medium cycle component.

These results indicate that mining-dependent economies put countercyclical measures in place based on innovation to cope with shorter-term downturns of the business cycle. It also means that, in the upturn, they are less reactive than more diversified economies. The latter are likely to have more technologically diversified innovation systems composed by innovative METS firms able to adapt new technologies to the mining sector.

References

Acs, Z. J., L. Anselin an, A. Varga (2002). Patents and Innovation Counts as Measures of Regional Production of New Knowledge. *Research Policy*, 31 (7), 1069–1085.

Balaguer, A., A. Palangkaraya, T. Talgaswatta and E. Webster (2018). "Which Australian Industries Produce Most Knowledge External Benefits," *Asian-Pacific Innovation Conference*. Delhi School of Economics, 13–14 December.

Barlevy, G. (2007). On the Cyclicality of Research and Development. *American Economic Review*, 97 (4), 1131–1164.

Barlevy, G., and D. Tsiddon (2006). Earnings Inequality and the Business Cycle. *European Economic Review*, 50 (1), 55–89.

Bartos, P. J. (2007). Is Mining a High-Tech Industry? Investigations into innovation and productivity advance. *Resources Policy*, 32 (4 December), 149–158.

Batterham, J. R. (2004). Has Mineral Industrial Technology Peaked? in E. C. Dowling Jr. and J. Marsden (eds.). *Improving and Optimizing Operations: Things that actually Work!* Littleton: Society for Mining, Metallurgy, and Exploration, Inc.

Canton, E., and H. Uhlig. (1999). Growth and the Cycle: Creative destruction versus entrenchment. *Journal of Economics*, 69 (3), 239–266.

Cogley, T., and J. M. Nason (1995). Effects of the Hodrick-Prescott Filter on Trend and Difference Stationary Time Series: Implications for business cycle research. *Journal of Economic Dynamics and control*, 19 (1–2), 253–278.

Comin, D., & Gertler, M. (2006). Medium-Term Business Cycles. *American Economic Review*, 96 (3), 523–551.

Cuddington, J. T., and D. Jerrett. (2008). Super Cycles in Real Metals Prices?. *IMF staff Papers*, 55 (4), 541–565.

Daly, A., D. Humphreys, G. Valacchi and J. Raffo (2019a). Innovation in the Mining Sector and Cycles in Commodity Prices. *Economic Research Working Paper* 55. World Intellectual Property Organization.

Daly, A., G. Valacchi and J. Raffo (2019b). Mining Patent Data: Measuring Innovation in the Mining Industry with Patents. *Economic Research Working Paper* 56. World Intellectual Property Organization.

Dunbara, W. S., et al. (2016). "Paths for Innovation in the Mining Industry." Working Paper, March.

EUROSTAT (2018). http://ec.europa.eu/eurostat/data/database

Fatas, A. (2000). Do Business Cycles Cast Long Shadows? Short-run persistence and economic growth. *Journal of Economic Growth*, 5 (2), 147–162.

Feenstra, R. C., R. E. Lipsey, H. Deng, A. C. Ma and H. Mo (2005). World Trade Flows: 1962–2000 (No. w11040). National Bureau of Economic Research.

Francis, E. (2015). *The Australian Mining Industry: More than just shovels and being the lucky country*, s.l.: IP Australia Economic Research Paper No. 4.

Geroski, P. A., and C. F. Walters (1995). Innovative Activity over the Business Cycle. *The Economic Journal*, 916–928.

Gomes, J., J. Greenwood and S. Rebelo (2001). Equilibrium Unemployment. *Journal of Monetary Economics*, 48 (1), 109–152.

Griliches, Z. (1998). Patent Statistics as Economic Indicators: A Survey, R&D and productivity: The econometric evidence, in Griliches, Z. (ed.). *R&D and Productivity: The Econometric Evidence Volume*. Chicago: University Chicago Press, pp. 287–343.

Gurmu, S. and F. Pérez-Sebastián (2008). Patents, R&D and Lag Effects: Evidence from flexible methods for count panel data on manufacturing firms. *Empirical Economics*, 35 (3), 507–526.

Howrey, E. P. (1968). A Spectrum Analysis of the Long-Swing Hypothesis. *International Economic Review*, 9 (2), 228–252.

IMF (2015). World Economic Outlook.

Hall, B. H., Z. Griliches and J. A. Hausman. (1984). *Patents and R&D: Is there a lag?* NBER Working Paper Series No. 1454. Cambridge, MA: National Bureau of Economic Research.

Jaffe, A. B. and Trajtenberg, M. (1999). International Knowledge Flows: Evidence from patent citations. *Economics of Innovation and New Technology*, 8 (1–2), 105–136.

Labys, W. C., A. Achouch and M. Terraza (1999). Metal Prices and the Business Cycle. *Resources Policy*, 25 (4), 229–238.

Lerner, J., and A. Seru (2017). *The Use and Misuse of Patent Data: Issues for corporate finance and beyond*. No. w24053. Cambridge, MA: National Bureau of Economic Research.

OECD (Organisation for Economic Co-operation and Development) (2005). Oslo Manual The Measurement of Scientific and Technological Activities: Proposed Guidelines for Collecting and Interpreting Technological Innovation Data. http://www.oecd.org

Radetzki, M. (2006). The Anatomy of Three Commodity Booms. *Resources Policy*, 31(1), 56–64.

Rafferty, M., and M. Funk (2004). Demand Shocks and Firm-Financed R&D Expenditures. *Applied Economics*, 36 (14), 1529–1536.

Scherer, F. (1984). Using Linked Patent and R&D Data to Measure Interindustry Technology Flows, in Griliches, Z. (ed.). *R&D, Patents, and Productivity*. Chicago: University of Chicago Press, pp. 417–464.

Solow, R. M. (2000). Toward a Macroeconomics of the Medium Run. *Journal of Economic perspectives*, 14 (1), 151–158.

Tilton, J. E. (2006). "Outlook for Copper Prices: Up or Down?" Paper presented at the Commodities Research Unit World Copper Conference. Santiago, Chile.

WIPO (2011). World Intellectual Property Report: The Changing Face of Innovation.

IP Use and Technology Transfer in the Brazilian Mining Sector

DOMENICA BLUNDI, ANA CLAUDIA NONATO DA SILVA
LOUREIRO, SERGIO MEDEIROS PAULINO DE CARVALHO,
MARINA FILGUEIRAS JORGE, FELIPE VEIGA LOPES,
GUSTAVO TRAVASSOS PEREIRA DA SILVA
AND VITORIA ORIND

8.1   Introduction

The importance of the role of the mineral sector in Brazil's economy is beyond doubt. The mining sector accounted for 21 percent of Brazil's total exports in the first quarter of 2017 (PortalBrasil, 2017). In 2015, metallic minerals accounted for 76 percent of total sales of Brazil's mineral output (DNPM, 2016a). The country's balance of trade has been positive owing to the contribution of mineral exports over the past years, which attests to the positive role of the mining industry in national economic growth (Brazilian Mining Institute (IBRAM), 2015a).

While the mining sector is economically strategic to the country, mining output has an unbalancing effect on the economy, since it is concentrated both geographically and in the hands of few producers. This characteristic may be considered contradictory by those who attempt to describe and analyze Brazil's mining activities, not only because of the country's size, but also because of its geological diversity.

The "concentrated" pattern warrants the Vale S.A. case study. In 2015, the company and its subsidiaries ranked either first or second among the leading production companies in Brazil's mining sector for various minerals (Figure 8.1). Vale is outstandingly not only a producer but also the operator of a large and sophisticated logistical system of railways and ports, which strongly distinguishes it from its competitors. Besides, it is Brazil's leading iron ore producer and exporter and the country thus features in the global ranking of iron ore mining companies.

Top Producing Companies

Aluminium (Bauxite)

Company	Share (%) (*)
MINERAÇÃO RIO DO NORTE	47,38
MINERAÇÃO PARAGOMINAS	33,19
ALCOA WORLD ALUMINA BRASIL	14,18
OTHER COMPANIES	5,25

Copper

Company	Share (%) (*)
SALOBO METAIS	47,43
VALE	26,32
MINERAÇÃO MARACÁ INDPUSTRIA E COMÉRCIO	19,04
OTHER COMPANIES	7,21

Tin

Company	Share (%) (*)
MINERAÇÃO TABOCA	52,84
COOP MINERADORA DOS GARIMPEIROS DE ARIQUEMES	11,33
COOPERATIVA DE GARIMPEIROS DE SANTA CRUZ	19,04
OTHER COMPANIES	16,79

Iron

Company	Share (%) (*)
VALE	73,77
COMPANHIA SIDERÚRGICA NACIONAL	4,49
SAMARCO MINERAÇÃO	3,98
OTHER COMPANIES	17,76

Manganese

Company	Share (%) (*)
VALE MINA DO AZUL	53,75
MINERAÇÃO CORUMBAENSE REUNIDA	28,75
MINERAÇÃO BURITURAMA	14,08
OTHER COMPANIES	3,42

Niobium

Company	Share (%) (*)
ANGLO AMERICAN NIÓBIO BRASIL	51,17
COMPANHIA MINERADORA DOPIRICLORO DE ARAXÁ	41,11
MINERAÇÃO TABOCA	3,55
OTHERS COMPANIES	4,17

Nickel

Company	Share (%) (*)
ANGLO AMERICAN BRASIL	37,85
VALE	28,22
VOTORANTIM METAIS	20,47
OTHER COMPANIES	13,46

Gold

Company	Share (%) (*)
KINROSS BRASIL MINERAÇÃO	18,88
ANGLOAMERICAN ASHANTI CÓRREGO DO SÍTIO MINERAÇÃO	17,33
SALOBO METAIS	8,43
OTHER COMPANIES	55,36

(*) Share in the total value of the mineral production.

Figure 8.1 Leading producing companies in Brazil (2015)

Source: Brazil National Department of Mineral Production (DNPM) (2015)

Characteristics of Brazil's mining sector will be outlined in the following sections, with emphasis on its competitive dynamics, strategic challenges, technological needs and institutional innovation-promoting arrangements. The chapter aims to describe patterns and distinctive features of Brazil's mining sector's technological agenda and proximity to or distance from global sector-specific innovative trends. To that end, answers will be provided to the following research questions:

- In which technological areas is the patent system being used by the mining sector in Brazil?
- How intensively do the mining equipment, technology and services firms (METS) use the patent system?
- How does Brazil's mining sector import technology? What role do the mining firms and METS play in this process?

Methodologically, two approaches were taken in reviewing innovation in Brazil's mining sector. First, patents and technology import contracts for metallic minerals, involving mining companies and METS in Brazil, were analyzed. The analysis covered the 2000 to 2015 period and both resident and nonresident stakeholders. Second, a case study was conducted of Vale S. A., Brazil's largest mining company, with emphasis on its strategies to mitigate challenges and meet technological needs. This qualitative research exercise has sought to highlight and give examples of real-life experience.

8.2   Overview of Brazil's Mining Sector

From colonial times, the history of Brazil's development has always been linked to mining. As from the sixteenth century, the pioneers' search for precious metals and gems, especially gold, silver and diamonds, was a major means of opening up the country's territories to settlement, leading to the formation of villages and cities that bore witness to the discovery of new metallic mineral deposits, especially iron and manganese. The main regions thus explored were São Paulo, Minas Gerais, Goiás and Mato Grosso. Only a small amount of iron was produced artisanally in Brazil until the nineteenth century in some steelworks (known as Catalan forges) established in Minas Gerais to reduce iron ore directly and to produce iron and steel. Mineral-extracting tools were rudimentary and nonresistant, usually made of cast iron. Veins were worked manually, with pointers and, when necessary, home-made blasting powders were used. The ore was transported in wheelbarrows and, over longer distances, by animal-drawn wagons (Center for Management and Strategic Studies (CGEE), 2002). The most sophisticated mines were the Minas Gerais gold mines, in which techniques brought

Table 8.1 *Brazilian ore production (2015)*

Mineral	Tons	World Rank	World Share
Niobium	84,189	1	92.29%
Iron	275,589,840	3	17.52%
Bauxite (raw ore)	37,057,000	3	12.77%
Manganese	1,226,458	5	6.74%
Tin	18,824	6	5.87%
Nickel	89,302	9	4.24%
Gold*	83,127	12	2.69%
Copper	359,463	14	1.86%

* Gold output in kg
Source: World Mining Data (2017). *NB: Figures concern the main reserves and not the total national reserves for each mineral.*

by English (probably from Cornwall) and German miners, trained in their home countries, were used (CGEE, 2002).

The country's industrialization began early in the twentieth century and was driven by aluminum, copper, lead, iron, manganese and tungsten metallurgy. The major mining enterprises were managed by foreigners during that period, owing primarily to the war effort, with scheelite being mined in the north-east by United States Vachang engineers and manganese at Lafaiete, in Minas Gerais, by the United States Steel Company (CGEE, 2002).

As shown in Table 8.1, Brazil is now one of the world's largest mineral producers, playing a major competitive role internationally. Its mineral resources are considerable, both in abundance and diversity, and it produces 72 minerals, of which 23 are metallic, 45 are nonmetallic and four are energy minerals (IBRAM, 2015a). Most minerals in Brazil are produced in open-pit mines, as there are few underground mines. Few operations are conducted on a scale higher than 400 t/d (CGEE, 2002).

Since 2005, growing world demand for minerals, in particular iron, bauxite, manganese and niobium ores, has boosted the value of Brazilian Mineral Production (PMB),[1] which has risen sharply in less than a decade.[2]

[1] The PMB methodology adopted by the IBRAM is based on the arithmetic mean of the price of the mineral good x production and is used for all minerals produced in the country (except petroleum and gas) (IBRAM, 2015b and 2017).
[2] www.mdic.gov.br/noticias/9-assuntos/categ-comercio-exterior/486-metarlurgia-e-siderurgia-10

In 2000, PMB values amounted to less than 10 billion USD, but rose to 53 billion USD in 2011. That "commodities boom" period gave way, however, to a major international foreign-market ore price crisis, triggered by falling growth rates in large global economies, especially China. The fall in the PMB (from 44 billion USD in 2013 to 24 billion USD in 2016) was due to a downturn in the international prices of Brazil's primary mineral commodities, namely gold, copper, nickel, zinc, bauxite and, in particular, iron ore which is the flagship of Brazilian exports. That decline was not reflected in the volume of ore produced, which demonstrated the impact of external factors on the mining industry. These fluctuations were not trivial: prices rose by 392.46 percent between 2002 (34.77 USD) and 2011 (136.46 USD), according to World Bank data, but had fallen to 39.78 USD by the end of 2015.

Despite these foreign market fluctuations, the characteristics of Brazil's mining sector contributed to its competitiveness on the international mineral market. Generally, despite falling mineral commodity prices in relation to output (PMB), the mineral industry still added value to its product. The logistical structure is, moreover, integrated into the international market. Brazil's iron ore has remained competitive for these reasons (Ministry of Mines and Energy (MME), 2016).

There are sharp contrasts in mining in Brazil. High-technology mining companies operate in some regions alongside artisanal enterprises that use rudimentary and improvised mining techniques. In addition, the country's mineral capacity is under-explored: less than 30 percent of the national territory has been mapped geologically on a scale appropriate for the activity.[3] Brazil's mining sector therefore still holds great potential for investment in exploration and mineral production technologies.

8.2.1   The Role of Metallic Minerals in the Brazilian Mineral Economy

Brazil has metallic mineral reserves in 17 of the country's 27 federal units.

Metallic minerals accounted for 76 percent of the total value of Brazil's marketed mineral output in 2015. Eight minerals – aluminum, copper, tin, iron, manganese, niobium, nickel and gold – accounted for 98.5 percent of that value, at 17.3 billion USD. Iron ore, produced mainly in the states of Minas Gerais and Pará, was the main metallic ore marketed in 2015, accounting for 61.7 percent of the total for that class of mineral

---

[3] Idem.

(DNPM, 2016b). Niobium, another strategic mineral considered rare worldwide, abounds in Brazil, and its known niobium reserves, totaling some 842 million tons, are found in the states of Minas Gerais (75 percent), Amazonas (21 percent) and Goiás (3 percent), constituting 98 percent of world reserves. In 2015, Brazil ranked first in niobium production, with 92.29 percent of the world total, followed by Canada and Australia (World Mining Data, 2017).

8.2.2   Mineral Industries and Foreign Trade[4]

The mining sector achieved an 11.5 billion USD surplus in the first quarter of 2017, accounting for 21 percent of all of Brazil's foreign market sales (PortalBrasil, 2017). This performance was owing to sales of iron ore, which accounted for 44 percent of mineral-sector exports and 9.3 percent of all Brazilian exports. Gold and niobium, too, performed well at 1.4 billion USD and 766.8 million USD, respectively, in that period. Imports grew concurrently by 53 percent, totaling 3.9 billion USD, as imports of metallurgical coal and potassium had risen in volume and in value.

The mining sector has contributed greatly to Brazilian exports in recent decades. Metallic minerals rank among the first four exported goods. The main countries that purchased ores from Brazil in 2015 were China, Japan, Netherlands, the United States of America and Canada, in that order. China is the largest customer for Brazil's minerals, in particular iron. In 2015, some 31.93 percent of the main metallic substances exported by Brazil were bound for the Chinese market (DNPM, 2016a).

Brazil has imported metal commodities from Chile, Peru, Argentina, the Russian Federation and China. In 2015, some 43.58 percent of metallic substances imported into Brazil, in particular copper, originated in Chile (DNPM, 2016a).

8.2.3   Trends and New Policies for Brazil's Mining Sector

Innovation is important to effective exploitation of natural resources, but issues concerning the actual impact of innovation on the sector and the factors that stimulate innovation in individual countries remain controversial (Figueiredo et al., 2016).

---

[4] Here, data of the mineral sector are shown as a whole, including the extraction of metallic and nonmetallic ores and the mineral transformation.

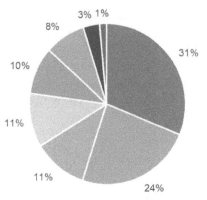

- 3% 1%
- 8%
- 10%
- 11%
- 11%
- 24%
- 31%

■ Aquisition of machinery and equipment

■ Training

■ Software acquisition

■ Introduction of innovations technologies in the market

■ Industrial design and others technical preparations

■ Acquisition of others external knowledge

■ External Acquisition of R&D

Figure 8.2   Innovative activities developed by extractive companies and degree of importance
Source: IBGE (2016).

The Innovation Survey (PINTEC) conducted by the Brazilian Institute of Geography and Statistics (IBGE) on the sector's primary ways and means of acquiring technology, shows that Brazil's extractive industry has innovated primarily by acquiring machinery and equipment and secondarily by training personnel, which may be deemed complementary.[5] The survey sample consisted of 47,693 innovation-implementing companies, 1,138 of which were in the extractive sector.

Figure 8.2 shows part of PINTEC's findings, highlighting the scale of innovative activities conducted by extractive companies from 2012 to 2014. Machinery and equipment acquisition and training accounted for 55 percent of the extractive companies' innovative activities. These findings spotlighted the importance of reviewing the technology transfer role of METS in Brazil's mining sector. The mineral sector innovation rate (42 percent) had doubled in comparison with the average for the previous five innovation surveys (21 percent). This increase was mirrored by activities such as machinery and equipment acquisition and research and development (R&D), both of which had doubled in value since earlier research (Lins, 2017, in Oliveira, 2018).

With regard to the sector's commitment to the promotion of innovation, companies, government representatives and trade associations have discussed the challenges faced by Brazil's mining sector. During the 17th Brazilian Mining Congress (Belo Horizonte, Minas Gerais,

---

[5] These findings apply to petroleum and gas extraction.

Table 8.2 *Mining sector challenges and technological demands*

Unlocking productivity and operational efficiency	Social license to operate
Digitalization and the Internet of Things in mining	Mining tailings dams
The fully connected mine	Mining waste management
Autonomous vehicles for the mining industry	Water resources
Blasting strategies for increased mill productivity	Climate change
Safety and health in mining	Mining and communities

Source: Adapted from the 17th Brazilian Mining Congress – Exposibram 2017. Belo Horizonte, September 18 to 21.

September 2017), those groups highlighted two major drivers of innovation, namely higher productivity and operational efficiency and the social license to operate, with emphasis on environmental sustainability and relations with local communities (Table 8.2).

In raising productivity and operational efficiency, the sector has tended to focus on technologies conducive to greater automation of activities, in particular those that are occupational safety hazards, and to lower operating costs. Digital and satellite connectivity technologies are other factors of investment in innovation through which companies seek process-efficiency gains.

Brazil's mineral industry has increasingly integrated the social license to operate agenda into its investments, with emphasis on improvements that can enhance sustainable behavior, not only environmentally, but also in relation to communities in the vicinity of operations.

Priority has been given to dam management in particular, by including it not only in the sector's agenda, but also in the agendas of local governments and the legislature. This resulted from the Bento Rodrigues accident, which occurred when the Samarco Fundão Dam burst in Minas Gerais in November 2015. It shows the extent to which the mining sector reacts to events rather than adopt a more proactive stance conducive to a structuring and long-term approach by anticipating innovative solutions for potential future problems.

Furthermore, Brazil's mineral sector faces challenges inherent in the national scenario. It was not by coincidence that the Ministry of Mines and Energy (MME) published the 2030 National Mining Plan – Geology, Mining and Mineral Transformation (MME, 2011), in May 2011 as guidance for medium and long-term policies for progress in mining activities. The challenges mapped cover matters such as infrastructure and logistics, sustainability, occupational safety and health, and micro and small local businesses.

Moreover, the Brazilian Government made changes to the mineral sector's rules in Provisional Presidential Decree No. 790 on June 25, 2017 (MP 790). Brazil's current Mining Code was established in 1960 and updated in 1996, but has been superseded by current market demands. The federal government wishes to implement new rules to make the sector more competitive and to attract more investors by increasing transparency and legal security.

Highlights of the new rules include: (a) an increase in the sector's royalty rates (CFEM); (b) establishment of the National Mining Agency (ANM) to replace the current DNPM in regulating and overseeing the sector; (c) a higher ceiling for fines; (d) inclusion of rehabilitation of degraded environmental areas and mine decommissioning plans in miners' responsibilities; and (e) extension of the mineral prospection and exploration period. Conceptually, MP 790 broadens the scope of the federal government's competences and of regulated activities. The regulation now covers the entire life cycle of the mining activity, from prospection and extraction to ore marketing and mine decommissioning. The new rules seek to boost the sector's dynamics and, consequently, its modernization and to intensify the country's mineral production through new investments and thus new technology.[6]

The propensity to incorporate innovative activities has been rising gradually in Brazil's mineral sector and its representatives have displayed higher levels of commitment. The sector's revamping has included a legislative overhaul, highlighting the diversity of forces that have driven Brazil's mining companies to rethink their forms of action.

8.2.4   Institutional Collaboration for Innovation

Some of the behavioral characteristics of Brazil's mining companies when acquiring technological capabilities and technologies will be considered

---

[6] http://revistamineracao.com.br/2017/10/09/mineracao-brasileira-precisa-se-renovar-afirmam-especialistas

in this section. These dynamics are very important if it is borne in mind that the innovation environment can be improved by institutional collaboration and linkages rather than isolationist behavior and aversion to sharing content and experience.

Figueiredo et al. (2017) has stressed the importance of collaboration among companies in building their technological capabilities. Research has confirmed that, between 2003 and 2014, much of Brazilian miners' innovative technological capabilities were accumulated in partnerships with universities and local research institutes, consultants and agents along the production chain (suppliers and clients).

Institutional collaboration in the mineral sector has sound historical foundations in Brazil. The sectoral innovation system was formed through a long process of technological and scientific skills building and accumulation, involving feedback and interaction among companies, research institutions and universities. It is not by chance that undergraduate and postgraduate courses in mining engineering, materials engineering and metallurgy have flourished and are well established at the Federal University of Minas Gerais (UFMG) (Suzigan and Albuquerque, 2008).

Brazil's mining companies and academic community (universities and research centers) collaborate considerably under cooperation agreements and formal partnerships. This has been achieved incrementally, as some confidentiality and intellectual property issues are yet to be resolved in order to smooth out such relations. Vale S.A. exemplifies the way in which such obstacles can be overcome. It has broadened its portfolio of academic partners since 2010, by issuing calls for proposals for partnership with governmental science promotion agencies, and has thus gained access to a broad spectrum of research groups that were previously unknown to the company (Mello and Sepulveda, 2017).

METS are equally crucial innovation stakeholders in the mining sector, as noted in studies abroad (Francis, 2015). Mining is a catalyst of technical progress and the capital goods industry has emerged to provide solutions that meet the mining companies' technological demands (Furtado and Urias, 2013).

This has held true for Brazil, too. Throughout its history, as noted at the beginning of this chapter, the technological development of Brazil's mining corporations has drawn both on the direct participation of foreign producers and on various engineering services. New mining technologies have frequently been brought into Brazil by outside companies and the foreign technicians who came to work in the mines brought what was best known in their home countries (CGEE, 2002).

Furthermore, it was common practice to send Brazilian professionals abroad to complement their studies, and machine and equipment manufacturers sometimes promoted visits to open mines worldwide as a means of observing products and more efficient production processes (Bertasso and Cunha, 2013). In addition, returning Brazilian technicians, having worked in foreign companies and absorbed their practices, actually disseminated new technologies.

Even though a significant part of Brazil's technological base is imported, domestic machinery, equipment and engineering services were used to modernize much of its mining industry. It is noteworthy that, since the 2000s, the machine and equipment sector has mirrored the concentration and internationalization of the mining sector. This shows that the companies are interdependent. As mining companies became stronger and more complex, thus demanding more comprehensive technological solutions from suppliers, the latter began to build alliances with the mining companies in order to develop new products jointly. This association took the form of knowledge and competency transfers. Machine and equipment suppliers provided training for mineral sector workers and monitored and maintained (preventively and remedially) the machines and equipment supplied (Bertasso and Cunha, 2013). However, in comparison with other countries such as Australia, South Africa, Chile and the United States of America, the trend in Brazil is still nascent, owing to the dearth of examples, which are confined to the major mining companies (Figueiredo et al., 2017).

Brazilian miners seem to be more willing to interact with external players. Brazil's mining companies have been driven to search for solutions outside their own gates in order to acquire different experience and skill sets.

8.3 Use of the Patent System and Technology Transfer in Brazil's Mining Sector

This section will consider the main two mechanisms used by mining companies and METS in Brazil to build their technological capabilities, namely technology development and technology acquisition from abroad. It will identify the main technological innovation areas and stakeholders in Brazil's mining sector and the ways in which companies have been importing new technologies. Both analyses have drawn on a sample of patent and technology import contracts involving resident and nonresident mining companies and METS.[7]

8.3.1   Technology Protection

A sample of 130 resident and nonresident mining companies and METS that filed patents at INPI from 2000 to 2015 was analyzed. As Table 8.3 shows, these companies filed 7,933 patents and utility models, including 4,273 for mining technologies filed by 21 mining firms and 83 METS.

As shown in Figure 8.3, nonresident METS predominate in applications for patents in Brazil's mining sector. They account for nearly all of the mining patents filed from 2000 to 2015.

METS are more likely to file patents for mining and metallurgy technologies, while mining firms focus on refining and transport technologies, as can be seen from Figure 8.4.

It can be seen that most of the METS applicants were from Japan, as they accounted for 36 percent of the 3,978 patents filed in the period under review, followed by North American and German METS. Although Brazilian METS hardly feature in these results, they seemed more concerned to protect technology in Brazil than Canadian or Australian METS, for instance (Figure 8.5).

The major two METS applicants were Nippon Steel and Mitsubishi, from Japan. They focused on metallurgy and mining technologies. The leading applicants among resident METS were Terex Cifali and Ciber, both of which deal with transport and processing technologies (Figure 8.6).

Figure 8.7 shows applicant mining firms. There is a wide gap between Vale S.A. and the other mining firms. While Vale filed 46.8 percent of patents from 2000 to 2015, the remaining firms filed 53.2 percent of patents altogether. This confirms the aforementioned concentrated nature of Brazil's mining sector.

Vale has filed for patents mainly in transport and refining technologies. Transport is crucial to Vale's patenting strategy because of its logistics business and demand for railway technologies. In addition, Vale has protected technologies in seven of the eight mining technology areas present in the WIPO Mining Database, and has not applied for patents in blasting technology only. Here, too, Vale's representativeness

---

[7] For methodology details, see Blundi et al. (2019)

Table 8.3 *Patents applications: 2000–15*

	Mining firms			METS			TOTAL
	RES	NRES	Total	RES	NRES	Total	
Number of applicants	15	10	25	35	70	105	130
Total patents filed	234	131	365	106	7,462	7,568	7,933
No. of applicants (only mining patents)	11	10	21	22	61	83	104
No. of patents (only mining patents)	182	113	295	73	3,905	3,978	4,273

Source: BADEPI, INPI (2018).

Notes: RES = Resident; NRES = Nonresident.

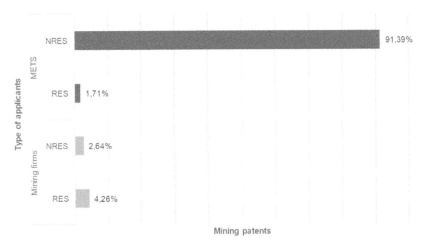

Figure 8.3   Mining patents, by type of applicant (2000–15)
Source: BADEPI, INPI (2018). NB: RES = Resident; NRES = Nonresident.

Figure 8.4   Mining patent applicants, by mining technology groups
Source: BADEPI, INPI (2018).

warrants a more detailed analysis, which will be provided in the Section 8.4.

The Anglo-Australian Broken Hill Proprietary Company Limited (BHP Billiton) was the leading applicant among non-resident mining firms, followed by a Rio Tinto Canadian subsidiary. BHP Billiton applied for patent protection mainly in refining technologies. The company did not seek to patent transport, environment, automation and blasting technologies in Brazil. Here, too, this mining firm's patenting strategy focused on refining technologies in Brazil's mining sector, in the same way as its Brazilian competitor, Vale S.A.

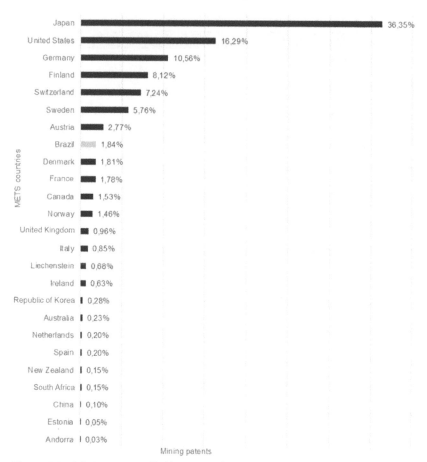

Figure 8.5   Mining patents filed by METS, by country of origin (2000–15)
Source: BADEPI, INPI (2018).

According to Figueiredo et al (2017), Brazil's mining sector's techno-logical capabilities are greatest in mineral processing (refining), which is warranted by the need to maximize productivity and minimize costs. Companies are consequently more concerned about being competitive in those areas and, therefore, protecting such technology.

Of the 255 Brazilian patent applications relating to mining technolo-gies, including both resident mining firms and METS, only 11 patents were filed jointly with academic institutions (see Table 8.4)

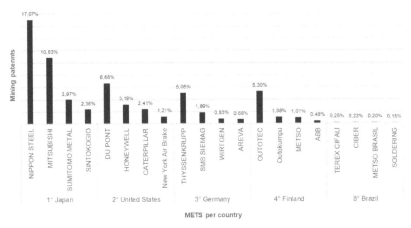

Figure 8.6   Leading METS applicants (2000–15)
Source: BADEPI, INPI (2018).

8.3.2   Technology Transfer

Two systems for innovation are known: the so-called open and closed innovation systems. While in a closed innovation system all the R&D is done within the firm, in an open innovation system external cooperation among different entities is promoted to accelerate internal innovation and expand the markets for external use of innovation (Chesbrough et. al., 2006). The Brazilian economy seems increasingly oriented toward the open innovation system.

As an example of that, some nonresident METS that used the patent system in Brazil had been contracted by resident mining firms to provide technological service or technological know-how. The sample of 18,252 import contracts registered in INPI's database showed that 707 concerned mining companies and METS. As Table 8.5 shows, 26 mining firms and 14 resident METS were recorded as technology contractors. Only two METS contracts did not involve a parent company and its resident subsidiary. Resident METS (the subsidiaries) assumably acted as intermediaries between non-resident METS and resident mining firms in order to operationalize technology transfers.

Table 8.6 shows technology import contracts, by type, by contractor and by supplier. Technical assistance services contracts were the type of contract most used, mainly by resident mining firms. This finding assumably flows naturally from the previously mentioned point on nonresident METS' key role in providing technical services to Brazil's mining enterprises (Bertasso and Cunha, 2013; CGEE, 2002).

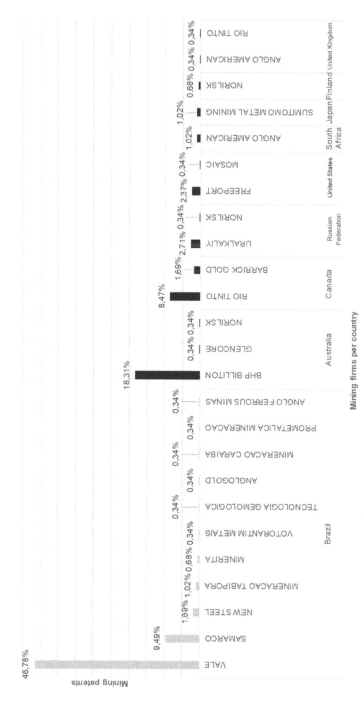

Figure 8.7 Leading applicants among mining firms (2000–15)
Source: BADEPI, INPI (2018).

Table 8.4 *Coapplications and foreign inventors, by mining technology*

Resident firms		Coapplications with universities		Foreign inventors	
Nippon Steel	METS	N/A	0	Metallurgy	1
Samarco Mineracao	Mining firm	Exploration	1	Processing	1
Vale S.A.	Mining firm	Environmental	2	Environmental	1
		Exploration	3	Exploration	3
		Mining	1	Mining	3
		Processing	2	Refining	3
Anglogold Ashanti Brasil	Mining firm	Environmental	1	N/A	0
Mineração Caraiba	Mining firm	Metallurgy	1	N/A	0
TOTAL			**11**	**TOTAL**	**12**

Source: BADEPI, INPI (2018). NB: N/A = Not applicable.

Table 8.5 *Research sample (technology import contracts) (2000–15)*

	Mining firms			METS			TOTAL
	RES	NRES	Total	RES	NRES	Total	
Import contracts (No. of contracts)	N/A	N/A	N/A	N/A	18,252	18,252	18,252
Import contracts (No. of contracts within Brazil's mining sector)	N/A	N/A	N/A	N/A	707	707	707
Import contracts (No. of contractors)	26	n/a	26	14	n/a	40	40
Import contracts (No. of providers)	N/A	N/A	N/A	N/A	295	295	295

Source: BADEPI, INPI (2018). NB: N/A = Not applicable.

Table 8.6 *Technology import contracts by type, by contractor and by supplier (2000–15)*

Type of contract	Contractor		Supplier
	RES Mining Firms	RES METS	NRES METS
Technical assistance services	82%	10%	92%
Know-how agreement	1.5%	5.5%	7%
Patent licensing	0.00%	1%	1%
Total	**83.5%**	**16.5%**	**100.00%**

Source: BADEPI, INPI (2018).

Figure 8.8 shows that Vale S.A. is the leading contractor, accounting for more than half of the INPI-registered technology import contracts. If the parent companies are taken into consideration, then it can be said that four mining groups, namely Vale S.A., Anglo Gold Ashanti, Kinross and Yamana Gold, are represented by their Brazilian subsidiaries in technology-transfer contracts negotiated with nonresident METS, as observed in Table 8.7.

Figure 8.9 shows that the suppliers of most technology import contracts are from North America. Metso's and Komatsu's subsidiaries are the major suppliers from the United States of America and, as can be seen from Figure 8.9, they have been contracted by their own subsidiaries, MetsTao Brasil and Komatsu do Brasil, both acting as technology transfer intermediaries. Another two major suppliers are Chile's Elementos Industriales y Tecnologicos and Canada's SBVS Mine Engineering.

In view of the major role of Vale S.A. in Brazil's mining sector, this company's technological strategies will be the subject of a case study in the next section.

8.4   Vale S.A. Case Study

Companhia Vale do Rio Doce (CVRD) was founded in 1942, as a state-owned company (Vale, 2012).[8] In 1974, it took the lead in iron ore

---

[8] The brand and the company's name became Vale S.A. in 2007, name for which it was always known on the stock exchanges, but the original corporate name was kept. In 2008, Companhia Vale do Rio Doce no longer used the acronym CVRD, starting to use the name Vale.

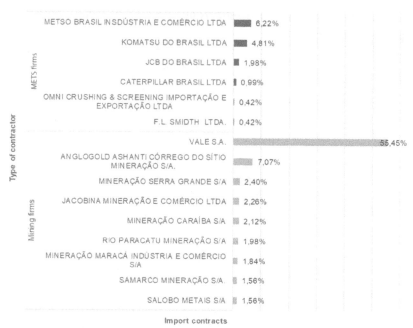

Figure 8.8   Leading contractors (2000–15)
Source: BADEPI, INPI (2018).

exports, which it has not relinquished since. Two decades later, in 1997, CVRD was privatized and, in 2006, it made other giant step by acquiring INCO, a Canadian firm, and thus became the world's second-largest mining company after the Anglo-Australian BHP Billiton. Vale S.A. is a now a multinational company; it is active on six continents and is one the largest iron ore producing companies in the world, as the world leader in the production of pellets. Vale produces coal, copper, fertilizers, manganese and ferroalloys. Its iron ore production flagship, Carajás deposits, in the state of Pará, is the world's largest open-pit iron mine and produces the world's best quality iron ore. On average, the Carajás rocks have a 67 percent iron ore content, which is considered a very high grade.

8.4.1   Science, Technology and Innovation at Vale

Like any big mining company, Vale faces major technology and innovation challenges. Producing hundreds of millions of tons of ore yearly, Vale's operations involve complex and sophisticated logistics and

Table 8.7 *Mining firm contractors (subsidiaries and parent companies)*

Contractor (Mining firms)	Parent company
Salobo Metais S/A	Vale S/A
Samarco Mineração S/A	
Anglogold Ashanti Córrego Do Sítio Mineração S/A	Anglo Gold Ashanti
Mineração Serra Grande S/A	Anglo Gold Ashanti and Kinross
Rio Paracatu Mineração S/A	Kinross
Jacobina Mineração E Comércio Ltda	Yamana Gold
Mineração Maracá Indústria E Comércio S/A	
Mineração Caraíba S/A	N/A

Source: Based on mining firms' websites (accessed 2018).

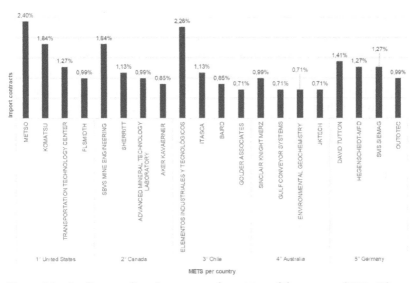

Figure 8.9   Leading suppliers, by country of provision of the contract (2000–15)
Source: BADEPI, INPI (2018).

increasingly advanced energy-intensive prospection, exploration and mineral-processing technologies, while minimizing environmental, health and safety impacts.

In taking up these technological challenges, Vale has established several internal R&D facilities. The first facility, the Mineral Development Center (CDM), was founded in 1965 in order to develop technological improvements to the extraction and processing of itabirito, a low-iron-content ore extracted from Minas Gerais deposits. CDM was instrumental in making the technological change through which Vale became the world's largest iron ore exporter (Mello and Sepulveda, 2017). At the time, in a technological leap forward, Vale pioneered the use of magnetic separators that raised the productivity of itabirito (Vale, 2012). Present-day CDM's specialists use state-of-the-art equipment to investigate production and processing methods for different types of ores and to ensure mineral project viability. The second facility, the Ferrous Metals Technology Center (CTF) was established in 2008 to focus research on the use of iron ore and coal in steelmaking. Both CDM and CTF are located in the southeastern state of Minas Gerais.

The third facility, the Logistic Engineering Center (CEL), was established in 1997 with three units based in Espirito Santo (southeast), Maranhão (north) and Minas Gerais (southeast), respectively. Its main characteristic is its combination of lectures and practical lessons in providing port and railway technical training to employees and market professionals.

In 2009, Vale Institute of Technology (ITV) was founded under a broader science, technology and innovation (ST&I) strategy designed to take up technological challenges over the long term.[9] ITV is a major link between Vale and the scientific and technological community (Mello and Sepulveda, 2017). It is a nonprofit research and postgraduate teaching institution with two units, one in Pará and the other in Minas Gerais. We can say that the new R&D configuration has complemented those that already exist, giving the company a longer-term view of its innovation strategy. In this sense, since 2009, Vale has been more in touch with external partners, such as universities and funding agencies, which have gradually shifted the ST&I from a closed toward a more and more open innovation system.

8.4.2   Vale's Institutional Collaboration to Foster R&D

As mentioned, ITV began to coordinate the company and ST&I community more broadly and methodically in 2009. Since 2010, Vale has entered

---

[9] The Department of Vale Institute of Technology was renamed Department of Technology and Innovation in 2013 and Executive Management of Technology and Innovation in 2015. In 2018, the department was divided up and technology portfolio management was decentralized to some of the company's other departments.

into major partnerships with Brazilian funding agencies in order to launch calls for proposals to promote R&D projects in states in which Vale operates. State Research Foundations (FAPs) are National Science and Technology System entities attached to state governments.

Through these partnerships, Vale has expanded its portfolio of R&D partners and related research themes. From 2010 to 2018, these partnerships have involved the ST&I community in six Brazilian states, namely Minas Gerais, Pará and São Paulo (in 2010), Espírito Santo and Rio de Janeiro (in 2016) and Maranhão (in 2017).

In addition to State funding agencies, Vale has acted in coordination with federal government agencies, such as the National Council for Scientific and Technological Development (CNPq), which plays a significant role in national science and technology policy formulation (in 2009 and 2011), and the Brazilian Development Bank (BNDES) in 2012. In each agency, Vale shares financial resources with the government, thus improving the purpose and strength of the collaborative model. This was, moreover, a means by which both sides – the company and the public authority – leveraged resources from each other. Vale's BUs are in contact with a variety of R&D institutions in order to exchange information and practices that will enable both sides to learn from each other and, consequently, devise more innovative solutions to meet technological demands. It is a virtuous circle, from which the company and the ST&I community benefit. Highlights of partnership outcomes include the project on the use of biotechnology to accelerate environmental solutions in the field and the project implemented to automate routine mining activities in order to optimize operational processes (Vale, 2017). In addition to new technologies, other important findings comprise the number of new researchers recruited under research grants. For example, under the partnership with FAPs in Minas Gerais, Pará and São Paulo, 621 research scholarships are active in 30 universities and research institutes (Vale, 2017).

8.4.3   Vale's Intellectual Property Strategy

Vale's IP strategy is recent and it has been extensively discussed in Oliveira (2018). We now summarize and discuss some of her main findings. Before 2009, Vale did not have a structured and coordinated IP process. IP was not treated globally but piecemeal, under a restricted strategy. In fact, IP was a small, almost isolated, area involving administrative and bureaucratic activities rather than those evocative of a consistent IP strategy. During that period, Vale's patent application practice focused on what might be termed "tooling," encompassing small incremental technologies involving equipment and tools used in day-to-day activities. The company did not focus on technology per se, but on minor operational improvements. It can be said that documentary and administrative management was geared to protecting developments, but no strategy was in place to evaluate whether inventions were actually being used in operations or whether they could be licensed or made available to third parties. However, even though it lacked a coordinated IP strategy, Vale did acquire new knowledge and technologies from some inventions during that period, as some had been applied in operations and had generated value for the company.

In acquiring INCO and its highly renowned R&D center in 2006, Vale also acquired a substantial technological hard core, owing to INCO's mining patents, and Vale's portfolio increased by approximately 1,500 active processes, brands and patents. In 2010, as Vale INCO, the company began to manage the entire portfolio of Canadian patents, all of which concerned nickel operations. As a result, the IP department was obliged to implement more robust procedures.

In 2009, IP activities began to be more structured and to focus on technology rather than minor improvements.[10] This change was consistent with the new company's ST&I position. ITV hired a specialized team, with employees who could effectively address IP issues and formulate an integrated IP strategy for the company. Strategically, Vale files patent applications primarily in Brazil. The company uses the Patent Cooperation Treaty (PCT) system, which gives access to the results of international search reports, in order to decide whether to file patent applications in other countries. Operationally, the IP Management department has structured and centralized the entire technology protection process into technology evaluation, patent search, protection and maintenance and has adopted specific forms and tools in order to coordinate the BUs' IP activities. Vale considers that it is vital to protect technologies that are integrated into its core business. The strategy under the current model is to protect inventions that are aligned with the company's business in Brazil and in the

---

[10] The new approach was taken in Brazil rather than Canada, as INCO already had extensive patent portfolio experience.

world, rather than simply expanding its IP portfolio without any specific focus.

8.4.4 Technology Import Contracts and Technology Transfer at Vale

Despite being part of Vale's activities from its beginning, the technology transfer are not structured in a specific area. As can be seen from Figure 8.7, Vale registered the highest number of import contracts with INPI between 2000 and 2015, according to the Innovation Survey (PINTEC) results.

As to the other side of the technology transfer coin, Vale does not have a structured process in place to license technology developed in-house or through R&D project partnership with external institutions. In view of the importance of a culture of technology transfer and in-house or external R&D project outcomes as a means of adding value to the business, Vale's IP Management department is planning to implement such procedures in the company (Oliveira, 2018).

As Vale is the major stakeholder in Brazil's mining sector, a trend that may augur a paradigm shift in other Brazilians mining companies, by pushing the entire sector in the same direction or even opening up new development pathways for Brazil's mining sector.

8.5 Innovation Patterns in Brazil's Mining Sector: Final Considerations

Despite the size and geological diversity of Brazil, mining activities are concentrated geographically and in the hands of a single company. Minas Gerais and Pará account for more than half of Brazil's mining output, and Vale S.A. is the predominant producing company. These factors are critically important to any analysis of innovation and technology transfer in the sector, as the same pattern of concentration is mirrored in decisions on the technology agenda of Brazil's mining sector.

In this last section, we'll try to answer the questions that were specifically presented before. The sector seems to focus more on protecting technologies that raise productivity and lower costs, such as mining (extraction), metallurgy, processing, refining and transport technologies, rather than on a technological agenda with an emphasis on long-term solutions that will actually change the way of doing things, such as automation and environmental protection. The perceptible underlying rationale gives pride of place to innovation that focuses on short-term matters, such as operational improvements and cost reduction, in setting a technological trajectory (Dosi, 1982).

Brazil's mining sector should invest in prospection for new deposits (greenfield projects) and in mineral extraction technologies in order to take advantage of the country's geology, size and diversity. In view of the role played by mining firms and METS in the technology protection agenda, it must be stressed that mining firms have not heretofore focused on the protection of exploration and mining technologies. That role has been played by nonresident METS, which have mainly protected mining technologies (extraction), while mining firms have mainly protected refining and transport technologies.

The analyzed data have shown the patterns of concentration of the few companies that are active in the mining sector in Brazil. Nonresident METS, from Japan and North America in particular, accounted for practically all applications filed for mining technology patents. The concentration pattern for mining firms shows that only one resident mining firm, Vale S.A., has patents in seven of the eight mining technology areas considered in this chapter.

We have also observed some historical collaborations among players in Brazil's mining sector. The analyzed data showed that some mining patents applied for by resident companies from 2000 to 2015 were results of coapplications generated from partnerships with universities, which corroborates that technologies and knowledge required for mining development were in part provided through this type of relationship.

Data analysis of the use of technology import contracts in Brazil's mining sector as a means of technology transfer has shown that non-resident METS are still the main suppliers of technology and technical assistance services to resident mining firms. Their role has been fundamental to mining technology development in Brazil. This characteristic has been corroborated by some global mining strategy studies, according to which companies, in times of crisis, choose to keep their main operations at the lowest possible cost and to focus on the operating cash flow ratio to ensure long-term profitability. Historically, the sector's innovative capability tends to be limited to short-term solutions, which in turn contributes to companies being "followers" of existing technologies (EY, 2016). Thus, mining companies became clients of existing technologies rather than investing in long-term, more disruptive research and development to deal with future challenges. This study shows that a shift from short-term to long-term innovation investments is happening in mining firms. Vale, the biggest Brazilian mining company, started to put in place a consistent and long-term-oriented IP strategy which replaced the old uncoordinated investments mostly aimed at small and short-term technology improvements.

References

Bertasso, B. F., and Cunha, A. M. (2013). *Segmento de máquinas e equipamentos para extração mineral.* Campinas: UNICAMP.IE.NEIT / ABDI.

Blundi, D., A. C. Nonato, S. Paulino et al. (2019). "Technology appropriation and technology transfer in the Brazilian mining sector." Geneva. WIPO Working Paper Series. Working Paper No. 53.

CGEE (2002). *A mineração no Brasil.* Secretaria Técnica do Fundo Setorial Mineral. Centro de Gestão e Estudos Estratégicos, Brasilia.

Chesbrough, H., W. Vanhaverbeke and J. West (2006). *Open Innovation: Researching a New Paradigm.* Oxford University Press.

DNPM (2015). *Sumário* Mineral. Vol. 35. Departamento Nacional de Produção Mineral, Brasília.

DNPM (2016a). *Anuário Mineral Brasileiro: Principais Substâncias Metálicas.* Departamento Nacional de Produção Mineral, Brasília.

DNPM (2016b). *Informe Mineral.* Departamento Nacional de Produção Mineral, Brasília, December.

Dosi, G. (1982). Technological paradigms and technological trajectories: A suggested interpretation of the determinants and directions of technical change." *Research Policy*, 11, 147–162.

EY (2016). *Top 10 business risks facing mining and metals, 2016–2017.* EYGM Limited.

Figueiredo, P. N., and M. Pinheiro (2016). Competitividade industrial brasileira e o papel das capacidades tecnológicas inovadoras: a necessidade de uma investigação criativa. *Technological Learning and Industrial Innovation Working Paper Series.* Rio de Janeiro: FGV/EBAPE, March, pp. 1–17.

Figueiredo, P. N., et al. (2016). Acumulação de capacidades tecnológicas e fortalecimento da competitividade industrial no brasil: breve análise empírica da indústria de mineração. *Technological Learning and Industrial Innovation Working Paper Series.* Rio de Janeiro: FGV/EBAPE, November, pp. 1–152.

Figueiredo, P. N., et al. (2017). "Acumulação de capacidades tecnológicas, inovação e competitividade industrial: alguns resultados para indústrias selecionadas relacionadas a recursos naturais no Brasil." *Technological*

Learning and Industrial Innovation Working Paper Series. Rio de Janeiro: FGV/EBAPE, February, pp. 1–25.

Francis, E., 2015. *The Australian Mining Industry: More than Just Shovels and Being the Lucky Country*, IP Australia Economic Research Paper No. 4.

Furtado, J., and Urias, E. (2013). *Recursos naturais e desenvolvimento: estudos sobre o potencial dinamizador da mineração na economia brasileira*. São Paulo: Ed. dos Autores/IBRAM.

INPI (2018). BADEPI - Intellectual Property Statistical Database, Instituto Nacional da Propriedade Industrial, edição 2018.

IBGE (2016). Pesquisa de inovação: 2014. Instituto Brasileiro de Geografia e Estatística, Coordenação de Indústria. Rio de Janeiro, 2016.

IBRAM (2015a). *Informações sobre a economia mineral brasileira*. Instituto Brasileiro de Mineração, Brasília, October.

IBRAM (2015b). *Relatório Anual*. Instituto Brasileiro de Mineração, Brasília.

IBRAM (2017). *Produção Mineral Brasileira Série Histórica*. Instituto Brasileiro de Mineração, Brasilia, February.

Mello, L. E. A., and Sepulveda, E. S. (2017). "Interação academia-indústria. Relato da experiência da Vale." *Estudos Avançados*. São Paulo: USP, vol. 31, n° 90, May/August, pp. 89–101.

MME (2011). *Plano Nacional de Mineração 2030. Geologia, Mineração e Transformação Mineral*. Ministério de Minas e Energia. Brasilia, May.

MME (2016). *Série Estudos Econômicos. Nota Técnica DEA 08/16*. Ministério de Minas e Energia. EPE: Rio de Janeiro, April.

Oliveira, C. S. (2018). "Estudo de caso: A evolução histórica da gestão de propriedade intelectual na Vale." Mestrado Profissional em Propriedade Intelectual e Inovação. Rio de Janeiro: INPI. Academia de Propriedade Intelectual, Inovação e Desenvolvimento. Rio de Janeiro: Programa de Mestrado Profissional em Propriedade Intelectual e Inovação do Instituto Nacional da Propriedade Industrial (INPI).

PortalBrasil (2017). www.portalbrasil.net, accessed August 31, 2017.

Suzigan, W., and E. Albuquerque (2008). A interação entre universidades e empresas em perspectiva histórica no Bral. Belo Horizonte: UFMG/Cedeplar. Texto para discussão no. 329. www.cedeplar.ufmg.br/pesquisas/td/TD%20329.pdf

Vale (2012). *Nossa História 2012*. Rio de Janeiro: Verso Brasil.

Vale (2017). MAIS Newsletter, n° 1. Rio de Janeiro: RJ.

World Mining Data (2017). *Minerals Production*. Vol. 32. Vienna: International Organizing Committee for the World Mining Congresses.

Innovation and IP Use in the Chilean Copper Mining Sector

CLAUDIO BRAVO-ORTEGA AND JUAN JOSÉ PRICE

9.1 Introduction

The importance of the copper mining sector in Chile is unquestioned and is reflected in many production, international trade and fiscal revenue indicators. The sector, however, faces major challenges, namely deeper mines, scarcity of (and consequently more expensive) key inputs such as water and energy, lower-grade ores, concern for neighboring communities and respect for the environment. Innovation appears to be key to tackling these issues.

Given the well-documented causal relation between innovation and productivity gains,[1] it is very important to determine whether there is also a correlation between intellectual property (IP) protection and innovation rates. Although this seems theoretically plausible (intellectual property rights are, in effect, temporary monopoly rights and thus incentives for innovation), there is little supporting empirical evidence.

We also thank the senior staff of the companies and universities who were interviewed for this project: Nury Briceño (Antofagasta Minerals), Oscar Castañeda (Codelco), Enrique Celedón (Rivet), Pamela Chávez (Aguamarina), Francisco Costabal (Freeport-McMoRan), Enrique Grez (Samsa), Aldo Labra (Innovaxxion), Cleve Lightfoot (BHP Billiton), Felipe Merino (Codelco Tech), Gaspar Miranda (Drillco Tools), Petar Ostojic (Neptuno Pumps), Miguel Peña (Enaex), Ximena Sepúlveda (Universidad de Concepción) and Brian Townley (Universidad de Chile).
We thank Sergio Escudero, María José García, Álvaro González, Isidora Insunza and Catalina Olivos, (all from the National Institute of Industrial Property, INAPI), Ricardo Morgado (Fundación Chile) and Osvaldo Urzúa (BHP Billiton). They all provided valuable data and feedback during this project. Of course, all errors and omissions are the sole responsibility of the authors.

[1] See Bravo-Ortega and García (2011) and the references quoted therein, particularly Grilliches (1998) and Hall et al. (2010).

This chapter contains the findings of an online survey of 300 resident mining equipment, technology and services suppliers (METS) that are covered by EXPANDE, a public–private program on open innovation in the mining sector. The main survey objective was to collect information on the number of patents and other intellectual property rights (IPRs) filed, the firms' consideration of IP protection in their commercial strategies and the factors that underpin decisions on IP protection.

The survey analysis was complemented by semi-structured interviews of senior executives from a sample of 13 entities (four mining companies, seven METS and two universities). Four case studies on the firms interviewed have been selected because they interestingly reflect different types of innovation that should thus relate to different IP management strategies.

The literature on the subject has hitherto focused on high-income countries. Little, and rather, anecdotal, evidence is available for middle-income countries (Hall et al. 2013). The only exception is the comprehensive report published by the National Institute of Industrial Property (INAPI) in 2010 and providing data on the patenting practices of companies participating in the Copper Mining Cluster Program from January 2000 to December 2009.[2] This chapter complements and updates INAPI's 2010 analysis and raises new questions.

This chapter differs from earlier endeavors by focusing on METS, while drawing on suggestions in the literature that they could play a major role in the mining sector's innovation patterns (see, Bravo-Ortega and Muñoz (2015, 2017), Navarro (2018), Meller and Gana (2016), Scott-Kemmis (2013) and references therein). METS' innovative capabilities have been largely confirmed, but the findings show that they hardly rely on IP protection mechanisms.[3] Some evidence of the likely underlying factors is provided and policy implications suggested.

It must be stressed, however, that the information gathered yields only preliminary evidence on the importance of IP as a driver of innovation practices in the mining sector. The chapter should generally be viewed as a starting point and an invitation to conduct new research in greater depth.

Section 9.2 highlights the importance of the copper mining industry in Chile, while Section 9.3 adduces some preliminary evidence on the

---

[2] See Navarro (2018) for a detailed analysis of this program.

[3] This may be so because only resident METS were considered; inclusion of multinational METS may lead to a different result.

sector's innovation capabilities, with particular emphasis on resident suppliers. Section 9.4 outlines the methodology and sources of information, while the fifth contains the main findings. The chapter ends with the conclusion and policy recommendations in Section 9.5.

9.2 The Mining Sector in Chile

The importance of the mining sector in Chile is reflected in many production, international trade, employment and fiscal revenue indicators. Chile holds 29.2 percent of the world's copper reserves and accounts for 30 percent of world output. The Chilean State owns the National Copper Corporation (Codelco), the world's largest copper producer, and the world's largest copper pit (Escondida, owned by Broken Hill Proprietary Company Limited (BHP) and Rio Tinto), is in northern Chile.

In 2016, mining production accounted for 11 percent of gross domestic product (GDP), with copper production amounting to 10 percent. These figures were stable throughout the 2013–16 period. Copper exports accounted for 45 percent of total exports in 2016.[4] The latter figure does give some cause for concern, as the high share of copper exports in total

Table 9.1 *Share of global production and reserves (%, 2015)*

	Production	Reserves
Chile	30	29
Peru	9	11
USA	7	5
China	9	4
Russia	4	4
Australia	5	12
Canada	4	2
Zambia	4	3
Congo Democratic Republic	5	3

Source: World Metal Statistics and Chilean Mining Council (based on COCHILCO and the US Geological Survey).

---

[4] Source: Chilean Copper Commission (COCHILCO).

exports leaves the country extremely sensitive to the international business cycle.

Mining companies in Chile face challenges in a wide variety of areas, all of which are critical to productivity gains. First, lower-grade ores and mines that are hard to exploit (the resources are at greater depth than in the past), the shortage of key inputs (mainly water) and relations with local communities (made more contentious, among other environmental problems, by air and water pollution) are all factors that raise production costs.

Moreover, the sector's total factor productivity (TFP) fell at an average estimated rate of 4.7 percent per year between 1993 and 2015, according to a recent report by the Organisation for Economic Co-operation and Development (OECD, 2018). It also fell in other "mining countries," but the negative trend was sharper in Chile, as stressed in the report, and seemed to be the main factor of TFP stagnation in Chile's economy.

Owing to all of these factors, firms should become more innovative (Báez, 2015) and, for that reason, it is very important to understand the factors that can raise the sector's innovation rate.

9.3   Innovation in the Mining Sector

9.3.1   Preliminary Observations

Interestingly, several authors have written that the sector (and extractive industries in general) is a canonical example of a noninnovative sector, at least in the case of big mining companies (Murphy, 2015). This view is consistent with the idea that it is more of a curse than a blessing for a country to be rich in natural resources (Sachs and Warner, 1995 and 2001), but it has been contested by Bravo-Ortega and De Gregorio (2007), Lederman and Maloney (2007) and Manzano and Rigobon (2007), among others. Suffice it to say here, without delving into the debate, that, other factors being equal, innovation seems to make a difference in resource-rich countries' reasons for taking differing development paths. It is therefore important to try to understand how innovation can be triggered in this sector.

The following issues appear to be critical in this regard: (i) development of linkages between end producers and input suppliers; (ii) collaboration by both end producers and input suppliers with universities and research institutes; and (iii) in-house innovation which, in the case of suppliers, is crucial to the development of knowledge-intensive mining services

(KIMS); for supporting evidence, see Chile Foundation (FCH) (2014), Fessehaie and Morris (2013) and Bravo-Ortega and Muñoz (2015). In Chile, public and private efforts have been made under these three heads. Examples of collaboration between the public sector and private firms include the World Class Mining Suppliers Program,[5] developed by BHP Billiton and Codelco (FCH, 2014), and the Alta Ley Mining Program, which is jointly administered by the Production Development Corporation (CORFO)[6] and the Ministry of Mining and is designed primarily to strengthen productivity, competitiveness and innovation in the national mining industry and to build national KIMS-exporting capacity.

9.3.2   The Role of Specialized Suppliers in Chile

Although the sector has been described as not very innovative, this might be an untenable view because it focuses only on end producers (mining firms) whereas most mining innovations seem to be actually developed by specialized suppliers rather than big mining operators (Murphy, 2015). Klevorick et al. (1995) point to the technological opportunities arising in various sectors as a major cause of poor innovative perform-ance and conclude that metal production is indeed one of the sectors in which technological opportunities are low.[7] Hall et al. (2013) reinforce this point and attribute Chile's low patent intensity partly to an industrial specialization pattern dominated by sectors with a low propensity to patent, such as the mining sector.

Suppliers have grown in importance as innovation drivers, moreover, because mining firms are increasingly outsourcing nonstrategic tasks such as transport, by-products, information technology (IT) services and equipment maintenance so that they can focus on their core business areas (FCH, 2014). According to FCH (2014), METS innovation rates are higher than recorded national economy and mining industry averages.[8] Moreover, 25 percent of the companies surveyed, by category, were classified as Essential Innovators, which are companies (METS) that have high levels of innovation and capabilities for new technology and equipment development.

---

[5] For further details, see Navarro (2018).
[6] This is the national development agency and it is attached to the Ministry of Economy, Development and Tourism.
[7] See Klevorick et al. (1995) for further details.
[8] This confirms the findings of the 2012 edition of the study.

Table 9.2 *Percentage of firms that innovate (mining suppliers vis-à-vis the industry and the economy)*

Type of innovation	METS firms	Mining firms	National economy
Product	60	12	12
Process	41	35	16
Management	51	27	14
Marketing	31	10	10

Source: FCH (2014).

In terms of innovation capabilities and performance, however, this sample might not be considered very representative of the METS universe. As a matter of fact, the sample covered companies which had taken part in the World Class Supplier Program and which are characterized by being more sales- than mining-intensive and by having higher levels of professionalization and of innovation and export capacity than the average supplier.

Despite this likely bias, the findings have been largely confirmed by a recent report by the Industrial Mining Suppliers Association (APRIMIN) and the Chilean Copper Commission (COCHILCO) on the innovative behavior of 108 resident METS (APRIMIN/COCHILCO, 2017). According to the report, innovation is highly valued by companies, 75 percent of which reportedly have an innovation budget, and there are no apparent differences between national and foreign companies, although foreign companies had higher innovation rates. Among other findings, most of the respondent companies (83 percent) reported that they had experience of piloting, although there was scope for even greater cooperation with other competitors and research centers. Lastly, CORFO was most widely recognized as the institution that channeled public support for innovation activities.

According to FCH/PROCHILE (2017), METS' exports to a total of 39 countries in 2016 amounted to nearly 3 billion dollars. The main destinations were Peru (43 percent), the United States of America (28 percent) and Mexico (6 percent). The supplier sector mainly exported mining design and engineering consultancy services, which accounted for 44 percent of services exported in 2016. Original software design services ranked second at 25 percent and IT consultancy services and technical support ranked third at 22 percent. Export capacity was high, despite the low copper cycle (prices), as local companies had maintained product development and international mining market share and had exported significant amounts.

9.3.3 IP in Chile's Mining Sector

As stated, the mining sector faces major efficiency, productivity and sustainability challenges. Innovations leading to improvements in one or more of these areas may give a great competitive edge to firms and, to retain that advantage, consideration must be given to IP protection.

IP protection not only constitutes an effective tool for resolving appropriability issues,[9] but also affords an opportunity to raise a firm's commercial value because IPRs are an asset that can be used strategically. For instance, patents can be licensed and even sold. This added value can also be used as fund-raising collateral. Codelco's experience illustrates this point. IP comes into play when Codelco develops mining equipment prototypes and enters into supplier agreements. Once tested, the prototypes are incorporated into Codelco's production processes. Under the agreements, Codelco transfers IPRs to its commercial partner in order to optimize product development. Moreover, IP plays a major role in a firm's network of alliances with various companies, research centers and universities (Báez, 2015).

Mining is one of the sectors that contribute most to patenting in Chile, together with the chemical and pharmaceutical sectors. Codelco and its technological division (Codelco Tech), both included in the sample of companies interviewed for this chapter, are the leading patent holders (see Table 9.3). Box 9.1 covers Codelco's innovation and IP strategy.

In the preceding nine years (2000–9), 1,090 patents were filed (INAPI, 2010). In the period under review, 1,731 patents were filed, an increase of 58 percent. In 2000–9, 41 percent of the applications filed were national patent applications, which fell in the following nine years to 26 percent but remained higher than the average for national applications within the economy as a whole.[10] Most national patent applications therefore originated in the mining sector.

According to INAPI (2010), in the 2000–9 period, 93.3 percent of applications were filed by firms domiciled in 10 different countries. Chile led the ranking with 41.4 percent, followed by Finland (12 percent) and the

---

[9] Trade secrets and know-how are probably of some importance in mining, since many innovations concern process, rather than product, technologies (Murphy, 2015).

[10] The percentage was 14.5 in the 2000–9 period (INAPI, 2010). Figures for the latter years are not available.

Table 9.3 *Mining-related patents filed in the Chilean Patent Office*

		Residents	
Year	Non- Residents	Total	Of which Codelco
2009	85	59	11 (19%)
2010	35	49	12 (24%)
2011	130	49	2 (4%)
2012	187	41	1 (2%)
2013	188	41	2 (5%)
2014	200	55	10 (18%)
2015	177	67	4 (6%)
2016	169	43	1 (2%)
2017	117	39	8 (21%)
Total	1.288	443	51 (12%)

Source: INAPI.

BOX 9.1 CODELCO'S INNOVATION STRATEGY (THE ROLE OF CODELCO TECH)

Codelco's importance to mining in Chile merits further examination of how the company is organized for innovation.

In 2016, Codelco merged its technological companies (IM2, BioSigma and Codelco Lab) into a single division known as Codelco Tech.

The new company is wholly owned by Codelco and has devised an open solutions development model that incorporates and promotes contributions by suppliers, research centers, start-ups and other entities.

Each of Codelco Tech's many units is tasked with seeking solutions in areas such as pyrometallurgy, hydrometallurgy, water, energy, underground mining, pit mining, biotechnology, automation, robotization, remotization, data science and new uses of copper, lithium, molybdenum, sulfuric acid and by-products.

The company has established an innovation management system in order to measure its impact over time in relation to a 2016 baseline.

By 2015, Codelco had filed 250 national and international patent applications, 134 of which have been granted in Chile and 21 in other countries. The company has focused its innovation strategy on developing smart mining technologies for use at every stage of production in order to raise productivity and operational efficiency and achieve significant cost savings. These technologies include remotely controlled mineral-extracting robotic machinery that considerably reduces miners' occupational hazards, and new digital technologies for ever greater integration and automation of remotely managed processing operations (Source: Báez, 2015 and interview of senior Codelco Tech and Codelco executives).

United States of America (11 percent). The most recent data for the 2009–17 period paint a similar picture, with the United States of America replacing Finland in second position. Table 9.4 shows the 10 countries that have filed the greatest number of patents in Chile in the last nine years.

9.3.4   INAPI's Role

INAPI is Chile's IP Office. Its current policy agenda, of relevance to the mining sector, includes statistical data (Analiza),[11] capacity-building, awareness-raising, advice to small- and medium-sized enterprises (SMEs) and public policy. Under the first component, INAPI conducts surveys and issues reports on the current status of IP in the mining sector, as exemplified by the aforementioned publication (INAPI, 2010), which complements other reports on mining issues.

The second component consists of training programs for mining sector entities, including operational and innovation management staff. The achievements of the "INAPI in the field" project have been considerable in the north of the country, which is the predominant mining region. For example, INAPI provides training in IP strategies to member companies of the Antofagasta Industrial Suppliers Association that are at the technology-development and product-packaging stage (an advanced stage of the innovation pipeline).

Lastly, INAPI contributes to public policy formulation on the subject as a permanent advisor on CORFO-based programs that provide funding for large-scale and long-term innovation in mining sector projects. This is the case of the Innova Chile committee, the Technological Capabilities subcommittee and the Alta Ley Council, through which the major stakeholders (academia, suppliers and mining companies) meet to draw up a roadmap to solve industry-wide problems (the roadmap is used by CORFO in drawing up its technological support programs). On INAPI's recommendation, all beneficiary companies under CORFO-administered innovation support programs are required to have IP management strategies in place and to keep available technologies under technological surveillance. These rules are necessary because many mining industry technologies have not been protected owing primarily (if not only) to a lack of awareness of IP protection mechanisms and the myth about their costs and complexity (lack of knowledge leads naturally to immobility).[12]

---

[11] www.inapi.cl/portal/publicaciones/608/w3-propertyvalue-12030.html
[12] Interview with María José García (Deputy Director, INAPI Knowledge Transfer Unit).

Table 9.4 *Major 10 nonresident (NR) firms filing patents in Chile, by country of origin*

	2009	2010	2011	2012	2013	2014	2015	2016	2017	Total
United States	23	11	22	47	44	43	43	32	25	290
Germany	7	2	19	24	25	26	14	19	6	142
Finland	3	2	15	13	8	23	18	26	12	120
Australia	8	2	14	12	11	14	11	10	6	88
Switzerland	1	1	6	10	16	16	8	14	10	82
Canada	3	1	7	12	8	10	8	9	11	69
Japan	14	2	3	9	7	4	12	4	3	58
France	1	1	9	4	7	12	5	10	2	51
Brazil	3	3	2	7	7	7	4	2	8	43
United Kingdom		3	5	5	11	2	4	6	1	37
Total	*63*	*28*	*102*	*143*	*144*	*157*	*127*	*132*	*84*	*980*
(percent of NR)	*74*	*80*	*78*	*76*	*77*	*79*	*72*	*78*	*72*	*76*

Source: INAPI.

9.4 Methodology

Inputs were gathered from three main sources, namely online surveys, semi-structured interviews and case studies. Each information source is covered below.

9.4.1 Survey: EXPANDE Program

An online survey was conducted of 300 resident suppliers that form part of EXPANDE, which is the first ever open-innovation mining program. Led by BHP, AMSA, Codelco and FCH, the program was established in 2017 and builds on the lessons learnt from the World Class Suppliers Program (2008–16). EXPANDE seeks to link mining companies that require technological solutions not only to suppliers but also to other stakeholders in the ecosystem such as investment funds, banks, export promotion agencies and international knowledge nodes.

The firms were interviewed about their innovation practices, their use of IP instruments (if any) and their opinion of the IP protection system in Chile. Basic corporate financial information, such as gross domestic expenditure on research and development (GERD), exports and number of employees, was gathered. As Figure 9.1 shows, most firms produce both goods and services, followed by those that only produce services. A small proportion of firms (7.5 percent) produce only goods.

Table 9.5 shows some descriptive corporate statistics. The sample was restricted to the 42 firms recorded in the database as having positive sales.[13] Although the standard deviation (column 3) suggests that the firms are highly heterogeneous, closer examination shows that only a few "outliers" influence the result. The four biggest firms effectively account for 83 percent, with a single firm accounting for 37 percent, of total sales (Figures 9.2 and 9.3 illustrate the highly skewed distribution of the data on sales and number of workers). If the sample is narrowed down to 38 firms (excluding the largest four), the resultant statistics are those shown in the last three columns.[14]

One result that does not significantly change from one table to the other is the GERD-to-sales ratio, which is higher than that of the mining sector as a whole and that of the general economy. This finding is

---

[13] The full sample (57 firms) is considered in all tables except Table 9.5, as the remaining 14 firms answered all of the other questions and only omitted the "economic data" questions.

[14] The mean values for sales and number of workers are very similar to economy-wide SME values, as reported by the National Bureau of Statistics and Chile's National Tax Agency.

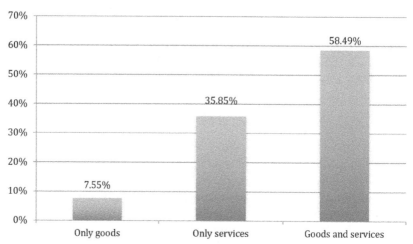

Figure 9.1   Types of firms surveyed by products supplied
Note: Out of the 57 firms that responded the survey, 53 gave an answer to this question.
Source: Survey applied to the firms of EXPANDE.

consistent with the tendency for METS to be more innovative than other firms in the sector and in other industries.

Most respondent METS engaged in product innovation (81 percent) and process innovation (55 percent). Mining companies seem to require these types of innovation the most, as illustrated in the case studies in Section 9.5.4.

9.4.2   Semi-structured Interviews

In an analysis of mining industry patents, Francis (2015), mindful of the wide array of technologies involved, classified patent applicants into three groups, namely miners, METS and major publicly funded entities such as universities. This classification was followed when conducting semi-structured interviews of senior executives from a sample of four mining firms, seven METS and two universities.[15]

All of these organizations consider themselves to be innovative, have collaborated on innovation projects with universities or nonacademic research centers at least once and are active users (beneficiaries) of public innovation-supporting instruments. As to IP protection mechanisms, most

[15] For further details on the companies and universities interviewed, see Bravo-Ortega and Price (2018).

Table 9.5 *Descriptive statistics (in US dollars)*

	Full sample			Excluding five larger firms		
	(1) Mean	(2) Median	(3) St Dev	(4) Mean	(5) Median	(6) St Dev
Sales	4,100,835	463,333	11,723,221	775,133	425,000	1,023,938
Exports*	211,024	50,000	333,055	163,940	45,412	322,443
Workers	47	9	110	15	7	16
GERD	81,718	8,333	124,774	80,607	12,500	140,183
GERD / Sales (percentage)	12	2.1	23.8	13.3	2.3	24.8

Source: Survey of EXPANDE firms.
* Among exporters

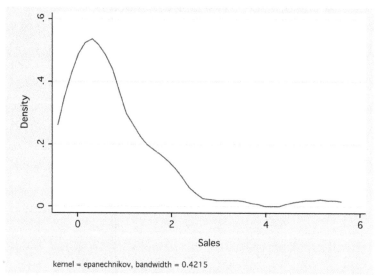

kernel = epanechnikov, bandwidth = 0.4215

Figure 9.2   Sales (frequency distribution, excluding the largest four firms)
Source: Survey applied to the firms of EXPANDE.

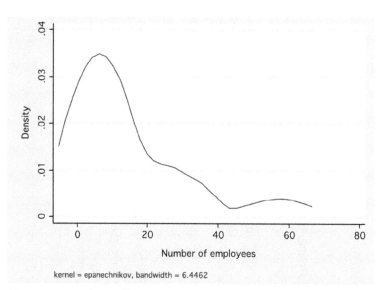

kernel = epanechnikov, bandwidth = 6.4462

Figure 9.3   Employees (frequency distribution, excluding the largest four firms)
Source: Survey of EXPANDE firms.

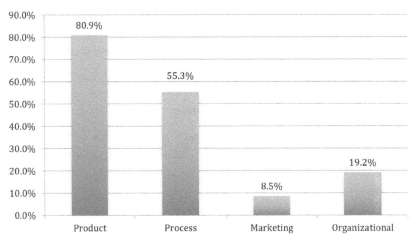

Figure 9.4   Type of innovation
Note: Of the 57 survey respondent firms, 47 answered this question.
Source: Survey of EXPANDE firms.

rely on patents, which they have registered both nationally and internationally through procedural formalities delegated to external lawyers.[16]

The interview questionnaire contained questions designed to elicit information on these organizations' innovation and IP protection practices. The interviews usefully corroborated some survey findings. It is noteworthy, however, that although the sample is very small, the companies were not selected at random.

9.4.3   Case Studies

Two case studies are similarly structured. They set out the innovation idea and its expected impact, any difficulties encountered during the innovation process and the way in which each organization has handled related IP matters.

The two METS were selected from the sample of interviewees. The case studies are particularly interesting because they concern different types of innovation for which different kinds of protection could be sought. The

[16] Only South American Management (SAMSA) responded that it did not hold any IPRs (this company had never applied for any IP protection). This is understandable because it is a mining prospection consultancy firm and, according to INAPI (2010), exploration does not require much IP protection and is one of the three areas in the mining value chain in which both resident and nonresident companies require the least protection.

scope of application, too, varies: the first concerns a process innovation that is applicable to all copper mines worldwide, while the second concerns a product innovation that is tailored to the particular mine and could hardly be sold abroad.

9.5   Analysis

This section provides some preliminary ideas on the IP protection practices of the suppliers surveyed. The interviews yielded valuable complementary information.

9.5.1   Do METS Rely on IP Protection Mechanisms?

As noted earlier, the METS surveyed considered themselves to be innovative. This has been borne out by their responses on the type of innovation and the average GERD.

The next question of interest was whether the firms protected their innovations. As shown in Table 9.6, the answer to this question is in the negative: METS do not protect the outcome of their innovation efforts. Most firms have not filed IP applications either in Chile or abroad.[17] This is particularly true of industrial designs and utility models.

Although most METS do not protect their innovations, nearly 90 percent of them stated that they take IP issues into account when appraising new business opportunities, as Table 9.7 shows. The table also shows that most METS are fully aware of IP protection costs and regulations.

9.5.2   Why Do Innovative METS Not Rely on IP Protection Mechanisms?

The literature suggests that the major reasons for this situation are patent costs, the perceived complexity of the patent system and some companies' preference for soft forms of protection such as trade secrets.[18] As shown in Table 9.8, the analysis has confirmed that this holds true for METS, as respondents have pointed to costs as the major reason for not

[17] The figures shown in this document concern filed IPRs only (as do details on granted IP mechanisms, but emphasis is laid on companies' interest in securing protection, which is measured by the percentage of firms applying for protection).

[18] See Kalanje, Christopher. Role of Intellectual Property in Innovation and New Product Development. SMEs Division, WIPO. (Accessed 17/09/17, www.wipo.int/sme/en/docu ments/ip_innovation_development_fulltext.html and the evidence quoted thereon).

Table 9.6 *IP applications filed in the Chilean Patent Office and abroad, by instrument (%)*

	In Chile			Abroad		
	0	1	2 or +	0	1	2 or +
Patents	52.9	26.5	20.6	60.9	17.4	21.7
Utility models	91.3	4.4	4.4	90.0	0.0	10.0
Industrial design	87.5	12.5	0.0	85.0	0.0	15.0
Trademarks	79.2	16.7	4.2	84.2	0.0	15.8

Source: Survey of EXPANDE firms.
NB: Of the 57 survey respondent firms, 41 answered this question. The likelihood of "self-selection bias" relating to this omission certainly cannot be ruled out.

Table 9.7 *Questions on IP practices and regulation (%)*

	Yes	No
Do you know the legislation that regulates IP in Chile?	74	26
When appraising new business opportunities, do you consider the IP involved?	88	12
Do your company's employment and supplier contracts contain any clauses on confidentiality and/or other IP ownership matters?	74	26

Source: Survey of EXPANDE firms.
NB: Of the 57 survey respondent firms, 50 answered this question.

protecting an innovation. It has also been confirmed by Figure 9.5, which shows that 69 percent of respondents identified costs as a major factor in their protection decision, possibly because resident METS in Chile tend to be SMEs. Conversely, protection is standard practice (especially through patents) among large mining companies, as confirmed by some mining firms' senior executives during the interviews.

Moreover, Table 9.8 shows that nearly one fifth of the firms surveyed lacked knowledge of IP protection mechanisms and utilization; this

Table 9.8 *Innovating firms' reasons for not protecting innovations (%)*

The cost (including money spent and time involved) is too high	40.0
Not applicable to this innovation (e.g. software)	33.3
Does not know of IP protection opportunities	16.7
Another (softer) type of protection (e.g. trade secret or copyright)	10.0

Source: Survey of EXPANDE firms.
NB: Of the 57 survey respondent firms, 31 answered this question.

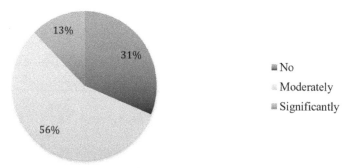

Figure 9.5   Do IP registration costs affect protection decisions in Chile?
NB: Of the 57 survey respondent firms, 48 answered this question.
Source: Survey of EXPANDE firms.

interesting finding casts light on the need for information and training policies in this area to be more effectual.[19]

As noted above, some METS preferred "softer" forms of protection. METS surveyed seem to rely on trade secrets as a form of soft protection. Figure 9.6 indicates that 55 percent of the respondent firms actually have trade secrets.

Interest in IP protection differed among firms, depending on whether they were exporters and on their export intensity. The number

---

[19]   Mindful of the importance of this activity, INAPI held two patent-drafting courses in the preceding ten months (Source: interview of senior INAPI staff).

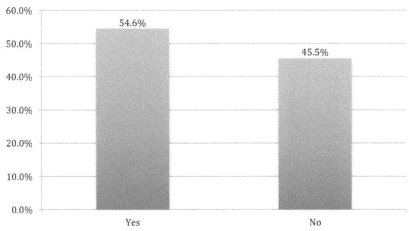

Figure 9.6 Does your firm have trade secrets?
NB: Of the 57 survey respondent firms, 44 answered this question.
Source: Survey of EXPANDE firms.

of exporting firms is so small that this point could not be tested in the analysis. A survey question was nonetheless drafted to gather information on firms that intended to export goods or services. Figure 9.7 shows that most METS (73 percent) that wished to sell goods/services abroad were interested in filing for a patent through the international IP registration system and in other means of IP protection such as trademarks (58 percent) and industrial designs (33 percent). The importance ascribed to trademarks is consistent, moreover, with most respondent METS' tendency to invest in product innovation, inasmuch as the significance of trademarks becomes apparent when a new or improved good is to be marketed and a mark is to be devised for that purpose.

9.5.3 Does the Capacity for IP Protection Suffice?

The interviewees seemed to share the view that Chile's expertise for proper legal and technical advice on IP strategy management sufficed.

Some interviewees considered, however, that the country lacked the required capabilities to develop business models to take full advantage of the economic potential of IP assets and that IPRs should be regarded as assets which had a clearly defined life cycle and which must give a return on time. For instance, many innovators of process and product

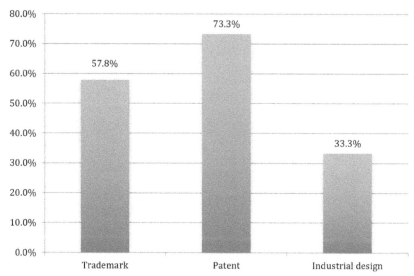

Figure 9.7   IP instruments of apparent interest to potential exporters
NB: Of the 57 survey respondent firms, 45 answered this question.
Source: Survey of EXPANDE firms.

innovations should consider ways and means of finding new markets and/or of licensing or even selling their IPRs. Capabilities must be built to take up those challenges effectively.

Universities are a good example of the country's efforts to develop such skills and they are major stakeholders in the transfer of new knowledge and technologies to the production sector. They develop new knowledge, some of which is protected by IPRs. Engineers and managers with advanced knowledge of innovation business models are being recruited in order to take full advantage of those rights.

9.5.4   Case Studies

As it has been previously suggested, resident METS (which are probably less internationalized) don't rely much on the patent system. This could be because they mostly work with local firms developing location-specific technologies. But there are some METS that are more oriented toward and internationalization strategy, and for them the IP system might appear more beneficial. In what follows, we analyze two good examples of this type of METS.

iFlux (Innovaxxion)

Innovaxxion has excelled as a supplier of innovative solutions based on technology and applied engineering. It operates mostly in the mining sector, although it also develops applications for other industries (defense, energy and agro-industry). It has filed 15 patents in the past 24 months in the 10 countries in which the 20 largest copper operations are concentrated.

The firm has developed a knowledge creation model under which it generates and patents innovations and then forms companies to market the new good. It invites investors to enter into the ownership of the new companies, but it retains the controlling share.

This company's innovation model is based on the "design thinking" method, which relies on seven steps and five scales, from identification of the innovation challenge to hypothesis testing. The company works with other firms and with universities. Initial ideas undergo digital prototyping, which roughly 15 percent survive and move to the next stage (three-dimensional prototyping). The idea that best meets requirements is selected, a full-size prototype is made and large-scale testing (in an industrial environment) is conducted. If all is successful, a spin-off is formed and Innovaxxion outsources manufacturing to a "partner company." The firm usually files two patents – one to protect the specific solution (which has a clearly determined physical appearance) and the other to protect the formulation (i.e. the specific range of parameters); this is common practice in the pharmaceutical industry when laboratories protect new drugs.[20]

Applying its innovation model, the company has devised and successfully marketed iFlux, an innovative solution that optimizes processes in foundry furnaces. iFlux is based on components that, under a briquette format, penetrate the surface of the bath inside furnaces and generate a series of chemical reactions to recover a higher percentage of copper than is usually possible in the smelting process.

The product is sold in sacks of different tonnages. Its proposed value also factors in expert professional services provided throughout the injection of the solution into smelting furnaces, as well as special industrial dosing equipment designed by the company to inject the product efficiently into the copper smelting furnaces.

The innovation was developed in response to a problem of competitiveness. Chile's foundries were in the last quartile of global industry in

---

[20] In the pharmaceutical industry, these are known as primary and secondary patents, the former protecting an active ingredient and the latter protecting a range of related chemicals.

terms of unit costs and they even exhibited negative cash margins. Why were they losing money? This question drew the attention of Innovaxxion. As the innovation team noticed that copper recovery capacity was very low, thorough research was conducted into the state of the art. With its team of lawyers, the firm reviewed copper-recovery processes in foundries and found that the problem had not been properly addressed worldwide. It led the research for two years and the related applied R&D was performed by pyrometallurgy experts based at Federico Santa María Technical University (UTFSM), a Chilean university well known for the reputation of its Science and Engineering faculty.

iFlux is expected to increase copper recovery and to raise smelting efficiency: in initial testing, the percentage of "left over" copper fell from 38 percent to 20 percent and currently accounts for only 10 percent of residue. iFlux could, moreover, lead to improved and cleaner operation of foundry furnaces.

The first difficulty was encountered at the beginning of the innovation process. Innovaxxion had applied for public funding, which had been denied; it therefore decided to risk its own capital. Second, owing to conflictual relations with academia, the innovation advanced slowly.

Potential customers to which Innovaxxion plans to roll out the solution include nineteen smelters found in Chile, Peru, Brazil, Mexico, the United States of America and Canada, which have an overall output capacity of 3.4 million tons per year. Chile holds 50 percent of that capacity. The project is currently in its first implementation stage in three Chilean furnaces. The objective was to serve the entire market in Chile by the end of 2018. The commercial model was supposed to be validated in 2019 so that it could be launched internationally.

Patents (both national and under the PCT) are being filed for the product. Furthermore, the company expects to be granted a triadic patent (registered in the United States of America, Europe and Japan). It understandably wishes to protect this process innovation internationally because it seems to be applicable to all copper mines worldwide. IP registration has been conducted ably both nationally and abroad. Lastly, the firm is open to the possibility of licensing or selling patents as an option conducive to developing new businesses abroad.

Intelligent Skids (RIVET)

RIVET supplies equipment and components to the mining sector. With more than 100 years on the market, RIVET is currently the main supplier of metal mesh to mining companies in Chile and has a leading position in the conveyor-belt business.

Conveyor belts are the most economical means of transporting ore. They can transport a large quantity of ore over long distances and great heights, while keeping energy consumption low. The spotlight here is on RIVET's work in this area, particularly in the manufacturing of one of the key conveyor-belt system components, the skids.

Skids must be reliable and durable because they bear the belts. The company manufactures skids to withstand extreme mining conditions in Chile, such as harsh environments, high tonnages and high speed. RIVET has launched a series of intelligent skids with integrated sensors that form part of a data analysis platform for ascertaining operating conditions and predicting failures.[21] Mining companies can thus save resources by reducing the number of unscheduled plant shutdowns.

As to the main innovation difficulties encountered, it is noteworthy that it was difficult to find the appropriate technologies and to train a suitable technical team. Data transmission technologies that met specific energy consumption and signal reliability criteria were required but were not available on the market. This hurdle could be overcome only by working with electrical engineers (RIVET specializes in mechanical engineering). Working relations with the initial team of expert engineers broke down owing to lack of agreement on ownership of IPRs in the innovation. A team of experts, with whom the innovation was developed, was ultimately found.

The potential customers are large and medium-sized mining firms. RIVET intends, first of all, to market this innovation in the countries in which it has operated with other products, namely Chile (where most of its output is sold), and Peru.

RIVET is at the final patent application stage. From the beginning, it seemed clear that it was a radical innovation and, for that reason, the firm opted for patent protection (rather than a utility model). RIVET, which first applied for a patent in Chile (INAPI), is now filing for PCT registration and plans to apply for protection in other countries. The company is very open to licensing the patent afterwards.

According to Enrique Celedón, the company's Chief Executive Officer (CEO), it was very difficult to draft the patent. "It is as if it were a new literary style," Celedón said. RIVET was therefore obliged to hire an

---

[21] This technology is also known as "intelligent roller," "smart roller" and "smart idler." The original (commercial) Spanish term is *polín multisensor inalámbrico inteligente*.

engineer expert in patent drafting. Celedón has suggested that INAPI "organize and/or subsidize training courses so that firms can acquire the necessary patent drafting skills."[22]

9.6   Conclusions and Recommendations

This chapter has provided information on the IP protection practices of METS in Chile's mining sector. The analysis was based on an online survey of approximately 300 mining suppliers that were covered by the EXPANDE Program. The information pointed to some preliminary conclusions, some of which were corroborated by opinions gathered from semi-structured interviews of executives from mining companies and suppliers, including universities.

Most of the firms are small and medium-sized (in terms of sales and number of employees). They consider themselves to be innovative and their self-reported opinions are consistent with both the GERD-to-sales ratios and earlier surveys and literature. Nevertheless, only a minority of these seemingly innovative companies relies on IPRs to protect their innovations. The most crucial factors that account for this finding are the cost and expected complexity of registration.

We have also presented two case studies describing innovation efforts of two mining providers, the partners with which those bodies have engaged, the difficulties that they have encountered and the IP protection strategies that each has implemented. Some of the firms had established cooperation agreements with researchers based in universities or research centers, while one firm had relied mainly on its own research expertise. The form of IP protection selected and firms' sale or licensing intentions related largely to the type of innovation and the market served.

Outcomes from the interviews indicate that in Chile there is enough legal expertise and that it is relatively easy to get that sort of advice in the area of IP rights. However commercial capabilities (expertise in innovation management and business plans addressing the questions of commercialization and licensing of IP rights) are much less developed. Universities are expected to play a role in order to tackle this skills shortage.

---

[22] As noted, INAPI is aware of the importance of this activity and held two courses on patent drafting in the past year.

References

APRIMIN/COCHILCO (2017). "Encuesta de Innovación en Empresas Proveedoras de la Gran Minería." www.cochilco.cl/Listado%20Temtico/ Encuesta%20de%20Innovaci%C3%B3n%20VF3%20Enero%202017.pdf

Báez, F. (2015). "Mining innovation." *WIPO Magazine* 5. September. https:// www.wipo.int/wipo_magazine/en/2015/05/article_0006.html.

BIS (2012). "UK Innovation Survey 2011 – First Findings." https://www.gov .uk/government/publications/uk-innovation-survey-2011-first-findings

Bravo-Ortega, C., and de Gregorio, J. (2007). "The Relative Richness of the Poor? Natural resources, human capital, and economic growth," In Lederman, D., and Maloney, W. (eds.). *Natural resources: Neither Curse nor Destiny*. Washington, DC: Stanford University Press and the World Bank, pp. 71–103.

Bravo-Ortega, C., and García, A. (2011). "R&D and Productivity: A two way avenue?" *World Development*, 39 (7), pp. 1090–1107.

Bravo-Ortega, C., and Muñoz, L. (2015). "Knowledge Intensive Mining Services in Chile: Challenges and opportunities for future Development." *IADB Discussion Paper 418*. Washington, DC: Inter-American Development Bank, October.

Bravo-Ortega, C., and Muñoz, L. (2017). "A Toolkit for R&D Policy Choice with an Application to Chilean Mining." *International Journal of Technological Learning, Innovation and Development*, 9 (4), 333–352.

Bravo-Ortega, C., and Price Elton, J. J. (2019). "Innovation and IP Rights in the Chilean Copper Mining Sector: The Role of the Mining, Equipment, Technology and Services Firms." Economic Research Working Paper No. 54. WIPO Economics & Statistics Series.

FCH (2014). *Proveedores de la Minería Chilena. Estudio de Caracterización 2014*. Santiago, Chile: FCH. https://corporacionaltaley.cl/wp-content/ uploads/2019/09/Estudio-de-Caracterizacion-de-Proveedores-de-la- mineria-2014.pdf

FCH/PROCHILE (2017). *Proveedores de la minería chilena: Reporte de Exportaciones 2012–2016*. PROCHILE and FCH. https://corporacionaltaley .cl/wp-content/uploads/2019/09/Reporte-Exportaciones-2012-2016-VD.pdf

Fessehaie, J., and Morris, M. (2013). "Value Chain Dynamics of Chinese Copper Mining in Zambia: Enclave or linkage development?" *The European Journal of Development Research*, 25, 537–556.

Francis, E. (2015). *The Australian Mining Industry: More than just shovels and being the lucky country*, s.l.: IP Australia Economic Research Paper No. 4.

Griliches, Z. (1998). *R&D and Productivity*. Chicago: University of Chicago Press.

Hall,B., Mairesse, J., and Mohnen, P. (2010). "Measuring the Returns to R&D." In Hall, B., and Rosenberg, N. (eds.). *Handbooks in Economics. Economics of innovation*, Vol. 21. Elsevier, pp. 1033–1082.

Hall, B., Abud, M. J., Fink, C., and Helmers, C. (2013). "The use of intellectual property in Chile." *Economic Research Working Paper No. 11.* WIPO Economics & Statistics Series. July.

INAPI (2010). "*Patentamiento en el cluster minería del cobre: Análisis de presentaciones realizadas en Chile*" Chilean IP Office. Santiago, March. www.inapi.cl/portal/publicaciones/608/articles-738_recurso_1.pdf.

Klevorick, A., Levin, R., Nelson, R., and Winter, S. (1995). "On the Sources and Significance of Interindustry Differences in Technological Opportunities." *Research Policy, 24*, 185–205.

Lederman, D., and Maloney, W. (2007). "Trade Structure and Growth." In Lederman, D., and Maloney, W. (eds.). *Natural Resources: Neither curse nor destiny*. Washington, DC: Stanford University Press and The World Bank, pp. 15–39.

Manzano, O., and Rigobon, R. (2007). "Resource Curse or Debt Overhang." In Lederman, D. and Maloney, W. (eds.), *Natural Resources: Neither curse nor destiny*. Washington, DC: Stanford University Press and The World Bank, pp. 41–70.

Meller, P., and Gana, J. (2016). "*El desarrollo de proveedores mineros en Australia: Implicancias para Chile*" CIEPLAN, Chile.

Murphy, E. (2015). "The Chilean Mining Industry: The Role of IP in the Innovation Process." *IP Watch*. www.ip-watch.org/2015/06/09/the-chilean-mining-industry-the-role-of-ip-in-the-innovation-process/

Navarro, L. (2018). "The World Class Supplier Program for mining in Chile: Assessment and perspectives." *Resources Policy*, 58, 49–61. https://doi.org/10.1016/j.resourpol.2017.10.008.

OECD (2018). *Production Transformation Policy Review of Chile: Reaping the benefits of new frontiers*: Paris: OECD Publishing.

Sachs, J., and Warner, A. (1995). "Natural Resource Abundance and Economic Growth." NBER Working Paper, 5398, Cambridge, MA.

Sachs, J., and Warner, A. (2001). "Natural Resource Abundance and Economic Growth" in Meier, G., and Rauch, J. (eds.). *Leading Issues in Economic Development*. Oxford: Oxford University Press, pp. 161–168.

Scott-Kemmis, D. (2013). "How about those METS? Leveraging Australia's mining equipment, technology and services sector." A public policy analysis produced for the Minerals Council of Australia.

WIPO (2011). *World Intellectual Property Report*. Geneva: WIPO.

10

The MINER Act of 2006: Innovating for Safety and Health in US Mining

ANDREW A. TOOLE, JAMES FORMAN AND ASRAT
TESFAYESUS

Disclaimer: The views expressed in this article are the authors' and do not necessarily represent the views of the United States Patent and Trademark Office. The authors would like to thank Reza Noorani, Mine Safety and Health Administration, US Department of Labor, for providing the US mine accident data used in this chapter and Alexander Giczy for excellent research assistance.

10.1 Introduction

Mineral mining jobs are among the most dangerous in the world. According to the International Labour Organization, mining accounts for about 8 percent of the world's work-related fatalities but only represents 1 percent of the global workforce (ILO, 2015). However, while mining is unquestionably a dangerous industry, the long-run trend in the United States (USA) shows a significant decline in mine-related fatalities. US fatalities peaked in 1917 at 3,679 people. This total includes a disastrous electrical fire at Granite Mountain's Speculator Mine that resulted in 163 deaths. By 1954, the number of annual fatalities had dropped to 535 people and continued to fall to 28 by 2017. This long-run decrease surely reflects a number of changes, but technological innovations are likely to be one of the most important sources of improvements in health and safety outcomes at US mining operations.

This chapter uses patent data to explore the levels and trends in technological innovations in US mineral mining with a particular focus on safety and health. Starting with the World Intellectual Property Organization (WIPO) set of mining patents discussed earlier in this volume, our chapter introduces a modern data refinement for grouping patents into thematic areas or industries, so-called patent landscaping. We apply a machine-learning approach to identify patents granted by the US Patent and Trademark Office (USPTO) related to mineral mining as well as those patents directed at technical innovations in mine safety.

After forming our patent database using the machine-learning approach, our chapter focuses on the impact of the Mine Improvement and New Emergency Response (MINER) Act of 2006. With this Act, the US Congress tried to mitigate risks in underground mining and to ensure worker safety. Importantly, the Act created a competitive grant program to stimulate mine safety- and health-related innovations. We present four types of evidence on the impact of the MINER Act: graphical, case studies, text-based similarity and regression analysis. While this evidence does not include a randomized or natural experiment to establish causality, all four types of evidence point to a positive and significant effect of the MINER Act on patenting in safety-related mineral mining technologies, as well as reduced injuries and lost workdays among mine workers.

Section 10.2 provides a quick overview of the major US laws related to mining safety and health and describes the 2006 MINER Act. Section 10.3 describes our machine learning approach to identifying mineral mining patents and the subgroup related to safety[1]. Section 10.4 gives a brief overview of our data on mineral mining while Section 10.5 contains the evaluation of the MINER Act using our patent database. Concluding remarks appear in Section 10.6.

10.2   Health and Safety Legislation in US Mining

Mineral mining has always played a key role in US economic activity. In 1900, US production of metallic and nonmetallic minerals amounted to over $1 billion (equivalent to over $29 billion in 2017 dollars) (Day, 1902). Moreover, despite some important downturns, the role of mineral mining and its share in US economic activity has seen dramatic increases throughout the twentieth century. In 2017, total mineral mining production in the USA reached nearly $100 billion (Ober, 2018).

Similarly, mineral mining has contributed significantly to employment in the USA. As shown in Figure 10.1, at its peak in 1923, the mineral mining industry employed over 860 thousand miners. While we observe continuing decline in mineral mining jobs, primarily due to

---

[1] See Toole et al. (2019) for technical details on the machine-learning approach.

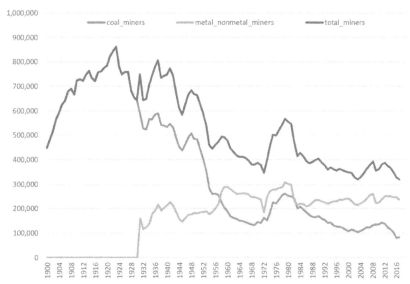

Figure 10.1   US mining employment (1900–2017)
Source: www.cdc.gov/niosh/mining/data/default.html

technological advances, the mining industry remains a major employer with nearly 320 thousand miners employed in the USA in 2017.

Unfortunately, mineral mining is also an inherently dangerous job that exposes miners to high risks of accidents that are sometimes fatal. Each mining accident can have disastrous consequences, claiming the lives of hundreds of miners in a single instance. As shown in Figure 10.2, the highest number of fatalities occurred in 1917 when 3,679 miners lost their lives due to mining accidents.

The dangerous nature of mineral mining activities prompted the US federal government to enact laws aimed at improving the safety and health of miners. The following provides a short synopsis of the US legislative history leading up to the 2006 MINER Act, which is the main focus of our analysis.

- The first safety and health-related Congressional initiative became law in 1891. Among other things, this federal statute established minimum ventilation requirements at underground coal mines and prohibited the employment of children under 12 years of age.
- In 1910, in light of the rising fatality rates in the previous decade, Congress established the Bureau of Mines as an agency in the

Figure 10.2   Fatalities in US mining (1900–2017)
Source: www.cdc.gov/niosh/mining/data/default.html

Department of the Interior. Led by Dr. Joseph A. Holmes as its first director, the Bureau was responsible for research and the reduction of accidents in coal mining. The Bureau focused on training and educational efforts and successfully trained over 50 thousand miners in its first year on first aid, mine rescue, and fire-fighting skills.

- The Federal Coal Mine Safety Act was passed in 1952. This statute, and its more comprehensive 1966 version, provided for annual inspections of coal mines, gave the Bureau of Mines additional enforcement authority, including issuing violation notices and withdrawal orders, and authorized the assessment of civil penalties against noncomplying mine operators.
- In 1966, the Federal Metal and Nonmetallic Mine Safety Act became the first federal statute directly regulating non-coal mines. Although it gave only minimal enforcement authority to the Bureau, the statute called for advisory standards and allowed for inspections and investigations of non-coal mines (Breslin, 2010).
- A few years later, Congress passed the Federal Coal Mine Health and Safety Act of 1969 (known as the Coal Act). Up to that date, this was the most comprehensive and stringent mining law targeting safety. Among other things, the Coal Act significantly increased the

enforcement authority of federal agencies, required the imposition of monetary penalties for all violations, and established criminal penalties for knowing and willful violations.

- A year later, in 1970, Congress passed the Occupational Safety and Health Act, which created the National Institute for Occupational Safety and Health (NIOSH). This newly created agency has the mandate to "conduct . . . research, experiments, and demonstrations relating to occupational safety and health" and to develop new methods and approaches increasing occupational safety and health. While not intended exclusively for the mining industry, NIOSH has contributed and continues to contribute significantly to the advancement of health and safety in mining.

- In 1977, Congress again passed a statute regulating health and safety in mining, the Federal Mine Safety and Health Act, also known as the Mine Act. It amended the 1969 Coal Act and consolidated all federal health and safety regulation in mining. This statute also transferred responsibilities from the Department of the Interior to the Department of Labor and called the new agency the Mine Safety and Health Administration (MSHA). Along with the new agency, the statute created a committee that provides an independent review of MSHA's enforcement actions. Furthermore, the Mine Act gave miners stronger and broader rights with enhanced protection from retaliation for exercising these rights.

From 1977 to 2005, the US Congress did not pass any new mining legislation related to safety and health. However, things changed in 2006. On the morning of January 2, 2006, West Virginia suffered its worst mining disaster in over half a century due to a coal mine explosion in the Sago Mine. Located near the Upshur County seat of Buckhannon in Sago, West Virginia, the mine had an explosion followed by a collapse that trapped 13 miners. Only one survived. A few days later, on the morning of January 19, 2006, another mine accident in West Virginia claimed two more lives. In this case, a conveyor belt in the Aracoma Alma Mine in Logan County, West Virginia, caught fire releasing a heavy cloud of smoke. The two miners died of carbon monoxide poisoning. A few months later on May 20, 2006, another mine disaster killed five more miners. This time the accident was at the Darby Mine in Harlan County, Kentucky, where an explosion that investigators attribute to methane occurred with only one survivor.

Spurred by these tragedies, the Health, Education, Labor, and Pensions (HELP) Committee in the US Senate spearheaded an initiative to manage risks in underground coal mining and to ensure worker safety. The HELP Committee identified six areas of particular concern: post-accident communication, post-accident tracking, post-accident breathable air, lifelines for use in post-accident escape, training and local emergency coordination (Breslin, 2010, p.5). They believed improvements in mine safety were possible through "innovation, vigilance, adaptability and resources."

On June 15, 2006, President George W. Bush signed the resulting Congressional bill to pass the MINER Act. One of the most important sections of this law, section 6, permanently established the Office of Mine Safety and Health within the National Institute for Occupational Safety and Health (NIOSH). The purpose of this new office was "to enhance the development of new mine safety technology and technological applications and to expedite the commercial availability and implementation of such technology in mining environments."[2] To fulfill this purpose, the Office was to establish a competitive financial award program to facilitate research, development, and testing of new technologies and equipment. This new technology-oriented public financing program could award grants or contracts to research institutions or private companies to stimulate new mine safety technology and equipment. Within 10 years of the passage of the MINER Act, the Office of Mine Safety had awarded over "120 technology development and commercialization or interagency agreements in its execution of the MINER Act."[3]

The MINER Act is the primary focus of the empirical work in this chapter. Our objective is to evaluate the evidence that the 2006 MINER Act improved US miner safety and health.

10.3   Data Sources and Data Processing

As described in Daly et al. (2019), the World Intellectual Property Organization (WIPO) developed an algorithm that identified the set of global patents (applications and grants) related to mineral mining. This effort exploited the European Patent Office's PATSTAT product and used a traditional patent landscape methodology. Specifically, WIPO identified patent documents that correspond to mineral mining

---

[2] www.govinfo.gov/content/pkg/CRPT-109srpt365/html/CRPT-109srpt365.htm
[3] www.cdc.gov/niosh/mining/researchprogram/contracts/index.html

inventions based on detailed technology classification codes (from the International Patent Classification system) and Boolean text-based searches of patent document titles and abstracts. WIPO applied these methods to PATSTAT and identified over 1.6 million patent applications. Of these 1.6 million patent applications, which cover a variety of countries, we determined that 123,853 of these applications were submitted to the USPTO with application dates reaching as far back as the early 1960s.

As described in Toole et al. (2019), we used a machine-learning approach to refine the original WIPO patent dataset. This approach improves on the traditional patent landscape methodologies by more fully exploiting the rich text-based information contained in published patent documents (i.e. patent specifications). We augmented the traditional approach with machine learning to identify US patents granted in the area of mineral mining and in the subarea of safety-related patents in mineral mining. In this section, we provide a high-level overview of our approach and data.

Starting with the US applications contained in the WIPO patent dataset (123,853), we used the patent application numbers to match to PatentsView, which is a public visualization and analysis tool for US-granted patents (www.patentsview.org). We determined that 91,818 of the 123,853 unique US patent applications were granted and the remaining 32,035 were published applications without a corresponding patent number.[4] Inspection of these 91,818 patents revealed a fairly large number of patents that did not belong in a group of mineral mining patents.[5] We found patents directed toward technology improvements related to oil & gas wells, robotic household vacuums, data mining techniques, nucleotide sequences (including amine groups) and motorcycle fuel pumps.

Based on this, we developed a machine-learning approach to refine our set of US-granted patents in mineral mining (see Toole et al. (2019) for details).[6] This involves three steps: (1) identifying a "training set" of

---

[4] We assume that the applications with no patent number have not been granted. Either these applications have been abandoned or they are still undergoing the patent examination process.

[5] We defined "mineral mining" patents as those directed to an improvement related to the extraction or refinement of either minerals (both metallic and nonmetallic minerals) or coal.

[6] Of the 92k patents, we could only use those that had patent owners identified in the data. This was 78,173 (85.1 percent).

patents; (2) allowing a computer algorithm (i.e. a machine-learning statistical procedure) to learn how to identify mineral mining patents from the training set; and (3) using the machine-learning results to classify patents into mineral mining and nonmineral mining. The training set is a group of patents that we identified as mineral mining and nonmineral mining. We formed a training set of 22,813 patents using a variety of information and manual checking. Then, based on statistical performance criteria, we decided on a machine-learning algorithm.[7] Finally, we then applied the machine-learning results to classify each of the remaining 68,503 patents from the WIPO patent dataset, which resulted in classifying 43,815 patents as mineral mining patents and 24,688 patents as nonmineral mining.[8] Our final dataset of US patents granted in mineral mining contains 45,572 patents (43,815 + the mineral mining patents from the training set of 1,757) out of the 91,818 patents from the WIPO Patent Dataset.

To determine safety-related mineral mining patents, we undertook another three-step process (see Toole et al. (2019) for a detailed description). First, we applied Boolean searches to identify a starting group. This is the traditional patent landscape method. Second, we refined this set based on language in the patent documents. The patent language was analyzed using an established multi-task convolutional neural network classifier. Third, we restricted our set of safety-related mineral mining patents to those appearing in our refined version of WIPO's patent dataset described previously. This intersection produced 1,311 patents – our final group of US granted patented for safety-related mineral mining.

10.4   US Patents in Mineral Mining

While imperfect, economists and policy makers often use patents as an indicator of innovation. The rationale is that patented technologies often facilitate or are used to define and construct new products and services. Taking this perspective, the level and trend in granted patents can provide information on the technological evolution of an industry, even its "innovativeness."

Figure 10.3 provides a perspective on innovation in mineral mining using our refined dataset of 45,572 US patents. The patents are displayed

---

[7] We used a linear Support Vector Machine classifier with stochastic gradient descent.
[8] We could not run 527 patents through the classifier because their specification text was missing in the data.

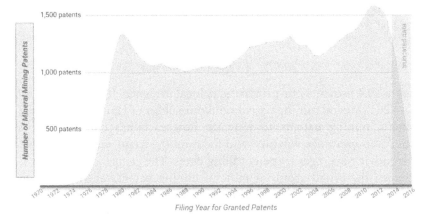

Figure 10.3   USPTO-granted patents in mineral mining (three-year moving average by filing year)
Source: Author's calculations.

by filing date to better reflect the date of invention discovery. We also use a three-year moving average to smooth the time series. It is clear from the figure that our coverage is most comprehensive for patents filed during the period 1979–2014.[9] During that period, we observe that filing rates were over 1,200 applications annually. We also observe an overall increase in the filing rates with a peak of 1,616 patent filings in 2012. This shows that innovation in the US mining industry remains strong and is even increasing. We show later that a number of these innovations reflect a significant rise in safety-related mineral mining patents, particularly following the 2006 MINER Act.

10.5   The MINER Act of 2006: Safety Innovation and Health Outcomes

In this section, we explore the impacts of the 2006 MINER Act on innovation in mineral mining safety and health. We present four types of evidence: graphical, case studies, text-based similarity and regression analysis. While this evidence does not include a randomized experiment or natural experiment to establish causality, all four types of evidence point to a positive and significant effect of the MINER Act on patenting

---

[9] Our data provides limited coverage of earlier years and suffers from truncation in later years. Note that we report a three-year moving average to focus on overall trends.

in safety-related mineral mining technologies as well as reduced injuries and lost workdays among mine workers.

10.5.1   Graphical Evidence

Figure 10.4 presents our primary graphical evidence. It displays the set of 44,261 mineral mining patents and our subset of 1,311 safety-related mineral mining patents to visualize how each has changed across time.[10] To minimize volatility and focus on the trend, we report three-year moving averages by patent filing dates. The critical comparison is between the broad group of mineral mining patents and the safety-related subgroup. The broad group experienced a wave of new patent filings starting around 1995 and ending in 2003, while safety-related patent filings declined over this period. If one looks at the window of time around the 2006 MINER Act, the period from 2004 to 2012, mineral mining patent filings increased by 36 percent, but safety-related patent filings grew by 113 percent. That is, the filing rate for

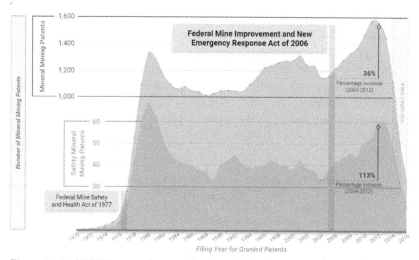

Figure 10.4   USPTO-granted patents in mineral mining separated into safety-related and non-safety-related groups (three-year moving average by filing year)
Source: Author's calculations.

---

[10]   The 44,261 mineral mining patents in this set exclude the 1,311 mineral mining safety patents (i.e. 45,572 − 1,311 = 44,261).

safety-related mineral mining patents increased by more than triple other mineral mining patents for the same period. This evidence suggests that the 2006 MINER Act stimulated growth in safety-related patenting. The growth rate difference between these two groups can be loosely interpreted as the "treatment effect" from the MINER Act. It suggests the MINER Act led to a 77 percent increase in safety-related USPTO patent filings. While this point estimate is probably too high, the effect of the MINER Act appears to be positive and economically meaningful.

We also examined two key technologies relevant to the 2006 MINER Act that relate to improvements in accident preparedness and emergency responsiveness. In particular, the Act specifically mentions the need for more effective means of *through-the-earth communication* for trapped miners and *refuge chambers* in which miners can safely wait.[11] These two areas are defined as:

(1) **Refuge Chambers**

- An emergency shelter installed in an underground mine intended to provide mine workers access to clean air, food, and water until they can be rescued.[12]

(2) **Two-way, 'through-the-earth' (TTE) wireless communications**

- A wireless communication through the earth surface under which a miner is trapped and where regular radio transmissions cannot operate.[13]

To evaluate the extent to which the MINER Act helped advance innovation in these two areas, we identified all of the keyword occurrences for "refuge chamber" and "TTE communication" for the period before and after the Act. We conducted keyword searches on all 45 k mineral mining patents in our dataset as follows:

- The keywords used to identify refuge chamber related mineral mining are: "refuge chamber"; "refuge shelter"; "refuge alternative"; "emergency

---

[11] For more detail, see sections 2, 6 and 13 of the MINER Act. file:///C:/Users/atesfayesus/Desktop/All%20Files/Projects/Early%20Projects/Mining/Legislative%20History/2006mineract.pdf

[12] www.cdc.gov/niosh/mining/topics/refugechambers.html

[13] No suitable through-the-earth technologies (for communication between underground miners, mine rescue teams, and a surface command center) existed when the MINER Act was enacted. www.cdc.gov/niosh/mining/features/throughtheearthcommtech.html

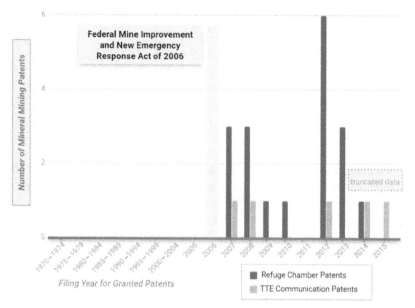

Figure 10.5   USPTO-granted patents in mineral mining for refuge chambers and TTE communications
Source: Author's calculations.

shelter"; "emergency chamber"; "rescue shelter"; "outby refuge"; "outby shelter"; "hardened room"; "in place shelter".[14]
- The keywords used to identify TTE communication related mineral mining are: "through the earth" and any["tte," "(tte)," "'tte'"].[15]

As shown in Figure 10.5, we find that all of the patenting activity in both areas occurred after the MINER Act in 2006. There were eighteen patent filings related to "refuge chamber" (shown in blue) filed in 2008 or later. Similarly, five patents related to "TTE communication" (shown in red). Again, we find that all of these patents were filed in the period after the MINER Act.

---

[14] We selected these keywords using two NIOSH publications as reference: www.cdc.gov /niosh/mining/works/coversheet1695.html; www.cdc.gov/niosh/mining/Works/cover sheet1886.html
[15] These selections rely on NIOSH-sponsored research paper summarizing TTE wireless communication (Yenchek et al., 2011)

10.5.2   Case Studies

Case Study #1: *Battelle Memorial Institute & Emergency Mine Refuge Alternatives*
Battelle is a private nonprofit applied science and technology company
headquartered in Columbus, Ohio, and founded in 1929. Initially funded by
Ohio industrialist Gordon Battelle, the original focus was research, development
and commercialization of metals and material science technology. Battelle has
expanded to offer solutions in medical devices, public health and safety,
agrifood, industrial products, pharmaceutical and biotechnology, and national
laboratory management.

Event Timeline

February 2006: One month after the tragic Sago Mine disaster, Ohio formed the
Underground Mine Task Force to evaluate Ohio's underground mine emergency
response program. Subject-matter experts were invited to give presentations on
state-of-the-art safety equipment and technological advancements. **Battelle's
Jim Reuther and Rick Givens** gave a presentation on **a new type of mine
refuge alternative**: *"Breathing Curtain: New Mine-Fire Survivor Rescue Tool."*
August 2007: Battelle was awarded a NIOSH grant to further develop, design and
demonstrate its new mine refuge alternative. At contract completion, Battelle
was pursuing commercialization and field testing of the prototype in an operating underground coal mine.[16]
June 2013: The US Patent & Trademark Office granted a patent[17] to Battelle for
a "Mine Barrier Survival System," wherein both Jim Reuther and Rick Givens
were included as inventors.

Technology Description (Figure 10.6)

How It Works: After an explosion or collapse, miners unroll, inflate and connect
lightweight plastic alls (see Item 100 in Figure below) in order to create a wall-to-
wall barrier (400). Two wall-to-wall barriers are erected in order to provide safe
volume (410) for the survivors. In this safe space, breathable, filtered-air (CO_2
absorption, O_2 generation, CO reduction, flammable methane reduction) is
provided by a unique air-scrubbing system attached to the inside walls of the
inflatable barriers.

---

[16] www.cdc.gov/niosh/mining/researchprogram/contracts/contract_200–2007-22067.html
[17] US Patent 8,469,781 had the highest avg. refuge cosine similarity score of the identified
WIPO refuge chamber patents.

Case Study #2: *Stolar, Inc. & TTE Emergency Communications*

Stolar is a research and development company based in Raton, New Mexico, and founded in 1983 by Dr. Larry Stolarczyk. Stolar specializes in radio geophysics development for the underground mining industry with the mission to improve underground coal mining health, safety and productivity.

Event Timeline

1980s: Starting in the early 1980s, the New Mexico company pioneered the development of through-the-earth imaging of coal seams using electromagnetic waves.

January 2006: A methane gas explosion in the Sago Mine trapped its miners without a way to communicate with surface personnel 85 m (280 feet) above. The trapped miners believed that the mine's escape-way was blocked. If communications had been available, the miners could have been given instructions for a 700-foot walk to fresh air.[18] Only 1 of the 13 trapped miners survived.

March 2006: In response to both the tragic Sago Mine and Aracoma Alma No.1 Mine fatalities in January 2006, the Mine Safety and Health Administration (MSHA) held a "Mine Rescue Equipment and Technology Forum" in Washington, DC. At the forum, **Stolar** gave a presentation on a new, proposed emergency communication and tracking system utilizing ultra-low frequency (ULF) radio waves that can travel up, through the earth, to a surface receiver.

June 2006: The Mine Improvement and New Emergency Response Act (the "MINER Act") was enacted, and called for underground coal mines to develop post-accident emergency response plans that specify two-way wireless communications and electronic tracking systems. "No suitable through-the-earth (TTE) communication systems existed when the MINER act was enacted."[19]

September 2009: Stolar was awarded a NIOSH contract to design a two-way, TTE emergency communication system, fabricate the hardware and test the prototype. A demonstration in a southwestern Pennsylvania commercial coal mine achieved two-way text messaging at a vertical range of nearly 244 m – with an extrapolated maximum vertical range at this mine site of nearly 335 m.[20]

September 2013: The US Patent and Trademark Office granted a patent[21] to Stolar for an improved underground radio communications and tracking system.

---

[18] www.cdc.gov/mmwr/preview/mmwrhtml/mm5751a3.htm
[19] www.cdc.gov/niosh/mining/features/throughtheearthcommtech.html
[20] www.cdc.gov/niosh/mining/researchprogram/contracts/contract_200–2009-32117.html
[21] US Patent 8,115,622 holds the highest avg. TTE cosine similarity score in the WIPO dataset.

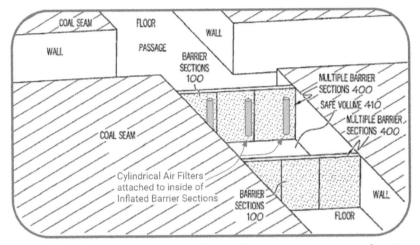

Figure 10.6 Schematic diagram of a wall-to-wall barrier in a passageway of a mine
Source: Author's calculations, based on Figure 4 in US Patent 8,469,781.

Technology Description (Figure 10.7)

How It Works: A software definable transceiver integrated into the cap lamp of
a mining hardhat allows a miner to communicate via voice or text-message
using carrier waves ranging from ultra-low frequency (suitable for sending/
receiving through-the-earth text messages) to ultra-high frequency (suitable for
voice calls). Additionally, a Blackberry-type PDA can be connected to the
hardhat transceiver via Bluetooth so as to enable the miner to receive and view
foreman's reports, maintenance advisories and location information of mine
assets and roaming miners on the PDA display.

10.5.3   Text-Based Similarity

Another approach to explore the impact of the 2006 MINER Act on
innovation in mineral mining safety and health relies on establishing
a link between innovation efforts driven by the MINER Act and patenting activity. Recall that the Act established a competitive funding program administered by National Institute of Occupational Safety and
Health (NIOSH). We analyzed all 105 awarded NIOSH mining safety
contracts to determine which of our 45 k mineral mining patents contained similar language to the awarded NIOSH mining safety contracts.

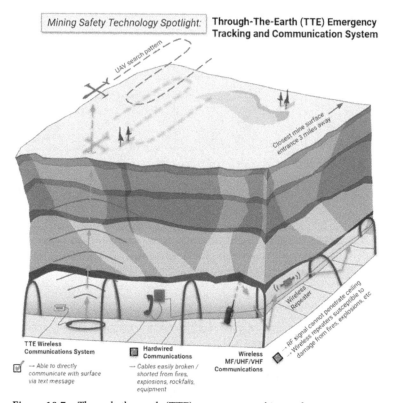

Figure 10.7   Through-the-earth (TTE) emergency tracking and communication system
Source: Author's calculations.

Specifically, we collected the text descriptions from each awarded NIOSH mining safety contract.[22] These descriptions were combined with our dataset of 92 k patent documents from WIPO. Recall that patent documents contain a lot of text describing the invention. Next, we calculated the importance of particular words in each individual document (contract and patent) by using a method called "term frequency, inverse document frequency (TF-IDF)," which is very commonly used for text analysis. This method provides a "content characterization" for each contract and patent based on the text of the document. By looking at the content based on TF-IDF, we calculate the similarity between two documents. The similarity metric we used is called the cosine similarity score.

---

[22]   The data were obtained from the NIOSH-Contract csv file generated from the contract data located at: www.cdc.gov/niosh/mining/researchprogram/contracts/index.html

We posit patents that are more similar to NIOSH contracts (as measured by higher cosine similarity scores) are more likely to be patents directed toward safety technologies as compared those that are less similar (lower cosine similarity scores). To test this hypothesis, we plotted the cosine similarity scores from lowest to highest – least similar to most similar. These histogram plots are constructed using the "kernel density" over the distribution of cosine scores, which we abbreviate as kdensity.

Figure 10.8 shows four kdensity histogram plots. The first and tallest, shown in blue, plots the similarity between NIOSH contracts and all mineral mining patents. It is the tallest of the four plots with most of the scores in the leftmost portion of Figure 10.8. This means most mineral mining patents have a low similarity to the NIOSH mining and safety & health contracts (the mean score is 0.0037). Similar plots are shown for safety patents (brown curve), TTE communications patents (green curve) and refuge chamber patents (orange curve). The overall takeaway is that safety-related mineral mining patents are more similar to NIOSH contracts because the brown curve is to the right of the blue mineral

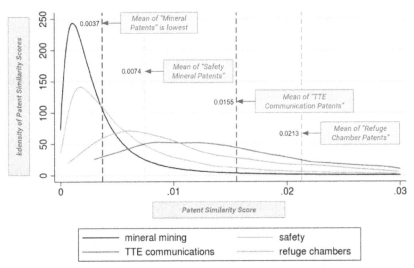

Figure 10.8 Distributions of similarity scores for NIOSH granted patents in four mutually exclusive groups (mineral mining, safety-related mineral mining, TTE communications and refuge chambers)
Source: Author's calculations.

mining patents curve. This substantiates our prediction that patents with higher cosine similarity scores vis-à-vis the NIOSH contracts are more likely to be patents directed toward safety technologies. We also show that both TTE communication and refuge chamber patents have higher cosine similarity suggesting that they are more likely to be safety related as well as within the scope of the MINER Act.

10.5.4   Regression Analysis

Unlike the previous forms of evidence presented, regression analysis allows us to identify a systematic relationship between the passage of the 2006 MINER Act and health outcomes of mineral miners. Up to this point, our results suggest the MINER Act spurred technological innovations as measured by safety-related patents. But the Act also imposed a number of non-technological requirements on mine owners, such as data collection, training and local emergency coordination. Did the technological and nontechnological aspects of the MINER Act have economically impactful results? Specifically, did the MINER Act result in fewer injuries at mines or fewer workdays lost?

To evaluate this question we constructed a mine-level longitudinal dataset covering the years 1995–2014. This means our data contains repeated observations on individual mines over time. The data, which come from the public records of the Mine Safety and Health Administration (MSHA), contain various injury and work loss records for each US mine for various years. For our analysis, we restricted attention to about 2,200 underground mines. The key variables used in the regression models are:

(1) Health Outcome "injuries": any injury of a miner at the worksite (MSHA injury codes 1–6)
(2) Health Outcome "lost work": number of miners with lost workdays (worker production codes 1–4)
(3) MINER Act: an indicator that captures the effect after the passage of the 2006 MINER Act

The results of the regression model are shown in Table 10.1.[23] The regression model holds constant any mine-specific characteristics that

---

[23] The regression model is as follows: $Injuries_{it} = \beta_0 + \beta_1 MINERAct_t + \gamma_t + \mu_i + e_{it}$. The regression model was estimated using STATA's xtpoisson command controlling for unobserved mine-specific effects and using robust standard errors.

Table 10.1 *MINER Act on health outcomes, 1995–2014*

	Injuries		Lost Work	
	Coef.	Std. Err.	Coef.	Std. Err.
MINER Act	–0.709***	(0.079)	–0.705***	(0.095)
Year dummy variables	YES		YES	
Observations	16,463		15,830	

Robust standard errors. Significance: * $p < 0.1$, ** $p < 0.05$, *** $p < 0.01$.
Source: The mining injury data for the years 2000–14 was downloaded from
https://arlweb.msha.gov/OpenGovernmentData/OGIMSHA.asp

are time constant. These characteristics include, for instance, the type of mine (e.g. coal, metal or nonmetal mine), location, different levels of state regulation, management policies and so forth. The regression model also accounts for time-changing factors that affect health outcomes of all mines using year dummy variables (e.g. medical advances that are available to all US miners that may reduce injuries or time away from work for all mines). The key variable, MINER Act, captures the influence of the MINER Act on injury and lost work. In Table 10.1, the variable MINER Act has a negative and highly statistically significant coefficient indicating a systematic decline in injuries and lost workdays following the passage of the MINER Act in 2006. The coefficient sizes are quite similar and suggest about a 51 percent (1-exp(–0.709)) decline in injuries and lost workdays.

10.6 Conclusion

This chapter explores the level and trends in technological innovation for the US mineral mining industry using patent data. Within this industry, we investigate the impact of the **M**ine **I**mprovement and **N**ew **E**mergency **R**esponse (MINER) Act of 2006 on US patenting, innovation and economic outcomes. The analysis offers a general approach for creating curated patent collections related to particular themes or industries (called patent landscaping) and applies it to US mineral mining. Our approach augments the traditional approach used by WIPO to identify global mineral mining patents, which uses patent classifications and Boolean queries with keywords, with machine learning (see Toole et al. (2019) for a technical description). This approach identified 45,572 US mineral mining patents and a subset of 1,311 mine safety-related patents out of an initial set of 91,818.

Our investigation examines four types of empirical evidence on the impacts of the MINER Act. The first type of evidence graphically displays the level and trends in US mineral mining patents as well as the subset of those related to mine safety. Visual inspection shows the growth in safety-related patents is much greater than the growth overall mineral mining patents following the MINER Act. Next we examine two case studies: refuge chambers and "through-the-earth" wireless communications. Both of these illustrate useful technologies that emerged following the MINER Act. Our third form of evidence uses the similarity in the text contained in NIOSH contracts and text contained in US granted patents to assess if patents were more similar to mining safety following the MINER Act. The data analysis supports this conjecture. Finally, we offer regression evidence based on longitudinal data from US underground mines between 1995 and 2014. That analysis finds that the MINER Act is associated with a 51 percent decrease in both injuries and lost workdays. We conclude that the 2006 MINER Act improved technological innovation related to mine safety and resulted in improvements in health outcomes among US miners.

References

Breslin, J. (2010). "One Hundred Years of Federal Mining Safety and Health Research," Information circular 9520, Center for Disease Control and Prevention, US Department of Health and Human Services. https://www.cdc.gov/niosh/mining/UserFiles/works/pdfs/2010–128.pdf

Day, D. T. (1902). "Mineral Resources of the United States, 1901," USGS Publications Warehouse. https://doi.org/10.3133/70175771.

Daly, A., Valacchi, G., & Raffo, J., 2019. *Mining patent data: measuring innovation in the mining industry with patents*, s.l.: WIPO Economics Research Working Paper No. 56.

ILO (2015). "Mining: A hazardous work," www.ilo.org, Safety and health at work, Hazardous Work, https://www.ilo.org/safework/areasofwork/hazardous-work/WCMS_356567/lang–en/index.htm

Ober, J. A (2018). "Mineral Commodity Summaries 2018." Report. Mineral Commodity Summaries. Reston, VA. USGS Publications Warehouse. https://doi.org/10.3133/70194932.

Toole, A. A., J. Forman and A. Tesfayesus (2019). "The Miner Act of 2006: Innovating for Safety and Health in U.S. Mining," USPTO Economic Working Paper No. 2019-01, http://dx.doi.org/10.2139/ssrn.3376091

Yenchek, M., G. Homce, N. Damiano and J. Srednicki (2011). "NIOSH Sponsored Research in Through-the-Earth Communications for Mines: A status report," Conference Paper ·in 2011 IEEE Industry Applications Society Annual Meeting, doi: 10.1109/IAS.2011.6074387

Innovation in the Canadian Mining Sector

BAHARAK COURTNEY DOAGOO, ELIAS COLLETTE, SEAN
MARTINEAU, AMIRA KHADR, MARC NEVILLE AND
MAZAHIR BHAGAT

11.1 Introduction

The mining sector is an important industry to Canadians and the
Canadian economy. The mining industry at large is a significant contributor to prosperity for Canadians as it is responsible for providing
jobs, supporting communities, and attracting investment. In 2015, the
mining industry contributed $56 billion (approximately 4 percent) to
Canada's gross domestic product (GDP).[1] Canada is internationally
recognized as one of the leading mining countries in the world. Some
of the largest Canadian and international mining companies have chosen
to headquarter their companies in Canada as it is one of the largest
producers of minerals and metals. Moreover, almost 60 percent of the
world's publicly listed mining companies are listed on the Toronto Stock
Exchange (TSX) and the TSX-Venture Exchange, which is a stock
exchange for emerging companies. The Government of Canada's department of Natural Resources Canada indicated that for Canada to create
and maintain a competitive advantage, it is essential to ensure the
sustainable development of our minerals. Sustainable development will
in turn help Canada attract investment, avoid project disruptions,
enhance technological advancements, and strengthen domestic and
international partnerships for the benefit of Canadians.[2]

Research and development (R&D), innovation, and commercialization are key challenges for the Canadian mining sector. In 2013,

[1] MAC (2016).
[2] NRCan (2017b).

investment in R&D in the mining sector reached $677 million, surpassing that of the machinery sector, the pharmaceutical sector, and the wood products and paper sector. It should be noted that 2013 was a rather difficult year for the mining industry and the resources invested in R&D may underrepresent the average annual resource allocation. Nevertheless, Canada faces a challenge in facilitating a robust environment to foster innovation and enhance R&D.[3]

Intellectual property assets are also an important component of the Canadian mining sector. Mining is the sixth largest sector in Canada for firms filing patents. Moreover, the number of Canadian firms in the mining sector with more than one type of IP asset (patent, trademark, or industrial design) is high compared to other sectors and comparable to Canadian firms operating in the pharmaceutical and transport equipment industries.[4]

To further promote innovation in the mining sector, the Canada Mining Innovation Council has developed a strategy to stimulate innovation in Canada toward achieving zero waste in mining and mineral processing within 10 to 20 years. This strategy focuses on four key areas: exploration projects, underground mining projects, energy and processing projects, and environmental stewardship projects. The Canada Mining Association states that for the Canadian mining sector "to remain sustainable, progressive and profitable, the industry must innovate." What is noteworthy is that certain technological advances have considerably improved the ability of firms to perform exploratory work while minimizing the impact on the environment, such as GPS surveying, airborne technologies, and down-hole seismic imaging. These technologies have facilitated locating new deposits that would not have been possible using traditional methods.[5]

Patent data is a good starting point for the analysis of the development of new technologies as it provides important information on the specific technical knowledge embedded in the invention. This chapter, resulting from a collaborative effort between the Centre for International Governance Innovation (CIGI) and the Canadian Intellectual Property Office (CIPO), examines the importance of patenting in the mining sector from a Canadian perspective following WIPO's methodology (Daly et al., 2019).

---

[3] MAC (2016).
[4] OECD, STI Micro-Data Lab: Intellectual Property Database and Orbis, version10.2016, Bureau van Dijk, June 2017.
[5] MAC (2016).

The structure of this chapter is as follows: Section 11.2 broadly examines the use of intellectual property in the Canadian mining sector and provides an overview of the latest developments around promoting innovation in the sector based on qualitative interviews, and additional primary and secondary sources.[6] Section 11.3, which is based on EPO PATSTAT data, presents the patent landscape and the Canadian companies leading in terms of patenting activity. Section 11.4 dives deeper into the patent data, exploring patenting activity in the mining sub-sectors, examining collaboration[7] between firms, and identifying industry clusters based on patenting activity. Section 11.5 concludes by highlighting the main findings.

11.2   Intellectual Property in the Mining Sector

Intellectual property rights are generally used to protect intangible assets in the mining industry, as they are in other industries. Mining technologies include a wide range of innovation in exploration, mining methods, and processing, and even "aim to improve worker safety, increase efficiency, and minimize environmental impacts."[8] Due to the range of innovation taking place in the mining sector, there is a mixed approach to the type of intellectual property strategies used. For example, patents can be used for inventions, confidential information for "know how," and copyright for software, plans, and designs.[9]

Even though it is not widespread, some companies within certain segments of the mining industry may apply for patent registration to

---

[6] There were four qualitative interviews conducted by telephone. The participants were asked four general questions: (i) whether intellectual property law was used in the mining industry (i.e. patents, confidential information, industrial design, copyright), (ii) whether there was collaboration between firms, and if so, what type of collaboration (e.g., intellectual property rights or innovation) was the norm, (iii) whether companies in the mining industry have an intellectual property strategy, and, (iv) whether it was common to license intellectual property rights within the mining industry. Note that not all the questions were asked of each participant depending on their responses and other limitations.

[7] For the purpose of this chapter, the term "collaboration" refers to instances where two or more companies and/or individuals related to the mining industry (including but not limited to mining companies, suppliers, universities, technology start-ups) work together for any reason, such as to conduct any activities related to mining, including exploration, extraction, processing, refining, as well as for financing, the development of technologies, or software research and development generally. These relationships can be either formal or informal.

[8] Minalliance (2012), p.11.

[9] Emily Moore, Hatch, Interview December 18, 2017; Anthony de Fazekas, Norton Rose Fulbright Canada, Interview December 20, 2017.

protect inventions or processes.[10] New patented technologies in the mining industry can lead to increased efficiency, productivity, and innovation, from "LED mining headlamps" to "tele-mining" robots.[11] Companies apply for patents for a number of reasons, including to use the subject matter exclusively, to serve as evidence of prior art, to use in negotiations, and to mark clear boundaries of ownership in the case of collaboration.[12] On the other hand, patent registrations may be abandoned for reasons such as low return on investment or that the company has decided to invest in alternative inventions.[13]

Although this report predominantly focuses on data available from patent applications and registrations, patenting is not the only means by which mining companies protect their inventions and processes: an alternative to patenting frequently used in the mining industry is undisclosed or confidential information (trade secrets).[14]

Patenting requires disclosure of the claim of the invention or process, while confidential information can only be protected so long as the information remains confidential.[15] Furthermore, the protection afforded to confidential information is not as robust as patent law. For example, confidential information is not protected by reverse engineering or independent creation. On the other hand, companies can protect a wide range of proprietary information using confidential information. Therefore, the scope of protection offered by confidential information is broader because it can protect inventions and processes that may or may not ordinarily qualify for patent protection.[16] A mining company may, for example, require that the resulting data from the performance of new equipment remain

[10] Carl Weatherell, Canada Mining Innovation Council, Interview December 8, 2017.
[11] Minalliance (2012), pp. 173 and 189.
[12] Emily Moore, Hatch, Interview December 18, 2017. Companies may also publish the details of their invention where they may not have the means to patent it widely. Publishing allows them to stake a claim to use it and also serves as prior art, preventing others from restricting their use of it; see also Brierly and Kondos (2016), pp. 163–168.
[13] Emily Moore, Hatch, Interview December 18, 2017.
[14] The difficulty in understanding how widely trade secrets or confidential information protection is used relates to the fact that they are confidential and therefore gathering first-hand data is not possible unless it is deliberately disclosed. The information provided in this section was made public in case law, publications or interviews. Notably, other types of intellectual property protection such as trademarks, industrial design, and copyright law can also be used in the mining industry but were not the focus of this study.
[15] Hagen et al. (2013), pp. 573–574.
[16] Ibid., p. 575.

confidential.[17] Other uses of confidential information may include extraction methods or exploration data.[18]

In the context of patent-eligible inventions or processes, confidential information can be used where a competitive advantage (and not necessarily the intent to commercialize the invention or process itself) is sought.[19] Notably, determining whether to use patents or confidential information is always based on careful consideration and the overall objectives or strategy of the company.[20] Due to the nature of confidential information, without qualitative research and voluntary admission from those who use it, it's impossible to gauge exactly how widely and for what subject matter confidential information (trade secret) protection is used.

In order to appreciate the preference for certain intellectual property strategies, it is important to understand the environment within which innovation in the mining industry takes place. For example, as Brierly and Kondos (2016) observe, innovation can arise both from within the mining industry and from peripheral industries. It has been suggested that "evolutionary" innovation comes from the mining industry, whereas "revolutionary" innovation comes from secondary sources, such as manufacturers and suppliers of mining equipment, technology, and services (METS), government, and universities. Furthermore over the last few decades, there has been a shift in the Canadian mining sector.[21] Where mining companies traditionally invested in research and development internally, the landscape has shifted more to an outsourcing model, which has led to the development of a broad and growing

---

[17] Note that this can be either a supplier or buyer (Carl Weatherell, Canada Mining Innovation Council, Interview December 8, 2017).

[18] Examples of Canadian cases include *Lac Minerals Ltd. v. International Corona Resources Ltd., [1989]* 2 SCR 574; in this case, a junior and a senior mining company informally discussed a joint venture in relation to a property for exploration. The Court held that a breach of confidence was found when the senior company purchased the property to the exclusion of the junior company after the junior company disclosed confidential information relating to the property. Another example is in *Novawest Resources Inc. v. Anglo American Exploration (Canada) Ltd et al.,* 2006 BCSC 769, where confidential information was used to stake claims by Anglo American on property that was not a part of the area defined in a confidentiality agreement signed with Novawest. The Court held that "the Confidentiality Agreement supplanted any common law duty of confidentiality Anglo owed Novawest with respect to land outside the area of influence. As the claims staked by Anglo are all located outside the area of influence, Anglo acted in conformity with the Confidentiality Agreement and is not in breach of a common law duty of confidentiality," para 91.

[19] Carl Weatherell, Canada Mining Innovation Council, Interview December 8, 2017.

[20] Anthony de Fazekas, Norton Rose Fulbright Canada, Interview December 20, 2017.

[21] Don Duval, NORCAT, Interview December 22, 2017.

METS industry.[22] These newer firms have been developing technologies and sophisticated intellectual property strategies.[23]

Generally, the mining industry was and remains extremely competitive.[24] The competitive environment, coupled with the large magnitude and scale of operations in the mining industry, can create risks associated with investing, developing, and testing new technologies and innovation.[25] Ultimately, this can result in companies becoming proprietary and increasingly cautious about sharing their innovations.

In 2007, the federal, provincial, and territorial Mines Ministers met and "agreed to press forward in key areas to support the competitiveness of the mining sector."[26] In doing so, they "endorsed" the creation of the Canada Mining Innovation Council (CMIC). CMIC's mandate was to help the industry develop a strategy to increase research and innovation in the mining industry.[27]

In 2008, as part of their mandate, CMIC published the *Pan-Canadian Mining Research and Innovation Strategy*, setting the stage for collaboration and innovation systems within the industry.[28] The report also stated:

> Canada's mining and mineral processing sector faces key challenges related to R&D, innovation, and commercialization. There is a need for technological solutions to advance sustainable mining, meet environmental standards and regulations, reduce costs, increase the value added, and protect the health and safety of workers. There is a lack of efficient and cost-effective access to R&D capacity in Canada and globally. There are shortages of necessary engineers and scientists that are not being matched by increasing enrolment in most university mining departments.

[22] Ibid. Although there is a shift, some large mining companies continue to follow the internal research and development model.

[23] Ibid. Where most innovations used to be kept confidential, intellectual property strategies were not as prevalent other than to keep innovations secret. Newer firms are now becoming more thoughtful and strategic about their intellectual property strategies.

[24] KPMG LLP et al. (2017), p. 4. For example, in research, see Canada Mining Innovation Council (2008), "There have been a number of discrete initiatives over the years at both the regional and national level to encourage research collaboration. Yet today there remains fragmentation in research effort and competition, rather than collaboration in seeking research funding," p. 8; Brierly and Kondos (2016) suggest that while strategic partnerships or collaborations between "mining companies and R&D organizations" can be beneficial in several ways, "collaborations among mining companies, however, are only feasible in non-competitive spaces," pp. 171–172.

[25] Brierly and Kondos (2016), p. 170.

[26] Canada Mining Innovation Council (2008), p. 3.

[27] Ibid.

[28] Ibid., p. 1.

Furthermore, Canada is not fully capturing the commercial benefits of R&D for domestic and international markets.[29]

Since then, CMIC has been championing an "open innovation" approach to the development of technology platforms and developing consortiums involving various segments within the industry.[30] Notably, the term "open innovation" is industry and context specific. This can be a nuanced term as the definition and boundaries associated with "open" and "sharing" can vary among stakeholders.[31] It may be that in a consortium model, the intellectual property is still owned by the entity that brought it in but is open to being shared with project participants. Belonging to the consortium in some cases may give member companies the ability to access and share new inventions or innovations on a preferred royalty basis or even royalty free.[32] For the purpose of this analysis, the term "open" may be interchangeable with collaborative but should not be confused with "free."

However, despite these efforts, the culture of the mining industry has remained a challenge for collaboration in this industry. For example, "Openness to Sharing and Intellectual Property Considerations" was identified as one of the eight barriers in a report based on stakeholder inputs at the Energy and Mines Ministers' Conference in 2017:

> [G]iven the competitive nature of the mining sector, there is a lack of transparency and a closed culture of sharing information, including valuable intellectual property (IP), between industry and the supporting stakeholder groups. This results in a preference to develop ideas in-house or with a small group of partners, rather than sharing information and cross-pollinating ideas across the broader mining ecosystem.[33]

Furthermore, based on qualitative research carried out on the Canadian mining industry in 2016, it was revealed that companies "are also very reluctant to trust each other, since the concept of formalized collaboration is still new and constituents are protective of their intellectual property (IP) and competitive advantage" and that "[f]or many companies, the concept of collaboration simply isn't in their DNA."[34] As previously mentioned, the environment in which the mining industry operates

---

[29] Ibid., p. 8.
[30] Carl Weatherell, Canada Mining Innovation Council, Interview December 8, 2017.
[31] Don Duval, NORCAT, Interview December 22, 2017.
[32] Emily Moore, Hatch, Interview December 18, 2017.
[33] KPMG LLP et al. (2017), p. 4.
[34] Monitor Deloitte et al. (2016), p. 11.

is very competitive and there are some risks associated with the development of new technologies. While collaboration may seem like an interesting avenue, it is not surprising that some companies remain cautious or reluctant.

Due to the lack of evidence and indicators used to measure collaborative initiatives in this sector, there's a large variance in the value of the intellectual property in question from the perspective of companies. As more collaboration occurs, one would expect the perceived values to converge. Despite this, there have been initiatives that demonstrate the shift that mining and related extractive industries have been making toward collaboration.[35]

Many firms now desire to move toward riskier initiatives and breakthroughs or disruptive innovation and, due to the lack of internal capacity, are increasingly collaborating with external parties. This strategy is aligned with emerging evidence that such collaborations will enable them to accelerate innovation and be more competitive as opposed to firms remaining internally focused.[36] In line with this idea, the Government of Canada proposed a new intellectual property strategy in Budget 2018 that will enable better access to shared intellectual property so that small and medium-sized enterprises (SMEs) can grow their business.[37]

The following section presents the approach taken in this chapter to use patents as a metric of innovation.

11.3   Patented Inventions in the Mining Sector

Measuring innovation is a difficult task. Currently, a universal indicator for measuring innovative activities does not exist, as it is difficult to capture all of the elements that comprise the innovation process. However, patenting activity has been identified as a good proxy for measuring innovative activities. It was noted in the report, "*The Use of Intellectual Property Rights and Innovation by Manufacturing Firms in Canada,*" that world-first innovators patent more frequently and firms that patent infrequently tend to be imitators.[38] In addition, the study finds that firms that protect their intellectual property are more likely to increase their profits than those that do not. Moreover, SMEs that patent

---

[35] Canada Mining Innovation Council (2017) in the context of innovation; PWC (2017) in the context of financing, pp. 12–13.
[36] WEF (2015).
[37] Government of Canada (2018).
[38] Hanel (2008).

are more likely to be high-growth firms and are more likely to export, which is important for success.[39] These conclusions are reinforced by a Canadian study that noted that firms that are aggressive innovators, meaning that they introduced a radically new product that involves patent protection, have higher profits.[40] Finally, while some inventions are not patented, patents are obtained for almost all economically and historically significant inventions.[41]

Patent data, like most data sets, does have limitations. While patents measure the flow of new ideas, they only partially measure innovation for three important reasons: patents do not include non-patented innovations (e.g., trade secrets), not all patents result in commercialization, and many patents are strategic in nature.[42] It is important to understand that patent data will not provide a representation of innovation in the mining sector in its entirety, but rather a good approximation of the overall level of inventive activity.

This section takes a more in-depth look at the Canadian contribution to the patent landscape using patent families as the primary metric. Overall, Canadian patenting activity in the mining industry increased 159 percent between 1990 and 2014. As seen in Figure 11.1, in the early

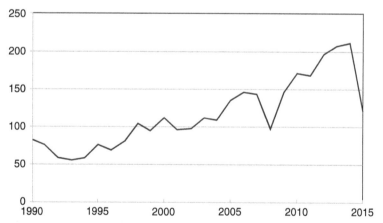

Figure 11.1   Canadian patenting activity in the mining sector between 1990 and 2015
Source: Author's calculations.

[39] ISED et al. (2014).
[40] Baldwin and Gellatly (2006).
[41] Dernis et al. (2001).
[42] Kleinknecht et al. (2002).

1990s, patent families filed by Canadian applicants, hereinafter referred to as "assignees," actually decreased before climbing in 1995. The increasing trend gradually continued until 2004, although with some degree of fluctuation over the years, before experiencing a significant uptick in 2005. In 2008, around the time of the Great Recession, patent families filed decreased considerably; however in 2009, those losses were negated as filing activity picked up and continued to grow until 2015. Although the drop in patenting activity in 2015 is generally consistent with slumping industry performance worldwide driven by lower oil and natural resource prices, it may also be partially due to data truncation.

In order to gain a better understanding of Canada's business and institutional strengths in relation to patenting in the mining sector, the following analysis examines the filing tendencies for the most active mining firms and METS. Note that the assignee name(s) on a patent are not always updated to the most recent entity assigned to the patent. Should a merger or takeover occur, for example, the decision is up to the acquiring firm about whether to update the information contained on the patent. As such, this analysis does not update the names of the patent assignees to reflect mergers and acquisitions, but rather maintains the information as presented in the data. For this reason, Inco Ltd., for example, still appears as the patent assignee in our dataset although it was acquired by a foreign company over a decade ago. Keeping the names as they appear on the patent documents is a good opportunity to show how some of the top companies performed prior to being acquired.

In Figure 11.2, we see that many of the leading Canadian patent filers, including Tesco, Shell, Imperial Oil, and Petro Canada are companies active primarily in the oil and gas field. Considering the methodology used to extract the patent data for this analysis follows the same approach used in the other chapters of this book and explicitly excludes oil and gas patents, this finding suggests that these companies are actively patenting in areas outside of their core business as the inventions being protected apply to many industry sectors that use similar instruments and practices. Notably, the patent families associated with these mining firms and METS are predominantly in the exploration and environmental categories. With respect to companies that operate primarily in the mining sector, Inco Ltd., the third-ranked company in terms of quantity of patent families filed, was formerly the world's leading producer of nickel. The Toronto-based company now operates as a subsidiary of Vale Canada Ltd. following its acquisition by the Brazilian mining company Vale in

Top Canadian Mining Firms & METS	Primary Category	Secondary Category
Tesco Corporation (CA)	Exploration	Mining
Shell Canada Energy (CA)	Exploration	Environmental
Inco Limited (CA)	Refining	Exploration
Imperial Oil Resources Limited (CA)	Environmental	Exploration
Alcan International Limited (CA)	Refining	Environmental
Packers Plus Energy Services Incorporated (CA)	Exploration	Mining
Hatch Limited (CA)	Refining	Environmental
Petro Canada Incorporated (CA)	Environmental	Exploration
Schlumberger Canada Limited (CA)	Exploration	Mining
Syncrude Canada Limited (CA)	Environmental	Processing
Natural Resources Canada (CA)	Mining	Refining
Noranda Incorporated (CA)	Refining	Exploration
University of British Columbia (CA)	Refining	Environmental
XAct Dowhole Telemetry Incorporated (CA)	Exploration	Environmental
Cominco Engineering Services Limited (CA)	Refining	Environmental
McCoy Corporation (CA)	Exploration	Mining/Transport
Placer Dome Incorporated (CA)	Refining	Mining
Precision Drilling Corporation (CA)	Exploration	Environmental
Cenovus Energy Incorporated (CA)	Exploration	Environmental
Rio Tinto Alcan International Limited (CA)	Refining	Environmental
Stream-Flo Industries Limited (CA)	Exploration	Mining
Suncor Energy Incorporated (CA)	Environmental	Exploration
Atlas Copco Canada Incorporated (CA)	Exploration	Mining
Sherritt International Corporation (CA)	Refining	Environmental
Canadian Downhole Drill Systems Incorporated (CA)	Exploration	Mining

Figure 11.2   Top Canadian mining firms and METS and their associated mining sector category, 1990-2015
Source: Author's calculations.

2006.[43] Inco's patent families are predominantly tagged to the refining category, but also to the exploration category. Alcan, the fifth-ranked mining company and one of the world's largest aluminum manufacturers, is also a significant patenting entity. In 2007, the company was acquired by Australian-British multinational Rio Tinto, and was subsequently renamed Rio Tinto Alcan. Also among the top Canadian filers in this field are two public entities: the Government of Canada's Department of Natural Resources and the University of British Columbia.

Understanding in which countries the leading Canadian mining firms and METS are seeking protection provides an indication as to what markets they see as strategic priorities. However, examining priority country shares for the top applicants shows a strong bias by companies to file first in countries in which they operate. Canadian companies do

---
[43] The Canadian Encyclopedia (2006).

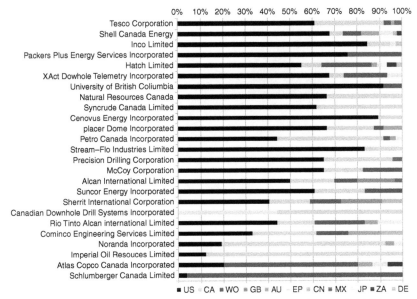

Figure 11.3   Priority country share for top Canadian mining firms and METS
Source: Author's calculations.

have a tendency to file predominantly in the United States, likely due to its large market size and the presence of competitors working in similar fields. In Figure 11.3, all of the leading Canadian mining firms and METS have priority filings in the United States.

Overall, the observed behaviour in priority patent family filings by the top Canadian mining firms and METS is consistent with the filing tendencies for all Canadian assignees. The United States and Canada account for more than 80 percent of all countries where patents are filed first. Patent Cooperation Treaty (PCT) patent families, represented by the WO country code, account for approximately 8 percent of all priority country filings. Other jurisdictions identified in Figure 11.4 that are targeted by Canadian assignees, but to a significantly lower degree, include the European Patent Office (EP), Great Britain (GB), Mexico (MX), Japan (JP), South Africa (ZA), and Germany (DE). Also highlighted is the distribution for other participating countries in this publication, specifically, Australia (AU), China (CN), Brazil (BR), Colombia (CO), and Chile (CL).

Patenting activity is an important indicator of innovation within an industry and can further explain the directions and types of technologies

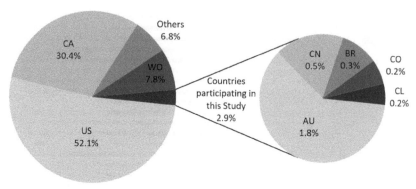

Figure 11.4 Priority country share for all Canadian mining firms and METS
Source: Author's calculations.

being created. The patent landscape map in Figure 11.5 is an interesting way to visualize patent data. The map is generated by an algorithm that uses keywords from patent documentation to cluster patent families according to shared terminology. The patent families are organized based on common themes and are grouped as "contours" on the map to identify areas of high and low patenting activity. The "snow-capped" peaks in white represent the highest concentrations of patented inventions, and each peak is labelled with key terms that tie the common themes together. Shorter distances between peaks indicate that the patented inventions they represent share more commonalities relative to those that are further apart. The distance between keywords helps to illustrate their relationship to one another. Keywords that are located closer together may refer to similar systems or technologies, whereas keywords located further apart have less of a relationship.

As noted previously, the use of the keywords presented in the map along with the most common International Patent Classification (IPC) codes found in the patents, allows for the identification of various technological areas under development in the sector. Note that many keywords are ubiquitous and would also be found in other industries and technologies. For this reason, the mining-specific keywords found in the landscape map are more useful. More widely used keywords could then be used to further refine the patent search. The opaque or less-visible keywords would provide a second level of detail. The intention is to facilitate the exploration of patent data for those interested in the technology or industry. Figure 11.5 shows that the highest concentration of patents in this Canadian dataset relates to patents comprising keywords

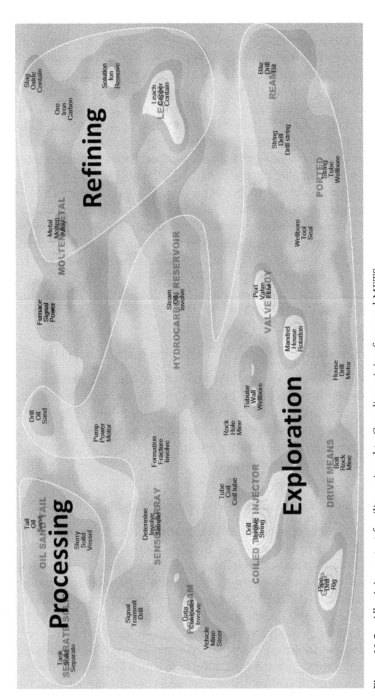

Figure 11.5 All mining patent families assigned to Canadian mining firms and METS

Source: Author's calculations.

such as "drill, involve, string," "pipe, drill, rig," "data, computer, involve," "mandrel, house, rotation," "tubular, wall, wellbore," "solution, ion, remove," "leach, copper, contain," and "port, valve, flow." The ocean separating the islands highlights technological areas of patenting activity that are very different from each other. The top IPC in this dataset is predominantly E21B (earth or rock drilling), which, not surprisingly, is tagged to the exploration mining category. Other IPCs found in the map include C22B (production or refining of metals) and B01D (separation) but to a much lesser extent. To facilitate a deeper understanding of specific mining industry subsectors, specific mining categories have been highlighted in yellow. The size of the grouping is representative of the breadth of patent families tied to a specific category. Groupings with multiple snow-capped peaks are indicative of categories with a larger number of patent families. In this case, the exploration category grouping also includes patent families that are categorized to the other mining sector categories as one patent family can be associated with many IPC codes.

Section 11.4 of this chapter examines patenting activity in the mining sector categories in more detail.

11.4   Patented Inventions in the Mining Sector Categories

The following section contains three subsections. The first presents the filing trends by mining category and highlights the mining categories in which the Canadian mining sector is relatively specialized. The second includes an analysis of collaborations that took place in specific mining categories and finally, the third presents a cluster analysis showing patenting intensity by provinces.

11.4.1   Specialization of the Canadian Mining Sector

Now that a high level overview of the patenting activity by Canadian assignees in the mining sector has been presented, this section dives deeper into the data and examines the categories of the mining sector, namely, and in no particular order, exploration, automation, mining, transport, refining, blasting, environmental, processing, and metallurgy. As explained in Chapter 2, the patent family data has been categorized according to designated sectors of activity in the mining industry.

Examining the trend in patent family filings for each of the mining categories can provide a better indication as to which ones are responsible for higher levels of inventive activity. It comes as no surprise that the

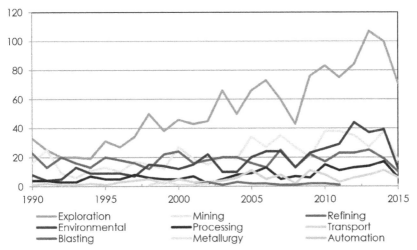

Figure 11.6   Canadian patenting activity by mining category between 1990 and 2015
Source: Author's calculations.

exploration category is tagged to the most patent families considering most of the leading Canadian assignees are involved in this field. The trend in patenting activity in this category follows very closely the trend for all categories combined in Figure 11.1. Overall, the trends observed for each of the categories in Figure 11.6 seem generally to follow similar growth patterns over time, but the magnitude of the growth does vary.

In order to gain a better understanding of Canada's performance in terms of patenting activity in the mining sector, we use the Relative Specialization Index (RSI) (additional detail in Annex). The measure uses patenting intensity to allow for industries to be compared between countries of different sizes on a similar basis. The RSI index provides a ratio of each country's share of patent families within the mining sector as a share of the country's total patent families produced within a given timeframe. In categories where the value is greater than zero, Canada is seen to be relatively specialized compared to the rest of the world. Figure 11.7 reveals that Canadian assignees are relatively specialized in the exploration, blasting and processing categories.

Figure 11.8 represents a more focused patent landscape map, created to determine the type of technologies that have been protected. This provides a deeper understanding of patenting activity within the exploration category and identifies the areas in which Canadian assignees are specialized. As noted previously, the use of the keywords presented in the

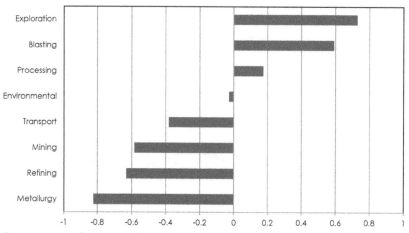

Figure 11.7   Relative Specialization Index (RSI)
Note: The automation subcategory has been removed from the RSI figure because
Canada holds only one patent family tagged to this category. The RSI figure is based on
patent family data used by WIPO rather than INPADOC patent families that are used
throughout this Canadian section of the chapter.
Source: Author's calculations.

map along with the most common IPCs found in the patents allows for
the identification of various technological areas under development in
this category.

In the exploration category, 1,385 patent families were identified, with the
prominent keywords being: "data, computer, base," "transmit, signal, transmitter," "reservoir, production, injection," and "pipe, handle, rig." These
keywords are not particularly mining-specific and neither are the second-
level keywords. The use of these keywords with the appropriate IPCs would
be required to identify mining patents related to this category. The IPCs
classified to the exploration category as identified in the methodology
section (WIPO section) include predominately E21B (earth or rock drilling),
and others such as C09 K (materials for applications not otherwise provided
for), G01 V (geophysics; gravitational measurements; detecting masses or
objects), and G01 N (investigating or analysing materials by determining
their chemical or physical properties), but to a much lesser extent.

Inventions around the "data, computer and base" as well as the "transmit, digital and transmitter" snow-capped peaks are related to data
transmitting and gathering methods and systems. Digital technologies,
now more affordable and available, are used to improve productivity in

the mining sector.[44] The snow-capped peaks characterized by "pipe, handle and rig" and "reservoir, production and injection" are related to technologies aimed at improving pipe handling and methods for lifting fluids. These peaks are related to drilling and extraction techniques often applicable to both the oil and gas and the mineral mining industry.

The red dots in Figure 11.8 represent patent families involving more than one company, hereinafter referred to as "collaborations." While these collaborations are scattered throughout the map, they seem to be concentrated around the "reservoir, production and injection" and "data, computer and base" peaks. The fact that there are a number of collaborations further away from these peaks could be an indication that the collaborative work is occurring outside of the main areas of research that many companies are involved in.

11.4.2   Analysis of Collaborations

As indicated in Section 11.2, there has been a shift in the mining sector recently, as the sector moves toward more collaboration. Patent data is one source of information that can be used to get an idea of the level of collaborative activity between companies in this sector. The increasing trend in the number of patent families involving two or more companies as observed in Figure 11.9 confirms the culture shift that the industry is said to be experiencing. The significant number of collaborations from 2013 onward is noteworthy. The increase in collaborations over the last few years may be a result of companies pooling resources to collectively pursue similar objectives during a downturn in the sector. Optimizing research efficiency and innovation potential through collaboration was one of five strategic goals of the Pan-Canadian Mining Research and Innovation Strategy in 2008 to help better maximize the limited pool of funding accessible.[45]

Figure 11.9 breaks down the number of patent families involving collaborations from 1990–2015 by category and highlights their share as a percentage of all patent families filed annually. Patent activity in the exploration category is an area where Canadians assignees who are collaborating, regularly seek protection. The environmental, mining, and refining categories are other categories involving collaborations where protection is sought, but to a lesser extent. Although on average between 1990 and 2015 patent families involving collaborations represent 4 percent

---

[44] Durrant-Whyte et al. (2015).
[45] NRCan (2008).

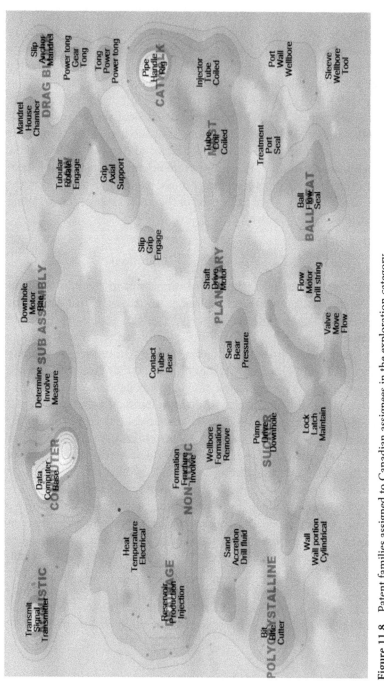

Figure 11.8 Patent families assigned to Canadian assignees in the exploration category

Source: Author's calculations.

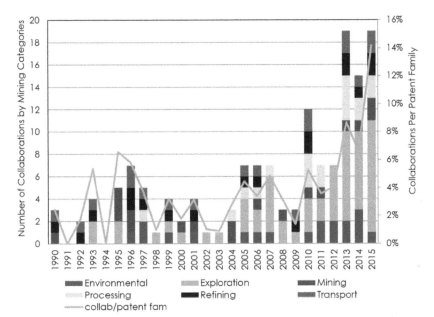

Figure 11.9   Collaborations and their distribution by mining sector category between 1990 and 2015

Note: The patent family counts represented by the trend line will not equal the sum of collaborations for all categories since some patent families are included in more than one category.

of the total number of patent families, we notice that collaborations are representing a growing share of patent families in more recent years.

Increases in innovation in the area of exploration may partially be attributed to incentives offered by the Canadian federal and provincial governments to attract investment in mining, including the Canadian Exploration Expense Claims (CEE) and Mineral Exploration Tax Credit (METC).[46] Exploration activities are both costly and risky and it has been suggested that incentives such as METC are the key to financing these activities and to sharing knowledge, especially where junior mining companies are concerned.[47]

[46] NRCan (2017a); FIN (2017); NRCan (2013); MAC (2008).

[47] NRCan (2013). For example, this report suggests that the Canadian mining landscape is "unique" in that junior companies account for the majority of exploration activities "and were the main drivers of increased investment in exploration and deposit appraisal between 2004 and 2008." It was suggested the focus of these junior companies is new explorations "greenfield" rather than existing or older ones.

As the Prospectors & Developers Association of Canada Report suggests:

> Canada's unique mining ecosystem is largely comprised of thousands of small-to-medium enterprises.
>
> . . .
>
> This subcontracting of risk from big mining companies to entrepreneurial small businesses is part of the unique system that keeps Canada's mining pipeline full.
>
> Unlike large companies, however, juniors cannot rely on revenues or on bank loans for financing – their development sites are not yet proven, and they are working with a potential for profit, not the certainty of one. As such, they rely heavily on equity investors who must weigh the possibility of high reward against the risk that nothing valuable may be found.
>
> **The METC & flow-through shares system is globally unique.**
>
> No other country has such a sophisticated, forward-thinking policy infrastructure in place to encourage investments in grassroots mining exploration, which in turn sustains its mining industry. The METC and flow-through shares system only applies to the grassroots exploration expenditures that junior companies undertake, and acts as an investment incentive.[48]

While it is not easy to quantify the number of collaborations between companies within the mining industry without conducting extensive empirical research, patent data may capture some relevant information about these collaborations as they relate to patentable subject matter. Collaboration maps are useful for visualizing patent data and facilitating the identification of collaborations. These maps are not only used to identify which companies are working together but can also be used to examine the data more closely to extract potentially valuable insights.

In the collaboration map in Figure 11.10, each yellow dot represents a patent family and the dots linking two applicants indicate that they are named as joint applicants on a patent application. This collaboration map highlights joint work between two of the top applicants in the Canadian mining sector, Inco Ltd. and Noranda Inc., before both were acquired by other companies. These two companies are associated with patent families categorised in multiple mining categories, but the patent family to which they are jointly assigned in this collaboration map is tied to the exploration category. These two companies also collaborated with other companies that patented in other mining categories. This demonstrates

---

[48] PDAC (2016).

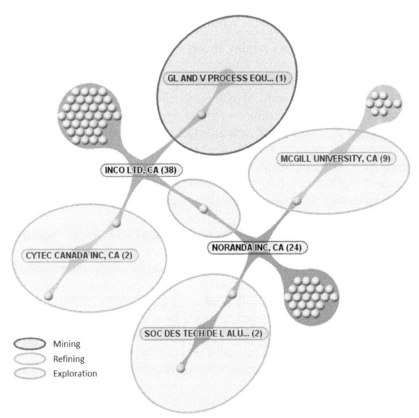

GL AND V PROCESS EQU... (1)

MCGILL UNIVERSITY, CA (9)

INCO LTD, CA (38)

CYTEC CANADA INC, CA (2)

NORANDA INC, CA (24)

SOC DES TECH DE L ALU... (2)

Mining
Refining
Exploration

Figure 11.10 Collaboration map involving mining firms and METS
Source: Author's calculations.

how these two large companies were actively working in various areas of the mining sector. Interestingly, Noranda also collaborated with McGill University, which is assigned to patent families linked to the environmental and refining categories. When two or more entities work together, they each bring to the table a specialization that, when combined, can lead to more advanced ideas if the proper synergies exist. In the case of Noranda Inc. and Inco Ltd., these two companies have leveraged their collaborative work and established a commercial agreement to refine copper anodes.[49]

---

[49] Marketwired (2005).

11.4.3   Cluster Analysis

In Figure 11.11, Canada's mining clusters are presented in a geographic map highlighting the active mining sites. Comparing this map to the geographic map in Figure 11.12, which highlights clusters based on the areas with a concentration of patent families identified by using the company address information on patents, we can observe some similarities in areas of activity based primarily in Canada's major cities as well as in more remote regions located closer to the mining sites. There are many benefits for firms in the same industry to cluster together, including increased productivity, faster innovation through collaborative research, and the creation of small businesses to cater to the niche needs of this industry.

The size of the clusters is also interesting. There are 12 business clusters, comprised of 10 or more companies, which emerge as key areas leading innovation in the Canadian mining sector. Nevertheless, there also appears to be a significant amount of patenting activity from individual companies outside of the clusters, as identified by the red dots overlaid on the map. The provinces have been color coded in different shades of blue, with provinces that have higher patent levels being darker. Most of the companies that have filed patent families in the mining field are located in Calgary, the largest of the clusters having 368 companies. This is not surprising considering the concentration of oil and gas companies in this area and the similarities in technologies used by the two industries.

Other cities with large clusters include Edmonton (127 companies), Toronto (123 companies), Vancouver (86 companies), and Montreal (71 companies). The fact that these clusters are major hubs of innovative activity is no surprise given that some of the largest international and Canadian mining firms and METS are headquartered or have a significant presence in these cities. For instance, Toronto, the second-largest cluster based on the number of patenting entities, includes companies such as Barrick Gold Corporation, Vale, and Glencore. It is also not surprising to find such large companies in this city, as it is the global center for mining finance. Toronto is also home to several dozen mining company head offices, as well as several hundred mining suppliers, consulting firms, and service providers.[50]

---

[50] MAC (2016).

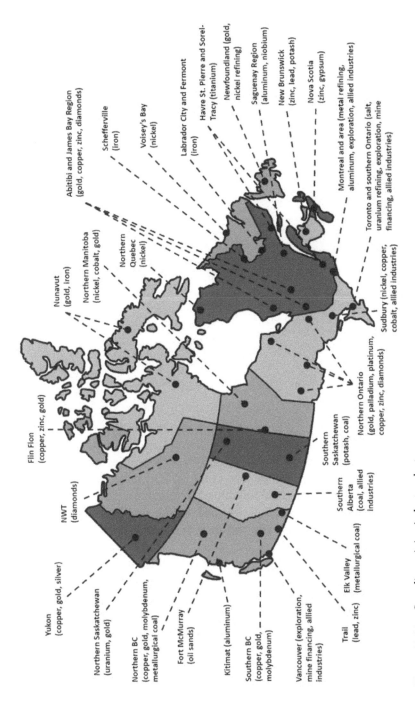

Figure 11.11 Canadian mining industry clusters

Source: The Mining Association of Canada – Facts & Figures 2016.

Abitibi and James Bay Region
(gold, copper, zinc, diamonds)

Schefferville
(iron)

Voisey's Bay
(nickel)

Labrador City and Fermont
(iron)

Havre St. Pierre and Sorel-
Tracy (titanium)

Newfoundland (gold,
nickel refining)

Saguenay Region
(aluminum, niobium)

New Brunswick
(zinc, lead, potash)

Nova Scotia
(zinc, gypsum)

Montreal and area (metal refining,
aluminum, exploration, allied industries)

Toronto and southern Ontario (salt,
uranium refining, exploration, mine
financing, allied industries)

Sudbury (nickel, copper,
cobalt, allied industries)

Nunavut
(gold, iron)

Northern Manitoba
(nickel, cobalt, gold)

Northern
Quebec
(nickel)

Flin Flon
(copper, zinc, gold)

NWT
(diamonds)

Northern Ontario
(gold, palladium, platinum,
copper, zinc, diamonds)

Southern
Saskatchewan
(potash, coal)

Southern
Alberta
(coal, allied
industries)

Yukon
(copper, gold, silver)

Northern Saskatchewan
(uranium, gold)

Northern BC
(copper, gold, molybdenum,
metallurgical coal)

Fort McMurray
(oil sands)

Kitimat (aluminum)

Southern BC
(copper, gold,
molybdenum)

Vancouver (exploration,
mine financing, allied
industries)

Trail
(lead, zinc)

Elk Valley (metallurgical coal)

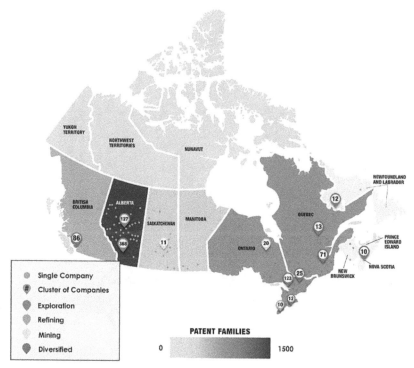

Figure 11.12   Geographical clusters of inventive activity in Canada
Source: Author's calculations.

Interestingly, the geographical map in Figure 11.12 can also be used to highlight centers of expertise based on clusters of companies specializing in a particular category of mining. For example, Vancouver is described as the global center of expertise for mineral exploration, with approximately 700 exploration companies located in the province of British Columbia. Among the many companies in Vancouver, Goldcorp and Teck Resources Ltd. are two of the largest players. Nevertheless, the patent families filed by Canadian companies in this city are tagged to a variety of categories including exploration. Interestingly, patent families linked to the exploration category are also present in other areas beyond the province of British Columbia, such as Calgary and Edmonton. Calgary, although primarily specialized in exploration, also has the highest number of patent families linked to the processing category of all the Canadian clusters; a category in which Canada has a specialization as per the RSI in Figure 11.7.

11.5 Conclusion

In this analysis, we have investigated patenting activity by Canadian mining firms and METS. The information presented provides a view of the innovative activity taking place in this sector. It provides a starting point for diving deeper into the patented inventions of the leading players and for exploring the data more closely. WIPO's methodology for categorizing mining sector patents has facilitated a more thorough analysis to identify areas where Canada is relatively specialized. Having an understanding of Canadian technological strengths helps policymakers develop targeted policies that can be designed to increase our performance in specific fields with the ultimate objective of advancing innovation. Collaboration is another useful indicator of innovation in the mining sector used in this analysis.

Section 11.2 of this chapter provides an overview of the mining industry as it relates to the use of intellectual property rights to protect various forms of innovation. It also highlights a general shift in culture toward collaboration despite the nature of the mining industry and the fact that companies remain protective of their intellectual property rights. Overall, it seems that the industry is moving toward a more open environment and the trends observed in Section 11.4 corroborate this recent movement of increased collaborative activity, especially from 2010 onward.

The analysis in this chapter also uses patent landscape maps and geographic maps to present a more holistic understanding of innovation in the Canadian mining sector. Keywords presented in the landscape maps, along with the most common IPCs found in the patents, allow for the identification of specific inventions in the technological areas. Geographic maps are used to locate companies that patent, and to determine if they are in locations where there is a cluster of companies. Overall, this analysis presents the value obtained from examining patent data to extend our understanding of innovative activity within the industry.

As environmental standards and regulations continue to increase, the challenge for companies operating in this sector to develop new technological solutions to advance sustainable mining becomes more important. Patent data is a good source of information to better understand the innovative activity that is occurring. The information extracted from patent data is an important resource available to policymakers and companies for use in decision-making.

ANNEX

Methodology

To conduct the Canadian-focused analysis from this chapter, a Canadian subset was created from the WIPO Mining Database. The dataset consists of 3,026 INPADOC patent families with a Canadian assignee that filed a patent between 1990 and 2015. The methodology used in this chapter deviates slightly from the one used more broadly in Daly et al. (2019) due to the availability of different tools. As such, the members of a patent family were not combined using the first family ID but rather Clarivate's Derwent Innovation INPADOC Family ID. Utility models and design patents were removed from the dataset, considering that CIPO does not offer utility models and because Canadian industrial design data is not included in the European Patent Office (EPO) PATSTAT database which was used to generate the data for this report.

The Clarivate's Derwent Innovation database was also used to create the patent landscape maps in this chapter. The approach taken to produce these maps involved a matching exercise to link the patent families extracted from the EPO PATSTAT database to the Derwent Innovation database. Once this exercise was completed, the publication numbers associated with the Derwent Innovation patent families were then loaded into the Derwent Innovation database to produce the landscape maps.

In order to better understand a country's strengths in each mining category, the Relative Specialization Index (RSI) was used. To ensure consistency throughout this chapter, the Canadian patent family data used to calculate the RSI is based on the methodology using EPO PATSTAT data to construct patent families using first family ID.

The formula used to calculate the RSI is as follows:

Numerator

The sum of patent families by Canadian assignees in a specific mining category is divided by the sum of patent families in the world in the same mining category.

Denominator

The sum of patent families by Canadian assignees in the mining dataset (all mining categories) divided by the sum of patent families for the world in the mining dataset (all mining categories).

$$RSI = ln\left[\left(\sum_{1990}^{2015}P_{Can,MiningCat} \middle/ \sum 1990^{2015}P_{World,MiningCat}\right)\middle/ \left(\sum_{1990}^{2015}P_{Can,Mining} \middle/ \sum 1990^{2015}P_{World,Mining}\right)\right]$$

, where P represents patent families.

An RSI greater than 0 suggests that Canadian assignees have a relative specialization in the particular mining category, while an RSI lower than 1 suggests the opposite. An RSI equal to 0 indicates that an economy's share of patents in that particular mining category equals its share in all mining categories.

Interviews

Anthony de Fazekas, Norton Rose Fulbright Canada, Interview December 20, 2017.

Don Duval, NORCAT, Interview December 22, 2017.

Emily Moore, Hatch, Interview December 18, 2017.

Carl Weatherell, Canada Mining Innovation Council, Interview December 8, 2017.

References

Baldwin, J. R., and Gellatly, G. (2006). Innovation Capabilities: The knowledge capital behind the survival and growth of firms. The Canadian Economy in Transition Research Paper Series, Statistics Canada.

Brierly, C. L. and P. D. Kondos (2016). Metallurgical Processing Innovations: Intellectual property perspectives and management. In Vaikuntam, I. L., Raja, R. and Ramachandra, V. (eds.). *Innovative Process Development in Metallurgical Industry: Concept to Commission.* Switzerland: Springer.

Bureau van Dijk (2017). ORBIS, version 10.2016, June 2017.

Canada Mining Innovation Council (2017). Clean Resources Supercluster. http://cmic-ccim.org/powering-clean-growth-mining-innovation

Canada Mining Innovation Council (2008). The Pan-Canadian Mining Research and Innovation Strategy: Strengthening the competitiveness of a responsible Canadian mining industry through excellence in research, innovation and commercialization. A Report to Federal, Provincial and Territorial Mines Ministers From the Canadian Mining Innovation Council. www.nrcan.gc.ca/sites/www.nrcan.gc.ca/files/mineralsmetals/pdf/mms-smm/poli-poli/col-col/2008/cmic-eng.pdf.

Daly, A., Valacchi, G., & Raffo, J., 2019. *Mining patent data: measuring innovation in the mining industry with patents.* WIPO Economics Research Working Paper No. 56.

Dernis, H., Guellec, D., and van Pottelsberghe, B. (2001). Using patent counts for cross-country comparisons of technology output. *STI Review*, 27, 129–146. www.researchgate.net/publication/312985498_Using_ patent_ counts_for_cross-country_comparisons_of_technology_output

Durrant-Whyte,H., Geraghty, R., Pujol, F. and Sellschop, R. (2015). How digital innovation can improve mining productivity. McKinsey & Company. www.mckinsey.com/industries/metals-and-mining/our-insights/how-digital-innovation-can-improve-mining-productivity

FIN (2017). Backgrounder: Mineral Exploration Tax Credit for Flow-Through Share Investors. Department of Finance Canada. www.canada.ca/en/ department-finance/news/2017/03/backgrounder_mineralexplorationtax creditforflow-throughshareinve0.html

Government of Canada (2018). Budget 2018: Equality and Growth for a Strong Middle Class. www.budget.gc.ca/2018/docs/plan/budget-2018-en.pdf

Hagen, Greg, Cameron Hutchison, David Lametti, Graham Reynolds, Teresa Scassa, and Margaret Ann Wilkinson (eds.) (2013). *Canadian Intellectual Property Law: Cases and materials.* Toronto: Emond Montgomery Publications.

Hanel, P. (2008). The Use of Intellectual Property Rights and Innovation by Manufacturing Firms in Canada. *Economics of Innovation and New Technology*, 17(4), 285–309.

ISED and STATCAN (2014). Survey on Financing and Growth of Small and Medium Enterprises. Innovation, Science and Economic Development Canada and Statistics Canada.

Kleinknecht, A., Van Montfort, K., and Brouwer, E. (2002). The Non-Trivial Choice Between Innovation Indicators. *Economics of Innovation and New Technology*. 11(2), 109–121.

KPMG LLP, Natural Resources Canada and the Green Mining Initiative Intergovernmental Working Group, Green Mining Initiative Advisory Committee (2017). National Collaboration Strategy for the Mining Industry: Driving Innovation in the Canadian Mining Industry. Natural Resources Canada. https://www.nrcan.gc.ca/sites/www.nrcan.gc.ca/files/ emmc/pdf/EMMC_Collaboration-Strategy-Mining_E_accessible.pdf

Lac Minerals Ltd. v. *International Corona Resources Ltd.*, [1989] 2 SCR 574.

MAC (2016). Facts and Figures of the Canadian Mining Industry F&F 2016. Ottawa: The Mining Association of Canada. mining.ca/wp-content /uploads/2019/03/Facts-and-Figures-2016.pdf

MAC (2008). Facts and Figures 2008: A Report on the State of the Canadian Industry. The Mining Association of Canada. mining.ca/wp-content /uploads/2019/03/FactsandFigures2008.pdf

Marketwired (2005). Noranda Inc. Confirms Agreement With Inco Limited to Refine Copper Anodes. https://web.archive.org/web/20180707101755/ http://m.marketwired.com/press-release/noranda-inc-confirms-agree ment-with-inco-limited-to-refine-copper-anodes-nyse-nrd-546957.htm

Minalliance (2012). 100 Innovations in the Mining Industry. Ontario Mining Association www.oma.on.ca/en/ontariomining/resources/minallian ce_100_innovations_en.pdf

Monitor Deloitte, Prospectors & Developers Association of Canada and Canada Mining Innovation Council (2016). Business Ecosystems in Exploration: Mining Edition 2016. Deloitte. www2.deloitte.com/content/ dam/Deloitte/co/Documents/energy-resources/ Business_Ecosystems_in_Exploration_Report_EN%20-%20Final.pdf

Novawest Resources Inc. v. *Anglo American Exploration (Canada) Ltd et al.*, 2006 BCSC 769.

NRCan (2017a). Mining-Specific Tax Provisions. Natural Resources Canada. www.nrcan.gc.ca/mining-materials/taxation/mining-specific-tax- provisions/8892

NRCan (2017b). Sustainable Mineral Development. Natural Resources Canada. http://www.nrcan.gc.ca/science-data/science-research/earth-sciences/earth- sciences-resources/earth-sciences-federal-programs/sustainable-mineral- development/16486

NRCan (2013). Mining Sector Performance Report 1998-2012. Natural Resources Canada. www.nrcan.gc.ca/sites/www.nrcan.gc.ca/files/minerals metals/files/pdf/MSP-report-eng.pdf

NRCan (2008). Performance Report: For the Period Ending March 31, 2008. Natural Resources Canada. www.nrcan.gc.ca/sites/www.nrcan.gc.ca/files/ mineralsmetals/pdf/mms-smm/poli-poli/col-col/2008/cmic-eng.pdf

OECD (2017). STI Micro-Data Lab: Intellectual Property Database. http://oe .cd/ipstats

PDAC (2016). The Mineral Exploration Tax Credit and the Future of the Mining Industry in Canada. Prospectors & Developers Association of Canada. www.pdac.ca/priorities/advocacy/federal-budget/budget-2015/ mineral-exploration-tax-credit

PWC (2017). Time for Change: Unconventional Strategies to Disrupt the Downturn. Price Waterhouse Cooper, Junior Mine 2015. www.pwc.com /ca/en/mining/publications/400293-junior-mine-2015.pdf

The Canadian Encyclopedia (2006). Inco Limited. www.thecanadianencyclopedia. ca/en/article/inco-limited/

WEF (2015). Collaborative Innovation Transforming Business, Driving Growth. World Economic Forum, August 2015. www3.weforum.org/ docs/WEF_Collaborative_Innovation_report_2015.pdf

12

Recent Trends of Innovation and IP Use in the Mining Sector in Australia

ROHAN AMBURLE, ALMA LACKEN, EMMA FRANCIS, DEANNA TRAINHAM, GREG MALONEY AND CATRIONA BRUCE

12.1 Introduction

Australia is a world leader in mineral resources, with the world's largest reserves of iron ore and gold, second largest reserves of bauxite and copper and fifth largest reserves of black coal. Australia is a top-five global producer of twenty important commodities, including gold, bauxite, iron ore, rare earths, mineral sands, zinc, lead and coal. In particular, it is the second largest producer of gold and alumina, third largest producer of uranium and zinc and fifth largest producer of nickel in the world. Australia is also the largest exporter of iron ore, metallurgical coal and bauxite (Britt et al., 2017).

These and other resources are a mainstay of the Australian economy. The Australian mining industry was valued at $138.2 billion in 2017–18 (Australian Bureau of Statistics, 2018a), with growth of 2.9 percent ($3.9 billion), in line with the overall growth of the economy (Australian Bureau of Statistics, 2018b). Mining accounted for around 8 per cent of Australia's gross domestic product (GDP) in the 2017–18 financial year. With around a quarter of a million people employed in the sector, and 72 per cent of Australia's exports of goods in 2017–18, Australia's resource and energy exports are likely to hit a new record

The authors would like to thank our colleagues for their assistance with consultation, discussion, and preparation: Paul Drake, Razib Tuhin and Benjamin Mitra-Kahn, Office of the Chief Economist, IP Australia; the R&D Tax Incentive team, Department of Industry, Science, Energy and Resources; and Alica Daly, WIPO.

high of $252 billion in 2018–19 (Australian Government Department of Industry, Innovation and Science, 2018b).

> Because Australia is a small open economy, its comparative advantage in minerals and energy exports makes the mining and mining equipment technology services (METS) sector an important driver of broader economic growth.

> We estimate that in 2015–16, the mining sector's total economic [i.e. direct and indirect] contribution to Australia was $236.8 billion, representing around 15% of the Australian economy. This economic activity supported a total of 1,139,768 FTE jobs across Australia, which represents around 10% of total FTE employment.
>
> (Deloitte Access Economics, 2017)

This chapter builds on our previous patent analytics study of the Australia mining sector, Francis (2015), which focused on determining who filed patents and in what technology areas. Francis analyzed mining inventions filed in Australia from 1994–2011, during the development of the Australian 'mining boom', finding that the METS sector accounted for the bulk of the mining patents.[1] Most patent filings in Australia originated from Japan or Germany, and the primary market for Australian patent applicants was the United States of America (USA). With the passing of the Australian mining boom, however, the overall picture of patent activity in the Australian mining industry has altered. Most patent filings in the mining sector in Australia are now originating from the USA, and the primary market for Australian patent applicants is now domestic.

This chapter uses patent data to analyze innovation in the Australian mining sector over the past two decades, with an emphasis on both Australian-led innovation and filings for patent protection in Australia.[2] The patent data analyzed in this chapter is leveraged from the technology search on mining completed by Daly et al. (2019). Finally, the chapter also discusses how government-supported expenditure in

---

[1] Francis (2015) identified mining entities using data supplied by the Resource Information Unit, mining equipment technology services (METS) sector firms by the Australian Government Department of Industry Science, Energy and Resources, publicly funded entities manually selected from a list of universities and Cooperative Research Centres (CRCs) in mining-rich states, as well as the Commonwealth Scientific and Industrial Research Organisation (CSIRO), or using Australian and New Zealand Standard Industrial Classification (ANZIC) divisions in the IPGOD database.

[2] Patent data for 2016–17 is incomplete due to the lag between earliest priority of a patent application and its publication and was included where available.

research and development (R&D) is linked to inventions in the mining industry and their commercialization.

12.2   Australian Miners

This section of the chapter focuses on Australian innovation in the mining sector by identifying patents that originate from Australia.[3] This analysis highlights the role of Australian innovation in the global mining industry.

12.2.1   Patenting by Australian Innovators over Time

Analyzing patent filings over time (Figure 12.1) can help to identify innovation trends. Such trend analysis is useful for informing R&D investment decisions and related activities such as collaboration and commercialization. The following section of this chapter, using data from the Australian Government's R&D Tax Incentive program, investigates R&D investment in the mining industry and compares this to patent filings to give a broader picture of Australian innovation in this sector.

As a basis for this study, we used the dataset of Daly et al. (2019), derived using a modular hierarchical search strategy of International Patent Classification (IPC) and Cooperative Patent Classification (CPC) classification symbols and keywords. The data used in this chapter includes 2,997 unique INPADOC patent families derived from PATSTAT 2017 Autumn Edition and IPGOD 2017 data, with earliest priority dates from 1 January 1997 onwards.[4]

The number of patents filed annually rose from 117 in 1997 to 169 in 2008, an increase of 44 per cent. A further 24 per cent increase from the level of 2008 was observed during 2010–12, averaging around 210 annual filings. This is in line with increased investment in the mining sector

---

[3] 'Australian' status or country of origin of an invention was attributed as follows.

The applicant/inventor address was used from PATSTAT where available (www .epo.org/searching-for-patents/business/patstat.html).

If the applicant/inventor address was available in IPGOD but not in PATSTAT then IPGOD was used (www.ipaustralia.gov.au/about-us/data-and-research/ip-government-open-data).

If the applicant/inventor address was not available in either PATSTAT or IPGOD, then country of origin was determined using the methods of Daly et al. (2019).

[4] Post-2015 data is incomplete due to the lag in patent publication, and therefore excluded in the analysis over time. The remnant sections report on all the available data from January 1, 1997.

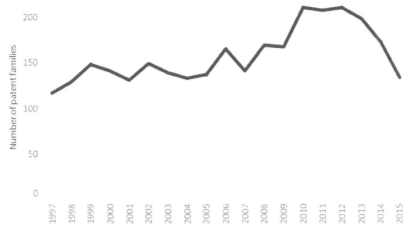

Figure 12.1   Patent families of Australian origin, by priority year, 1997–2015

during the latest Australian 'mining boom' period. Since the mining boom's peak, patenting activity has sharply declined from 2013, to 134 filings in 2015, comparable to the 1997–2004 period average.

12.2.2   Australia's Mining Boom

In a Reserve Bank of Australia research paper, Downes et al. (2014) used historical time series data to review and model Australia's 'mining boom', in which the world price of Australia's mining exports more than tripled over the 10 years to 2012, and investment spending in the mining sector increased from 2 per cent of GDP to 8 per cent during this period. Iron ore prices rose from about $20 a tonne in 2002 to peak at about $170 a tonne in 2011.

This mining boom had three phases: price rise, investment boom and production boom. The investment boom began as world commodity prices rose, driven largely by a Chinese demand to fuel its infrastructure investment. The boom in mining production lagged a few years until the capacity created by the surge in mining investment became available. While export prices have fallen from their peak in 2012, the volume of Australian mining production has remained high, thus maintaining strong export revenues, although the picture varies by commodity (Australian Government Department of Industry, Innovation and Science, 2018a).

Downes et al. (2014) portrayed the mining boom as a confluence of events that boosted world minerals prices and mining investment, and in turn the volume of Australian mining output. For example, the development of horizontal drilling and seam fracturing or fracking technology allowed the exploitation of coal seam and shale gas reserves that previously were difficult or impossible to tap. Together with the development of new technological capabilities and resources, a combination of factors in Asian energy markets, particularly concerns over energy security, pollution and greenhouse gas emissions, led to a demand for long-term contracts that allowed commitments to build large-scale projects. The boom can also be explained by less complex factors, such as growth in Chinese steel demands.

12.2.3 Top Australian Innovators

In Australia, a patent provides the owner of an invention an exclusive right for 20 years to commercialize the invention. Inventors file patents to protect their products and processes from imitation without compensation, and so the number of patent families filed by an applicant in a particular technology can be indicative of their interest, strength and market presence, or their desire to build and maintain a market share.

Figure 12.2 identifies the top innovators originating from Australia.[5] The top three patent filers contributed 15 per cent of total patent filings in the mining sector; about 59 per cent of these were related to metal refining technology.

While the multinationals Rio Tinto and BHP Billiton dominate Australian patent filing through their Australian subsidiaries, Australia's publicly funded Commonwealth Scientific and Industrial Research Organisation (CSIRO) is the third largest Australian filer.[6]

---

[5] This study identifies applicants that have each filed at least 11 patent families. Applicants and inventors are classified as Australian based on PATSTAT address data. Australian-based subsidiaries of multinational companies are included as Australian applicants.

[6] CSIRO is an independent Australian Government agency responsible for scientific research. One of its main purposes is to improve the economic and social performance of industry for the benefit of the community. CSIRO Mineral Resources works closely with industry partners to deliver innovation to grow Australia's resource base, increase productivity, and drive environmental performance. Their goal is to deliver science and technology options for the discovery and efficient development of Australia's mineral resource endowment that enable flow-on benefits to the wider national economy, with a focus on three key impact areas for industry and the nation: growing Australia's resource base, increasing productivity, and driving social and environmental performance. www.csiro.au/en/Research/MRF/Areas/Our-impact-strategy

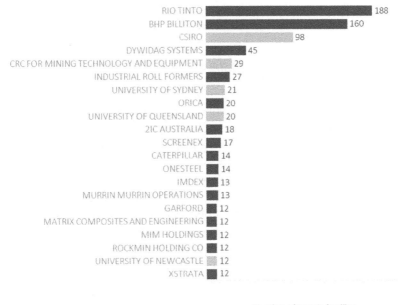

Figure 12.2   Top Australian patent filers

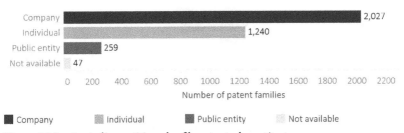

Figure 12.3   Australian entities who file patents, by entity type
Note: Data on entity type is not available for 47 Australian patent filers.

The relatively large number of patent filings by CSIRO demonstrates the importance of the mining sector in Australian publicly funded research. However, overall, patent filings in the mining sector are driven by corporate entities and individuals. Figure 12.3 shows that 67 per cent of patent filings are directly attributable to companies, in a total of 2,997 patent families filed by Australian innovators.[7]

12.2.4   Technology Specialization by Australian Innovators

So far, we have observed the volume of patents and patent filers over the past two decades. This section explores the different patenting technology areas with a view to understanding areas of strength and competitive advantage for Australian innovators. Patents are assigned a technology category based on the inventions they describe. This allows us to compare activity levels for different categories or subcategories in the technology.

Based on the IPC and/or CPC symbols, Figure 12.4 illustrates the total number of patent families by each broad technology category, while Figure 12.5 shows their movements over time. These broad groups are further subdivided in Table 12.1 and Table 12.2.[8]

Patents within the mining operations category make up 36 percent of total patent filings, with twice as many filings as the metal production

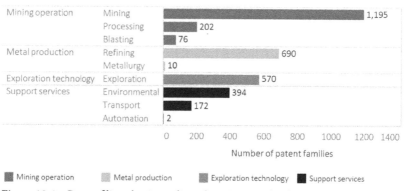

Figure 12.4   Patent filings by Australians, by mining technology

<hr />

[7] 'Individuals' and 'Not available' are grouped together into the category 'Other' in the subsequent sections referring to sector information.

[8] For the purpose of this analysis, definitions of technology sectors are as explained in Daly et al. (2019). Within the mining supply chain, environmental, transport and automation technologies are considered as support services for mining. Mining operation (blasting, mining, processing), metal production (refining, metallurgy) and exploration technology (exploration) are considered as the primary technologies.

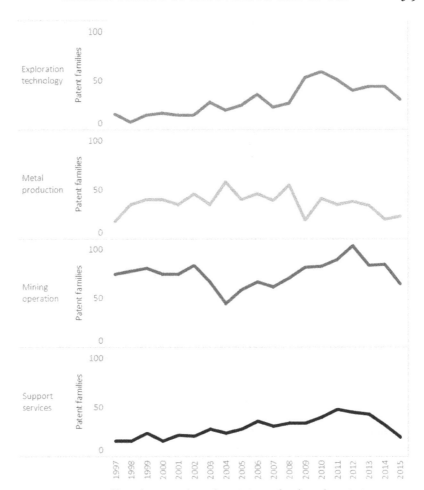

Figure 12.5   Patent filings by Australians, by mining technology, by priority year, 1997–2015

category, which is the second largest category overall. Filings over time in the metal production category do not reflect the overall pattern of the whole sector observed in Figure 12.1, of growth to 2010–12 followed by a sharp drop in 2015.

Table 12.1 (mining operation, production and exploration) and Table 12.2 (mining support services) show the number of patent families filed

Table 12.1 *Mining patent filings by Australians, by technology and entity type*

			Company	Other	Public Entity
Exploration technology	Exploration	Assays	15	20	9
		Core extraction	39	32	1
		Drilling	114	101	3
		Drilling tools	49	54	
		Exploration	83	74	25
		Methods or apparatus for drilling	96	91	8
		Surveying and testing	91	80	9
		Surveying and testing: automatic control	16	15	7
Metal production	Metallurgy	Casting/powder metallurgy	2	2	
		Coating		1	1
		Electrometallurgy	3	3	
		Metallurgy	2	3	1
	Refining	Ferrous	162	156	10
		Inorganic chemistry	19	14	3
		Non-ferrous	425	278	
Mining operation	Blasting	Blasting	66	59	5
		Fuses	4	3	
	Mining	Excavation	232	242	32
		Ground control support	267	220	8
		Other mining categories	266	234	47
		Safety/rescue	47	56	8
		Shafts	14	11	
		Subsea	30	27	
		Tunnels	47	48	4
		Ventilation	30	32	
	Processing	Bio-processing	1	1	
		Crushing/grinding	14	10	
			18	13	2

Table 12.1 (*cont.*)

	Company	Other	Public Entity
Crushing/grinding mineral			
Flotation	48	48	10
Processing	7	4	1
Separation	94	82	6

Source: PATSTAT 2017 Autumn Edition and IPGOD 2017.

within technology sub-categories by entity type. Corporate entities filed the highest number of patent families in most areas. This was closely matched by numbers of patent families filed by entity type 'other', which may be individuals or entities not identified as companies or public entities.

12.2.5   *Where Do Australians Seek Patent Protection?*

Applicants must file patent applications in each country or patent jurisdiction where they wish to have patent protection. This means that possible target markets for inventions in any technology can be indicated by the jurisdictions in which patent applications are filed.

Figure 12.6 shows the countries where Australian innovators file patent applications in the mining sector. Australian patents are primarily filed in Australia, with 2,571 patents filed since 1997. This represents 77 per cent more patent filings than those filed by Australians in the second largest target market, the USA, which highlights the importance of the domestic market for Australian-origin mining innovation. The relative number of filings into Australia by Australians has increased from the analysis of Francis (2015). The USA and Canada represent the second and third largest target markets for Australian innovators, respectively.

Table 12.2 *Mining support service patent filings by Australians, by technology and entity type*

			Company	Other	Public Entity
Support services	Automation	Automation	2	1	2
	Environmental	Biological treatment of soil	5	7	25
		Environmental	188	148	5
		Reclamation of mining areas	3	4	7
		Technologies related to metal processing	31	32	
		Technologies related to mineral processing	36	43	2
		Treatment of waste water	7	9	1
		Treatment of waste water- metallurgical processes	45	38	
	Transport	Waste disposal	10	12	1
		Containers	13	18	1
		Control	10	11	4
		Conveying	20	30	2
		Hauling	16	14	
		Hoisting	28	29	
		Infrastructure	11	12	
		Rail	15	16	4
		Shipping	5	5	
		Vehicles	15	17	2

Source: PATSTAT 2017 Autumn Edition and IPGOD 2017.

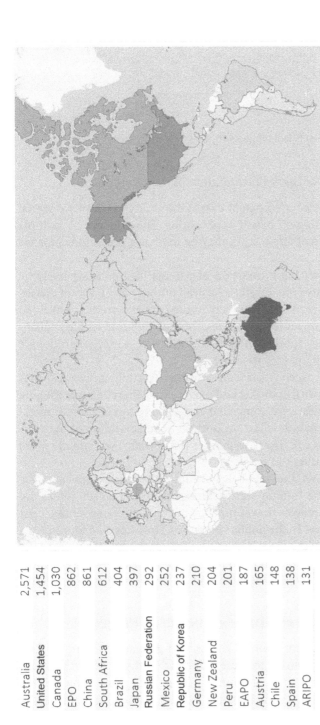

Australia	2,571
United States	1,454
Canada	1,030
EPO	862
China	861
South Africa	612
Brazil	404
Japan	397
Russian Federation	292
Mexico	252
Republic of Korea	237
Germany	210
New Zealand	204
Peru	201
EAPO	187
Austria	165
Chile	148
Spain	138
ARIPO	131

Figure 12.6 Jurisdictions in which Australian innovators seek patent protection

Note: The number of patent filings in the top nineteen target jurisdictions are listed in Figure 12.6, all target jurisdictions are shown on the map.

European Patent Office (EPO), Eurasian Patent Organisation (EAPO) and African Regional Industrial Property Organization (ARIPO) patents are enforceable in designated contracting states at the date of filing of the application. They are, therefore, included in the target market analysis, and are represented here by non-proportional dots over central Europe, central Asia and central Africa, for indicative purposes only. Patent applications can also be filed directly in individual European, Eurasian or African countries.

Figure 12.7   Australian patent filing collaboration by entity type

12.2.6   Research Collaboration in the Mining Sector

One advantage of analyzing patent data is the ability to identify research partners collaborating on patent applications. The presence of multiple applicants on a patent application may be used as a proxy indicator for collaboration.

Figure 12.7 shows the proportion of patents filed collaboratively by Australians by entity type. Overall, Australians have low levels of collaboration in the mining sector. Publicly funded entities are more likely to collaborate than companies. The proportion of applications filed collaboratively by publicly funded entities (12 per cent) is more than double those filed by companies (5 per cent).

Collaboration between Australians and non-Australians was also analyzed (data not shown); domestic and overseas collaboration was roughly equal. Public entities were somewhat more likely to collaborate internationally than companies. The proportion of collaboration of the publicly funded entities with overseas entities (53 per cent) was slightly more than that of companies (42 per cent).

Figure 12.8 shows the top collaborating Australian applicants for patent filings in the mining sector. Most of the top collaborators are companies, which reflects the dominance of companies in overall patent filings by Australians. In the public sector, Rio Tinto has filed four patents in collaboration with the University of Sydney and one with the University of Manchester, and two patent filings are three-way collaborations between CSIRO, BHP Billiton and the University of Queensland.

12.2.7   Case Study: Cooperative Research Centres

The Australian Government's Cooperative Research Centre (CRC) Program supports industry-led research collaborations between industry, researchers and the community. This is a proven model for connecting researchers with industry for the purpose of commercial

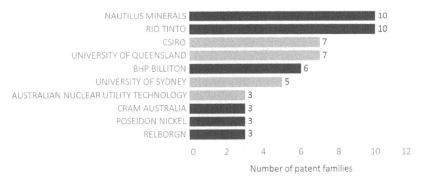

Figure 12.8   Top Australian collaborators in patent filings

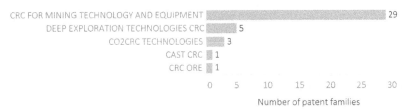

Figure 12.9   Australian patent filings by CRCs

R&D. The CRC Program is a competitive, merit-based grants program that supports industry-driven, multi-year research collaborations. Since its inception in 1991, the Australian Government has supported over 210 CRCs and committed over $4 billion in program funding (Australian Government Department of Industry, Innovation and Science, 2016).

Figure 12.9 shows patents filed by CRCs in the mining sector. Identifying CRCs is a complex task as they normally have a short life cycle (up to ten years) and can have multiple iterations where the collaborating entities may differ in some cases (Encyclopedia of Australian Science, 2010; Lever, P., 2014; Mining3, 2018a). As a result, the data may not capture all involvement of CRCs in the mining sector.

The CRC for Mining Technology and Equipment (CMTE), the Deep Exploration Technologies CRC (DET CRC) and the CRC for Greenhouse

Gas Technologies (CO2CRC) have each filed more than one patent family.

Established in 1991, CMTE was one of the first CRCs formed. This CRC had successful funding renewals in 1997 (CMTE 2), in 2003 (CRC Mining 1) and 2009 (CRC Mining 2). Its most current iteration, Mining3, is a partnership between CMTE and the CSIRO Mineral Resources group formed in July 2016. Their research includes areas such as fracture and damage mechanics, rock and coal characterization, and fragmentation and instrumentation. CMTE has filed 29 patent families, which is three times more than the combined number of filings by all other mining CRCs. Most of its patent filings are in technologies related to excavation, drilling, exploration and safety (Mining3, 2018b).

DET CRC was established in 2010 to address the challenge of decreasing mineral resource availability due to high production rates and low mineral exploration success. This CRC has filed five patent families broadly covering aspects of drilling, data logging, and sensing and targeting of mineral deposits. DET CRC was wound up in September 2018 at the end of its Commonwealth funding period. DET CRC licensed a number of its products and services to its company sponsors; these licences are now being managed by MinEx CRC.

The CO2CRC was established with the aim of researching and demonstrating carbon capture and storage as a major industrial emissions reduction technology. All three patent families filed by the CO2CRC are associated with carbon capture technologies.

RoXplorer®

RoXplorer® is an innovative success story developed by DET CRC. One of the major challenges in mineral exploration is to find evidence of mineralization. This is generally a painstaking drilling process. In practice, this means drilling more holes in the right places to give a higher chance of making a discovery. A conventional drill string is made up of individual steel rods that must be connected and disconnected as the drill hole deepens. The requirement for manual rod handling restricts drill rate and poses a risk to operator safety (Soe, 2017).

RoXplorer® is a technology developed by DET CRC to overcome this challenge. It is a coiled tubing drilling rig with a continuous malleable steel coil in the drill string. A motor within the drill string near the base of the hole drives the drill bit. This eliminates the need to add individual drill rods, making drilling quicker, cheaper and safer. RoXplorer® has a much lower estimated operational cost than diamond drilling or reverse circulation drilling (Deep Exploration Technologies CRC, 2018). DET CRC aims to lower the cost of drilling to about $50 per metre by advancing their RoXplorer® technology. Patents WO2018132861 (Mobile coiled tubing drilling apparatus) and WO2018132862 (Rotary drill head for coiled tubing drilling apparatus) are recent mining innovations filed by DET CRC.[9]

12.3   Australia's R&D Tax Incentive

Australia's R&D Tax Incentive is the Australian Government's primary means of supporting business investment in R&D, targeting areas likely to benefit the wider Australian economy. The R&D Tax Incentive, which replaced the former R&D Tax Concession in 2011, provides a company tax benefit to help offset costs of eligible R&D activities in companies registered with the scheme. For the 2016–17 income period, the program reported a $13.7 billion of R&D expenditure by 15,177 R&D performing entities across all industry sectors (Australian Government Department of Industry, Innovation and Science, 2018c).

Ongoing reform helps to ensure the effectiveness, integrity and financial viability of the program. There were 13,346 registrations across all technology areas in 2016–17, including 3,021 new registrants representing an annual increase of 21 percent. The R&D Tax Incentive was reviewed by Ferris et al. (2016), with recommendations to improve the effectiveness, integrity and additionality of the program. These recommendations have been reflected in reforms to the R&D Tax Incentive in the Australian Government Budget 2018–19 (Australian Government, 2018).

12.3.1   The R&D Tax Incentive and the Australian Mining Sector

To assess the impact of the R&D Tax Incentive on the mining sector, we analyzed data on mining companies registered with the program.[10]

---

[9]   Due to the publishing lag, these patents are not captured in the current data set analyzed.

[10]   The R&D Tax Incentive data was provided by the Department of Industry, Science, Energy and Resources. Mining sector companies were identified by Australian and New Zealand Standard Industrial Classification (ANZSIC) codes related to coal and mineral ore mining and exploration and other mining services. To align as closely as possibly with our patent dataset, industries relating to oil and gas extraction and non-metallic mineral mining and quarrying are omitted from this analysis.

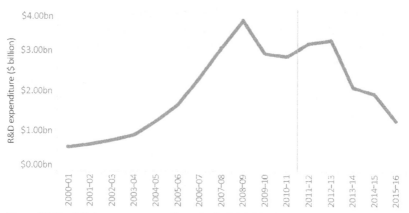

Figure 12.10   Mining sector expenditure in the R&D Tax Incentive, 2000–1 to 2015–16
Note: There is a break in the data in the 2011–12 income period, in moving to the R&D
Tax Incentive from its predecessor, the R&D Tax Concession; this transition is denoted
by the grey line.

Figure 12.10 shows R&D expenditure of registered mining entities
using data from the R&D Tax Concession (2000–1 to 2010–11) and the
R&D Tax Incentive (2011–12 to 2015–16) programs.

Under these programs, R&D expenditure in the mining sector has
grown six-fold from 2000–1. At its peak in 2008–9, the expenditure of
$3.74 billion was nearly 21 per cent of the total R&D expenditure of the
entire program that year. After a decline from 2008–9 to 2010–11, there
was a small recovery in expenditure to 2012–13, following a pattern
across the whole program (Australian Government Department of
Industry, Innovation and Science, 2018c). This was followed by further
decline, with a total decline of 67 per cent by 2015–16 relative to its peak
in 2008–9. This decline reflects the overall picture of investment over
time in the mining sector following the mining boom, as discussed in the
following sections of this chapter.

Company Size

An analysis of company size can provide insight into the differential
impact of the program on different business classes. The annual turnover
threshold of $20 million is used to separate small to medium-sized
enterprises (SMEs) from larger ones. The data on mining companies

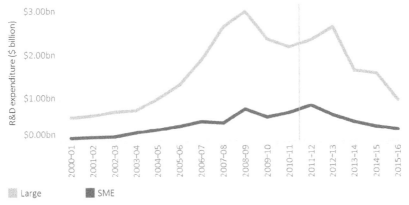

Figure 12.11   Mining sector companies by entity size, 2000–01 to 2015–16

registered with the R&D Tax Incentive was analyzed by company size (Figure 12.11).[11]

R&D expenditure of both SMEs and large firms followed the overall expediture trend from 2000–1 to 2015–16 shown in Figure 12.10. The R&D expenditure of large firms grew from 2003–4 to 2008–9, with a peak expenditure six times greater than that of SMEs. Since 2008–9, R&D expenditure by large firms has dropped to a ten-year low in 2015–16.

Mining by Industry Subdivision

We analyzed the data on mining companies registered with the R&D Tax Incentive by Australian and New Zealand Standard Industrial Classification (ANZSIC) code (Trewin and Pink, 2006) for two subdivisions: mining and exploration and other support services (Figure 12.12). While R&D expenditure of the registered companies in the mining subdivision drove the overall trend shown in Figure 12.10, companies in the exploration and support services industry subdivision did not conform to this trend, with a lower uptake of the program. Figure 12.4 also shows more patenting activity in the mining area compared with exploration and support services, although not such a marked difference as seen here.

---

[11] This analysis is limited to registered entities that have filed patents in the mining sector. The R&D Tax Incentive data fully matches 62 per cent of the patent data reported in this section. This is not an exact comparison between entities identified in the patent data and those in the R&D Tax Incentive data due to data confidentiality. The patent data is limited to business entities identified as Australian innovators in this chapter.

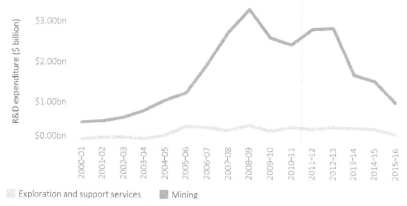

Exploration and support services   Mining

Figure 12.12   Comparison of mining sector industry subdivision trends under the R&D Tax Incentive by industry subdivision, 2000–1 to 2015–16

12.3.2   Patenting Activity and the R&D Tax Incentive

To explore potential correlations between R&D expenditure and patenting activity in the mining industry, we analyzed patent family filings and R&D expenditure of R&D Tax Incentive-registered entities (Figure 12.13).

R&D expenditure and patenting show similar patterns over time, with an overall increase from 2000–1 to 2009–10. Both the number of patents filed and R&D expenditure increased from 2009–10, with a peak in 2012–13.

R&D expenditure grew three-fold from 2009–10 to 2012–13, representing a stronger increase than the corresponding growth in the number of patent filings. This indicates the expenditure was not associated with innovation in products and processes requiring commercial protection to hold or build market share.

Both R&D expenditure and patenting activity declined steeply since 2012–13, which follows the overall decline after the peak of the Australian mining boom in 2012.

R&D Expenditure and Patent Filing by Australian State and Territory

Mining investment and activity varies considerably across Australia. To provide insight into the impact of the R&D Tax Incentive on the mining industry in different Australian States or Territories, we have compared R&D expenditure, patenting activity and the number of R&D Tax

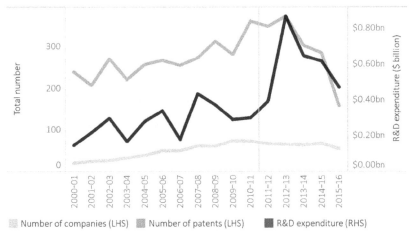

Figure 12.13   Mining sector R&D expenditure and patent filings for R&D Tax Incentive companies, 2000–01 to 2015–16
Note: Due to the lag in publication of patent applications, the number of patents for 2015–16, with a priority date after 1 January 2016, is incomplete.

Incentive-registered entities in the mining sector by State or Territory (Figure 12.14).[12]

This geographical analysis demonstrates considerable differences between the number of companies registered for the R&D Tax Incentive, R&D expenditure, and the number of patents originating from each state and territory.

Western Australia (WA) has the highest R&D expenditure under the R&D Tax Incentive ($2.55 billion) and the highest number (84) of R&D Tax Incentive-registered entities in the mining sector. WA also has the second highest number of patents (328) filed by matched companies. This may be attributable to the richness of the iron ore and gold resources of this region: the majority of Australia's gold exploration activity and iron ore deposits with operating mines are located in WA. This makes WA's mineral resources particularly valuable to the global market since Australia is the largest iron ore exporter in the world, holding 29 per cent of global iron ore reserves, and is the second largest producer of gold in the world, after China

---

[12]   State-level aggregated R&D Tax Incentive data for the period 2000–1 to 2015–16 includes combined data for South Australia (SA), the Australian Capital Territory (ACT), the Northern Territory (NT) and Tasmania (TAS) due to low or negligible mining activity in these regions. In contrast, the patent data is not aggregated and is plotted against each individual state or territory.

Number of companies

Number of patents

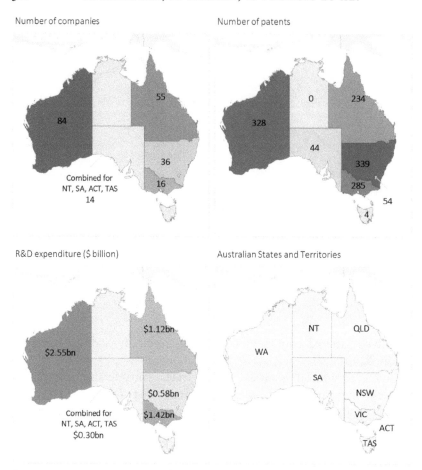

R&D expenditure ($ billion)

Australian States and Territories

Figure 12.14   Mining sector performance under the R&D Tax Incentive by State and Territory, 2000–1 to 2015–16

(Australian Government Department of Industry, Innovation and Science, 2018a).

Victoria (VIC) has the second highest mining R&D expenditure ($1.42 billion) and the third highest number of patents (285) filed by matched companies. However, only 16 R&D Tax Incentive-registered entities are located in Victoria. Queensland (QLD) has the second highest number (55) of R&D Tax Incentive-registered entities, third highest R&D expenditure ($1.12 billion) and is fourth in terms of the number of patents filed.

The overall disparity in the number of patent filings by state and the R&D Tax Incentive data could be a consequence of corporate headquarters filing both patents and R&D Tax Incentive claims. These corporate offices are usually located in metropolitan cities, with Sydney being a very popular choice. This might account for New South Wales (NSW) having the highest number of patent filings recorded in Australia, but much lower R&D expenditure than Victoria, Queensland and Western Australia.

This indicates that, while there is useful information to be derived from comparing matched R&D Tax Incentive data with patent data in the mining sector, geographical data does not appear to be directly comparable, likely due to differences in defining entity locations.

12.4   Patenting in Australia

While the focus of this chapter is to explore Australian innovation in the mining sector, we have also included an analysis of patent filings into Australia as part of a broader overview of the Australian mining industry. Patents are filed to seek patent protection in specific jurisdictions. As such, patent filings in a country can give an indication of how valuable a technology is considered to be in a particular market. The analysis of patent filings in Australia can therefore be used to infer the relative importance of Australia in the global mining landscape.[13]

12.4.1   Patent Filing in Australia over Time

Over the past two decades, a total of 16,374 patent families were filed in Australia in the mining sector. Figure 12.15 shows the annual number of patent families filed from 1997 through 2015. Patenting activity tripled between 2005 and 2012, with a decline since then. While this may be partly due to incomplete data for 2015,[14] the severity of the decline indicates that there may be further underlying factors.

---

[13] In this analysis, applicants were defined in accordance with the IPGOD database.

[14] Incomplete data in 2015 results from the Patent Cooperation Treaty (PCT) filing route, which allows for up to 30 months between PCT priority filing and national phase entry. This means there is incomplete data available from 2015 onwards (2016 and 2017 data is not shown in Figure 12.15). Data for the Autumn edition of PATSTAT is usually compiled with publications up until July of that year and release around October, so the full year of 2015 patent applications through the PCT route is not captured in this edition.

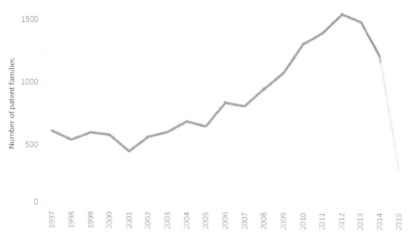

Figure 12.15   Patent filings into Australia, by priority year, 1997–2015

To understand the fall in mining sector patenting activity in Australia since 2013, we have investigated other proximate factors such as commodity prices as well as mining profits and investment. First, Figure 12.16 shows movements in commodity prices (Reserve Bank of Australia, 2018). Second, Figure 12.17 shows Australian mining sector profits as a share of GDP (Australian Bureau of Statistics, 2018c). Third, Figure 12.18 shows mining sector investment proportional to GDP (Australian Bureau of Statistics, 2018d). In all three Figures 12.16 to 12.18, we observe a sharp drop from a peak around 2012–13, which coincides with the fall in patenting activity in Australia.

While the decline in patent filings and R&D expenditure by Australian companies (Figure 12.13) coincides with the fall in commodity prices as well as mining profits and investment after 2012–13, this does not reflect the severity of the drop in patent filings into Australia from 2013–15. This suggests a number of other factors, including global issues, may have contributed to the decline in patent filings into Australia since 2012–13 (Kent, 2016).

While acknowledging that the patent filing data is incomplete for 2015 onwards, as discussed previously, it seems likely that a complex combination of factors has contributed to the dramatic drop in patent filings into Australia from 2013–15. This drop – to a 20-year low and with half the number of patent filings of 1997 – is particularly noticeable given the mining industry was much bigger in 2015 than in 1997. The drop in R&D

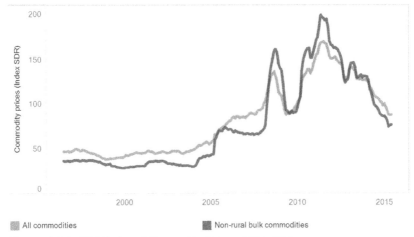

Figure 12.16   RBA Index of Commodity Prices, 1997–2015
Note: Commodity price is SDR; 2016/17 average = 100.

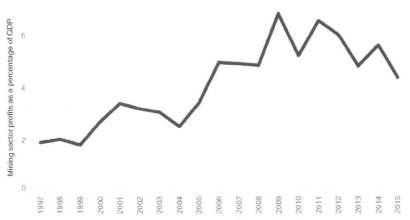

Figure 12.17   Mining sector profits as a share of nominal GDP, 1997–2015
Note: Gross operating profits, inventory valuation adjusted.

expenditure by Australian companies may be attributable to the overall
drop in mining investment, which is in turn attributable to the drop in
commodity prices and in corporation profits, none of these downturns
are as severe as that in patent filings into Australia. Revealing its underlying causes therefore warrants further research.

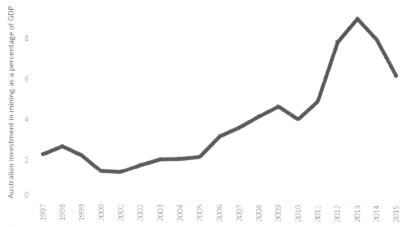

Figure 12.18   Australian investment in mining as a percentage of GDP, 1997–2015

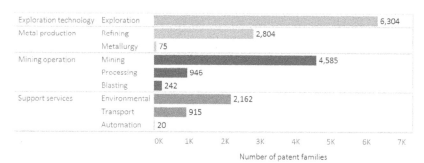

Figure 12.19   Patent filings into Australia by mining technology

12.4.2   Technology Specialization in Australia

An analysis of patenting in different technology areas provides an overall picture of innovation in the sector. In this vein, Figure 12.19 shows the number of patent families filed into Australia in different mining technology areas.[15]

---

[15] Patent data analyzed by INPADOC patent families derived from PATSTAT 2017 Autumn Edition and IPGOD 2017 data, with earliest priority dates from 1 January 1997. Post-2015 data is incomplete due to the lag in patent publication, all available data is included in our analysis, except for trend analysis over time where post 2015 data is excluded.

The top three technology categories for patent filings into Australia are exploration, mining and refining. This differs from global patent filings originating from Australian applicants, in which the top three technology areas are mining, refining and exploration, respectively (Figure 12.4). This reflects the differences between foreign and domestic patent applicants in terms of what they invent and want to protect in Australia.

12.4.3   Who is Filing Patents in Australia?

Patent filing data can be used as a proxy indicator of innovation performance of a nation; therefore, the analysis of patent applicant origin may reflect how innovative a country is. Figure 12.20 shows the total number of patent families filed in Australia in the mining sector by various source countries from 1997 onwards. Australia ranks second, with 1,968 domestic patent filings filed by Australian applicants. A total of 6,477 patent filings originate from applicants in the USA, by far the most from any country, and about three times more filings than the second-placed Australian applicants. The most prominent

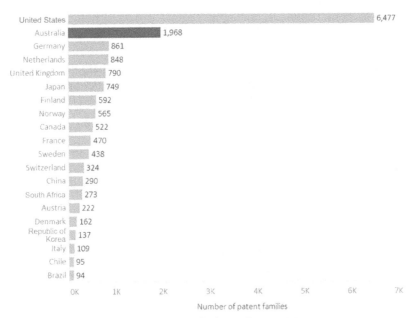

Figure 12.20   Patent filings into Australia by applicant origin

Australian companies filing into Australia are the Australian subsidiaries of Rio Tinto (139 patent filings) and BHP Billiton (103 patent filings).

12.4.4   Top Innovators Filing patents in Australia

The number of patent families filed by an applicant in a specific technology can be indicative of its strength, interest and market presence or desire to build and maintain a market share. Figure 12.21 shows the top applicants for inventions that were filed into Australia in the mining sector.

The core business for a number of these applicants, such as the top applicant, Halliburton, appears to centre on providing products and services predominantly to the oil and gas sectors, which are specifically excluded from the definition of mining technologies in this analysis. The fact that these companies are key players for patents in the mining technologies covered by this chapter indicates an overlap of technologies used by both the mining and the oil and gas sectors.

Halliburton

Halliburton, founded in 1919 and with its headquarters in the USA, is one of the world's largest providers of products and services to the global energy industry and in particular to oil and gas companies. Its services include locating resources, managing geological data, drilling, construction and supporting production throughout the life of a project (Halliburton, 2019; cf. Bloomberg, 2019b). Halliburton also owns Landmark, a technology solutions provider of data and analytics, science, software and services for the exploration and production industry (Halliburton Landmark, 2019). Patent filings by Landmark (194 families or 11 per cent) are a significant contribution to overall filings in Australia by Halliburton in the mining sector.

Halliburton has been a consistent patent filer in Australia to 2008, after which its filings increased strongly, particularly in 2012 and 2013. Halliburton's filings have predominantly been in the exploration area (89 per cent).

General Electric

Based in the USA, General Electric is a global company operating in diverse fields including power, renewable energy, oil and gas, aviation, healthcare, transportation and lighting (GE Australia, 2019; cf. Bloomberg, 2019a). The General Electric group includes Baker Hughes, a global company with operations in over 120 countries.

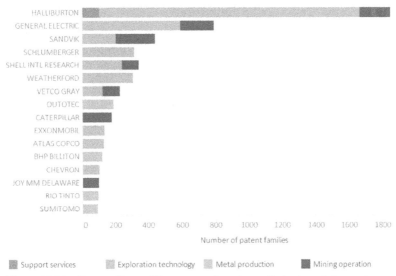

Figure 12.21   Top applicants filing patents into Australia in the mining sector

Baker Hughes is a provider of integrated oil-field products, services and digital solutions (Baker Hughes, 2019). Like Halliburton, the core Baker Hughes business appears to centre on providing products and services predominantly to the oil and gas sectors.

Patent filings in Australia by General Electric in the mining area have been mostly through the Baker Hughes company (650 families or 81 per cent). Like Halliburton, General Electric (Baker Hughes) was a consistent patent filer in Australia up to 2008, after which their filings increased dramatically, particularly during 2009–11. Its filings have also been predominantly in the exploration area (74 per cent).

Sandvik AB

Sandvik AB, with headquarters in Stockholm, Sweden, is a global high technology engineering group. It provides equipment and tools, service and technical solutions for the mining industry (Sandvik, 2019; cf. Bloomberg, 2019c). Sandvik AB has consistently filed for patents in Australia with increased activity here between 2003 and 2011, and in 2013. Its filings have predominantly been a mixture of the exploration and mining operations areas.

Schlumberger

Schlumberger, operating in over 85 countries, is a global provider of products and services for exploration and production of the oil and gas industry (Schlumberger, 2019). It has principal offices in Paris, Houston, London and The Hague. Schlumberger has consistently filed for patents in Australia with a sharp increase from 2008. Its filings have mainly been in the exploration area.

12.4.5   Collaboration in Patent Filings in Australia

The presence of multiple applicants on an application is indicative of collaboration. Figure 12.22 shows the top countries of origin for collaborative mining sector patents filed in Australia. The USA is the most collaborative country filing patents in Australia, with Australia ranking second. All the top collaborative countries have a mixture of domestic and international collaborations.

Figure 12.23 shows the top mining technology areas for collaborative patents; the top three areas are mining operations, exploration and refining technologies. Differences in collaboration in different technologies by country of origin are shown in Figure 12.24, which highlights patterns of specialization and indicates the resultant competitive advantage of countries.

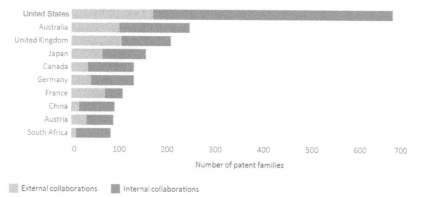

Figure 12.22   International collaboration on patent filings into Australia in the mining sector

Note: This figure compares collaborations between applicants in the same country (internal collaborations) and between applicants of different countries (external collaborations).

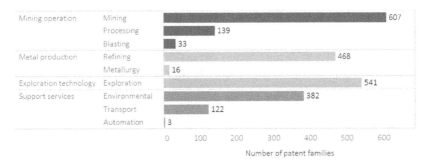

Figure 12.23 Collaboration on patent filings into Australia in the mining sector by technology

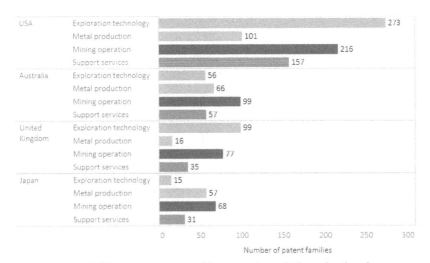

Figure 12.24 Collaboration on patent filings into Australia by technology by country. Note: Collaboration by the top four collaborating countries.

In summary, interest in the Australian mining market has been through a period of turbulence from 1997–2015, including strong collaboration and strong investment by domestic innovators. The market has a focus driven by USA firms on exploration, mining and refining technology development.

There has been a steep drop in patent filings into Australia during 2013–15, which does not appear to be purely cyclical. It is possible that factors not identified in the data used for this chapter have affected the perceived value and strength of this sector in Australia.

12.5 Conclusion

Australia is a global leader in the mining sector, both due to its rich resources and to its technological innovation and investment in this sector.

We have analyzed innovation in the Australian mining sector using patent data from 1997–2015, finding a total of 2,997 Australian mining sector patents filed during this period. Patenting activity by Australian entities increased from the early 2000s to peak during 2010–12. This was followed by a decline, returning to the 1998 level in 2015. The rise and fall in patenting activity coincides with similar movements in commodity prices, as well as mining profits and investment.

We analyzed patenting activity in the light of company participation in the Australian Government's R&D Tax Incentive program. Patenting activity and business R&D expenditure broadly followed similar patterns over time, peaking in the years around 2010 and then declining. R&D expenditure by entities registered for the R&D Tax Incentive grew six-fold from 2000–1, peaking in 2008–9 with an expenditure of $3.74 billion. By 2015–16, this declined by two thirds.

A similar picture is observed in patent filings into Australia. These peaked in 2012, and declined strongly thereafter. This indicates a decline in patent protection in the Australian market from both domestic and international applicants, which could reflect the perceived value and strength of this sector.

Overall, patenting activity and R&D expenditure followed the rise and fall of the Australian mining boom, peaking in 2012 and declining thereafter to 2015. However, the Australian mining industry is well positioned to fuel a growing demand for electric vehicles. Australia has the world's largest reserves of nickel, and is the world's largest producer of lithium. Australia is the fourth largest global producer of manganese ore and cobalt, and the fifth largest producer of nickel and copper (Britt et al., 2017). These are essential inputs for the production of electric vehicle batteries. The demand for these metals is forecast to rise steeply by 2030 in the lithium-ion battery supply chain for electric vehicles (Bloomberg New Energy Finance, 2018).

To realize the opportunities, Australia will need enough targeted investment in R&D in different mining technologies. This will not only support efficient use of resources but also build investor confidence in the Australian market.

References

Australian Bureau of Statistics, 2018a, 5204.0 – Australian System of National Accounts, 2017–18, Table 51, Gross Fixed Capital Formation by Type of Asset. www.abs.gov.au/AUSSTATS/abs@.nsf/DetailsPage/5204.02017–18?OpenDocument

Australian Bureau of Statistics, 2018b, 5204.0 – Australian System of National Accounts, 2017–18. www.abs.gov.au/AUSSTATS/abs@.nsf/DetailsPage/5204.02017–18?OpenDocument

Australian Bureau of Statistics, 2018c, 5676.0 – Business Indicators, Australia, Sep 2018, Tables 11–12, Company Gross operating profits. www.abs.gov.au/AUSSTATS/abs@.nsf/DetailsPage/5676.0Sep%202018?OpenDocument

Australian Bureau of Statistics, 2018d, 5204.0 – Australian System of National Accounts, 2017–18, Table 5, Gross Value Added by Industry. www.abs.gov.au/AUSSTATS/abs@.nsf/DetailsPage/5204.02017–18?OpenDocument

Australian Government Department of Industry, Innovation and Science, 2018a, Resources and Energy Quarterly, June 2018, Office of the Chief Economist, Australian Government Department of Industry, Innovation and Science, Canberra. https://publications.industry.gov.au/publications/resourcesandenergyquarterlyjune2018/index.html

Australian Government Department of Industry, Innovation and Science, 2018b, Resources and Energy Quarterly, September 2018. Office of the Chief Economist, Australian Government Department of Industry, Innovation and Science, Canberra. https://publications.industry.gov.au/publications/resourcesandenergyquarterlyseptember2018/index.html

Australian Government, 2018, Budget 2018–19 Fact Sheet: Reforming the R&D Tax Incentive. https://archive.budget.gov.au/2018-19/

Australian Government Department of Industry, Innovation and Science, 2018c, Innovation and Science Australia Annual Report 2017–18, Australian Government Department of Industry, Innovation and Science, Canberra. https://www.industry.gov.au/sites/default/files/2018-11/innovation-and-science-australia-annual-report-2017-18.pdf

Australian Government Department of Industry, Innovation and Science, 2016, Innovation Australia Annual Report 2015-16, Australian Government Department of Industry, Innovation and Science, Canberra.

https://www.industry.gov.au/data-and-publications/innovation-australia-annual-report-2015-16

Baker Hughes, 2019, "Our Company." www.bhge.com/our-company

Bloomberg, 2019a, General Electric Co https://www.bloomberg.com/profile/company/GE:US

Bloomberg, 2019b, Halliburton Co https://www.bloomberg.com/profile/company/HAL:US

Bloomberg, 2019c, Sandvik AB. https://www.bloomberg.com/profile/company/SAND:SS

Bloomberg New Energy Finance, 2018, Electric Vehicles Outlook: 2018.

Britt, A., et al., 2017, "Geoscience Australia 2017. Australia's Identified Mineral Resources 2017". Geoscience Australia, Canberra. https://ecat.ga.gov.au/geonetwork/srv/eng/catalog.search#/metadata/116001

Daly, A., Valacchi, G., and Raffo, J., 2019, "Mining patent data: measuring innovation in the mining industry with patents", WIPO Economic Research Working Paper No. 56.

Deep Exploration Technologies CRC, 2018, "Uncovering the Future." https://ecat.ga.gov.au/geonetwork/srv/eng/catalog.search#/metadata/116001

Deloitte Access Economics, 2017, "Mining and METS: engines of economic growth and prosperity for Australians", Report prepared for the Minerals Council of Australia, 2017. www.minerals.org.au/sites/default/files/Mining%20and%20METS%20engines%20of%20economic%20growth%20and%20prosperity%20for%20Australians.pdf

Downes, P., Hanslow, K., and Tulip, P., 2014, "The effect of the mining boom on the Australian economy". Research Discussion Paper RDP 2014–08, Reserve Bank of Australia. https://www.rba.gov.au/publications/bulletin/2014/dec/3.html

Encyclopedia of Australian Science, 2010, CRC for Mining Technology and Equipment (1991–2003). www.eoas.info/biogs/A001916b.htm

Ferris, B., Finkel, A., and Fraser, J., 2016, Review of the R&D Tax Incentive. www.industry.gov.au/sites/g/files/net3906/f/May%202018/document/pdf/research-and-development-tax-incentive-review-report.pdf

Francis, E., 2015, "The Australian Mining Industry: More Than Just Shovels and Being the Lucky Country", IP Australia, Canberra. www.ipaustralia.gov.au/sites/g/files/net856/f/the_australian_mining_industry_more_ than_just_shovels_and_being_the_lucky_country.pdf

GE Australia, 2019, www.ge.com/au/

Halliburton, 2019, "About Halliburton." www.halliburton.com/en-US/about-us/default.page?node-id=hgbr8q6o

Halliburton Landmark, 2019, "About Landmark". www.landmark.solutions/About

Kent, C., 2016, "After the Boom", Speech at Bloomberg Breakfast, Sydney 13 September 2016. www.rba.gov.au/speeches/2016/sp-ag-2016–09-13 .html

Lever, P., 2014, "Transforming mining". https://crca.asn.au/transforming-mining/

Mining3, 2018a, "Who we are". www.mining3.com/about-us/who-we-are/

Mining3, 2018b, "What we do". www.mining3.com/about-us/what-we-do/

Reserve Bank of Australia, 2018, Index of Commodity Prices, November 2018. https://crca.asn.au/transforming-mining/

Sandvik, 2019, "About Us. www.home.sandvik/en/about-us/

Schlumberger, 2019, "Who We Are". www.slb.com/about.aspx

Soe, S., 2017, "The coiled tubing drilling rig for mineral exploration: the Roxplorer®", Australian Institute of Geoscientists Bulletin No.64, Conference Proceedings, Drilling for Geology II, 26–28 July 2017, Brisbane, Australia, Extended Abstracts, pages 25–26, 2017. www .csaglobal.com/wp-content/uploads/2017/08/D4G2_Extended-Abstracts-Volume.pdf

Trewin, D., and Pink, B., 2006, Australian and New Zealand Standard Industrial Classification 2006, ABS Catalogue No. 1292.0, Australian Bureau of Statistics, Canberra. www.ausstats.abs.gov.au/ausstats/sub scriber.nsf/0/19C21C5659BCAE73CA2574C8001474E4/$File/ 12920_2006.pdf

INDEX

Academic institutions. *See* Universities and academic institutions
African Regional Industrial Property Organization (ARIPO), 319
Aguamarina, 102
Alcan, 288
Aluminum
  in Australia, 308
  in Brazil, 205, 206–7
  environmental impacts, 142
  processing stage, 7
  "pull effect" of innovation, 11
Anglo American Exploration, 282
Anglo Gold Ashanti, 221
Angola, FDI in, 62
Aplik, 102–3
Argentina, mineral trade with Brazil, 207
Artisanal and small-scale miners (ASMs), 4–5
Austmine, 4
Australia
  generally, 323
  automation, patent filings and, 44
  automation subsector in, 316–18
  blasting subsector in, 314, 316–18
  Canadian company patent filings in, 289
  clean patents in, 149–50
  coal imports and exports, 121
  collaboration in, 320–1, 336–8
  Commonwealth Scientific and Industrial Research Organisation (CSIRO), 21, 312–14, 320, 322
  Cooperative Research Centres (CRCs), 21, 45–6, 320–3
  Deep Exploration Technologies CRC (DET CRC), 321–3

Department of Industry, Innovation and Science, 323
environmental impacts of mining industry in, 142
environmental technology, patent filings and, 44
environment subsector in, 316–18
exploration, patent filings and, 42
exploration subsector in, 314, 316–18
FDI and, 58
German company patent filings in, 309
government support of mining industry in, 178
Greenhouse Gas Technologies CRC (CO2CRC), 321–2
importance of mining industry in, 308–9
innovation in, 309
innovators, patent filings by, 312–13, 334–5
Japanese company patent filings in, 309
longer transit distances of mining products and, 121
measurement of environmental policy stringency in, 158
metallurgy subsector in, 314, 316–18
METS sector in, 4, 212
Mining and Technology CRC (CMTE), 321–2
mining boom in, 311–12
mining innovation ecosystem in, 14
mining patents as share of total patents, 39
mining specialization in, 183
mining subsector in, 314, 316–18
New South Wales, R&D expenditures in, 329

342

Printed in Australia
AUHW011919140422
362293AU00003BA/6